A FRAMEWORK FOR

SUPPLY CHAINS

Dedication

To those who endured disruption to their lives so this book could be written: Renuka, who provided the support for Roger, as she has done for so many years, through our different ventures; Katia thanks her husband Greg for the endless support and encouragement and takes inspiration from little Cooper, who loves presenting logistical challenges of his own. We thank you.

ROGER **OAKDEN**

KATIA **LEONAITE**

A FRAMEWORK FOR

SUPPLY
CHAINS

LOGISTICS OPERATIONS IN THE ASIA–PACIFIC REGION

The **McGraw·Hill** Companies

Sydney New York San Francisco Auckland
Bangkok Bogotá Caracas Hong Kong
Kuala Lumpur Lisbon London Madrid
Mexico City Milan New Delhi San Juan
Seoul Singapore Taipei Toronto

National Library of Australia Cataloguing-in-Publication Data
Author: Oakden, Roger.
Title: A framework for supply chains : logistics operations in the
                  Asia-Pacific region / Roger Oakden, Katia Leonaite.
Edition: 1st ed.
ISBN: 9780070997783 (pbk.)
Notes: Includes index.
Subjects: Business logistics–Pacific Area–Textbooks.
Other Authors/Contributors:
                  Leonaite, Katia.
Dewey Number: 658.7091823

Published in Australia by
McGraw-Hill Australia Pty Ltd
Level 2, 82 Waterloo Road, North Ryde NSW 2113
Acquisitions editor: Michael Buhagiar
Editorial coordinator: Fiona Howie
Art director: Astred Hicks
Cover design: We Buy Your Kids/The Jacky Winter Group
Internal design: David Rosemeyer
Production editor: Claire Linsdell
Permissions editor: Haidi Bernhardt
Copy editor: Tim Fullerton
Proofreader: Leila Jabbour
Indexer: Olive Grove Indexing Services
Typeset in 10pt Scala by Midland Typesetters, Australia
Printed in Australia by Griffin Digital

Contents

PART 1   LOGISTICS AND SUPPLY CHAINS

CHAPTER 1 | The enterprise, its logistics and supply chains   2

CHAPTER 2 | Business planning, risk and sustainability   19

CHAPTER 3 | Logistics in practice   31

CHAPTER 4 | Supply chains in the Asia–Pacific region   45

Preface

This book is designed to address the need for a text that considers the specifics of supply chains and logistics in the Asia–Pacific region, covering issues that are not included in books written for North American or European regions.

Our approach has been to provide a framework in which to understand the scope of supply chains and logistics, and a foundation that informs the reader of the principles behind a topic. It is designed so that the reader can understand where individual elements fit into the larger picture and grasp the scope of supply chains and logistics as they apply to specific business models and economies.

The book's main theme, reinforced and revisited throughout, is that supply chains and logistics ensure the *availability* of products and services for the customers of an enterprise. A second theme is that organisations have multiple supply chains, both internal and external. In reality these are a complex network of independent, and possibly interdependent, product and service suppliers and customers. The result of this need for availability—and for working within the supply network processes—is a heightened requirement for planning and scheduling, while recognising the importance of managing risk.

The book's four parts consider different themes and the four chapters within each part are linked. Each chapter serves as an introduction to the topic and can be selected as required. The key terms in each chapter help readers build their own electronic information pack on the topic, based on the framework provided.

A Framework for Supply Chains is designed for readers from a variety of backgrounds: students new to the logistics discipline; those with experience working in just one aspect of supply chains who need to understand the broader concepts; and those who have worked and studied in other disciplines and have been promoted or transferred into a logistics role. It is also of value to those working in disciplines that interact with logistics and who need to understand why supply chains are important to the business.

We view supply chains and logistics as a critical part of a business but our experience has shown that many companies have yet to understand and embrace this criticality—it is far more than trucks and boxes! The exciting aspect of studying and working within supply chains is that the theory and real-world experience inform each other—this is not a discipline that stands still, in any sense.

We invite feedback on your experiences from reading and using this book; please send your views and suggestions to us at authors@learnaboutlogistics.com. We continue the learning experience at www.learnaboutlogistics.com.

Roger Oakden
Katia Leonaite

Acknowledgments

Our thanks go to Kerrie-Anne McPhee for encouraging us to write a book that addresses the issues and challenges specific to the region. We would also like to thank Jenny Dick for her help in determining the best approach to meet the learning needs of our diverse reader groups.

We thank our many colleagues in various supply chains for their tireless contribution by way of reviews and feedback, and for being excellent sounding boards for ideas and case study material; also our students, past and present, on whom much of the material has been tested over time.

Special thanks go to the chapter reviewers who provided the knowledgeable feedback required for us to improve each chapter— although, of course, responsibility for the contents of the finished chapter remains with us. Our esteemed reviewers are: Melissa Bayley, Guy Callender, David Grieve, Kerry Hammond, Shaun Hodgson, Peta Irving, Tiong Lee, Pieter Nagel, Stephen Paull, Tom Rafferty, Chris Rowlands and Sue Schmid.

To those who took the time from their busy schedules to write the case studies and exercises that provide such a wide range of scenarios concerning supply chains and logistics as practised in the Asia–Pacific region, we are enormously grateful. They are: Jwalant Batavia, Antoinette Brandi, Tony Clarke, Laurie Le Fevre, Gen Ford (www.ithacabusiness.biz), Kerry Hammond, Mark Kluver, Carter McNabb (www.gra.net.au), Stephen Pereira (www.gs1.org.au), Derrick and Grace Phua, Chris Rowlands, Ranjeet Singh (www.transecopl.com) and George Zhou.

Thank you all.

Roger Oakden
Katia Leonaite

Roger Oakden

Roger is the Principal of REN Services, a consulting firm that works with clients to improve their supply chains, business systems and processes. Formerly at RMIT University in Melbourne, Roger was the Program Manager responsible for development of the largest postgraduate supply chain logistics program in the Asia-Pacific region, with centres in Australia, Singapore and Hong Kong. While at RMIT, Roger was appointed Ford Motor Company Procurement Fellow in Australia.

Roger's extensive industry background includes significant high-level roles. As Associate Director at a global consulting firm, he led teams in assisting clients to improve their manufacturing operations, systems, logistics and strategic procurement. Earlier, at a multinational computer company, he provided pre-sales analysis of manufacturing industry customer requirements throughout the region and project management for the implementation of ERP/MRP and other applications.

His industrial management experience covers industrial engineering, management accounting, procurement and operations in the shipping, chemical, metals and food industries.

Roger holds a Masters degree in Logistics Management, a first class honours degree in Finance and Accounting, is certified in Production and Inventory Management (CPIM) and is a Certified Purchasing Manager (CPM). He is also certified in Assessment and Workplace Training.

He is a past president of the Australian Production and Inventory Control Society (APICS), has written articles for the business press and presented papers at logistics industry conferences in Australia, Asia and Europe.

Katia Leonaite

Katia is a supply chain professional with industry experience ranging from agricultural to retail and is passionate about managing change in the complex supply chains context.

She began her career in a 'point-to-point' transport courier environment. Upon completing her MBA at the Macquarie Graduate School of Management, she managed a key logistics services portfolio in a government enterprise as it went through the privatisation process. Since then she has been successfully engaged in various supply chains and logistics management roles, ranging from large events to contract management with some of Australia's leading organisations.

Katia is currently the Course Convenor for the Graduate Certificate in Supply Chains at Swinburne University in Melbourne. Through her firm L5 Consulting, she has provided development of learning materials and lecturing services in the area of supply chain and logistics for Monash University, University of Ballarat, Central Queensland University and Victoria University.

Katia holds an MBA (Operations and Logistics) from Macquarie University and a BA/BEd (Maths/Computer Science) from the University of NSW.

How to use this book

Links to other chapters
Each chapter opens with a visual representation of how it relates to the other chapters. This encourages students to develop a 'mind-map' of where each chapter fits in.

Learning outcomes
A set of learning objectives at the beginning of each chapter outlines the core skills and knowledge students are expected to derive from the chapter. They are also designed to assist with student revision.

Key terms
A list of key terms used and highlighted in the text is located at the beginning of each chapter. Students are encouraged to develop their own notebook by downloading information from the internet about each term.

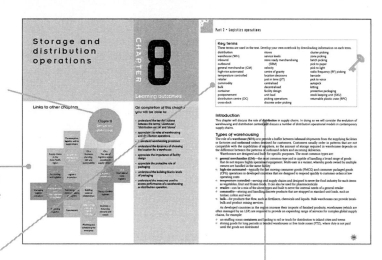

Introduction
The introduction, combined with the learning outcomes, helps to set a clear path for learning and a foundation for the key principles of the chapter.

Chapter questions and exercises
A series of practice questions can be found at the end of each chapter. Divided into three progressive categories—Operational, Planning and Management—to suit diploma-level, undergraduate and postgraduate students respectively. Exercises are also provided where relevant.

References and links
There is list of references and links at the end of each chapter where students can seek further information.

Case studies appendix
Ten case studies in transport and logistics derived from Australia and the wider Asia–Pacific region are provided. The case study questions have the same format as the end-of-chapter questions, listed in the three categories of Operational, Planning and Management.

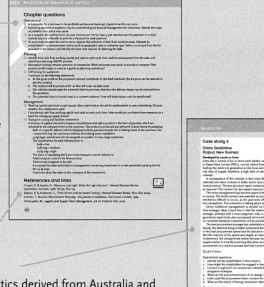

E-STUDENT

The online Learning Centre (OLC) that accompanies this text helps you get the most from your course. It provides a powerful learning experience beyond the printed page.

www.mhhe.com/au/oakden

PowerPoint® presentations

A series of PowerPoint® presentations summarises the key points of each chapter. They can be downloaded as valuable revision aids.

E-INSTRUCTOR

In addition to the student resources, instructors also have password-protected access to:

Instructor resource manual

The instructor resource manual provides chapter summaries, solutions to end-of-chapter questions and additional quality teaching resources. It saves time for instructors and helps provide consistency across teaching teams.

Artwork library

Illustrations and tables from the text are available in an online artwork library as digital image files. Instructors thus have the flexibility to use them in the format that best suits their needs.

EZ Test Online

EZ Test Online is a powerful and easy-to-use test generator for creating paper or digital tests. It allows easy 'one click' export to course management systems such as WebCT and Blackboard, and straightforward integration with Moodle.

EZ Test Online gives instructors access to the testbanks of this text and a range of others from one point of entry, and also permits instructors to upload or edit their own questions. More information is available via the Online Learning Centre.

Testbank

A bank of test questions written specifically for this text lets instructors build examinations and assessments quickly and easily. The testbank is available in a range of flexible formats: in Microsoft Word®, in EZ Test Online or formatted for delivery via Blackboard or WebCT.

Useful websites for logisticians

Websites can provide additional information about supply chains and logistics. Additional links are also provided at the end of chapters under 'References and Links'. There are more sites available but to have confidence in the information consider the following:

- Go to trusted sources such as government, university, library, quality newspaper and magazine sites. Follow their links.
- Cross-check the information against other sources.
- Check the source of a web page if you have concerns about its authenticity and independence.
- Check if the information is current.

Wikipedia at www.wikipedia.com is a good resource for commencing the research using the key terms provided for each chapter

Associations

www.laa.asn.au—Logistics Association of Australia
www.sclaa.com.au—Supply Chain and Logistics Association of Australia
www.apics.org/default.htm—APICS
http://cscmp.org—Council of SCM Professionals
www.supply-chain.org—Supply Chain Council (SCOR)
www.cipsa.com.au—Chartered Institute for Purchasing and Supply in Australasia (CIPSA)
www.supplychains.com—Global Supply Chain Council of China; publishes *ChaINA* online magazine
www.chinawuliu.com.cn—China Federation of Logistics and Purchasing
www.ism.ws – Institute for Supply Management in America

Information

www.wikipedia.com—Wikipedia information resource
www.gartner.com/resources/201200/201212/the_amr_supply_chain_top_25__201212.pdf—Gartner report on the top Logistics services companies
www.logisticsmagazine.com.au—online *Logistics Magazine* in Australia
http://resources.bnet.com/topic/supply+chain.html—online business resources
http://logistics.about.com—reference concerning logistics and supply chains
www.sloanreview.mit.com —MIT Sloan Management Review
www.bcg.com—Boston Consulting Group publications
www.mckinseyquarterly.com—online journal of McKinsey & Co.
www.transportintelligence.com—weekly newsletter
www.nztransport-logistics.co.nz—newsletter
www.unescap.org—United Nations Economic and Social Commission for Asia and the Pacific (ESCAP). Based in Bangkok.
www.aberdeen.com—Aberdeen Group research industry reports
www.lean.org—Lean Enterprise Institute
www.eft.com—Eye for Transport information source
http://knowledge@whartonschool.com—Wharton Business School

USA-based newsletters

www.supplychainbrain.com—*Supply Chain Brain Today*, online newsletter
www.sdce.com—*Supply & Demand Chain Executive*
www.scdigest.com—*Supply Chain Digest*
www.scmr.com—*Supply Chain Management Review*
http://scm.ncsu.edu—*Supply Chain Resource Digest*. Based at NC State University

Undergraduate and postgraduate-level courses presented by the business or engineering faculties of universities may provide an overview of supply chains and logistics as a core or elective subject. This book provides a framework within which the subject content can be learned.

At the vocational level, information regarding industry trends, workforce development and changes to qualifications and units of competency can be accessed via the Industry Skills Council website at www.isc.org.au. For qualifications and units relevant to business, access Skills for Australia at www.skillsforaustralia.com.

Qualifications and the units available which address operational logistics for the commercial and military sectors are prescribed by the Transport & Logistics Industry Skills Council (TLISC) in Australia at www.tlisc.org.au.

For industry and logistics service providers (LSP):
• Diploma of Logistics

For the military and service companies engaged in the re-supply of continuing operations:
• Diploma of Deployment Logistics
• Advanced Diploma of Deployment Logistics

For whole-of-life support for military capability platforms, including ships, aircraft and tanks, from acquisition to decommissioning:
• Diploma of Matériel Logistics
• Advanced Diploma of Matériel Logistics

This book provides a framework for the Diploma of Logistics and the Diploma of Deployment Logistics, within which the study of individual units is undertaken with the assistance of unit learner guides. The units that link to the chapters in this book are listed in the table below.

Chapter number	Chapter title	Unit number	Unit title
Part 1	**Logistics and supply chains**		
Chapter 1	*The enterprise, its logistics and supply chains*	TLIL5055	Manage a supply chain
		TLIX4028	Apply knowledge of logistics
Chapter 2	*Business planning, risk and sustainability*	TLIU4001	Implement and monitor environmental protection policies and procedures
		TLIP5004	Develop a transport and logistics business plan
		TLIP5011	Develop and evaluate strategies for transport and logistics enterprises
		TLIU5006	Conduct environmental audits
		TLIX4028	Apply knowledge of logistics
		BSBCOM501	Identify and interpret compliance requirements
		BSBRSK501	Manage risk
		TLIP5006	Establish international distribution networks
Chapter 3	*Logistics in practice*	SITXEVT605	Develop event transport plans
		TLIP5011	Develop and evaluate strategies for transport and logistics enterprises
		TLIB5010	Plan and implement maintenance schedules
		TLIX4028	Apply knowledge of logistics
Chapter 4	*Supply chains in the Asia–Pacific region*	TLIP5006	Establish international distribution networks
		BSBRSK501	Manage risk

Chapter number	Chapter title	Unit number	Unit title
Chapter 15	*Improving logistics*	BSBWHS501	Ensure a safe workplace
		TLIF0003	Develop and implement policies and procedures to ensure chain of responsibility compliance
		TLIF4064	Manage fatigue management policy and procedures
		TLIP5008	Manage a transport and logistics business unit
		TLIX4028	Apply knowledge of logistics
		BSBCOM501	Identify and interpret compliance requirements
		BSBMGT516	Facilitate continuous improvement
		BSBPMG522	Undertake project work
		TLIP5007	Contribute to the development of a workplace learning environment
		TLIJ5007	Conduct internal quality audits
Chapter 16	*Managing logistics operations*	TLIF0002	Administer chain of responsibility policies and procedures
		BSBWHS501	Ensure a safe workplace
		TLIF0003	Develop and implement policies and procedures to ensure chain of responsibility compliance
		TLIF4064	Manage fatigue management policy and procedures
		TLIP5008	Manage a transport and logistics business unit
		TLIX4028	Apply knowledge of logistics
		TLIX5040	Manage contracted support services
		BSBCOM501	Identify and interpret compliance requirements
		BSBHRM405	Support the recruitment, selection and induction of staff
		BSBINN502	Build and sustain an innovative work environment
		BSBMGT502	Manage people performance
		BSBMGT517	Manage operational plan
		BSBWOR502	Lead and manage team effectiveness
		BSBWRK510	Manage employee relations
		PSPGEN048	Support workplace coaching and mentoring
		TLIF5020	Manage emergencies
		TLIJ5007	Conduct internal quality audits
		TLIL4009	Manage personal work priorities and professional development
		TLIM4004	Mentor individuals or small groups
		TLIU0001	Develop workplace policy and procedures for environmental sustainability
		TLIO5005	Plan and manage security procedures for the enterprise

PART 1

Logistics and supply chains

1

The enterprise, its logistics and supply chains

Learning outcomes

On completion of this chapter you will be able to:

- understand the role of an organisation in adding value for its customers

- appreciate the distinction between a supply chain and a value chain

- distinguish between logistics and supply chains

- understand the structure and connections of supply networks

- discuss the importance of logistics and supply chains to the success of the enterprise

- recognise the importance of logistical trade-offs in the design of supply chains.

Links to other chapters

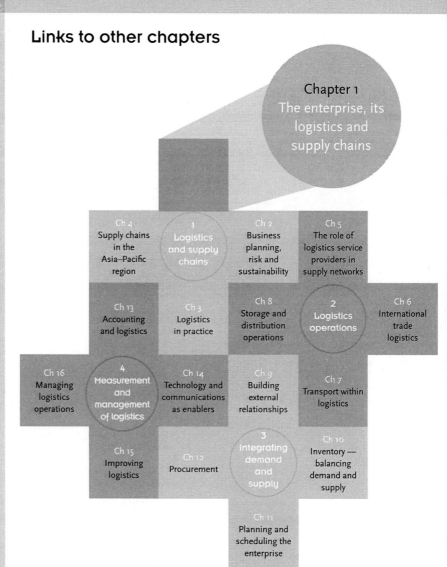

Chapter 1
The enterprise, its logistics and supply chains

1 Logistics and supply chains

Ch 4 Supply chains in the Asia–Pacific region

Ch 2 Business planning, risk and sustainability

Ch 5 The role of logistics service providers in supply networks

Ch 13 Accounting and logistics

Ch 3 Logistics in practice

Ch 8 Storage and distribution operations

2 Logistics operations

Ch 6 International trade logistics

Ch 16 Managing logistics operations

4 Measurement and management of logistics

Ch 14 Technology and communications as enablers

Ch 9 Building external relationships

Ch 7 Transport within logistics

Ch 15 Improving logistics

Ch 12 Procurement

3 Integrating demand and supply

Ch 10 Inventory — balancing demand and supply

Ch 11 Planning and scheduling the enterprise

Key terms

These terms are used in the text. Develop your own notebook by downloading information on each term.

cash flow	demand	original design manufacturer
business flows	supply	(ODM)
added value	fast-moving consumer goods	original equipment manufacturer
value chain	(FMCG)	(OEM)
inbound	consumer packaged goods	power
outbound	(CPG)	dependency
supply chain	full container load (FCL)	availability
logistics	supply network	tier 1 suppliers
core supply chain	logistics service provider	cash-to-cash
extended supply chain	(LSP)	logistical trade-off
sales and operations planning,	third-party logistics (3PL)	
(S&OP)		

Introduction

This chapter provides an overall framework within which to position an organisation's logistics operations and supply chains. It identifies a business and the flow of materials and services from suppliers, through the enterprise to its customers. The network surrounding the enterprise becomes more complex as the business becomes larger and ventures into multiple markets. You will identify the main features of supply chains and logistics and how they must be tailored to suit the business model of the enterprise.

The enterprise and adding value

A business is an economic system in which goods and services are exchanged on the basis of their perceived worth and typically for money. The *Business Dictionary* states, 'every business requires some form of investment and a sufficient number of customers to whom its output can be sold at a profit on a consistent basis' (www.businessdictionary.com).

The income generated provides a **cash flow** for the business, enabling it to purchase goods or services from other businesses, which are called suppliers. There is now a flow of materials and services from suppliers to their customers and a flow of money in the reverse direction. To ensure the required materials and services are supplied and the agreed money is paid, there is a flow of data and information between the parties to the agreement. These **business flows** are shown in Figure 1.1.

Adding value

In providing a product or service that customers want to buy, a business adds value to the supplies that it has purchased.

A coffee shop is an example of a small business that adds value. It has a range of product suppliers, including distributors of beverages and cakes as well as suppliers of services, such as the landlord from whom the premises are rented, utility companies and a bank, which provides financial services such as EFTPOS, a credit card facility and a business loan. In addition, there are one-off suppliers of goods such as furniture and shop-fitting services.

The coffee shop provides food and drinks and a pleasant ambiance.

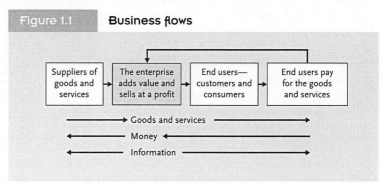

Figure 1.1   Business flows

Suppliers of goods and services	The enterprise adds value and sells at a profit	End users— customers and consumers	End users pay for the goods and services

→ Goods and services →

← Money ←

← Information →

Customers may pay $3 for a coffee and $10 with cakes. In paying these prices, customers will mentally evaluate the **added value** being provided over the input costs of the coffee and cakes in a form that is of use, and at a time and place that is convenient.

These same customers could probably make the coffee in their office for free and bring cakes from home for substantially less cost. However, the ability to get away from their workstation for a few minutes is a factor in the customers' positive cost–benefit analysis that justifies paying the price demanded.

For an example of added value in a larger organisation, consider the cost of the Google Nexus One mobile phone. This was discussed in an article published by *ChaINA* magazine (2010) and is summarised in Table 1.1.

In this example, the total cost of the materials and freight is US$189. HTC has used the intelligence of its staff to design and produce the mobile phone and Google is willing to pay US$281 for the finished item.

To provide this new product, HTC has therefore added value of US$92 to the purchase cost of material items. The US$92 is then available for HTC to pay its staff, keep the business established, pay the banks, pay the government and provide a dividend to its shareholders.

Where is the added value in services? An example is a car insurance company; it provides a risk management service, such that if the insured driver damages a car valued at $40 000, it is repaired at full cost, even though the driver has paid only, say, a $1000 premium. The administration cost may be a 10th of the premium and the difference can be considered the added value provided by the insurance company.

Table 1.1 Mobile phone added value

Component	Comment	Cost US$
Processor		30.50
Memory		20.40
Electrical		16.30
Camera		12.50
Mechanical		2.80
Total material cost		174.15
Manufacturing cost	Estimated cost: HTC (Taiwan) is the original design manufacturer (ODM)	27
Airfreight to USA	Estimated cost: sent to Brightpoint Inc, the logistics service provider (LSP) in North America for HTC	5
Fulfilment	Estimated cost: including final configuration and packaging (5–8 minutes per unit) and inventory holding cost	10
Total delivered cost	Estimated	216
Sale price by HTC to Google	Estimated 30% gross margin	281
Added value by HTC		92
Sale price by Google to consumers	Estimated 87% gross margin	530

Source: Based on *ChaINA* magazine, March–April 2010, www.supplychains.com.

Value chain

The concept of added value was initially promoted by Porter (1985) in which he defined value as the amount that a buyer is willing to pay for an item. He considered the **value chain** as a combination of nine activities that work together within any business to provide value for customers.

The nine activities are divided into a primary and support focus. The primary activities are:

* operations – logistics (inbound, internal and outbound) plus production
* sales and marketing.

The support activities are:

* administrative infrastructure
* human resource management
* information technology
* procurement.

The value-adding process and the concept of economic exchange between organisations are at the core of business relationships.

Supply chains and networks

The terms **supply chain** and **logistics** have gained popularity over time and are often used interchangeably. Although linked, the terms do have different meanings; these concepts will be examined in relation to their part in adding value within and between organisations.

Supply chain

The term 'supply chain' entered the business language in the early 1990s, although it was first used in an article about ten years earlier. The concept was developed to reflect the complex arrangements that take place in getting goods from their initial raw materials to the ultimate finished product and so provide benefits for the end user.

Commencing with the final end user for an item and stepping back through each link, there are purchases by each party in the chain back to the raw materials purchased from mines and farms. This provides the supply chain for an item, as represented in Figure 1.2.

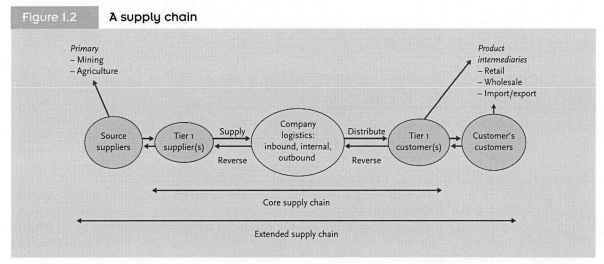

Figure 1.2   A supply chain

The transactions within a business and between a business and its immediate (tier 1) suppliers and customers are referred to as the **core supply chain**. The **extended supply chain** includes all the suppliers' suppliers back to the farm and mine and all of the customers' customers (product intermediaries) that handle an item through to the end user or consumer.

An example of a supply chain is that of aluminium cans, shown in Figure 1.3 overleaf.

Here, the elapsed time from the bauxite mine to the retail shelf in Europe is about 300 days. However, the time when value is being added to the material is about three hours: that is, to convert the bauxite through all stages to finally become a can containing a beverage.

What is occurring for the balance of the time? The material is either in transit through transport links (arrows in the diagram) or is resting as inventory in the multiple inbound and outbound storage areas. Because bauxite is mined in remote locations, it can be argued that transport from the mine to the alumina refinery is adding value—what do you think?

Other examples of time taken through supply chains are:

* cars—from iron ore to vehicle for sale at a dealer: 12 months
* medical grade plastic tubing used in hospitals—from completion of manufacturing in America to customer hospitals throughout Asia: 11 months
* clothing—from the wool fleece shorn from a sheep to clothing at a retailer: 18 months.

Time increases costs in supply chains—planning the added-value stages, planning to move the item, transport time and holding inventory. The total cost is not only the money paid directly to the business and to other parties in the supply chains, but the cost of time, especially at bottlenecks: 'What you do takes time and costs money—the longer it takes, the more it costs' (Goldratt & Cox 1984).

Supply chain and value chain

The difference between a supply chain and value chain is defined by Feller, Shunk & Callarman (2006), who see a supply chain as being focused on 'integrating supplier and producer processes, improving efficiency and reducing waste, while value chains' focus is downstream, on creating value in the eyes of the customer'. This is illustrated in Figure 1.4 overleaf.

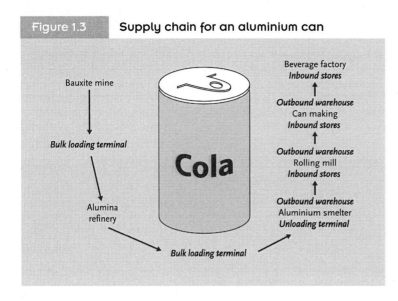

Figure 1.3   Supply chain for an aluminium can

Bauxite mine

Bulk loading terminal

Alumina refinery

Bulk loading terminal

Beverage factory
Inbound stores

Outbound warehouse
Can making
Inbound stores

Outbound warehouse
Rolling mill
Inbound stores

Outbound warehouse
Aluminium smelter
Unloading terminal

Although the illustration in Figure 1.4 (below) indicates two parallel lines for the value chain and supply chain, they can meet through an integrative planning process, called **sales and operations planning (S&OP)**, as shown in Figure 1.5 opposite.

The S&OP process is vital to the improved performance of a business and is discussed in Chapter 11.

Multiple supply chains

A business has two external components—the **demand** side and **supply** side. For each product type on the demand side and each material type on the supply side, there could be a different supply chain; a business will actually deal with multiple supply chains.

The demand side of the enterprise is driven by the customer and their requirements. For industrial products, the end user is more likely to be the business that buys the item, but for consumer products, the end user can be a commercial customer or a consumer. As an example, for **fast moving consumer goods (FMCG)** such as mobile phones, and **consumer packaged goods (CPG)** such as breakfast cereals, the customer is a retail chain, which buys the product in large quantities from the brand company, whereas the consumer is the person who purchases a single unit of the item, such as a box of cereal to consume at breakfast time.

Wholesalers are customers that act as intermediaries between manufacturers or importers and smaller retailers. Manufacturers or importers may only supply large deliveries, for example a full truckload or **full container load (FCL)**, while smaller retailers require a specific mix from the total product range being offered. The role of the wholesaler is to promote the products within categories that suit different customers and then break the bulk delivery received into the smaller deliveries required.

Figure 1.4   Value chain and supply chain

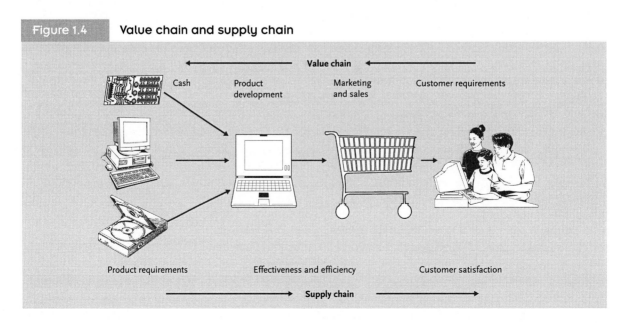

Value chain

Cash   Product development   Marketing and sales   Customer requirements

Product requirements   Effectiveness and efficiency   Customer satisfaction

Supply chain

Consider pharmaceuticals in Australia. These are predominantly sold through the approximately 4000 pharmacies (or chemists). There are about 150 manufacturers and importers of pharmaceutical products, so for each chemist to buy from each manufacturer once per month would be a substantial task. Instead, there are three 'full-line' wholesalers (with about 90 per cent of the market) who supply the pharmacies on an 'as required' basis, which can be within a few hours for certain types of drugs.

Another type of customer is the distributor, which brand companies use to distribute their products through specific market channels; for example, the food services channel supplies breakfast cereals in different packaging to hotels, hospitals and catering companies.

On the supply side are the products, materials, components and services procured from the immediate, or tier 1, suppliers. These suppliers in turn source their own products and services from their suppliers (referred to as tier 2 suppliers) and so on. Sometimes a tier 2 or tier 3 source supplier can have a direct relationship with the principal brand name business to supply a specific item.

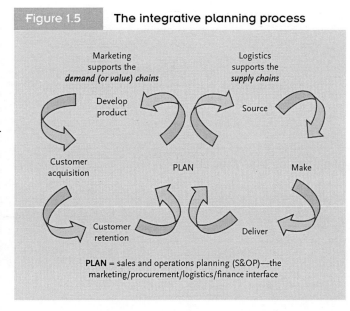

Figure 1.5   **The integrative planning process**

PLAN = sales and operations planning (S&OP)—the marketing/procurement/logistics/finance interface

Similar to the supply side, the brand company's direct customers are referred to as 'tier 1' and their customers are referred to as 'tier 2'. Again, it is possible for the brand company to have a direct relationship with some non-tier 1 customers.

Supply network

As discussed, a business will have multiple supply chains for its outbound finished goods, inbound materials, components and purchased products. Figure 1.6 (overleaf) represents these as a network of relationships for a business.

In this diagram, the enterprise will have its tier 1 material suppliers and customers (which have their own **supply networks**), and **logistics service providers (LSP)**, which undertake contracted roles in:

- goods movement: often referred to as **third party logistics (3PL)**, while governments may refer to 3PL services as the transport and logistics (T&L) industry
- material services such as buying services
- professional firms such as IT services.

'Logistics service provider' is a collective term that identifies the wide range of logistics services available. This is discussed in Chapter 5.

The supply network can also include contract manufacturers and **original design manufacturers (ODM)** that produce products on behalf of the brand owner, which are known in this instance as **original equipment manufacturers (OEM)**. The OEM will coordinate with the contract manufacturers and component suppliers for delivery of materials and components to the contract manufacturers. They in turn provide finished products to distribution contractors, for delivery to customers on behalf of the brand owner.

The supply network for the business has both physical and communications links. The transmission of standardised data through supply chains is being assisted by the development of communication standards and implementation of technologies, such as mobile and radio frequency. The communications capability will be a vital element of supply networks into the future, and is discussed in Chapter 14.

One of the first references to the term 'supply network' was by Rosenbaum and Kuglin (2000), but a definition of the term is provided by Slack et al. (2007):

Figure 1.6 **A supply network**

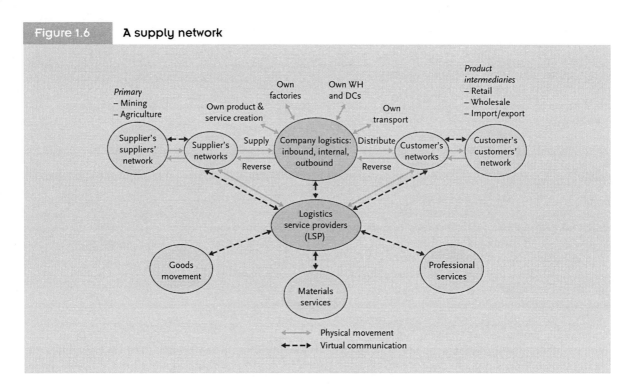

A supply network perspective means setting an operation in the context of all the other operations with which it interacts, some of which are its suppliers and its customers. Materials, parts, other information, ideas and sometimes people all flow through the network of customer–supplier relationships formed by all these operations.

A supply network consists of four components:

- physical locations: the 'nodes' of the network. Locations can be factories, warehouses, distribution centres, ports and intermodal terminals.
- transport: movement between nodes of the network (the links). Transport can be by trucks, trains, aircraft and marine vessels (deep sea and river).
- systems: flows of data, systems software applications and tools that support activities within the network. Examples are order management systems, warehouse management systems, transport management systems, logistics modelling and simulation, and inventory optimisation tools.
- relationships: the business and personal relationships developed within and between organisations, recognising the similarities and differences between peoples and their cultures. This is illustrated in Figure 1.7 opposite.

As an example, Confucianism has *Xiao* as a moral imperative (meaning filial piety—that is, benefiting a son or daughter and respect for parents). Therefore, in a business setting:

- family members are trusted, within reason
- friends, colleagues and associates are trusted to the extent that a mutual dependence has been established
- all others will have no assumptions made about their goodwill.

However, within a Christian and Western business relationship, more support is given to legal and contractual approaches, which establish the boundaries of the business relationship.

The basis of these business relationships is the use of **power** and **dependency**. As Cox (2000) argues, 'the freedom to develop advantageous terms is limited by the reality of exercising power and dependency in dealings between organisations'.

Logistics and availability

Unlike the term 'supply chain', the term 'logistics' is very old, but only entered regular vocabulary following the 1990 Gulf War, which various media portrayed as the 'logistics' war.

However, many years earlier, the French military campaigns led by Napoleon Bonaparte, especially into Russia, and those of the British in both the American War of Independence and the New Zealand Maori wars, could also be considered 'logistic'. These campaigns extended over long distances. In the case of the British, they obtained the majority of their supplies from England. The supply chains were therefore long and their management was too complex. The resultant failure to provide a continuous supply of military materiel contributed to the loss of each campaign.

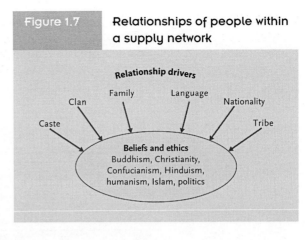

Figure 1.7 Relationships of people within a supply network

The term 'logistic' is derived from the Greek words *logizesthai* (to compute) and *logistikos* (skilled in calculating). In Roman times there was a military administrative official called Logisa and by Napoleon's time, with the advent of organised military campaigns, the French word *loger* (to lodge) was in use. Logistics in the military sense therefore required the moving, lodging and supplying of troops and their equipment.

The development of logistics ideas remained in the military until the advent of the Dutch and English trading companies of the 17th and 18th centuries, which organised cargoes and voyages between Asia and Europe and were the forerunners of the multinational companies of today.

At a presentation concerning the positioning of logistics and supply chains, the consultant and educator Kerry Hammond (c. 2001) stated:

> Logistics provides the underpinning theories and techniques which drive supply chains, as mathematics and physics underpin engineering. Hence, in logistics the theories and techniques used within transport, warehousing, procurement and inventory planning underpin supply chains and are similar to learning about and using calculus and algebra as the pillars of engineering.

Further, the US Council of Supply Chain Management Professionals (CSCMP) gives the following definition:

> Logistics is that part of the supply chains that plans, implements and controls the efficient, effective forward and reverse flow and storage of goods, services and related information between the point of origin and the point of consumption in order to meet customers' requirements ... Logistics Management is an integrating function which co-ordinates and optimises all logistics activities, as well as integrates logistics activities with other functions ...

Logistics is therefore what an organisation does; the supply chain for an item is the environment within which the item and its constituent parts move. While these terms have become buzz words, used liberally and interchangeably, they are different.

The equivalent Chinese term for logistics is *wu liu* (flow of goods); however, as with those who use the term 'logistics' in the English-speaking community, the term is not well understood by Chinese speakers.

Logistics management in business is continuing to evolve, primarily due to:

- the availability and decreasing cost of IT and communications hardware and applications, which allow the development of technologies and applications that enable and hasten the collaboration and integration of parties in supply chains
- the development of a body of knowledge since the 1960s concerning the discipline.

Figure 1.8 overleaf illustrates the stages to date.

Figure 1.8   **Stages in logistics evolution**

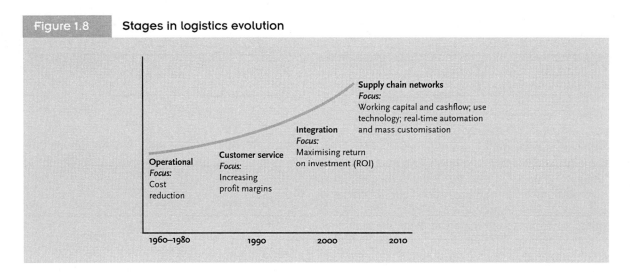

Availability

In practical terms, satisfying customer needs means the time-related positioning of resources (internal and external, including immediate suppliers) to provide **availability** of goods and services for customers at the lowest total cost.

If availability is the objective of logistics, then the measurement of logistics performance at each stage of a supply chain is 'delivery, in full, on time, with accuracy' (DIFOTA). This measure is holistic—while it measures the physical capability of the business, the wider administrative and systems capability must also be considered. It is of little value to deliver in full and on time if the customer's order has the wrong address for delivery, or the invoice is incorrect. DIFOTA is discussed in chapter 15.

PRODUCT LOGISTICS

Logistics within a product business contains four subsets that together provide availability:

1. *Customer service logistics*
   a. Inventory: how many and what value of products to hold, where and in what form and for what function, what materials to acquire and when, what to make (or import) and when
   b. Material movement: importing, materials storage, finished goods warehousing and distribution operations (provided through the organisation's own resources or providers of distribution services)
   c. Transport: owned by the organisation or operated by a provider of transport services.
2. *Conversion logistics*—planning of manufacturing or the final assembly, pack and test of inputs. In conversion logistics the planning of inventory is the main component of availability.
3. *Reverse logistics*—the return of goods, which typically involves packaging (primary and secondary), parts (warranty items) or whole products (recalled items).
4. *Support logistics*—the post-sales support of products and services. Also the planning and scheduling for the life-cycle support of an organisation's internal infrastructure and capital equipment. The United States military adopted the term 'integrated logistics management' (ILM) in the 1960s, which addressed the need for managing the total cost of ownership throughout the life cycle of weapons systems. ILM uses the techniques and tools of integrated logistics support (ILS) and logistics systems analysis (LSA). The underlying reason for support logistics is that design decisions and actual operational expenditure can be at widely spaced intervals, requiring management of the process that reflects the approximate situation at each stage of the product life cycle:
   a. Concept and specify stage: only about 50 per cent of supportability decisions are made
   b. Design and development stage: only about 20 per cent of support decisions can be changed without considerable effort

c. Use stage: only about 5 per cent of support decisions can be changed without considerable effort
d. Planned maintenance stage: 70 per cent of total costs are incurred.

Each of these four subsets of logistics contains a planning (thinking and calculating) and physical (doing) function. They can be performed internally by the enterprise or contracted externally to specialist service providers, which is commonly called outsourcing.

SERVICES LOGISTICS

Services logistics is the process of providing availability for non-material activities and associated materials required in the delivery of a service. Services logistics can be applied in a wide range of businesses, for example in fast-food outlets, hospitals and health delivery, finance and insurance and in the entertainment sector.

The factors addressed in planning for services that are different from those of a product company are capacity and costs. Service capacity is mainly about planning for the availability of people, which have the same role as inventory in a product environment. Features of planning for service delivery are:

- People must be available for peak period demands.
- Capacity planning is often by defined groups or teams that operate in fixed sizes.
- Groups are often dedicated to a location, so are difficult to re-allocate.

The cost structure in services generally has labour and other resources as fixed, at more than 75 per cent of operating costs:

- There is a low marginal cost to adding an additional customer.
- The loss of revenue from a disaffected customer has a greater effect than in a product environment.

Logistics strategy background—providing the products and services

Business model

The discussion concerning supply chains and logistics has highlighted that there is not a single or best way to design supply chains and implement logistics; it depends on multiple elements, including the industry, markets, products, processes and locality.

The most suitable business model (that is, most profitable) for a commercial business is, in part, dependent on how it interacts with its core supply chains (see Figure 1.2) and supply network (see Figure 1.6). As the global influence of supply chains is so pervasive, companies need to undertake a regular review (say, annually) and if need be, adapt the business model to take advantage of changes in the supply chains.

Industry and product type

Logistics strategy and operations will differ by broad industry type. These are shown in Figure 1.9 overleaf.

Within each industry type, there are different influences and pressures at the inbound, internal or outbound parts of their core supply chains. Even in primary industries such as mining and agriculture there are input supply chains, such as equipment, fuel, seed and fertiliser. There is also the availability and capacity of transport modes to move the product in bulk, especially at harvest time or when there is high international demand for minerals.

The handling, storage and transport of discrete and bulk products are very different, although companies can have bulk products as inputs and discrete products as outputs.

'Owning' the product

Within a company, ownership of the product has a strong influence on the business model, because it is the product 'owner' who is responsible for making money for the business. How the ownership is structured will influence the logistics operations. Responsibility for sales and profit can be assigned by:

- divisions or subsidiary companies, each with their own sales teams, which could even compete with other divisions of the same business
- geographic areas, in which region or area managers are responsible for all that happens within their allocated geographic zone—within the Asia–Pacific region, businesses may define the sub-regions of East

Figure 1.9 Industry types

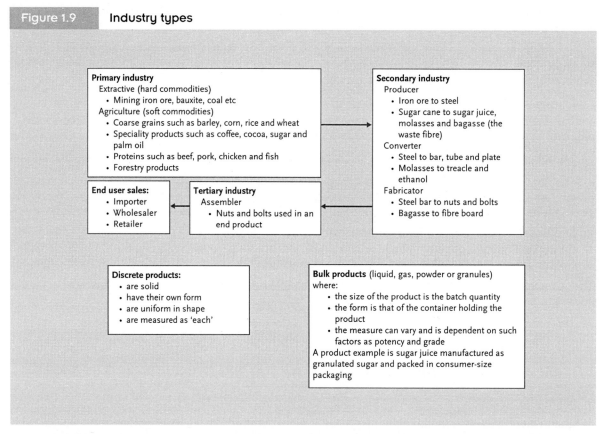

Asia (greater China, Japan and Korea); South-East Asia (the ASEAN countries); South Asia (India, Pakistan, Bangladesh and Sri Lanka) and Oceania (Australia, New Zealand and the Pacific island states). Within the South-East Asia sub-region, there could be smaller sub-regions such as the Greater Mekong region, consisting of Thailand, Vietnam, Cambodia and Laos
- product group, where a particular product group is manufactured in its own facilities and 'sold' (at an internal transfer price), to the company's sales group.

How a business views its markets
Businesses operate with their own view of how they relate to their markets; therefore, businesses in the same industry can operate in quite different ways, including their logistics; for example:
- Domestic—the business only operates within a local or country market.
- Multi-domestic—the domestic business model is copied for all countries where the business operates.
- International—the approach is that all countries operate as subsidiaries of head office; therefore policies and plans are centrally generated, although products and operations may differ in individual countries.
- Global—there is one company image, with standard product lines and standardised processes. There are few manufacturing locations (or outsourced contract manufacturing) that serve all markets.
- Transnational—the brand image is of high importance, but the approach is to 'think global, act local'. An objective is to effectively balance local and global sourcing, manufacturing and distribution.

Business structures and supply chains
Each approach noted below defines the links in the supply chains and has an impact on the supply network configuration, the **cash-to-cash** cycle and organisation structure.

1   *Core or focused business*—where the objective is to have a focused business (narrow product range or market), concentrate on the highest value adding parts of the supply chains and outsource the balance. This results in a network of logistics service providers (LSP) that require managing and integrating into the business.

2 *Horizontal integration*—where the aim is to sell a type of product or service in numerous markets through subsidiary companies. Each provides variations of the product to a different market segment or geographical area. It is common in the retail apparel sector. This approach will hopefully increase total sales, but lower the exposure to any one market segment and fully utilise the company's own or outsourced production facilities.

   Conglomerate organisations have a horizontal integration focus, but instead of being in one type of product or service, they can be in many. In this model, the company owns a collection of non-related businesses, with the holding company acting as a central bank. This business model went out of fashion in the 1980s, when 'focused' businesses became the accepted model. It is worth noting, however, that one of Australia's major businesses, Wesfarmers, is a conglomerate. Khanna and Palepu (1997) argued that conglomerates can be a useful model for developing countries, because the wider institutions of business (for example distribution and training) may not be widely available in the country. Strong conglomerates with trusted corporate brands could therefore best address the multiple needs of a developing economy.

3 *Vertical integration*—where consideration is given to the amount of a supply chain that an organisation owns, controls or influences. Vertically integrated businesses share a common owner and are united through an administrative hierarchy, but each member of the hierarchy produces different products or services, which are combined through a specific supply chain to satisfy a customer need.

   Manufacturers or importers can forward (or downstream) integrate towards the retail demand side (an example is IKEA furniture); manufacturers or importers can also integrate backward (or upstream) towards the supply side, by acquiring supplier businesses. This can be driven by actual or potential supply shortages, such as the need for rare earths in the manufacture of electric cars and mobile phones.

4 *Virtual integration*—where the company forms a network of business that are drawn together to meet a specific customer need in a project management structure. When the need has been satisfied, the company will form new networks to address different requirements or contracts. An example is when major construction projects are carried out.

5 *Supplier alliance*—where a formal relationship exists between two or more parties for a set period of time. The objective is to pursue a set of agreed-upon goals or to meet a critical business need, while remaining independent organisations. The alliance is a collaboration that aims for a synergy between the parties, where the total gain is greater than the sum of the individual business parts.

   The parties to the agreement may participate by providing the alliance with resources such as products, distribution channels, manufacturing capability, project funding, capital equipment, knowledge, expertise and intellectual property.

   Public–private partnership (sometimes referred to as PPP or P[3]) is a special case of strategic alliance, where a government venture is funded and operated through a contract between a government and one or more private sector companies.

   Unfortunately, the terms 'partner' and 'partnership' have become a part of the business vocabulary, even though they should be rarely used. *Encyclopaedia Britannica* defines the term 'partnership' as 'a voluntary association of two or more parties for the purpose of managing a business enterprise and sharing its profits or losses'.

   The sharing of risk and reward is the defining measure of a partnership, but contracts between parties in supply chains rarely meet this criterion. On the basis of the above definition, all supply chain relationships known by the authors and referred to as 'partnerships' are in fact customer–supplier contracts; with some contracts written as alliances to achieve an agreed objective.

Positioning the business

The business model (and therefore logistics) will differ for enterprises within the same industry, depending on how the company decides to address its customers' needs. Hayes and Wheelwright (1979) argue that although each business has the same steps in its business flow (Figure 1.1), the means to implement these steps is very different. It depends on the products and the processes used to produce the product or service for sale. Figures 1.10–1.13 enhance the work of Hayes and Wheelwright.

Figure 1.10 overleaf illustrates the matrix of product types and processes that are common to both product and service businesses.

Figure 1.10	Positioning an organisation—products and services

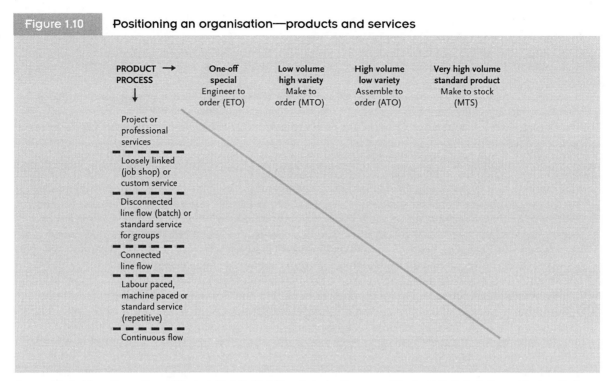

Source: Adapted from Hayes, R. and Wheelwright, S.C., 'Link Manufacturing Process and Product Life Cycles', *Harvard Business Review*, January–February 1979.

The explanation for the different product sectors is as follows:

1. Design is based on customer's specification and then 'engineered to order' (ETO).
2. Provide a design service (can be for options to a base product) and 'make to order' (MTO).
3. Assemble final products to order = Assemble to order (ATO) is based on orders from either customers or sales. Make or buy materials, components, sub-assemblies and options to:
   a. immediately assemble into finished goods and deliver. Can use just in time/lean/flow models.
   b. stock materials, components, sub-assemblies, etc. as inventory, then assemble items or mix ingredients and deliver, based on a customer order (this is called 'postponement').
4. Sell from finished goods inventory = Make to stock (MTS):
   a. Make finished goods from multiple components and hold in inventory.
   b. Make finished goods from one or a few ingredient materials that are processed into end products, co-products and by-products, then hold in inventory.
   c. Import finished items and hold in inventory.
   d. Make and distribute 'short shelf life' (perishable) products, such as dairy and seafood.

In positioning a business, its resources are focused on either the process or the product:

* Towards the top left-hand corner of the diagonal (ETO and MTO), the focus is on the process, so that customer orders and products compete for the available resources.
* In the bottom right of the diagonal (ATO and MTS), the focus is on the product, with the workforce and equipment (can be duplicated) organised around the product or service.

Figure 1.11 Positioning an organisation—examples

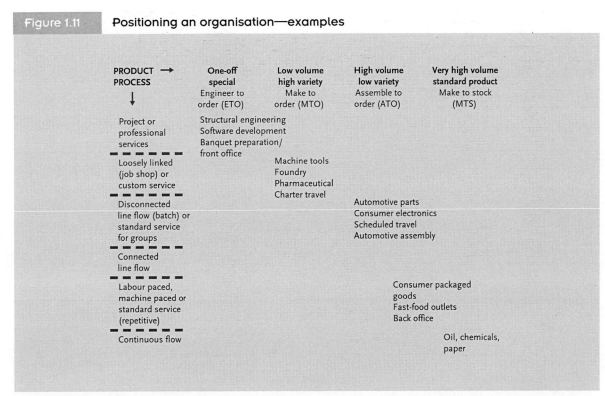

Source: Adapted from Hayes, R. and Wheelwright, S.C., 'Link Manufacturing Process and Product Life Cycles', *Harvard Business Review*, January–February 1979.

Examples of enterprises in each of the sectors are shown in Figure 1.11. The characteristics and complexity of these organisations is shown in Figure 1.12 overleaf. The challenges for each of these types of business are identified in Figure 1.13 on page 17.

The essential point to note is that the challenges in each sector are very different; therefore, approaches to overcoming these challenges will also be different in terms of organisation structure, use of technology, plus logistics and planning and scheduling methods.

Logistical trade-offs

When considering the business model, the challenge of **logistical trade-offs** is something that supply chain professionals grapple with on a daily basis. In lay terms it can be represented by the phrase 'you can't have everything', because there is a relationship between the variables of a supply chain—performance, service level, cost and so on.

When these are separated into relationship pairs such as performance to cost, or service levels to cost, or staff training to customer satisfaction, there can be a statistical correlation between the variables. For example, as service levels for customers improve, costs will most likely increase. Conversely, as costs are reduced, performance tends to deteriorate.

Another example is the trade-off between transport costs and the number of warehouses, as shown in Figure 1.14 on page 17.

Figure 1.12   Positioning an organisation—characteristics

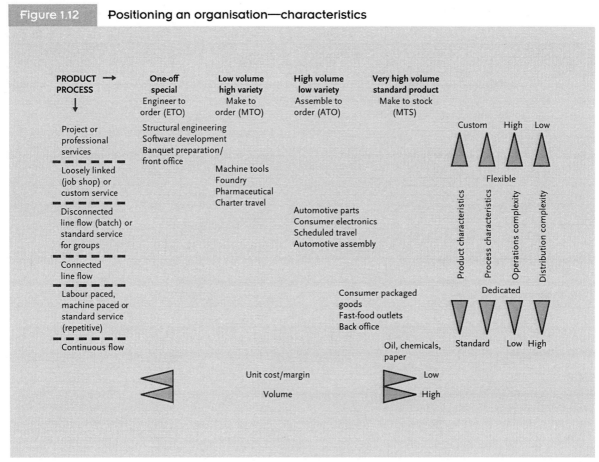

Source: Adapted from Hayes, R. and Wheelwright, S.C., 'Link Manufacturing Process and Product Life Cycles', *Harvard Business Review*, January–February 1979.

Global supply chains make the trade-offs in logistics more acute. For example:

- The reduced cost of globally sourced materials is traded off against the increased cost of holding additional inventory caused by the longer lead times.
- The lower cost of manufacturing in a particular location may be offset by the transport costs incurred and the administrative burden of importing/exporting.

There is a point at which the equation can be optimised and the 'best value for money' combination of the variables is achieved. Creating the balance between these variables is an applied problem of supply chains and can become very complex when considering supply networks.

Figure 1.13 Positioning an organisation—challenges

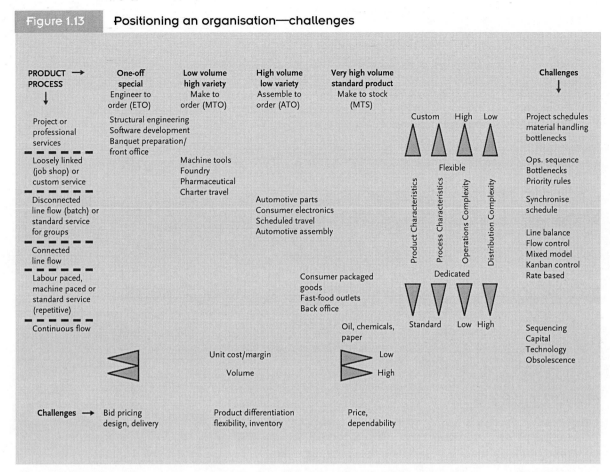

Source: Adapted from Hayes, R. and Wheelwright, S.C., 'Link Manufacturing Process and Product Life Cycles', *Harvard Business Review*, January–February 1979.

Figure 1.14 Example of a logistical trade-off

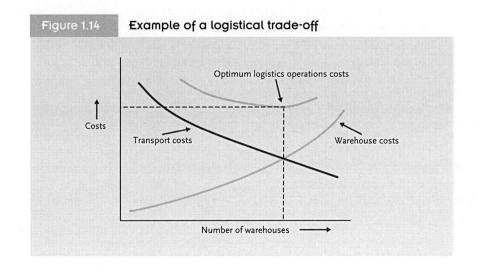

Chapter questions

Operational

1. Explain the difference between logistics strategy and logistics operations.
2. What are some of the common causes of the misalignment of logical and physical supply chains? What are the consequences of such misalignments?
3. Select a routine process in a supply network from which you can obtain the necessary information. Map the physical process. Then map the corresponding logical process.

Planning

4. Are there any undesirable consequences of the terms 'supply chain' and 'logistics' being used interchangeably?
5. Draw a map of a supply chain network (of multiple supply chains) from which you can obtain the necessary information. Are there any peculiarities of this network?
6. Develop a map of a value chain from which you can obtain the necessary information. Where do you see opportunities to add further value to the process?

Management

7. Is a supply chain strategy different from a logistics strategy? If so, how?
8. In the real world, few organisations are purely horizontally or vertically integrated. Companies can mix the two types of integration in their supply chain network. Identify some examples of such combinations and why these companies chose their specific combination of horizontal and vertical integration.
9. What model of integration (or combination of them) is found in a business from which you can obtain the necessary information? Discuss how this business model affects the supply chain design and logistics operations. In particular, consider the impact on customer service levels, response to the market and quality of data collection and reporting.

References and links

Cox, A., Sanderson, J. & Watson, G., *Power Regimes*, Earlsgate Press, Boston, 2000.

Feller, A., Shunk, D. & Callarman, T., 'Value chains vs. supply chains', *BP Trends*, March 2006, www.ceibs.edu/knowledge/papers/images/20060317/2847.pdf.

Goldratt, E.M. & Cox, J., *The Goal*, North River Press, New York, 1984.

Hayes, R.H. & Wheelwright, S.C., 'Link manufacturing process and product life cycles', *Harvard Business Review*, January–February 1979.

iSuppli, in *ChaINA* magazine, published by the Global Supply Chain Council March–April 2010, at www.supplychains.com.

Khanna, T. & Palepu, K.G., 'Why focused strategies may be wrong for emerging markets', *Harvard Business Review*, July–August, 1997.

Porter, M., *Competitive Advantage: Creating and Sustaining Superior Performance*, Free Press, New York, 1985.

Rosenbaum, F.A. & Kuglin, B.A., *The Supply Chain Network @Internet Speed: Preparing Your Company for the E-Commerce Revolution*, AMACON, New York, 2000.

Slack, N., Chambers, S. & Johnston, R., *Operations Management*, 5th edn, Pearson Education, New York, 2007.

The Business Dictionary, www.businessdictionary.com.

Council of Supply Chain Management Professionals (CSCMP), https://cscmp.org.

Business planning, risk and sustainability

Links to other chapters

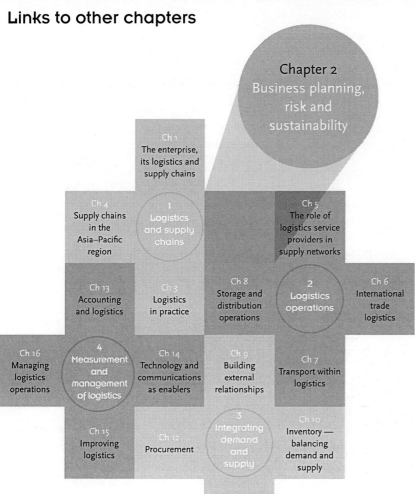

On completion of this chapter you will be able to:

- recognise the necessity for a business plan

- identify key elements of the logistics strategy and contribute to its development

- follow a framework for evaluating risk in a supply chain

- understand the importance of sustainability in supply chain environments

- appreciate the role of reverse logistics and how it is distinct from forward logistics

- conceptualise the connections between multiple supply networks

- explain the rationale behind the enterprise's choice of supply network structure.

Key terms

These terms are used in the text. Develop your own notebook by downloading information on each term.

strategy	variability	network mapping
logistics strategy	contingency plan	distribution centre (DC)
business plan	complexity	competitive advantage
mergers and acquisitions (M&A)	risk assessment	outsourcing
customer	vulnerability (supply chain)	sustainability
power	volume:weight	reverse logistics
disintermediation	value:weight	environmental logistics
consumer	life cycle	peak oil
market share	efficiency	just in time (JIT)
uncertainty	effectiveness	dense trade cluster (DTC)

Introduction

An important question concerning supply chains and logistics is how strategic this concept and discipline are to the future of a commercial business. Views differ, based on how various enterprises interpret the roles. This chapter introduces some ideas about adopting a strategic approach to thinking about and planning for supply chains and logistics. It considers the role of understanding and minimising risk and approaches to sustainability, as a major component of risk, which should be considered for all the strategic factors discussed in the chapter.

Strategic approach

Few companies have a strategic plan for their supply chains and logistics. The reason could be that supply chains are currently viewed with a cost focus and that efficiency in the individual disciplines of purchasing, production and distribution is the main requirement. It can also be reasoned that supply chains are a cross-organisational concept that is not under the control of any one function.

For companies that do develop a **strategy**, the variable use in industry of the terms 'supply chains' and 'logistics' means the strategy may be called by either of the terms or even the terms 'supply chain logistics' or 'operations strategy'. The name is immaterial, so long as the longer-term planning process is structured for outcomes that can be implemented and are achievable.

This chapter will consider the elements that product companies may consider in planning the optimisation of their supply chains so, for consistency of explanation, we will use the term **logistics strategy**. Strategic planning in logistics service provider (LSP) companies is discussed in Chapter 5.

Business plan

Due to change being a constant source of pressure on companies, management has two linked but very different tasks that need to be done in parallel; the first is planning to take advantage of current opportunities and the second is positioning the business for future opportunities. The **business plan** addresses the second task.

The business plan is developed to provide a focal point for thinking about the future of the business, so that executives understand the context in which they operate and are able to respond more rationally to the inevitable competitive and economic pressures they will experience.

This approach allows management to make informed choices concerning the 'best' portfolio of regions or countries and products, and to focus on possible actions in two areas to develop the business:

1. Define steps to gain market share through organic growth of the current business–invest in the fastest growing business sectors in each region and country and, essentially, the fast-growing parts of each sector.
2. Buy growth in markets through **mergers and acquisitions (M&A)**.

These actions need to be based on the long-term objectives of the business and not short-term targets. They should not have an inappropriate time horizon (for example the financial year) or be so specific that middle managers and employees are limited in using their initiative to identify better approaches to the challenges. The business plan provides the guide to building on future or longer term opportunities. As one of its inputs, it is informed by the logistics strategy for the medium term. This in turn links to the planning process called sales and operations planning (S&OP), which is directed at the near-term opportunities.

Logistics strategy approach

A model has been developed by Professor Pieter Nagel that describes the link between supply chains, logistics strategy and logistics operations and is shown in Figure 2.1.

Figure 2.1   Logistics strategy model

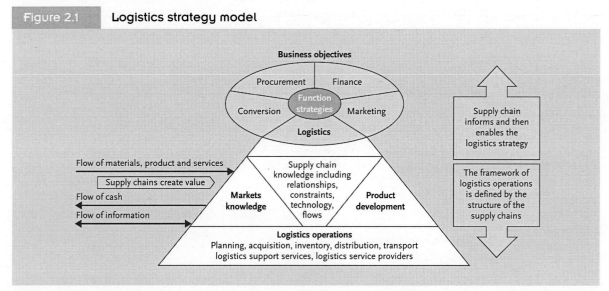

Source: Courtesy of Pieter Nagel.

The logistics strategy of the enterprise is informed by the current and future structure of the supply chains that interact with the business. This structure also defines the framework within which the logistics operations can execute the strategy, including the extent to which logistics operations will be provided by logistics service providers.

The updated logistics strategy will then be *enabled* by the revised supply chains for, as much as they have informed the logistics strategy, they may and probably will be subject to revision.

The logistics strategy is driven, in part, by the strongest influence on the strategy; either the brand, the **customers** or the suppliers. This provides an overview of the **power** structure within the supply network and therefore the degree of freedom the business has in designing and controlling each of its core supply chains, as shown in Figure 2.2 overleaf.

Power and its impact on supply chains

Power is the capability of a party in a relationship to make the other parties take action they otherwise would not do. The concept of power was explored by Porter (1979) who proposed that five forces shape industry competition, as illustrated in Figure 2.3 overleaf.

One aspect of the logistics strategy will identify how power is being used in the business relationships through the supply chains. Examples of how companies may increase their power are:

- restricting the availability of supply for an item in high demand
- incorporating product(s) into a superior service package that is not easily duplicated
- gaining influence through contacts in government
- providing a continual flow of innovative ('must have') products and services that customers have to stock
- obtaining a licence to operate from government
- promoting reputation and prestige by the seller or buyer

- increasing the size of the organisation and its buying strength
- promoting specialised knowledge, e.g. commodity trading
- eliminating dependency on a few powerful customers
- being a technology leader, e.g. holding patents
- developing superior information, optimisation and modelling systems.

Figure 2.2   A supply chain

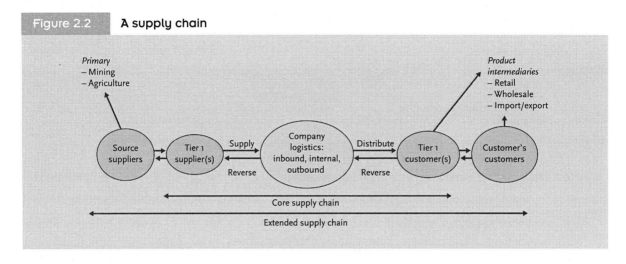

Figure 2.3   The five forces of competition

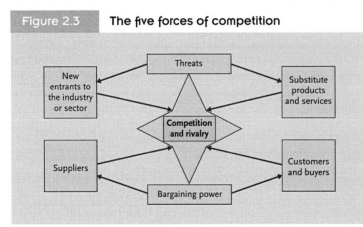

Source: Adapted from Porter, Michael E., 'How Competitive Forces Shape Strategy', *Harvard Business Review*, March–April 1979.

However, an established power base can be weakened. Approaches for this include implementing superior technologies, **disintermediation** (removal of intermediaries in the buying and selling process), e-procurement techniques, creating joint ventures and joint purchasing initiatives.

An example of power shift and response is in **consumer** goods retailing. In the past the manufacturers of consumer goods in developed countries had the power to dictate the supply terms and the retail price for their products. However, there has been a substantial power shift, with large retailers gaining market power.

Figure 2.4 indicates the concentration of retailers by country in grocery retailing.

This graph indicates there will be different outcomes in terms of power between global and local manufacturers, distributors and domestic retailers within each country.

Consider Australia and New Zealand, with a comparatively small market size but high consumer disposable income and a concentrated **market share** between few retailers. Conversely, other countries in the region with a low market share held by each of the large retailers have a situation of comparatively low individual disposable income with a large population.

Under these scenarios, changes in a power relationship between buyers and sellers will have different impacts on the total cost of the supply network. One of the consequences of power-shifting activities is that changes in supply chain processes can redistribute costs at the links in each chain.

The business plan needs to recognise that relationships within supply chains are complex and the use of power and dependencies between companies is common.

Figure 2.4 Concentration of grocery retailers

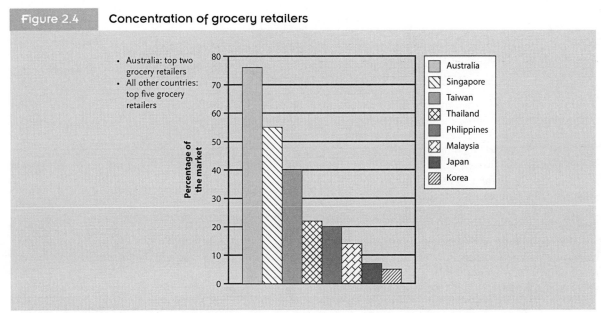

- Australia: top two grocery retailers
- All other countries: top five grocery retailers

Legend:
- Australia
- Singapore
- Taiwan
- Thailand
- Philippines
- Malaysia
- Japan
- Korea

Percentage of the market

Source: Based on National Association of Retail Grocers of Australia, 2002, www.narga.net.au.

Supply chain risks

A current fashion in business is the mantra of 'better, cheaper and faster'. Whether and how this can be built into the strategy and implemented will be influenced by the company's supply chains and logistics structure, relationships and operations.

From the discussion of supply chains, it is evident there can be a high level of **uncertainty** concerning the events that may occur. A supply chain can be complex and, due to the time, distances and range of assets used, subject to **variability**. This means that access to timely data and information is critical and that 'Plan B' must always be resourced should 'Plan A' fail; this is called the **contingency plan**.

Uncertainty is the totality of all the variables, constraints and **complexity** that can exist in a supply chain. The level of uncertainty is high when we know that a current supply chain situation may change, but we do not know exactly when and to what extent. Uncertainty is low when the most likely limits of change in a supply chain are known, based on observation and analysis.

These pressures on supply chains can all be called risks. The risks are amplified by the current acceptance of:

- distance from suppliers and customers
- focus on speed of operations
- disruption of natural and political disasters
- elimination of 'safety margins' concerning time, inventory and working capital.

Risk management requires a structured process that identifies, assesses and mitigates the risks. Risk management helps to answer the question, 'What is the likelihood of X happening, and what are the possible consequences?'

Risk assessment is the important initial process in risk management for supply chains. It consists of the following steps.

- Identify potential supply chain risks.
- Observe the process.
- Identify and document the criticality of risks.
- Assess the likelihood of the event occurring.
- Assess the consequences.
- Develop a risk management plan.
- Implement.
- Evaluate.

A basic risk assessment chart is shown in Figure 2.5 overleaf. A risk assessment using Figure 2.5 will relate directly to the nature of a specific supply chain. For example, in operating a city courier business, the likelihood of a delivery bike rider being involved in an accident may be at level C and the consequences will be at level 2.

This rating recognises the time involved with insurance claims, but also a court summons and bad publicity if a rider is killed or badly injured, which could take the consequences to level 4.

Now consider a global express freight company that has a freighter aircraft full of customers' valuable products, which crashes at a major airport in Asia. The likelihood of this could be rated at level D, but the consequences are at level 4.

The risk level for the courier company at C4 could be extreme, yet for the express freight company, the risk level is lower, at high. The preventative, or risk mitigation, action taken by both companies will depend on what their exposure will be and loss if the event occurs.

Supply chain **vulnerability** is an extension of risk likelihood, which is receiving increased attention. The effects on a company's business can be severe when caused by events in either the extended or core supply chains. However, the risks from activities in the core supply chains will take a higher profile in the logistics strategy due to the more immediate effect they can have on operations and profitability.

Product analysis

The logistics strategy should be considered by each product group, concerning where products will be made or sourced and how they will be moved and stored. The main product factors that affect design of a supply chain are shown in Figure 2.6.

Based on Figure 2.6, the **volume:weight** and **value:weight** ratios enable decisions about how close to markets the product should be made and the modes of transport to use. Availability indicates the immediacy of delivery requirements and therefore the requirements for holding inventory. The product security risk defines the type of storage security required.

Figure 2.5   **Risk assessment**

Consequences					
	1	2	3	4	5
A	H	H	E	E	E
B	M	H	H	E	E
C	L	M	H	E	E
D	L	L	M	H	E
E	L	L	M	H	H

Likelihood (vertical axis)

Risk level
E: Extreme risk—action
H: High risk—management attention
M: Moderate risk—specify responsibility
L: Low risk—process and procedures

Likelihood
A: Almost certain to occur
B: Will probably occur
C: May occur
D: Unlikely to occur
E: Rare occurrence

Consequences
1: Insignificant
2: Minor impact on the business
3: May compromise the business
4: Will seriously compromise the business
5: Will cause loss of business

Figure 2.6   **Supply chain design—product analysis factors**

Volume: weight ratio
Low: rolled steel
      printed material
      canned food
High: beach balls
      feather doona
      lampshades

Value: weight ratio
Low: coal
      iron ore
      bauxite
High: electronic equipment
      jewellery
      musical instruments

Supply chain design considerations

Availability required by the end user
Consumer products
• immediate and frequent buying—CPG
• time to seek and compare—cars
• wait for custom made—furniture
Industrial products

Product security risk
• perishable
• flammable/explosive
• high value/theft
• contamination

In developing the logistics strategy, assumptions must be made relating to future demand requirements, based on the quality of data. Some additional questions relating to the logistics strategy are:

- What is the fit between **life cycle** stages of products and the design of specific logistical activities? For example, in the introduction and decline stages of a product, a more agile, flexible and responsive logistical structure is required. Alternatively, a mature product requires a stable, predictable and low-cost solution.
- How can customer service be improved, with reference to the 'cost to serve'?
- Where should the various parts of the manufacturing process be performed?
- From where should materials and components be sourced?
- Should the enterprise have ownership or control of the upstream and downstream links?
- What global collaborations will assist the **efficiency** and **effectiveness** of the supply chains?

Supply network mapping

To gain additional understanding of the supply network, **network mapping** can be of value in providing a visual structure for a business. An example of a simple network diagram for a company is shown in Figure 2.7.

In this example, the company manufactures in Victoria and has a **distribution centre (DC)** in Sydney and another in Perth. The Sydney DC services customers in New South Wales, Queensland and South Australia, and the Perth DC services the West Australia market. The customer in South Australia services the Northern Territory, and the customer in Victoria services Tasmania.

For other options, this network could instead have a DC in each State that only supplied customers in that State, or a single DC servicing the entire country or some other variation.

Network mapping requires the capture of extensive information, with examples being:

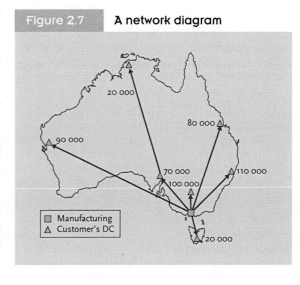

Figure 2.7   A network diagram

* the direction and volume of materials flowing through each supply chain
* details of core suppliers and customers and their respective locations
* ownership or control of specific links and nodes
* contractual responsibilities.

The benefits of using network mapping to better understand a supply network are threefold:

1. It shows how value is being driven through each of the supply chains. By taking a network-wide view and identifying the highest value-added segments of each supply chain, a logistician is able to rationalise the redundant links in the network.
2. It maintains the big picture of the business. For example, a particular link in a network may become weakened as a result of internal issues at a supplier, such as the supply of materials from the supplier's suppliers or industrial disputes. The decision to support the weakest link or eliminate it from the chain would be based on an overall assessment of the relative costs and benefits of the possible alternatives available.
3. It assists in maintaining competitiveness. It provides a customer-centric view of each supply chain through addressing customer demand patterns.

As the attributes of the product group are developed, the **competitive advantage** for that group, based on time and place utilities, can be identified. Slack et al. (2004) defined the utilities as shown in Figure 2.8.

As noted in the diagram, the five attributes of time and place (availability) are the basis of supply chain competitiveness. These can, however, be constrained by where in the total supply chain the business is located, the ease of handling and storage for the material, the basis on which orders are won and the essential qualifiers to be met before obtaining an order.

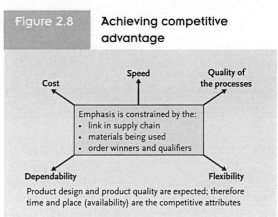

Figure 2.8   Achieving competitive advantage

Source: Based on Slack, N., et al. *Operations Management*, 4th edn, FT Prentice Hall, Harlow, 2004.

Logistics strategy elements

Using the data and information about the product groups and supply chains, the logistics strategy can be considered within five elements:

1. *Customer service strategy*—the appropriate level of service for customers, by product group or segment, considering: order fulfilment, enquiry and investigation, information availability
2. *Inventory location strategy*—centralised or decentralised approach; fast- and slow-moving stock split to different facilities or kept together; location of sites; use of specific technologies and layouts; use of company-owned or contracted facilities
3. *Inventory management policy*—the appropriate amount of stock to hold for various groups of inventory; planning structure that links outbound and inbound materials; in-house control or outsourced
4. *Cost strategy*—trade-off analysis between cost and service
5. *Transport and distribution strategy*—affected by whether the company imports or exports and the size and structure of conurbations being served (transport modes, delivery patterns and storage location considerations based on time taken for deliveries).

These elements are illustrated in Figure 2.9.

An additional element is the **outsourcing** strategy, that is, the degree to which the business will 'make' (do something within the business) or 'buy' (contract another party to do something). While contracting out may be treated as an operational transaction, strategically it relates to decisions concerning the degree of vertical integration within the enterprise. Terms used within 'make or buy' decisions are:

- *Outsourcing*—became part of the business lexicon during the 1980s and is the most prominent form of make vs buy decision. It relates to contracting out a complete process, such as product design, manufacturing or distribution to a services company.
- *Off-shoring*—the transfer of an organisational function to another country; this decision is likely to be outsourced.
- *Near-shoring*—signifies outsourcing or relocating operations to a lower cost country that is within a few hours' distance. Examples of near-shoring are Mexico to North America and Eastern Europe to Germany.
- *In-sourcing*—the term being used to signify that a function that has been outsourced is being brought back within the enterprise.

The objective should be to 'right-shore', that is, integrate the domestic, near-shore and off-shore processes so that logistics can operate within one plan for all the supply chains.

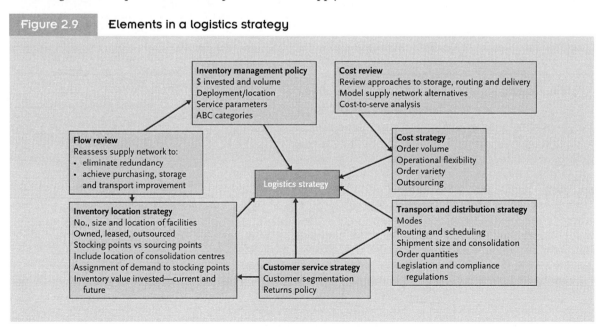

Figure 2.9   Elements in a logistics strategy

Sustainability and logistics strategy

Sustainability and business

An increasingly important element of the logistics strategy will be the future **sustainability** of supply chains. This is a relatively new area of consideration, but companies that are early adopters of the concept are already identifying that improving sustainability can increase profits, not just increase costs.

The Boston Consulting Group and the Sloan Management Review Sustainability Initiative report of September 2009 entitled *The Business of Sustainability* was an international survey of 1500 business leaders. It reported:

> There is a strong consensus that sustainability is having—and will continue to have—a material impact on how companies think and act.
>
> ...
>
> A small number of companies are acting aggressively on sustainability—and reaping substantial rewards ... practitioners with more knowledge about sustainability expanded the definition for sustainability well outside the 'green' silo. They tended to consider the economic, social and political impacts of sustainability-related changes in the business landscape. Simply put, they saw sustainability as an integral part of value creation.

Sustainability is therefore not a fringe issue, but a strategic business concern, beyond just maintaining the viability of the business and driven by government legislation, consumer concern and employee opinion. A critical element of sustainability is the operation of supply chains, which has generated terms such as 'food miles', used to signify the distance a food item has to travel (and therefore consume energy) to find its way onto a retail shelf awaiting purchase.

Responding to sustainability concerns (or are they opportunities?) requires a comprehensive strategy that considers all supply chains in the business. An approach that is an ad hoc collection of tactical actions designed to address a particular area will not be effective. The strategy requires an overall statement of purpose that is the basis for action.

The electronics brand company Hewlett Packard has the following statement of purpose concerned with the greenhouse gas element of sustainability:

> HP will reduce Greenhouse Gas (GHG) emissions from HP-owned and HP-leased facilities 20 per cent under 2005 levels by 2013 on an absolute basis. This goal is independent of organic business growth and will be accomplished by reducing the worldwide energy footprint of HP facilities and data centers.
>
> Our goals help us to provide products and services that are safe and environmentally sound throughout their life cycles, conduct our operations in an environmentally responsible manner and create health and safety practices and work environments that enable HP employees to work injury-free.

HP has also implemented a Supply Chain Social and Environmental Responsibility (SER) Program with its suppliers across all supply chains.

Linfox is an Australian-owned logistics service provider that operates throughout the Asia–Pacific region. It states it has 'set a goal to reduce our rate of greenhouse gas emissions by 15 per cent by 2010 based on 2006–07 emissions. We are reducing our greenhouse emissions through improved business practices, environmentally friendly technologies and the behaviour of our people ...'. In November 2009 Chairman Peter Fox announced that Linfox had cut carbon emissions by 28 per cent, well ahead of schedule.

These examples illustrate that both product and service companies can incorporate sustainability objectives within their overall business and supply chain logistics strategy.

Carbon measurement and reporting

Carbon measurement and reporting is a relatively new aspect of supply chain sustainability. The *National Greenhouse and Energy Reporting Act 2007* (Cth) (NGER) obliges all Australian corporations that control facilities and consume or produce energy or emit greenhouse gases above specified thresholds to supply data for the Greenhouse and Energy Data Officer at www.climatechange.gov.au.

The New Zealand Business Council for Sustainable Development provides information concerning sustainable supply chains. It also provides a guide to the NZ Emissions Trading Scheme (ETS) and a sustainable development e-book called *Hatched*.

The EU has implemented an Emissions Trading Scheme but many other countries are still deciding about the structure and approach to a scheme that requires industrial polluters to pay. The two methods of payment are 'cap and trade' and 'carbon tax'. An article, 'Understanding Cap and Trade and Carbon Taxes' at www.thegreensupplychain.com provides an explanation of the difference between the two approaches.

Peak oil

In December 2009, the BP Oil *Statistical Review of World Energy* recorded the January 2015 oil futures contract at US$95 a barrel and the January 2017 contract at more than US$100 per barrel. Assessing previous futures prices against the actual price provides some concern for the accuracy of these forward expectations of prices; however, the consensus is that oil prices will increase over time and affect the design of supply chains and networks.

Speaking to *The Independent* newspaper in London on 6 August 2009, the International Energy Agency's (IEA) chief economist, Dr Fatih Birol, stated:

> The first detailed assessment of more than 800 oil fields in the world, covering three-quarters of global reserves, has found that most of the biggest fields have already peaked and that the rate of decline in oil production is now running at nearly twice the pace as calculated just two years ago. On top of this, there is a problem of chronic under-investment by oil-producing countries, a feature that is set to result in an 'oil crunch' within the next five years. The IEA estimates that the decline in oil production in existing fields is now running at 6.7 per cent a year compared to the 3.7 per cent decline it had estimated in 2007, which it now acknowledges to be wrong.

Transport, including the movement of both people and freight, currently accounts for over 60 per cent of all oil consumed globally, and global trade has expanded in part because of the availability of cheap oil. A risk assessment of a company's exposure to supply chain interruptions and price increases caused by availability of oil should therefore be a part of the logistics strategy process.

Reverse logistics

Reverse logistics will become an essential part of sustainability for product companies and in some companies has become an integral part of **environmental logistics**, which aims to reduce all sustainability-based logistics costs.

Reverse logistics is the process of handling items as they travel back through a supply chain for one of the following reasons:

- recall (faulty)
- repair (service)
- returns (warranty)
- recycle (convert)
- refurbishment (end of lease or rental period)
- remanufacturing (hours of operation or trade-in).

An entire supply chain is designed and built around 'progressive disaggregation'; that is, as the materials progress through the inbound chain and then products through the outbound chain, the parcel size is progressively reduced. The reverse logistics process does the opposite and, as such, is counter-intuitive to the way supply chains normally work.

Reverse logistics is an area that has received publicity in recent years due to increasing consumer expectations, the environmental lobby and government legislation (particularly in Europe and Japan). However, it appears that unless there is legislation and an associated recycling market, companies are not forthcoming in establishing a reverse logistics culture, because it is seen only as a cost. Reverse logistics is currently a 'poor cousin' in business—a process that often does not have an owner, is not allocated resources and not professionally managed in the way companies expect of their outbound logistics.

Developments in freight movement

The assessment of **peak oil** effects on a company's supply chains will need to incorporate the likely government regulations that may limit road transport movements. These regulations will be constructed on a desire that wherever possible, only full trucks and containers are moved.

This will require re-evaluating **just in time (JIT)**/'lean' assumptions and the incorporation of sustainability parameters into calculations of order and container size, so as to reduce the number of deliveries.

To also reduce the number of deliveries and control inbound costs is the move towards customers (mainly retailers) buying free on board (FOB) at the factory gate of suppliers (also called 'factory gate pricing') and organising the transport. The collection operates as a 'milk round', whether within the country or in offshore countries, whereby the buyer's vehicle collects from all suppliers on a planned basis and delivers to the customer's facility. This reduces the number of part-loaded delivery vehicles required.

In the past, much attention has been paid to the improvement of specific elements of transport, goods movement and storage; however, it is now opportune to focus on the transfer points between transport modes. An approach to improving and consolidating freight movements is the **dense trade cluster (DTC)**.

A definition of a DTC by Leitner & Harrison (2001) is, 'a site or nodal point, located away from traditional land, air and coastal borders. It facilitates and processes international trade through strategic investments in multimodal transport assets and by promoting value-added services as goods move through the supply chains.'

Clusters designated for logistics activities have been an internationally proven concept since the 1980s. They counter traffic congestion, increase transport and distribution efficiency and bring speed, visibility and flexibility to importer and exporter supply chains. Hubs have been established in America; likewise in Europe, where there are more than 200 such clusters of varying sizes in 18 countries. In the Asia–Pacific region, development has been less evident, but could become a feature in countries with a good rail network and a need to clear containers from urban areas.

The main difference in DTCs is size and therefore the range of activities (value added services) that can be undertaken. They have four typical designations:

- freight village: an example is Te Rapa Freight Village in Hamilton, New Zealand
- inland port: an example is Duisport in Germany at www.duisport.com
- logistics hub: an example is the Global Alliance Logistics Hub at www.alliancetexas.com
- logistics city: an example is Dubai Logistics City at www.dwc.ae.

As there is not a standard terminology, a DTC can have any name, an example being that in Australia, the Victorian State government uses the term Freight Activity Centre.

While a DTC is designed to handle international and interstate freight movements, the consolidation of movements in urban areas will also take on greater urgency, due to traffic congestion. Terms such as Metropolitan Freight Activity Centre (Melbourne) and Urban Consolidation Centre (Europe) are used to describe centres that consolidate freight deliveries for, say, all shops in a street or a section of the central business district (CBD) of a city or town. This operational structure is expected to dramatically reduce the number of part-filled trucks currently delivering to retail outlets.

Chapter questions

Operational

1. How may upstream replenishment performance measure the impact of sales and marketing decisions?
2. Are there limits to the flexibility of production and distribution operations, with regard to fluctuating customer demand?
3. In relation to a company from which you can gain sufficient information, identify three key risks to that company. Rate and provide reasons for their likelihood, severity and consequences. On the basis of this, rank the three risks in order of priority and propose some mitigation strategies.
4. What role does power shift in supply chains have in managing relationships within a value chain?
5. Can a supply chain network really be flexible? If so, identify some of the logistical trade-offs in constructing a flexible supply chain network.
6. Consider the Australian business Visy Industries (www.visy.com.au), which has a substantial reverse logistics operation for waste paper, cardboard and plastic drink containers. Consider the main factors of the company's business model and map the possible supply chains.

Planning

7. How may a business ensure that its pricing and promotional activities do not adversely affect the upstream supply chains?
8. Identify the nature and extent of risk management and contingency planning in a business about which sufficient information is available to you.
9. What are the major issues associated with planning the supply chains of a branded product manufacturing company? Consider issues associated with various stages of a product life cycle—introduction, growth, maturity and decline.

Management

10. How are the sourcing strategy and inventory rules adjusted to take into account the effects of dynamic product pricing and customer margins?
11. How may sales and marketing IT applications be linked with critical supply chain factors such as lead times, inventory and capacity constraints?
12. A grocery retailer sells private label goods manufactured by independent suppliers, which may include manufacturers of major brands. Identify the impacts on supply chains of a major brand manufacturer when contracting to manufacture a private label range for a retailer.

References and links

Boston Consulting Group and the Sloan Management Review Sustainability Initiative, *The Business of Sustainability*, www.bcg.com, September 2009.

Leitner, S.J. & Harrison, R., *Identification & Classification of Inland Ports*, Centre for Transportation Research University of Texas, August 2001.

McKinsey & Co., 'Demystifying corporate growth', *McKinsey Quarterly*, www.mckinseyquarterly.com/newsletters/2008_07.htm, July 2008.

Porter, M.E., 'How competitive forces shape strategy', *Harvard Business Review*, March/April 1979.

Slack, N., Chambers, S. & Johnston, R., *Operations Management*, Prentice Hall, 2004.

Sustainable business resources links

An online hub on sustainability, www.sustained.com.au.

The Australian Research Institute for Environmental and Sustainability based at Macquarie University, www.aries.mq.edu.au/projects/SupplyChain/.

An online hub on 'green' supply chains, www.thegreensupplychain.com.

Reverse logistics resources links

Reverse Logistics Association, www.rltinc.com.

Logistics in practice

Links to other chapters

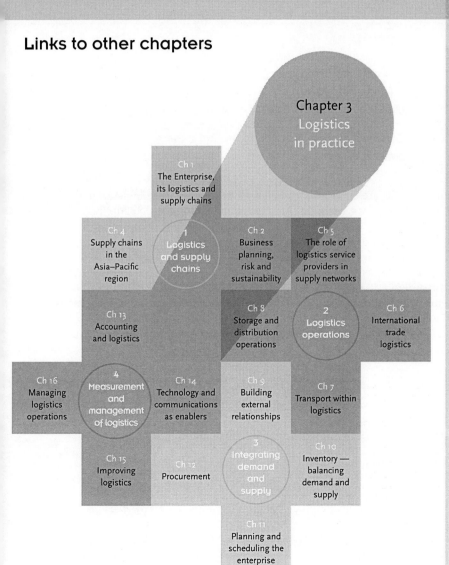

Chapter 3
Logistics
in practice

Ch 1
The Enterprise,
its logistics and
supply chains

Ch 4
Supply chains
in the
Asia–Pacific
region

1
Logistics
and supply
chains

Ch 2
Business
planning,
risk and
sustainability

Ch 5
The role of
logistics service
providers in
supply networks

Ch 13
Accounting
and logistics

Ch 8
Storage and
distribution
operations

2
Logistics
operations

Ch 6
International
trade
logistics

Ch 16
Managing
logistics
operations

4
Measurement
and
management
of logistics

Ch 14
Technology and
communications
as enablers

Ch 9
Building
external
relationships

Ch 7
Transport within
logistics

Ch 15
Improving
logistics

Ch 12
Procurement

3
Integrating
demand
and
supply

Ch 10
Inventory —
balancing
demand and
supply

Ch 11
Planning and
scheduling the
enterprise

On completion of this chapter you will be able to:

- recognise the main types of logistics applied in product and service organisations

- understand the essentials concerning logistics within different industries and sectors

- appreciate the various approaches required to understand and overcome logistics challenges

- comprehend the broad range of skills that a logistician should possess

- understand the possible career choices available in logistics.

Key terms

These terms are used in the text. Develop your own notebook by downloading information on each term.

business logistics	short shelf-life products	warehouse management system
reverse logistics	cool chain products	(WMS)
environmental logistics	fast moving consumer goods	product traceability
support logistics	(FMCG)	industrial products
service logistics	original design manufacturer	product service
event logistics	(ODM)	military logistics
disaster and emergency logistics	contract manufacturer (CM)	integrated logistics support (ILS)
humanitarian logistics	stock keeping unit (SKU)	performance-based contracts
logistics service provider (LSP)	first in first out (FIFO)	(PBC)
branded products	first expiry first out (FEFO)	mean time between failure
consumer packaged goods	just in time (JIT)	(MTBF)
(CPG)	lean manufacturing	

Introduction

This chapter provides an overview of logistics within different industry sectors. It illustrates that the structure of supply chains and how logistics is managed differs in its application, depending on the circumstances. The role of logisticians will therefore differ between organisations, and this is also discussed.

Different types of logistics

Logistics can be broadly categorised as being within either product-based or service-based organisations.

Product-based logistics

Enterprises that make and sell consumer goods are engaged in **business logistics**; they use logistics to drive improvements in their core supply chains and, if large enough, may influence their extended supply chains on a global scale.

Reverse logistics involves retrieving from customers and consumers the products and materials that for many reasons are no longer required. It also incorporates the capability to render the returns into useful output at the lowest cost to the environment. Words concerned with reverse logistics often begin with 're', such as return, remanufacture, refurbishment and recycle.

Reverse logistics is being incorporated into a new discipline known as **environmental logistics**. This is responsible for identifying and driving sustainability-related change that assists in creating value along the organisation's supply chains. Included are ways to reduce reverse logistics activities and reduce the carbon-based inputs of a business.

Service-based logistics

Support logistics is integral in military environments, continuous production operations and major service facilities.

With any major capital expense, such as acquiring large equipment, aircraft, weapons systems or buildings, too much emphasis is placed on the initial purchase price. However, the installation, planning of servicing throughout the equipment's operational life, obtaining and storing replacement parts and developing staff capabilities are often the most expensive components.

Service logistics is a necessary part of the retail, banking and finance, insurance and other service sectors to ensure the service is delivered to meet customer requirements. Service organisations also use materials such as forms, letters, promotional items, vouchers and other physical items that need to be incorporated into and delivered with the service 'package'.

A motor show, music spectacular or exhibition requires the expertise behind **event logistics** to ensure that vehicles, artists or exhibits from anywhere around the world arrive safely and securely and are in place and in time for the event. The process continues as goods and people are moved to the next location or back to their places of origin.

Incorporating all the previous logistics disciplines are **disaster and emergency logistics** and **humanitarian logistics**. The former is usually a domestic-based operation and the latter is international. They support the relief operations that bring life-saving medicines, food and materials to people affected by a disaster. This involves everything from holding service parts to keep helicopters in the air in difficult conditions, to issuing supplies, organising for ground traffic to get through inhospitable country and maintaining communication links.

Within each of these logistics types, functions and tasks can be contracted out, or outsourced, to specialist **logistics service providers (LSP),** which cover a wide range of activities; the largest group is the transport and distribution service providers. LSP businesses are discussed in Chapter 5.

Logistics challenges within industry sectors

There is a need for the skills of logisticians across a broad base of industry segments. While their roles may vary between being operational, analytical or commercial, there are additional specifics that relate to particular industries. These are often dictated by the nature of either the market in which the enterprise operates or the materials and products used. A selection of industries follows that indicate some of the challenges for logisticians.

Branded products companies

A brand is a collection of symbols, experiences and associations connected with a product or service. Brands have become increasingly important components of culture within consumer economies, such that some brands have become a generic term for a product or service.

Companies with strong brands are likely to invest heavily in the development of their products. They will also upkeep the brand identity through promotion to consumers and building consumer loyalty—a concept referred to as building brand equity. Of course, there is the need to present the products for sale. This activity allows retailers to, in effect, rent their shelf or display space to the brand company that presents the most compelling business deal. This provides for intense competition between brand companies for retail shelf space.

Branded products are contrasted with 'private label' products (also referred to as 'own label' and 'homebrand' products), which are gaining favour with large retailers, as they provide higher margins. The products are sold under the retailer's brand name and may be (although not always) positioned as lower cost alternatives to the products of leading brands. They are produced by manufacturers under contract. Consumer products and automotive products are examples of branded products.

Consumer products

Within consumer product (or brand) companies there are two distinct product types:

1. **Consumer packaged goods (CPG)** companies make and sell non-durable (perishable) goods that are typically food-based and are controlled by a 'use by' date. Food products businesses can have multiple global supply chains; consequently there is a greater risk to product quality caused through inadequate handling or packing. For these reasons, many food companies deal directly with their ingredient suppliers and undertake their own manufacturing, but use logistics service providers for finished product distribution activities and sometimes for delivery of inbound materials.

    Sub-groups within CPG are:
    a. **short shelf-life products,** such as bread products, vegetables, herbs and fruit
    b. **cool chain products** (including chilled and frozen), such as meat, seafood, dips and milk. In the global trade in food products, about 50 per cent require refrigeration during production, storage, transport and distribution.
2. **Fast moving consumer goods (FMCG)** companies make and sell durable consumer goods, such as electronics, household products and apparel. Examples of FMCG products and their supply chains are:
    a. *Electronics.* **Original design manufacturer (ODM)** suppliers dominate the worldwide production of notebook and desktop PCs and are replicating this in other electronic product segments. These brand

companies may contract with **contract manufacturers (CM)**. While the majority of manufacturing is concentrated in Asia, the distribution and after-sales services, repair and end-of-life product recycling belong in the local geographic regions. Imports from ODMs and CMs are often undertaken by logistics service providers, who work with the logistics, sales and marketing groups within the brand company to identify product volumes and delivery timing. Evolving technologies mean regular product launches, with 'spikes' in demand, but also consequential obsolescence, which place additional pressures on logistics.

   b. *Apparel.* Companies contend with seasonality, consumer fashion trends and obsolescence. This can involve the provision of different stock for up to four seasons over a yearly cycle, in two hemispheres and over a range of latitudes. The supply chains involve design, multi-country manufacture and supply of items made from a range of materials in a collection of colours and sizes from global contract manufacturers and LSPs. It is not unusual for a relatively small apparel company to manage the movement of over 50 000 **stock keeping units (SKU)** relating to style, size, colour and fit.

Large retailers impose strict criteria on suppliers concerning delivery of products in full, on time and with perfect transaction accuracy. CPG and FMCG companies need to manage the product 'use by' date and stock rotation on a basis that is most relevant; for example:

- **first in first out (FIFO)** at the store level
- **first expiry first out (FEFO)** at the DC level.

For logisticians, the level of outsourcing by their companies is a major strategic challenge. They need to assess the potential risks of adopting the outsourcing option, for each product and category within its stage of the product life cycle, by each geographic region, and evaluate current and possible suppliers' capabilities.

Logistics in the FMCG and CPG sectors is never dull and, due to the competition between companies for retail shelf space, it forces implementation of the latest logistics techniques and technologies, so logisticians can be working at the leading edge of ideas.

Automotive

Unlike consumer products, cars are typically designed and assembled by brand companies and sold through their accredited dealers; supply chains can therefore be more controlled by the powerful vehicle assemblers.

Depending on the design, cars can consist of 10 000 parts or more. Some of these parts can be presented as options that provide consumers with a choice and logisticians with challenges: choice leads to complexity.

The automotive sector is one of the most globalised industries. As such it requires that a logistician be a global thinker with an awareness of new markets in developing countries, new and developing market segments such as hybrid engines and new competitors from emerging economies. Analysis and systems capabilities are key competencies required of an automotive logistician.

Once a component or sub-assembly has been purchased by the procurement specialists, logisticians at the assembly facility plan and schedule the movement of incoming sub-assemblies and components and finished vehicles to the dealers.

Their counterparts at the tier 1 suppliers will plan and schedule activities from their global operations and with their component and raw material suppliers, to ensure the sub-assemblies arrive at the assembly facilities in the quantity ordered and at the time required.

Since the 1950s, Toyota has progressively developed the Toyota Production System (TPS), also known as **just in time (JIT)**, with a focus on removing waste from the system. The concept is simple in theory, but its implementation requires a lot of skill, especially in managing the relationship with suppliers; even Toyota is making constant improvements, 60 years on! JIT has further evolved, with the term **lean manufacturing** being used, and it has expanded from automotive manufacturing to other industrial and service sectors.

Retail

Consumer expectations of customer service, product quality and availability and a range of payment options continue to change. This remains constant across the different modes of shopping, whether at a physical store, via a catalogue, a website or by responding to an 'infomercial' on television.

For the retailer, these expectations present a challenge of having enough stock to meet consumer requirements while reducing inventory carrying costs and minimising risks of obsolescence, spoilage and waste.

Retail distribution centres and warehouses receive products from multiple suppliers and then assemble deliveries for specific stores, in some cases by in-store location. Logistics managers therefore require visibility and information concerning models, styles, colours, production locations, order sizes, store assortments and transport schedules within each of the many supply chains with whom they communicate.

Retailers are investing in corporate logistics IT applications that provide an integrated planning and financial management system. This is to support the current **warehouse management systems (WMS)** and communication devices that identify the location and volume of stock keeping units. The logistics IT applications include:

* financial planning for the merchandise purchases
* buying and product assortment management
* store allocation of products
* inventory replenishment and analysis to forecast sales and optimise inventory volumes.

Using these systems, logisticians can more accurately forecast consumer demand, optimise the inventory and improve speed and agility of the supply chains, especially in exceptional circumstances, such as severe weather.

Traceability of products

An extension to the challenges for logisticians working in CPG and retail companies is the requirements of products that require specific traceability and recording through the supply chains. Examples of **product traceability** are pharmaceuticals and halal products.

The concept of halal, which means 'permissible' in Arabic, addresses food, cosmetics, pharmaceuticals and nutraceuticals. Halal certification aims for a 'farm to table' inclusion to test whether a product has been contaminated. This includes the analysis of preparation procedures, plus the logistics management of products, including ports, shipping and land transport, freight forwarding and warehousing facilities, packaging and labelling.

An example of halal traceability is the brand used by Meat & Livestock Australia (MLA) for Australian meat sold in the Middle East. Exporters that want to supply halal meat must source it from abattoirs operating within the Australian Government Muslim Slaughter (AGMS) program, which is under the control and oversight of the Australian Quarantine and Inspection Service (AQIS).

The separation of halal products is a critical component of an intact halal food chain process, therefore the MLA's priorities are:

* separation of halal-fed animals while transporting to slaughterhouses, after slaughter, during processing and storage, and shipping of chilled or frozen halal meat in enclosed shipping containers
* management of the cold chain infrastructure to transport, store and market the products
* separation of halal products from non-halal, such as alcohol- and pork-related products, throughout the entire supply chain.

Industrial products

These 'business to business' (B2B) products are purchased by industrial companies for their own use, such as machines to be used in the manufacturing process, or to be used as components in a larger product, say gearboxes for trucks.

A feature of **industrial products** is that they are less likely to be held in inventory; instead they tend to be 'engineer to order' or 'make to order' (see Chapter 1). This requires different relationships with suppliers, as orders will be based on changing customer requirements and contracts, with the backlog of work (or orders in hand) being a measure of prosperity for the business. Planning and scheduling through the supply chains is more likely to be project or contract based and transport requirements can require special packaging or handling.

One industrial product that is in the bulk category is chemicals. Companies positioned through the chemicals supply chain consider distribution of their products to be a core competency—transit costs and service are critical. The specialised nature of hazardous products requires very specific expertise and skills from logisticians.

Supply chain costs in global chemicals can be more than 40 per cent of the added value within the sector, the highest of all major industries. Very complex and therefore potentially inefficient supply chains incur higher cost, which results in reduced margins and unprofitable products.

Chemicals are transported using specialised storage and handling such as chemical parcel carriers, chemical tankers and specialist ships; the supply chains are subject to chemical inspection and surveying. Companies typically negotiate their own contracts for the receipt and delivery of materials and look to logistics service providers for the physical operations, with visibility at each step. Delivery to places where the product company does not have a strong presence requires freight forwarding and customs brokerage to assist with international shipments. In some cases, the service provider takes over responsibility from a customer for all processing—for example grinding and providing additives, then packing and shipping in containers or via bulk ships.

Chemical companies need a close relationship with their logistics service providers: having safe, reliable and environmentally sound operations, both inside and outside the refinery or factory, is critical. 'Responsible care' is a long-standing ethic in this sector, making the approach to the chemical supply chain more holistic; therefore, due to the hazardous nature of the industry, a lot of 'best practice' information is shared between companies. Responsible care provides a risk-based approach to logistics, and procurement staff use this as a criterion when selecting a carrier, terminal or other LSPs.

The chemical industry is mature, with all competitors having broadly the same competencies; due to high capital investment, companies must plan over the long term. The challenge for LSPs is to help chemical companies consider the end-to-end total costs of the supply chains over the next five years rather than focusing on individual functional excellence.

Product support and service comprises the group of logistics activities used to support products and assets over their life, following the purchase. It comprises **military logistics** and support logistics for commercial ventures.

Military logistics

In the military context, there are two types of support:

1. *Deployment logistics*: this incorporates the moving of and providing for troops with the necessary shelter, food, uniforms and munitions relating to the deployment of forces in hostile, peace-keeping and humanitarian situations. This has some similarity to business logistics. There is also the need to liaise and coordinate the capability of the national infrastructure and manufacturing base to equip, support and supply the defence forces and to resupply those forces once deployed.
2. *Materiel logistics*: the term 'materiel' is derived from the French *matériel*, meaning equipment or hardware, and incorporates **integrated logistics support (ILS)**. This addresses the lifetime support of expensive capability platforms, be they ships, aircraft or tanks, from acquisition to decommissioning. The operative terms used are reliability, availability and maintainability (RAM).

The discipline of ILS operates within a broader framework of legislation, regulatory requirements (including technical regulations) and contractual obligations. ILS management is the process of planning, directing, controlling, coordinating and monitoring ILS activities. This includes support elements to ensure that the integration objectives of ILS are achieved. The support elements are:

- engineering support
- maintenance support
- supply support
- training support
- packaging, handling, storage and transport
- buildings and infrastructure facilities
- support and test equipment
- personnel
- technical data
- computer support.

These elements use logistics support analysis (LSA), which is an analysis discipline developed to provide a more accurate risk assessment of support plans.

There is a great diversity of specialisations in military logistics, which makes people marketable within civilian organisations when they have completed their military service. For example:

- Risk assessment is vital in planning a military system; this will include activities such as balancing potential 'out of stock' situations against an over-investment in parts, yet support the inventory availability target at the system level.

- Logisticians need to deal with problems that require the use of optimisation applications and other IT support tools.
- Logisticians are able to model the tangible and intangible elements to best align the assets of the supply network in support of the required service levels and performance commitments.
- The procurement of complex systems can be a long and detailed process, requiring extensive development of specifications and negotiation with suppliers.
- Logisticians negotiate **performance-based contracts (PBC)**, which are called performance-based logistics (PBL) in the military, whereby the supplier provides ongoing support to maintain the specified level of readiness required of the system. The supplier can be paid on the basis of effective available time or other outcomes-based payments.

Jobs in military logistics are performed by people who are uniformed members or civilian staff of the military forces and, increasingly, by specialists working for logistics service provider companies.

Support logistics (commercial)

Industrial operations can be large and expensive, such as petrochemical, steel, aluminium and mining, and at large service facilities such as major airports and entertainment complexes. They cannot remain idle, as 'time is money' in business.

Support logistics companies provide on-site servicing and repairs and, depending on the urgency of the industrial item to the customer, may undertake repairs at any time, on any day (24/7). Planning for skilled technician availability and service parts location and availability is critical—what excuse can be made for a \$500 000 machine not working due to the lack of a \$10 part? As PBCs become more common, the demand for capable logisticians in support logistics companies will increase.

For higher-value capital items (earth-moving equipment, for example) there are additional logistics challenges concerned with sustainability, including the return of worn and damaged parts to re-manufacturing factories, where the parts are refurbished and returned to the service group for re-use on the company's equipment. This is an element of reverse logistics and can be more complicated to plan and schedule than the supply chains for the sale of the original equipment!

The logistics planning requirements for industrial products is similar to the ILS process undertaken in defence. This is illustrated in Figure 3.1.

Product service for consumer products (also called after-sales service)

This is often the forgotten part of customer service. Brand companies put much effort into selling the original item, but the total customer experience can be poor, due to the lack of product support.

Product service can be for home products such as electrical goods used in the kitchen (white goods), electronic and electrical goods used elsewhere in the house (brown goods) and motor vehicles. Typically the product must be taken by the consumer to a repair centre; the time taken for repair can range from days to weeks, depending on where the spare (or service) parts are located and how much work is awaiting completion (the backlog) in the repair centre.

Product service can be performed by a brand company as a part of its overall offering to customers, or by a specialist product service company that, through specialising in one aspect of the customer experience, attempts to perform the service task better.

The supply chains for support logistics can be very complex. Many products are sold

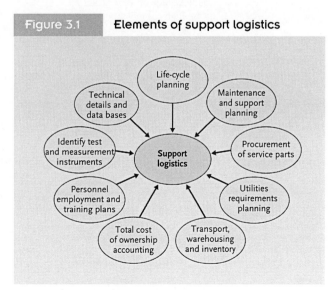

Figure 3.1 Elements of support logistics

on global markets—but a product sold in one country or region may not be sold in another. Furthermore, products are usually under continuous improvement, so parts can change over time within a product model and can be made by suppliers who are located throughout the world.

All these factors make the tracking of parts absolutely critical to the success of support logistics. In addition there is a need to calculate how often the products fail (called the **mean time between failure (MTBF)**) and for what reason, as this influences the planning of what spare parts are held, in what quantity and where. If this is done correctly, product support should be a very profitable part of the business.

Table 3.1 synthesises the industries discussed with the associated challenges and focus.

Table 3.1   Industry challenges and focus

Logistics application	Nature of goods	Associated services	Key challenges	Operational focus	Key terms
Branded products					
Consumer products: fast moving consumer goods (FMCG) and consumer packaged goods (CPG)	Various packaged goods (foods, medicines, etc.); nature of packaging varies—jars, bottles, boxes, bags, etc.	Logistics service providers (LSPs)	FMCG: low-cost country sourcing and technology; CPG: maintaining the freshness of products	Ensuring product availability to the distribution channels; matching the logistics model to product life-cycle requirements	FMCG, CPG; FIFO/FEFO; cold chain; short shelf-life; quick response (QR); efficient consumer response (ECR); sales and operations planning (S&OP); collaborative planning, forecasting and replenishment (CPFR)
Automotive manufacturing	Large number of component parts; obsolescence of parts; high value finished goods	Importing; customs clearance; contract manufacturing for an OEM; LSP	Pricing pressures	Reducing size of manufacturing batches; make to order	Original equipment manufacturer (OEM); just in time (JIT); lean
Retail	Varied— packaged, hanging, small, high value, etc.	Distribution centre and transport operations	Competition between suppliers for retail shelf space; managing the range of inventory in response to market demand	On-shelf availability; improving stock turns and managing obsolescence; spoilage, waste and minimising inventory carrying costs	Per consumer products

Table 3.1   Continued

Logistics application	Nature of goods	Associated services	Key challenges	Operational focus	Key terms
Industrial goods					
Industrial manufacturing	Various heavy equipment, e.g. packaging lines, mining equipment, FMCG production equipment etc.	Reverse logistics, after-sales service	Sustainability, including the return of worn and damaged parts to re-manufacturing		
Chemical and dangerous goods	Liquid, solid or gas substances in large quantities	Freight forwarding; customs brokerage; tracking and tracing	Scale of operations; specialist knowledge; high costs due to safety requirements	Safe product handing; ensuring reliable and environmentally sound operations; cost management	Responsible care
Product service					
Military logistics (materiel and deployment)	Capital equipment life cycle of weapons systems	Management of product and LSP contracts	Major capital and ongoing expenditure; security of information	Readiness of equipment; focus on reliability and maintainability	Integrated logistics support (ILS); logistics support analysis (LSA); Performance-based logistics (PBL)
Support logistics	Capital equipment life cycle: aerospace; industrial machinery; consumer products after-sales service	Specialist service companies; LSP	Mean time between failure (MTBF) records; scheduling of technical staff; availability of service parts inventory	Readiness of equipment; focus on reliability and maintainability; consumer after-sales processes	Mean time between failure (MTBF); performance-based contracts (PBC)

Role of the logistician

The role of the professional logistician is to 'meet availability objectives by reducing uncertainty and increasing strategic advantage through understanding the range of external variability that may affect the organisation and reducing the internal complexities caused by the conflicting objectives of corporate functions' (Giancarlo Chiodina, Director of Logistics at Benetton).

Success for a logistician is therefore the capability to identify, understand and, wherever possible, reduce uncertainty, variability and constraints (complexity in the supply chains) while managing risks.

The essential attributes required of a logistician are:

- a capacity for critical thinking—to cut through the three-letter acronyms and the latest hype associated with supply chains
- an ability to analyse the numbers and know when there is an error
- the skill to project manage the implementation of the proposed course of action, remembering that the proposal has to be first sold to senior management!

In Australia the Supply Chain Futures group (representatives from industry and academia), which is sponsored by GS1 Australia, has developed the Supply Chain and Logistics Graduate Skills Requirements

Matrix. This provides a broad set of 20 guidelines concerning the knowledge requirements of graduates from supply chain and logistics courses, as shown in Table 3.2.

Table 3.2 Supply chain and logistics graduate skills requirements matrix

Skill set	Skill set description
1. Communication skills	Is able to communicate effectively through different media and different styles, in accordance with the audience, including the ability to listen and disseminate learning and information
2. Social interaction skills	Exhibits the ability to manage relationships in diverse contexts, cross-culturally, intra- and inter-organisationally. Is a self-reliant communicator who works effectively with individuals, groups, teams and at an organisational level and instilling confidence in all concerned
3. Technology literacy	Is able to apply technology effectively at a personal and professional level and exhibits the ability to use application software commonly used in the management context. Understands the value of global standards, such as the GS1 System, in the coherent underpinning of technologies used in supply chains and supply networks
4. Analysis and problem-solving skills	Is able to apply appropriate numerical skills and techniques to understand, interpret and solve problems and undertake business analysis used in the context of supply chains
5. Knowledge of supply chains	Demonstrates a comprehensive knowledge of supply chains and integration with other disciplines through management of business relationships
6. Related knowledge to supply chains	Understands the interconnection of supply chains with other fields of knowledge; specifically, management thought in information science, physical science, industrial engineering, management science, including human resources, human behaviour and elements of emotional intelligence
7. Broad knowledge of supply chains and relationship management	Understands, from a national and global perspective, the applicability of supply chain and business relationship management as a disciplinary field
8. Practical application	Is able to integrate theoretical and practical knowledge to analyse and solve complex and novel supply chain problems e.g. issues of network planning and tracking and tracing
9. Knowledge of and the application of sustainable business practices	Understands the importance and value of deploying business practices that are sustainable, when considering the interplay of competing human, natural, technology, financial and time resources
10. Ethical application of knowledge	Has an awareness of the ethical dimensions, issues and relevant guidelines needed to work effectively with individuals, groups and organisations in a national and international context
11. Independent and collaborative knowledge transfer	Contributes to advancing knowledge in the supply chain domain through the clear and productive dissemination of information
12. Social responsibility	Engages responsibly in work and society with respect for diversity, social justice principles, the environment and corporate governance
13. Diversity management	Appreciates and respects individual differences in a cultural context and embraces this diversity to enhance organisational performance
14. Change management	Is able to identify the change involved, its impact on the organisation, alliances, systems and employees, to drive the change and manage implementation of the change appropriate to all stakeholders
15. Project management	Understands how project management is conducted and is able to participate and/or lead projects
16. Contract management and legal	Understands contractual and legal aspects of the business, its obligations and liabilities, issues of risk mitigation, including dealing with trading parties

Skill set	Skill set description
17. Strategic thinking	Is able to conceive and implement long-term strategies for the business, when considering global, environmental, industrial, social and economic impacts
18. Discernment and evaluation of best practices	Is able to evaluate and assess global and local operations, through site visits, benchmarking and economic and scientific evaluation, to determine appropriate 'best practice' implementation techniques in specific circumstances
19. Concept of continuous improvement	Understands the concept of continuous improvements with a specific focus on customers, using various measuring techniques, e.g. surveys and targeted feedback, including a focus on the environment, i.e. evaluation of carbon footprint and waste reduction as part of continuous improvement
20. Budget management	Understands accounting fundamentals in order to draw up a budget and manage the budget within resource, financial and capital constraints; recognises the limitations in accounting practice to measure the value of flows within and between organisations

Source: Adapted from GS1 Australia, 'Supply Chain and Logistics Graduate Skills Requirements Matrix', Supply Chain Futures group document, 2009.

Careers in logistics

The term 'logistician' is very broad, incorporating a range of industry applications and a variety of specific roles. Logisticians can be involved as:

- analysts who measure and interpret the performance of supply chains and analyse data to evaluate operating performance
- operational staff who make plans and schedules happen
- IT and communication technology staff
- management staff overseeing the relationship and performance of LSPs
- management staff overseeing the relationship with customers
- commercial staff who negotiate with suppliers
- sales logisticians working within LSPs.

Table 3.3 identifies some of the roles available for logisticians, likely qualifications required and the salary range in Australia.

Table 3.3   Careers map

Position	Qualification required	Salary range $'000
Product companies, importers and wholesalers		
Management		
Supply Chain Director	Postgraduate	150–200+
Supply Chain/Logistics General Manager	Postgraduate	95–195
Supply Chain Manager	Postgraduate	100–150
Logistics Manager	Diploma/Degree	75–135
Supply chain specialists		
Supply Chain Designer	Postgraduate/Degree	150–200
Logistics IT Applications Specialist	Postgraduate/Degree	130–150
Supply Chain Logistics Analyst	Degree	60–95
Planning and scheduling		
Sales and Operations Planning Manager	Diploma/Degree	90–130
Demand Manager	Diploma/Degree	75–110
Inventory Manager	Diploma/Degree	70–110
Demand/Inventory Planner	Diploma/Degree	60–75
Import/Export Specialist	Diploma/Degree	45–75

continued

Table 3.3 continued

Position	Qualification required	Salary range $'000
Procurement		
Director/GM Procurement or Strategic Sourcing	Postgraduate	170–200+
Procurement/Strategic Sourcing Manager	Postgraduate	90–150
Category/Commodity Specialist	Diploma/Degree	75–110
Purchasing Manager	Diploma/Degree	65–100
Contracts Specialist	Diploma/Degree	80–120
Senior Buyer	Diploma/Degree	65–80
Procurement Analyst	Diploma/Degree	60–90
LOGISTICS SERVICE PROVIDERS (LSP)		
Management		
Director/General Manager	Degree/Postgraduate	200+
National/Division Manager	Degree	130–160
State Manager	Degree	90–120
Sales		
Sales Director	Degree	200+
National Sales Manager	Degree	135–200+
State Sales Manager	Diploma/Degree	95–170
Account Manager	Diploma/Degree	75–105
Business Development Manager	Diploma/Degree	65–110
Sales Analyst	Diploma/Degree	50–75
Customer service		
Client Relationship Manager	Diploma/Degree	65–110
Warehousing and distribution		
National Distribution Manager	Postgraduate	95–150
Distribution Centre Manager	Diploma/Degree	75–140
Warehouse Manager	Diploma/Degree	65–130
Inventory Controller	Diploma/Degree	45–75
Distribution Analyst	Diploma/Degree	45–75
Freight forwarding		
Freight Forwarding Manager	Diploma/Degree	75–150
Customs broking		
Customs Manager	Diploma/Degree + Licence	75–110
Stevedoring		
Operations Superintendent	Diploma/Degree	100–120
Air cargo		
Operations Manager	Diploma/Degree + Licence	60–90
Rail intermodal		
Terminal Manager	Diploma/Degree	105–125
Road		
Line Haul Manager	Diploma/Degree	65–105

Source: Adapted from Department of Innovation, Industry and Regional Development, 'Careers Map', www.supplychainvictoria.com.au, Government of Victoria, June 2009.

Chapter questions

Operational

1. Examples have been provided in the text of logistics in consumer and industrial products and in product service. Complete Table 3.1 by identifying organisations that provide service logistics, event logistics and humanitarian logistics. Discuss and document their main features.

2. What are the major issues associated with developing the supply chains for a branded products company? Consider how the challenges evolve through the various stages of a product life cycle—introduction, growth, maturity and decline.

3. An evolving branch of logistics is called environmental logistics. Research the range of responsibilities under this heading and develop an outline job description for the role.

4. Reverse logistics covers a range of activities that include handling product and materials for the following reasons:
   a. recall (faulty)
   b. repair (service)
   c. returns (warranty)
   d. recycle (convert)
   e. refurbishment (end of lease or rental period)
   f. re-manufacturing (hours of operation or trade-in).
   Select one from the list and identify the logistics challenges that need to be addressed.

5. You have been appointed as the logistics manager for a vehicle financing company. Besides the activity of approving credit for vehicle purchases and raising finance, the other major activity of the business is influencing many dealers throughout the country to recommend finance for potential buyers of the vehicles. To do this, the finance company provides regular promotions. Identify the challenges of the logistics manager's role in this service business.

6. Large entertainment complexes that contain a casino, theatres, restaurants and other entertainment outlets are operating on a 24/7 basis in major cities, for example Melbourne, Sydney, Singapore and Macao. The major requirement is that all elements of the complex are working, and when maintenance activities are undertaken, the visiting public will not be inconvenienced. Define the possible role and responsibilities of the Logistics Manager.

Planning

7. Consider the business model of a grocery retailer that only retails private label goods. These products are sold in large pack and bulk formats. Evaluate the logistical impact on the supply chains of a major brand manufacturer after accepting a contract to manufacture a product in this range.

8. The supply of short shelf-life products must occur on a continuing basis. For a company producing a range of products, what are the critical planning elements that must be considered?

9. Humanitarian logistics must be managed based on risks and probabilities. As a logistics manager for a non-government organisation (NGO) based in the Asia region, what are the potential natural disasters to be prepared for? Provide examples of what items must be held in inventory at the highest readiness and what items can be contracted to be made by suppliers when an emergency occurs.

10. You are the country logistics manager for a non-government organisation (NGO) based in a country that has experienced both natural disasters and civil war. You are at a camp where approximately 10 000 refugees are located. They include people in family groups and individuals, from different religions and tribes. A part of the culture is that men do not prepare meals and are served food first; however, there are many women with young children. The numbers are as set out in the table below.

Group	Families			Individuals		
	Men	Women	Children	Men	Women	Children
Tribe 1	200	700	1600	100	50	400
Tribe 2	700	800	1200	250	100	300
Tribe 3	1000	600	1500	50	380	300

A food convoy has arrived, but due to the breakdown of some trucks, there are insufficient rations for distribution. You estimate there are sufficient rations for 8000 people to receive a full allowance of 1 kg per person; therefore the food must be allocated so that everyone receives something. As the people are hungry, some men are threatening to steal the food (and maybe kill you); you therefore have only a short time to organise how much food the different groups will receive without causing a riot. You have a laptop with a fully charged battery and a spreadsheet application.

Management

11 Reliability and maintainability are fundamental in promoting 'value for money' in the purchase of major capital equipment. Consider a specialist logistics support organisation that must reach an agreement with a client before committing to a performance-based contract (PBC). The client can be either a defence materiel organisation (DMO) or a commercial company running a 24/7 operation. What are the main points for discussion, and what position may the specialist logistics support organisation take?

12 The role of a retailer is to sell products from space in the physical or online store. Establish an argument why *all* links in the supply chains for product (except buying the products) should be managed by logistics service providers. What arguments could a retailer put against the proposals?

References and links

Department of Innovation, Industry and Regional Development, 'Careers map', www.supplychainvictoria.com.au, Government of Victoria, June 2009.

Other links at this site are for:

- Careers in Transport, Logistics and Supply Chain Interactive CD-ROM
- A Career and Course Guide for Victoria—Transport, Logistics and Supply Chain.

GS1 Australia, 'Supply Chain and Logistics Graduate Skills Requirements Matrix', Supply Chain Futures group document, 2009.

Port of Melbourne Supply Chain Awareness interactive website, www.supplychainvictoria.com.au/interactivetools/awareness.

Supply chains in the Asia–Pacific region

Links to other chapters

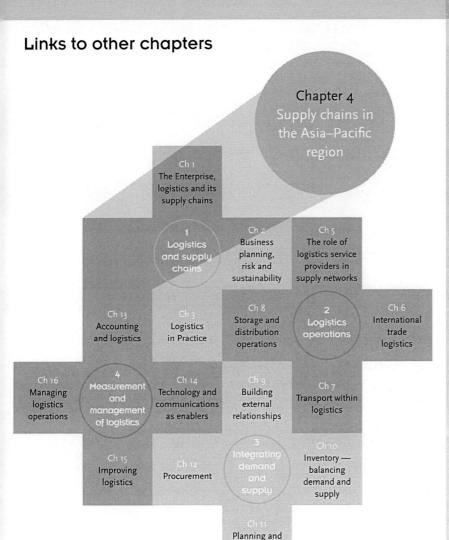

Chapter 4
Supply chains in the Asia–Pacific region

Ch 1
The Enterprise, logistics and its supply chains

1
Logistics and supply chains

Ch 2
Business planning, risk and sustainability

Ch 5
The role of logistics service providers in supply networks

Ch 13
Accounting and logistics

Ch 3
Logistics in Practice

Ch 8
Storage and distribution operations

2
Logistics operations

Ch 6
International trade logistics

Ch 16
Managing logistics operations

4
Measurement and management of logistics

Ch 14
Technology and communications as enablers

Ch 9
Building external relationships

Ch 7
Transport within logistics

Ch 15
Improving logistics

Ch 12
Procurement

3
Integrating demand and supply

Ch 10
Inventory — balancing demand and supply

Ch 11
Planning and scheduling the enterprise

On completion of this chapter you will be able to:

- understand the demographic and geographical properties of the Asia–Pacific region

- consider how these properties of the region can affect supply chain design and logistics operations

- recognise the differences between the logistics capabilities of countries at different levels of development

- explain the logistical specifics of your own country and that of the key trading countries in the region

- appreciate the changing nature of trading channels and infrastructure in the region.

Key terms

These terms are used in the text. Develop your own notebook by downloading information on each term.

Americas
EMEA
Asia–Pacific region
South Asia
South-East Asia
East Asia
Oceania
population density
gross domestic product (GDP)
development model

ASEAN
intermodalism
dense trade clusters (DTC)
TEU
Post-Panamax
point-to-point
hub-and-spoke
mergers and acquisitions (M&A)
free trade zone (FTZ)
Greater Mekong

Yangtze River Delta (YRD)
Greater Pearl River Delta (PRD)
small and medium-sized
    enterprise (SME)
store-ready merchandise (SRM)
food miles
refrigerated containers
Emissions Trading Scheme (ETS)

Introduction

This chapter provides an insight into the challenges of developing supply chain models within the Asia–Pacific region. As the International Monetary Fund (IMF) considers that the region's economy will become the world's largest by 2030, an increasing amount of trade and therefore supply chain planning will occur within the region.

The complexity of planning is heightened because countries are at different levels of development, with very different standards of infrastructure. Having an understanding of the region and its challenges makes for a more knowledgeable and informed logistician.

The Asia–Pacific region

Business has generally divided the world into three regions—the **Americas**, **EMEA** (Europe, Middle East and Africa) and the Asia–Pacific. From a business viewpoint, the **Asia–Pacific region** lies between the latitudes of 50°S and 40°N and the longitudes of 60°E and 180°E (the international dateline). A map of the Asia–Pacific region is shown in Figure 4.1.

The Asia–Pacific region incorporates the sub-regions of:

* **South Asia**: latitude 5°N to 40°N; longitude 60°E to 95°E
* **South-East Asia**: latitude 20°N to 10°S; longitude 95°E to 130E
* **East Asia**: latitude 20°N to 40°N; longitude 105°E to 150°E
* **Oceania**: latitude 0° (equator) to 50°S; longitude 105° to 180°E.

The Central Asia sub-region has been omitted from the discussion in this chapter; it comprises countries of the Russian Far East, Mongolia and the Central Asian republics.

| Figure 4.1 | The Asia–Pacific region |

The Asia–Pacific region

The geographical difference between the Asia–Pacific and other major regions is that it is not a continuous land mass, although individual countries such as Australia, China and India have substantial land masses of their own. Indonesia and the Philippines are countries with thousands of islands and Pacific island states may individually consist of only a few inhabited islands. Sea is the favoured mode in the region for transporting goods.

Countries in the region are at different stages of development concerning their logistics capability. The *Logistics Performance Index (LPI) Rankings* (2010), developed by the World Bank, provides a score by country based on a number of attributes. The listed countries of the Asia–Pacific region have been divided into three groups and identified in descending order according to their LPI ranking:

Group 1. Logistics developed
South Asia: Nil
South-East Asia: Singapore
East Asia: Japan, Hong Kong SAR, Taiwan, South Korea
Oceania: Australia, New Zealand

Group 2. Logistics developing
South Asia: India, Bangladesh, Mauritius, Pakistan
South-East Asia: Malaysia, Thailand, Philippines, Vietnam, Indonesia
East Asia: China
Oceania: Nil

Group 3. Logistics emerging
South Asia: Maldives, Sri Lanka, Nepal, Bhutan
South-East Asia: Laos, Cambodia, Myanmar (Burma)
East Asia: North Korea
Oceania: Papua New Guinea (PNG), Solomon Islands, Fiji (the remaining Pacific island states and economies were not ranked)

The LPI indicates that the level of logistics services capability in the Group 3 countries is about half that of countries in Group 1, which are able to provide the reliability and predictability required in supply chains.

Supply chain planning in the Asia–Pacific region

Population density

Euromonitor International (2010) stated that of the world's regions, Asia–Pacific had the largest growth of urban population between 2000 and 2010. Between 2010 and 2020, the Asia–Pacific urban population is expected to increase by more than 21 per cent.

The percentage of the population living in urban areas and the income per head between urban and rural areas of a country are factors taken into account when considering supply chain network planning for consumer goods within countries of the region.

Population density is expressed as people per square kilometre. Figure 4.2 identifies the density of selected cities in the region and their surrounding urban areas.

The logistics challenge of serving cities with extensive areas is illustrated by considering the current area of greater Sydney and the same conurbation if it were developed with the density of Hong Kong. The area used would only be 32 per cent of the current size! Extensive areas require additional warehouses and vehicles to support a high level of customer service over greater distances, which are becoming more congested and therefore increase the total logistics costs.

To overcome congestion in the major conurbations, governments can introduce urban road pricing and controls on traffic movement and companies may implement different transport arrangements. For example, in Bangkok, Pepsi distribution uses the river tides. Empty bottles are returned by barge on the incoming tide to the bottling facility; they are cleaned and refilled and then taken down the river with the outgoing tide to the main distribution centre.

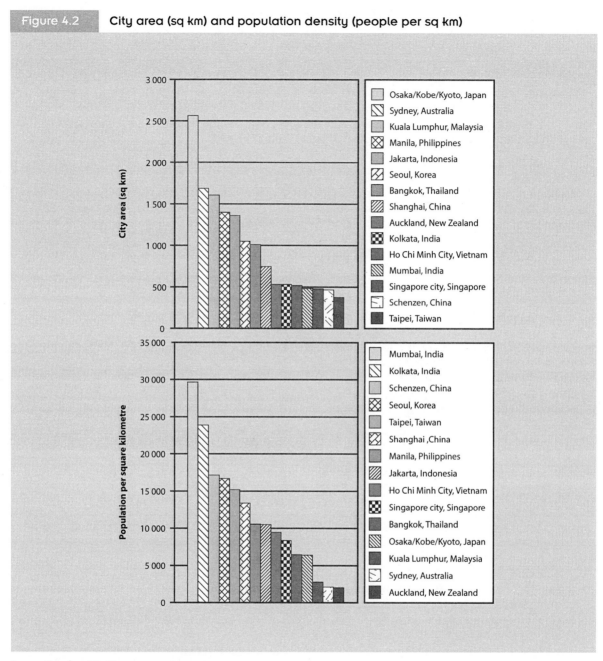

Figure 4.2 City area (sq km) and population density (people per sq km)

Source: Based on City Mayors, www.citymayors.com.

The CIA's *The World Factbook* (2010) identifies the urban population as a percentage of total population for some countries in the region as:

Australia	89%	Malaysia	70%	China	43%
New Zealand	87%	Philippines	65%	Thailand	33%
South Korea	81%	Indonesia	52%	India	29%

On this basis alone, distribution patterns are very different for countries with high urban population and to those with low, although there can also be wide differences between urban and rural development.

Examples of logistics challenges are:

1. Thailand has a low per capita income of about US$1400, but the per capita income of Bangkok is about US$6000. Bangkok provides about 60 per cent of Thailand's **gross domestic product (GDP)**, but the urban population is low at 33 per cent. Products to hold as inventory in rural areas will therefore most likely consist of basic and essential consumer goods, while the full range of consumer goods will be held in urban areas.
2. India's large rural and agrarian areas provide opportunities for small-size packaged consumer goods, mobile phones and two-wheeled vehicles. However, the challenge is that rural areas can be difficult to reach due to the poor state of road networks. The UN *State of World Population 2009* report noted that urban growth in India will mainly occur in intermediate cities with a population of fewer than 500 000 people. The challenge for future design of distribution networks will be the increasing need to service intermediate cities, but due to the state of roads, the number of warehouse facilities will need to be greater than if the infrastructure was capable unless the rail network is fully utilised.

Development model

Logistics capability can also be influenced by a country's **development model**. For example, China has developed since the 1980s through exports (in a similar way to Japan in the decades following World War II), while India promoted self-sufficiency for much of the second half of the 20th century. The China model (also used by **ASEAN** countries) requires development of infrastructure to assist exports, while the India model encouraged, domestic (and protected) manufacturing.

Inter-region trade has been increasing as exports (as a percentage of total trade) to the United States and the European Union (EU) have been decreasing. Growth of exports from countries in the sub-regions, generated by potentially high consumer demand in China and India, could become a significant trend. It will mean that countries in Asia can generate growth, even if consumption in the United States and Europe is static.

The demands of consumers during Chinese New Year celebrations are starting to compensate for the traditional post-Christmas downturn in spending that occurs in the United States and Europe, with its flow-on logistics effect through the supply chains.

Electronics exports are crucial to Asian economies, accounting for roughly one-third of the South-East Asia and East Asia sub-region's exports. Data from the *Global Trade Analysis Project* (GTAP) identifies that more than 70 per cent of intra-Asian trade consists of intermediate goods (components and sub-assemblies), which are sent from one Asian country to another before ultimately being shipped as the finished product for sale through retail stores. Of this volume, over 60 per cent is driven by demand from the G3 countries of Japan, the United States and the EU.

The logistics challenge can be that as distribution channels focus on the main export income area (electronics), it leaves the logistics capability for other products less developed; this can cause countries to become even more reliant on electronics. An example is in the Philippines, where the electronics sector comprises 64 per cent of total exports and 34 per cent of the country's domestic economy.

Australia and New Zealand are developed economies within the Oceania sub-region, with Australia providing bulk minerals and grains and New Zealand providing temperate-climate foods into the region. Both countries are reliant on consumer demand for much of their economic activity, so imports from the region are substantial and increasingly dominated by the activities of major retail chains.

Transport development

Details concerning transport infrastructure in Asia are taken, with permission, from the *Asia Pacific Transport and Logistics* (2008) report, compiled by Transport Intelligence Ltd of the United Kingdom.

The development of intermodal transport has been generally slow in the region, with minimal recognition until recently of the benefits gained from **intermodalism**—the linking of sea, air, road and rail facilities. Recognition is now occurring of the additional benefits from constructing **dense trade clusters (DTC)** (known by many names, including inland ports, freight villages, logistics cities etc.) that not only link transport modes but also provide associated businesses and services within a concentrated area.

Currently, nearly all container ships of more than 5000 **TEU** (twenty-foot equivalent units) are engaged on either the Asia to EU or Asia to North America trade routes. Port development is being dictated by the increasing size of container ships at 7000–9000 TEU (**Post-Panamax** ships that are currently unable to transit through the Panama Canal). This will dictate that bay- and river-based ports can only survive through extensive dredging—the $1 billion expenditure by the Port of Melbourne in 2009 being an example. Coastal deep-water, trans-shipment ports such as Singapore, Laem Chabang (Thailand), Hong Kong, Pusan New Port (South Korea) and Shanghai-Yangshan are likely to become the dominant ports of Asia. Ships of between 2000 and 5000 TEU would then provide feeder services to smaller ports.

The throughput of containers by major ports per country in the Asia–Pacific region for 2007 is shown in Table 4.1.

Investment in rail services for freight in the region has been low, except for China and South Korea. The *Region Action Plan (for rail)* (2006) for Asia, supported by the UN Economic and Social Commission for Asia and the Pacific (UN-ESCAP), has a focus on the integrated intermodal approach that incorporates financing, public–private participation (PPP) schemes and sustainability objectives.

Investment in roads should be enhanced through the *Intergovernmental Agreement on the Asian Highway Network* (2005), designed to coordinate the proposed 20 000 km of major highway developments that meet the Asian Highway Classification and Design Standards.

The challenge for airlines in the region is whether to pursue a **point-to-point** or a **hub-and-spoke** policy for air freight. Currently, the hub-and-spoke approach is favoured, with airports at Shanghai Pudong and Guangzhou (China), Narida (Japan), Incheon (South Korea) and Hong Kong in contention as a hub for East Asia. Singapore and Bangkok are the hubs for South-East Asia. In Oceania, it is Auckland as the New Zealand airport and in Australia it is Sydney, which handles twice the volume of Melbourne, even though the latter is a 24-hour airport.

Table 4.1 Container ports throughput 2007

Rank	Sub-region and port	Country	Throughput in TEU
South Asia			
15	Jawaharlal Nehru	India	4 060 000
42	Chennai	India	1 053 000
South-East Asia			
1	Singapore	Singapore	28 000 000
10	Port Klang	Malaysia	7 119 000
12	Tanjung Pelepas	Malaysia	5 470 000
13	Laem Chabang	Thailand	4 848 000
16	Jakarta	Indonesia	3 900 000
20	Ho Chi Minh	Vietnam	3 200 000
22	Manila	Philippines	2 800 000
29	Surabaya	Indonesia	2 110 000
35	Bangkok	Thailand	1 559 000
North Asia			
2	Shanghai	China	26 152 000
3	Hong Kong	HK SAR	23 998 000
4	Shenzhen	China	21 099 000
5	Pusan	Korea	13 260 000
6	Kaohsiung	Taiwan	10 257 000
18	Tokyo	Japan	3 721 000
19	Yokohama	Japan	3 428 000
34	Incheon	Korea	1 664 000
Oceania			
27	Melbourne	Australia	2 189 000
33	Sydney	Australia	1 696 000
No rank	Tauranga	New Zealand	568 000

Source: Adapted from Cargo Systems, www.containershipping.com, accessed 26 May 2010.

The market penetration rate for LSPs in the region has been low in comparison with Western Europe and North America, except for Singapore, Hong Kong, Australia and New Zealand. Difficulties for LSPs in most of the Asia–Pacific region have been due to the low acceptance of the LSP concept (mainly freight forwarding, distribution and storage services) by domestic manufacturers and the fragmented retail markets, which have a lower buying power than in the more developed countries.

LSPs that can provide multimodal services across multiple geographies could grow through **mergers and acquisitions (M&A)** and drive growth of the sector in Asia. While Japan is the major country for LSPs in Asia, it is substantially 'closed' to non-Japanese companies. For the remaining countries, the LSP market potential by size for 2011 is considered as:

- China
- South Korea
- India
- Australia
- Taiwan
- Indonesia
- Hong Kong
- Thailand
- Malaysia
- Singapore
- Pakistan
- Philippines
- New Zealand
- Vietnam.

Selected countries of the region

The logistics situation is forever changing (and hopefully improving) for countries in the region; therefore reference to the current situation is always advised. The following discussion is based on the Asia–Pacific Trasport and Logistics (2008) report compiled by Transport Intelligence Ltd.

South Asia

INDIA

The drivers of growth in India have been based on motivations that are different to those of other developing countries of the region:

* a focus on the domestic market, providing some insulation from global economic downturns
* an emphasis on private consumption, at 64 per cent of GDP, compared to China, at 42 per cent of GDP
* encouragement of higher technology, capital-intensive industry
* strength in services exports, which employ the more educated sector of society.

Logistics services costs in India are estimated at 14 per cent of GDP and will be difficult to reduce in the short term, as transport infrastructure has become a bottleneck to economic growth.

The road network handled about 65 per cent of the freight tonnage in 2007–08; however, the majority of main roads are narrow and congested, with poor surface quality. Delays are common due to accidents, breakdowns and stops at state and municipal checkpoints; overloading of outdated two-axle trucks is standard practice. Development of higher standard highways is occurring, but is a slow process, both to get started and during the construction phase.

The Indian rail network is the most extensive in the Asia–Pacific region. However, a government policy to subsidise passenger fares through freight charges has led to a decline in freight volumes. To counter the downward trend, the government has started to liberalise the rail freight system. Investment in rail will include dedicated freight corridors on the Western route (Mumbai to Dadri (near Delhi)) and the Eastern route (Ludhiana (north of Delhi) to Kolkata).

No ports match the large export container ports elsewhere in Asia. The 13 main ports handle about 90 per cent of India's trade, mainly via the trans-shipment ports of Singapore, Colombo (Sri Lanka) and Salalah (Oman). Port capacity utilisation is poor due to planning, scheduling and productivity deficiencies of both labour and equipment. Major port development will be a container trans-shipment port at Cochin (Kochi). For the bulk import of coal and metal ores, foreign investment in handling facilities is being encouraged. India has 14 000 km of waterways and navigable rivers, but these are underdeveloped.

Although there are 11 international airports, the four metro airports at Delhi, Mumbai, Kolkata and Chennai handle the majority of freight and all have received major upgrades. A new private airport has commenced operations at Bangalore (Bengaluru).

The primary centre for distribution is the Mumbai and Pune area, with Delhi, Chennai, Bangalore and Kolkata also popular. Secondary centres tend to be within each state, to accommodate an approximately 450 km radius for effective distribution, due to the infrastructure problems. Around 80 per cent of distribution revenue is earned by small family-owned transport concerns of less than five vehicles; freight forwarding also consists of thousands of small local concerns.

As consumption demand increases, private (but domestically financed) development of dense trade clusters (called logistics parks in India) has commenced around the major metropolitan cities and in some tier 2 and 3 cities.

South-East Asia

INDONESIA

Covering an archipelago of 6000 inhabited islands with 235 million people, the provision and use of logistics services in Indonesia is challenging and requires a thorough risk analysis.

Sea ferries and roads are the highway that links the country, although air services are extensively used. Rail only operates in the populous islands of Sumatra and Java, with the major new investment being the 800 km link between Jakarta and Surabaya.

The largest airport is located at Jakarta, which is adjacent to the port and is a distribution area, but flooding in the rainy season (late October to early May) can hamper the movement of goods.

Indonesia has 186 ports, with about 60 per cent of all port activity related to domestic movements. The largest port is Jakarta, which handles 42 per cent of imports and 28 per cent of exports, but the lack of port facilities at the eight main ports means that the majority of sea freight is trans-shipped through Singapore.

The operating cost of trucks is estimated at about 60 per cent more per kilometre than in comparable Asian countries. Major costs are the result of poor road maintenance and payment of illegal 'tolls' (paid through extortion).

While the development of dense trade clusters on the heavily populated islands is a government priority, the logistics challenges highlight the advantages of using Singapore as the hub and distributing direct to ports close to the required markets. This approach promotes the use of multinational LSPs over domestic companies, which do not have the required international and nationwide reach.

SINGAPORE

The value of traded goods (imports plus exports) in Singapore is 345 per cent greater than the GDP, due to the government policy of an open economy and the country's location. It is the major trans-shipment centre for South-East Asia, and handles half the world's crude oil and 25 per cent of global containers. The major export manufacturing sectors are electronics, pharmaceuticals and oil refining/chemicals.

Logistics activities are 8 per cent of GDP and logistics services are dominated by MNC companies of European and North American origin. The Logistics Enhancement and Applications Program (LEAP) of the Singapore government, which began in 1999, encourages cooperation between government ministries and authorities and the logistics services sector.

THAILAND

Thailand has an industrial base for export manufactured goods (mainly electronics components and cars) around greater Bangkok and an agricultural economy in the south and north. Similar to other countries in the Asia–Pacific region, poor logistics and multiple transfer points in agriculture have resulted in a high spoilage rate.

The National Economic and Development Board of Thailand states that logistics costs were about 19 per cent of GDP in 2007, but increased to 23 per cent in 2008; the aim is to initially reduce the figure to 15 per cent.

There is an extensive rail network, although much is single track and hardly used for moving goods, so the reliance on road transport has increased costs for all goods. The network of paved roads is extensive, with links to international connections: for example the Asian Highway 3 Chiang Khong Bridge, due to open in 2012, which goes over the Mekong River (one of four bridges across the river), through Laos and into south-west China.

The country's largest port is Laem Chabang in the Gulf of Thailand, 110 km south-east of Bangkok and located in the country's largest industrial area. There is a plan to develop two additional ports: one will be an inland port at Chiang Saen in the north, to enhance trade with the greater Mekong River economy and Yunnan Province in south-west China; the second port is to be on the west coast, to serve South Asia.

In South-East Asia, only Singapore airport is capable of handling more air cargo than Bangkok airport. The adjacent **free trade zone (FTZ)** and proximity to the Port of Laem Chabang, with its own distribution centre, provides the core of a multimodal hub for the **Greater Mekong** region.

VIETNAM

Its 3000 km long coastline and narrow width provides Vietnam with logistics challenges that raise the cost of logistics services to more than 15 per cent of GDP. The sea and air freight capability at Hanoi/Haiphong, DaNang and Ho Chi Minh, plus the network of inland waterways, have dominated goods movement, due to the poor state of road and rail infrastructure.

Even so, the lack of port infrastructure, inefficient customs and urban congestion have resulted in exports being trans-shipped through other Asian ports at additional cost. For example, shipping costs from Ho Chi Minh port to Los Angeles are 30 per cent more expensive than identical shipments from Hong Kong, which reduces the labour cost advantage of Vietnam over other countries in the region.

To reduce the logistics services cost base, it is intended to move the port from the current Ho Chi Minh City location to an area adjacent to the main industrial zone, which is also close to the proposed new airport. A dense trade cluster could be constructed close to the new port and airport; also a similar cluster can be developed close to the port of Haiphong, with its rail and road links to Hanoi and proximity to China.

East Asia

CHINA

The China Federation of Logistics and Purchasing (CFLP) states that logistics services costs are forecasted to be 17 per cent of GDP for 2010. In developed countries, the cost is generally between 9.5 per cent and 11 per cent of GDP, so the logistics services sector has substantial opportunities to improve productivity.

The primary locations for logistics services are clustered in three locations:

* Beijing/Tianjin in the north
* Greater Shanghai (the **Yangtze River Delta (YRD)**) on the central coast
* Guangzhou/Shenzhen in the south.

More than 70 per cent of all commercial warehouses in China are located in these three areas.

Centres that are developing comprise Dalian and Qingdao in the north, Suzhou and Ningbo in the Yangtze River region, and Xiamen in the southeast. As western China is developed, so centres of logistics services will grow in cities such as Wuhan and Chongqing.

The features of the logistics services market in China are:

* an oversupply of transport and distribution providers, with competition based on price and therefore with short-term objectives
* a limited number of logistics service providers that can offer a national, integrated services-delivery network. The outcome could be that:
  o non-asset–owning LSPs that rely on local operators with local connections could drive mergers and acquisitions (M&A) of domestic state-owned logistics service companies, to gain scale and improve profitability
  o SME logistics enterprises may differentiate themselves by offering customised services for different industries and join logistics services alliances
  o there is growth of foreign-owned companies with global connections and expertise
* developing infrastructure:
  o acceptable (some very good) but insufficient on the coast and reducing in quality further inland
  o difficulty in expanding port facilities quickly enough to meet increasing demand
  o the move to more centralised and higher quality facilities (i.e. dense trade clusters), thus improving the infrastructure and cost situation
* uneven enforcement of regulations with regional interpretation, which affects the efficient movement of goods between provinces
* undeveloped logistics networks, creating sourcing and delivery problems:
  o retailers and manufacturers need to support a distribution network of more than 250 cities as they penetrate the tier 2 and 3 category cities.

HONG KONG SAR

Hong Kong is a separate economy from China and a major trading and commercial services centre. Close to 50 per cent of exports and imports are traded with China. Hong Kong is tying itself more closely to Macao and Guangdong Province, through road and rail connections that will further develop the **Greater Pearl River Delta (PRD)** region.

Even with additional ports and airports in southern China, Hong Kong has expanded its cargo-handling capability, with the port terminals acting as a trans-shipment centre and hub for southern China. Chek Lap Kok airport, situated on Lantau Island, is the second busiest centre for air freight in the world.

JAPAN

As Japan is an archipelago, it has generated a view that transport by road is easier than by rail: more than 90 per cent of all freight in Japan is transported by road. With car ownership at 90 per cent, this puts an increasing strain on the road network.

The conservatism of Japanese manufacturing and retailing companies has meant that logistics activities have mainly remained in-house. A move towards outsourcing is occurring, with encouragement from the national government, through preferential tax treatment and subsidised financing arrangements.

Key distribution points are:

- Chiba for the Tokyo metropolitan area
- Nagoya for the industrial areas between Tokyo and Osaka
- Kagawa for mail order distribution
- Fukuoka City serving the south of Japan
- Hiroshima for the area between Osaka and Hiroshima
- Hyogo for the Kansai area.

The structural change in international trade has led to a fall in volumes through Japanese ports; in 1991 there were three Japanese ports in the top 20 world ports, but by 2008 there were none. The situation has been assisted by increased costs, due to the high manning levels and short shifts for port operations, especially in container terminals.

Air freight on a point-to-point basis between Japan and China is viable for high value items, such as electronic components and sub-assemblies, due to the cost of holding inventory to cover shipping time. The three main freight airports are Narida (Tokyo), Osaka and Nagoya, and a second freight terminal will be available at Tokyo from 2011.

SOUTH KOREA

With North Korea blocking land access to the Asian continent, South Korea is effectively an island that can be the strategic logistics hub located between China as the manufacturer and Japan as the consumer market, plus the developing Russian Far East.

The Port of Pusan is one of the world's largest ports, and is able to capitalise on the growth in numbers of Post-Panamax container ships. For air freight, Incheon airport can become a region air-freight hub for North-East Asia, as 40 cities, each with a population exceeding one million people, are within a three-hour flying time. This development plan must occur rapidly to counter the opening in China of large deepwater ports and the commissioning of additional cargo airports.

South Korea does not encourage foreign investment; therefore, logistics services are mainly undertaken in-house by manufacturing companies, with some outsourcing provided by domestic companies, which tend to be **small and medium-sized enterprises (SME)**.

The National Intermodal Transport Network Plan (2000–2019) was developed to improve national competitiveness for the 21st century. It includes incentives to reduce logistics costs through IT technology, such as the radio frequency identification device (RFID). The government construction of 39 dense trade clusters by 2011, will form a national distribution network linked to the comprehensive highway and rail system.

TAIWAN

Taiwan is a country with the same population as Australia but contained in half the area of Tasmania. Its internal transport and distribution system is extensive in the developed west side of the island. This is assisted by the presence of 11 000 registered companies providing logistics services, five free trade zones and a new dense trade cluster built alongside the main port. The logistics planning challenges are seasonal typhoons and occasional earthquake damage.

The majority of companies in Taiwan are SMEs, many of which have transferred their low-end electronics manufacturing and assembly to South-East Asia and China, to concentrate on higher technology such as semi-conductors and liquid crystal displays (LCD). The export volume of high-value electronic components has led to development of the main air-freight export point at Taipei, which is the fifth largest in Asia.

For air and sea travel, Taiwan is located at a shorter distance from more major centres in the region than any other developed infrastructure point. The main port of Kao-Hsiung, located in the south of Taiwan, is the eighth busiest container port in the world and handles over 65 per cent of the country's total sea cargo, with high-speed rail and road connections from the industrial centres.

Oceania

AUSTRALIA

Although Australia is the most urbanised country in the Asia–Pacific region, the Australian population is geographically dispersed, with people and businesses in rural and remote areas demanding the same services found in the large cities. Transport will therefore always to be a feature of doing business in Australia.

The distance between ports and the lack of a substantial interstate rail network has dictated that each State has its own container port. A future scenario is that shipping companies may use only Post-Panamax container ships on the Asia to Australia/New Zealand route and thereby reduce the number of ports serviced.

The competitiveness of rail along the east–west and north–south freight corridors is being improved (but slowly), to more evenly share the burden between road and rail of moving inland freight.

As Asian countries have expanded their infrastructure, so the demand for raw materials has increased. Major developments have occurred at some of Australia's main bulk minerals and agriculture ports, which are generally positioned away from centres of population—the main container ports are in Australia's south and the large mines and export ports are in the north. These locations present an added challenge for effectively managing operational materials, spare parts and consumer goods obtained from both domestic and international suppliers.

The reduction in Australia's manufacturing to about 10 per cent of GDP has resulted in an increase in imported consumer goods, which has resulted in a considerable imbalance of demand for containers.

The increasing power of large retail chains has led to the establishment of region-based buying offices in Asia. Cross-dock facilities operated by LSPs are being established in Asia, and some in Australia, which enable the delivery of ticketed and priced **store-ready merchandise (SRM)** direct into retail shops, via the lowest cost port of entry and intermodal services. This development could result in a situation whereby major supply-chain planning decisions for consumer goods destined for the Oceania region are centralised in Asia.

NEW ZEALAND

New Zealand is a trading nation with agricultural products as its main export; these present more challenges in international trade than manufactured products. An example is the increasing discussion in Europe and America concerning **food miles** (the amount of CO_2 consumed to bring food to a consumer's house). The threat to New Zealand is the potential for concerns about climate change being manipulated and used for the introduction of de facto protectionism in consuming countries.

Future supply chains and logistics challenges noted by the New Zealand Transport *Newsletter* are:

* Economic forecasts indicate a doubling in freight demand by 2040.
* More than 75 per cent of the national population and GDP are in the North Island, yet logistics infrastructure must be provided for both the North and South Islands. This can put pressure on decision makers concerning the allocation of infrastructure resources.
* New Zealand's requirement is for export-destined **refrigerated containers** (reefers). This demand can put exporters at risk if insufficient empty containers are bought to New Zealand by the (foreign-owned) shipping companies.
* There is a potential for eastern Australian ports to become hub ports for Oceania, with New Zealand trade handled by feeder ships into the hub ports, thereby potentially increasing costs and lead times.

In the North Island, the ports of Auckland and Tauranga handle about 60 per cent of the country's container trade. In the South Island the ports of Otago (Dunedin) and Lyttelton (Christchurch), which together handle less than 600 000 containers per year, will combine to operate as one entity. Action to rationalise the 11 container-capable ports will be assisted not only by decisions of shipping lines, but by shippers. This has occurred with the Fonterra Dairy Co-operative Group, one of the world's largest dairy companies, selecting Auckland, Tauranga, Napier and Lyttelton as its main export ports.

While rationalisation of container ports may be inevitable, there are unique features that need to be considered for some ports, including established routes used for bulk cargoes such as export logs and coal.

To exploit the value of larger ports, an effective inland rail and road network is required; however, since 1995, the share of domestic freight by rail has substantially decreased. The potential value of rail in the economy could be increased under the 2010 national **Emissions Trading Scheme (ETS)**; also by improved demand management and targeted road pricing. This last point is supported by claims in the *Coastal Shipping and Modal Freight Choice* study (2010) that road transport receives an effective subsidy of NZ$1.5 billion per annum.

PACIFIC ISLAND STATES

Countries in the region are widely dispersed and include Papua New Guinea (PNG), Solomon Islands and Fiji. All have small populations with minimal industry (except sugar in Fiji and mining in PNG). The taxation base can therefore be insufficient to maintain the legislative and regulatory control aspects of government. The problems are those of many developing countries:

- government involvement in commercial operations
- role of financial aid donors
- maintenance of donated infrastructure
- calibre of operating and financial management of transport concerns.

Countries have tended to own their own shipping and air services, rather than collaborating in a Pacific-wide service. There is limited coordination of timetables and available freight capacity between the different fleets. This results in inefficiencies and delays when ships or aircraft are removed from service at short notice for maintenance or repairs.

The Pacific Regional Transport study (2004) identified infrastructure problems in the Pacific islands states that result in the countries having a low performance in the LPI rankings. Specific issues are additional lead time, storage and handling limitations such as refrigeration and transport capabilities. In an island environment, there is a need to adapt large-scale operations to specific logistics projects for the benefits of a smaller country.

Using Chapters 1 to 4

Chapters 1 and 2 have provided an overview of the meaning of supply chains and logistics and where they fit into the structure of a business. They have also provided the basis for considering these concepts as strategic to the longer term success of an enterprise.

The chapters that follow will provide the framework for considering each element of logistics, its operational aspects and role within a supply chain and why it is a necessary part of the big picture called supply networks.

Chapter questions

Operational

1. Consider your own country and the infrastructure of a major city. Identify the impact on business logistics operations of CPG and FMCG companies caused by the current location and capacity of existing infrastructure.
2. Identify key government projects currently underway or approved in your State or province that are aimed at improving the logistics operations of companies. Comment on the effect these projects will have in a practical way on logistics operators. What other initiatives would you recommend and why?
3. It is noted in the chapter text (page 47) that if greater Sydney were developed with the density of Hong Kong, the area used would be 32 per cent of the current size. What advantages and disadvantages for logistics operations of CPG and FMCG companies will exist for cities with a high population density?
4. The chapter describes the features of the logistics services market in China. Consider that a company in a developed country has contracted for manufacture of their products with a producer located in the west of China. Manufacturing costs are low, but identify the areas of additional costs to get the products to Shanghai.

Planning

5. Consider the supply chains of a business of which you are aware. Identify the global location of the key nodes in the supply network of the business.
   a. Draw a network map of the supply chains for the business.
   b. Discuss the key constraints on this network. How could the business overcome or leverage these constraints?
6. When obtaining products and materials from countries ranked as *Logistics Emerging* in the *Logistics Performance Index (LPI) Rankings 2010*, what planning parameters should be put in place to ensure that there is sufficient supply?

7 The introduction of Post-Panamax container ships could progressively change the pattern of ship movements from a point-to-point to a hub-and-spoke pattern. The chapter text states on page 50 that 'coastal deep-water, trans-shipment ports such as Singapore, Laem Chabang (Thailand), Hong Kong, Pusan New Port (Korea) and Shanghai-Yangshan are likely to become the dominant ports of Asia'. If this approach is copied for Australia and New Zealand, what are the likely changes to logistics operations for importers of consumer goods?

8 Use the examples in question 7 of major ports in Asia, and note that 70 per cent of intra-Asia trade is the movement of intermediate goods (components and sub-assemblies) that are sent from one Asian country to another. Will the pattern of trade flows change with the greater use of Post-Panamax ships and, if so, how?

Management

9 Consider the situation of a business in Australia that is in the process of outsourcing its manufacturing to a contract manufacturer. Tender submissions have been received from three manufacturers, based in China, India and Thailand. The operating costs, product quality and reputation of the three manufacturers are very similar. Identify what supply chain and logistics parameters will be the key drivers in your decision process concerning which manufacturer should be awarded the contract.

10 To reduce congestion in cities, governments will progressively introduce road pricing, truck curfews and limited delivery hours to retailers located in commercial areas. As customers will be reluctant to pay increased prices (and if powerful, will refuse), what action will distribution service companies need to take to remain viable?

References and links

Asia Pacific Transport and Logistics, *Transport Intelligence Ltd*, report, www.transportintelligence.com, 2008.

Cargo Systems, 'Throughput of containers by major ports for 2007', www.containershipping.com.

Central Intelligence Agency, *The World Factbook*, www.cia.gov/library/publications/the-world-factbook/geos/my.html.

City Mayors, www.citymayors.com.

China Federation of Logistics and Purchasing (CFLP), www.chinawuliu.com.cn.

Euromonitor International, www.euromonitor.com, 2 March 2010.

United Nations, *State of World Population 2009*, www.unfpa.org and www.un.org/esa/population.

Global Trade Analysis Project (GTAP), www.gtap.agecon.purdue.edu.

Logistics Bureau for Logistics Association of Australia (LAA), *Supply Chain Report 2008*, www.laa.asn.au/pdf/ldaarticles/SE1.pdf.

National Economic and Development Board of Thailand, www.nesdb.go.th.

New Zealand Ministry of Foreign Affairs and Trade, *Global New Zealand*, report, 2009.

New Zealand Transport Newsletter, www.nztransport-logistics.co.nz.

Pacific Islands Forum, *Pacific Regional Transport Study*, www.forumsec.org.fj/resources/uploads/attachments/documents/Pacific%20Regional%20Transport%20Study,%20June%202004.pdf, 2004.

Rockpoint Corporate Finance, *Coastal Shipping and Modal Freight Choice*, study, www.rockpoint.co.nz, 2010.

UN-ESCAP, *Intergovernmental Agreement on the Asian Highway Network 2005*, www.unescap.org/TTDW/index.asp?MenuName=AsianHighway.

UNESCAP, *Korea National Intermodal Transport Network Plan (2000–2019)*, www.unescap.org/ttdw/ppp/reports/republicofkorea_21sept2007.pdf.

UN-ESCAP, Region Action Plan (for rail), supported by the UN Economic and Social Commission for Asia and the Pacific (UN-ESCAP), www.unescap.org, 2006.

World Bank, *Logistics Performance Index (LPI) Rankings 2010*, www.worldbank.org.

PART 2

Logistics operations

5

The role of logistics service providers in supply networks

Learning outcomes

On completion of this chapter you will be able to:

- understand the role of logistics service providers (LSP) in the supply networks of product companies

- consider the potential market for LSPs in the Asia–Pacific region

- evaluate the investment required by LSPs to improve their business and meet shippers' requirements

- understand the decision-making process required of a product company when it considers outsourcing, including the degree of collaboration and the performance-measurement criteria

- appreciate the selling process for an LSP and the potential benefits of performance-based contracts.

Links to other chapters

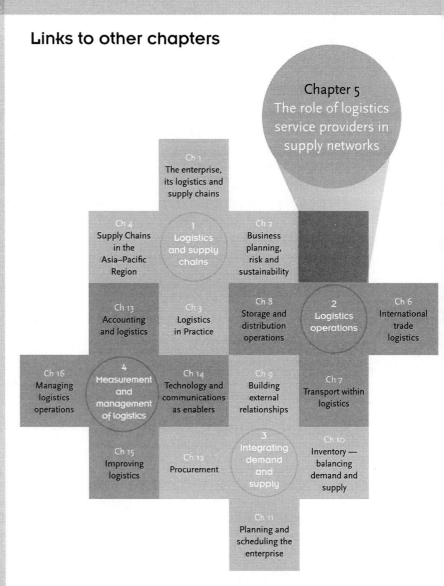

Chapter 5
The role of logistics service providers in supply networks

Ch 1
The enterprise, its logistics and supply chains

Ch 4
Supply Chains in the Asia–Pacific Region

1
Logistics and supply chains

Ch 2
Business planning, risk and sustainability

Ch 13
Accounting and logistics

Ch 3
Logistics in Practice

Ch 8
Storage and distribution operations

2
Logistics operations

Ch 6
International trade logistics

Ch 16
Managing logistics operations

4
Measurement and management of logistics

Ch 14
Technology and communications as enablers

Ch 9
Building external relationships

Ch 7
Transport within logistics

Ch 15
Improving logistics

Ch 12
Procurement

3
Integrating demand and supply

Ch 10
Inventory — balancing demand and supply

Ch 11
Planning and scheduling the enterprise

Key terms

These terms are used in the text. Develop your own notebook by downloading information on each term.

return on investment (ROI)
outsourcing
third party logistics (3PL)
multinational corporation (MNC)
logistics service provider (LSP)
shipper

multi-customer warehouse
electronic data interchange (EDI)
fourth party logistics (4PL)
business to business (B2B)
warehouse management system
(WMS)

transport management system
(TMS)
key performance indicator (KPI)
performance-based logistics
(PBL)

Introduction

In this chapter we will discuss the ability of logistics service providers, to positively impact the profitability of their clients. In doing so we will evaluate the key functional areas in which an LSP can add value and discuss various models for implementing the working relationship between the organisations. We will also consider the impact of outsourcing on the client's core business and evaluate the sales process to more closely align the objectives of the client and the LSP.

Developing supply chains and networks with LSPs

Beginning in the United States in the 1980s, large product-based public companies came under pressure from shareholders to provide higher annual dividends through improving their **return on investment (ROI)**. As part of their activities to achieve this, companies reduced their level of investment in fixed assets, the main elements being factories, warehouses and distribution centres.

To achieve this, companies looked to specialist providers who would not only undertake a whole function, but enter into a financial agreement to acquire the necessary assets from the client.

To have specialist work or tasks undertaken by other companies has been a feature of business for centuries. However, the new approach was different, in that it required a product company to contract out whole functions of its business. It received the new name of **outsourcing**.

An early function to be outsourced was road transport, as that is capital intensive, a commodity service and with a predominance of fixed and semi-fixed costs, such as insurance, fuel and drivers. This function was considered to be better performed by specialist businesses.

Outsourcing of distribution required a more thoughtful approach; this was not directly about distribution, but about capital investment and returns, labour relations risks and impediments to the business. The distribution market is a more variable service than road transport; therefore, companies that were already engaged in warehousing and had knowledge of managing these types of assets were most likely to adopt outsourcing contracts. Also, some transport outsourcing businesses added warehousing to their capabilities.

The typical arrangement was that a contractor entered into a financial contract to take over a client's distribution assets and would then provide a distribution service for a contract period. This activity was given the term **third party logistics (3PL)**.

Virum (1993) identified a 3PL firm as 'a middleman in the logistics channel that has specialised in providing, by contract for a given time period, all or a considerable number of logistics activities for other firms'. In the classical understanding, the two parties in a transaction are a supplier (the seller) and a customer (the buyer). When the supplier engages another organisation to act on its behalf in a way that has an interface with a customer, the contracted organisation becomes a third party to the transaction.

The situation today is that the service companies have developed their business to the level where they can often design and build warehouses and distribution centres that comply with clients' requirements. This direct interface with the client and their customer makes the third-party role so important. The visibility of its capabilities means that an LSP can affect customer satisfaction and potentially expose all parties to the risk of costly legal proceedings via chain of responsibility actions. In the physical sense, the third party connects its customer to their customer, and as such, facilitates their client's ability to generate revenue—a very important role in a supply chain.

As the concept of supply chains developed and **multinational corporations (MNC)** purchased increasing amounts of product from lower cost countries, the role of companies providing outsourced logistics services extended to cover the movement of materials, materials services and professional services. The term **logistics service provider (LSP)** is the collective term used to describe this wide range of businesses services, as shown in Figure 5.1 below and Table 5.1 opposite.

The development and growth of LSPs into all areas that address the movement of materials has resulted in governments and industry bodies talking about the 'logistics industry', which is better termed the 'logistics services industry'. This differentiates it from the logistics activities that take place within goods-producing and importing companies.

The core supply chain for an item is the inbound, internal and outbound activities of the product company (also called the **shipper**), plus the selection of suitable LSPs; therefore a company will have multiple supply chains that address its inbound and outbound needs, as shown in Figure 5.2.

Contracting a range of LSPs can be viewed as a reason for the product company not to employ its own specialist supply chain and logistics staff; however, this is a short-sighted view. Although the logistics operational services are supplied by LSPs, there are vital roles that should always remain within the brand-owning business. These are:

- development of the supply chain and logistics strategy
- improving the supply network
- negotiating and contracting supply chain relationships
- management of LSPs.

Role of LSPs within supply networks

The roles of some LSPs, noted in bold within Table 5.1, are expanded upon below.

Materials movement services

These companies invest in infrastructure and systems to provide warehousing and/or distribution services, including bonded warehousing for their customers. In addition to standard services, value added activities can be provided.

| Figure 5.1 | A supply network |

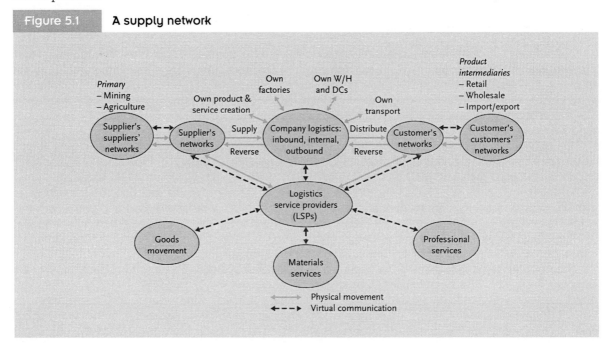

Table 5.1 Roles of LSPs in a supply network

Goods movement	Materials services	Professional services
Materials movement services including: • distribution including pack and label services (i.e. store ready merchandise) • order fulfilment—less than carton picking (also used for e-commerce–based sales delivery) • consumer products home delivery service • warehousing & storage services including bonded warehouses • quality inspection and testing • final assembly • **reverse logistics** services—bringing back products from the end user, repair and recycling	**Manufacturing services** including: • original design manufacturers (ODM) • contract manufacturing (CM) • product design services	**Financial services** including: • location and tax advice • futures market financing • financing accounts receivables • financing inventory • trade finance
Transport services including: • road • rail • air • sea and inland waterways • courier, express & parcel (CEP) services	**Procurement services**	**Freight insurance** including risk advice
Freight forwarding and customs broking	**Event logistics services** including concerts, exhibitions and trade shows	**International trade legal services**
Logistics infrastructure including: • intermodal services • freight services at airports • seaports, container terminals and parks plus container maintenance • dense trade clusters including logistics city, inland port, freight hub, logistics village, freight activity centre, etc.	**Logistics assets support services**	**Technology services** including: • software applications for supply chain, logistics and international trade • logistics IT and communications services
Materials handling services—for pallets, bulk bins, secure wrapping, strapping systems, etc.	**Lead logistics provider (LLP)** also called 4PL—consolidators of total logistics services for a client	**Education and training services**
	Freight managed services including: • transport consolidation • ship and aircraft brokering and chartering	**Government departments and agencies**—development of policy and administration of regulations in international trade, supply chains and logistics

As a subset of this model, a business may specialise in managing dedicated storage facilities where all the stock at the site is owned by a single customer; or they may operate **multi-customer warehouses** (called 'public warehousing' in the United States). Here, multiple customers from different and unrelated businesses store products in anticipation of their customers' orders.

There is not a requirement for an LSP to be involved in both the warehousing and distribution; however, many choose to do both to ensure a complete delivery service for their clients. Providers of warehousing services can subcontract other businesses to provide the transport services.

Warehousing and distribution service providers will invest in technology to facilitate communication with their clients, which can mean interfacing with multiple systems. In Australia, most large retail chains have

Figure 5.2   **A core and extended supply chain**

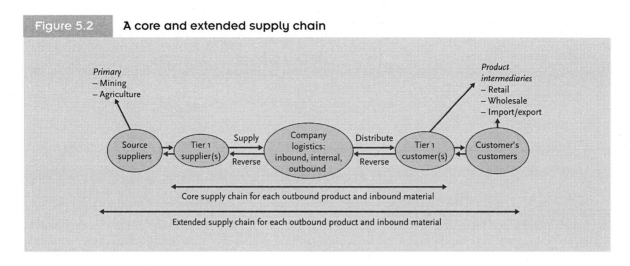

requirements for their suppliers to interface with them through **electronic data interchange (EDI)**. As smaller suppliers may lack the knowledge and skills in this area, distribution services providers can offer the EDI capability to process orders and invoices between the small supplier and retail chains, as shown in Figure 5.3 below.

Reverse logistics

Reverse logistics derives efficiencies in the reverse flow of goods, such as consolidating defective and returned products from retail chains and negotiating credits from suppliers in a systematic manner, including financial reconciliation and compliance.

Figure 5.3   **LSP communication services for small suppliers**

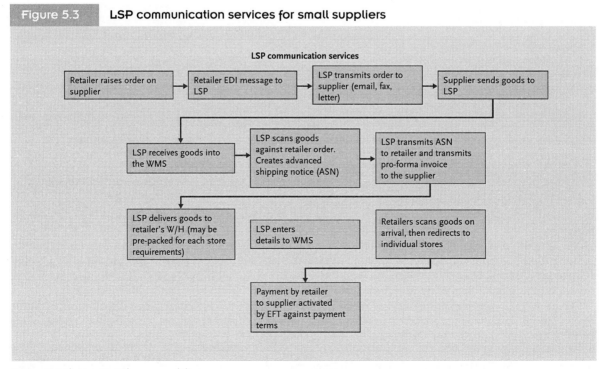

Source: Supply-Linq Pty Ltd, www.suppli-linq.com.au.

Also, a manufacturing company may have a line of business that benefits from reverse-flowing goods: for example offering paper or metal recycling services that are inputs to their packaging or smelting business. This service frees up working capital by improving the financial cycle time for customers, or relieving them of obligations and costs associated with disposing of waste materials. Examples of such organisations are The Ideas Company for clothing hangers and the Visy Group for paper.

Transport services

Transport services offered will include road, rail, shipping (ocean and river), air and specialist courier, express and parcel (CEP) services of which FedEx and DHL are the best known. Increasingly, national postal services are becoming competitors in this sector: for example the joint venture between Australia Post and China Post, trading as Sai Cheng Logistics.

As an example of the challenges facing transport services in developed countries, such as Japan and Australia, the transport and distribution sector in Australia has the following parameters:

* 1.25 million people work in the sector, which equates to 1 in 7 Australian workers
* 3 in 4 of them are male
* 1 in 2 is over 45 years old
* 1 in 3 has an education standard of Year 10 or below.

Some road transport business have recognised the long-term problems of this situation and are actively recruiting women and encouraging staff to gain qualifications.

Freight forwarding and customs broking

Both of these services are involved in international supply chains. The freight forwarder acts as the broker with transport companies to provide the physical movement of items between countries, plus support services for the required documentation. A long definition of freight forwarding can be found at the International Federation of Freight Forwarders Associations (FIATA) under 'Freight Forwarding and Logistic Services'. The customs broker provides services associated with clearing customs as the goods cross borders, including payment of the necessary duties, taxes and excises and obtaining any permits. It is now common for one organisation to provide both freight forwarding and customs broking services, but this is not necessary.

Logistics infrastructure

A logistics infrastructure operator provides facilities such as container terminals and parks, seaports, freight airports, rail terminals and multi-modal freight transfer terminals. These organisations can add value by developing trade clusters such as free trade zones, freight hubs, inland ports and similar concentrations of logistics and manufacturing services. Examples of such an organisation are:

* Port of Singapore Authority (PSA www.mpa.gov.sg)
* Melbourne Airport Corporation (www.melbourneairport.com.au)
* Duisport Inland Port in Germany (www.duisport.com)
* Global Alliance Logistics Hub (www.alliancetexas.com).

Lead logistics

Lead logistics providers (LLPs), also called **fourth party logistics (4PL)**, is a term developed by the consulting firm Accenture. These organisations are the consolidator and facilitator of all logistics services provided by multiple LSPs on behalf of their client, a shipper. An LLP adds value through intellectual property, industry knowledge and networks, computer systems and processes. An example of such an organisation is Li and Fung, based in Hong Kong, which specialises in apparel. The Exel Logistics division of DHL provides LLP services (which they call supply chain management) for a wider range of industries.

The LLP approach had an initial burst of enthusiasm, particularly in the automotive sector, but it has waned as shippers experienced problems. Contracts were not always clear as to where the LLP was adding value, rather than just adding an additional layer of costs and complexities; also, because the LLP has knowledge and systems, it can become the de facto decision maker for the shipper's supply chains.

Technology services

Technology services provide software applications and communications services for:

- internet-based, **business to business (B2B)** electronic markets for logistics services, including procurement portals that act as electronic brokers
- application tools for booking, monitoring, tracking and tracing items; **warehouse management systems (WMS)**; and **transport management systems (TMS)**
- applications to improve the productivity of supply chains, including supply network design tools, optimisation, modelling and simulation.

Technology in supply chains and logistics is discussed in Chapter 14.

Logistics services market

The LSP sector in all countries of the region is highly fragmented, with a large number of small, owner-operator companies, most of which operate in a defined geographic region and offer limited services. Even the largest distribution services business in Australia claims to have less than 10 per cent of the market.

Fragmentation forces the smaller companies to become successful through being proficient in a service category; this allows them to become contractors to larger LSPs. The questions for the smaller companies are:

- What is our business focus?
- In which product categories, industries and geographies should we operate?
- How much financial and intellectual capital should we invest?

As LSPs generally have a low earning-to-sales ratio on a pre-tax basis, larger LSPs in the warehousing, road transport and freight forwarding sectors will likely focus on expanding their customer base and reduce unit costs, through mergers and acquisition (M&A). This approach has consolidated business such that the largest 25 LSPs are considered to command in excess of 60 per cent of global expenditure in logistics services. The top 10 LSP companies in 2008 were considered by SJ Consulting Group as:

1. DHL Logistics, Germany
2. Kuehne + Nagel, Switzerland
3. DB Schenker Logistics, Germany
4. Geodis, France
5. CEVA Logistics, Netherlands
6. Panalpina, Switzerland
7. Logista, United Kingdom
8. CH Robinson Worldwide, USA
9. Agility Logistics, Kuwait
10. UPS Supply Chain Solutions, USA.

In the Asia–Pacific region, LLPs and large LSPs are the gateway between the product export-reliant economies of East and South-East Asia and the mostly offshore retail customers and importers; or between the component supply companies in South-East Asian countries and final assembly in China. The added value of the LLP/LSP role is bridging the gap between the mainly Western customer expectations and the operational and cultural constraints in the Asia region. Bridging the gap is enacted through the large LSP subcontracting with country-based LSPs for execution of the contract.

India is different; manufacturing is mainly for the domestic market. Therefore LSPs are either agents of international firms, independent domestic companies or divisions of the major domestic business 'houses', such as Reliance, that contract with divisions of the parent company.

In Oceania, the LSPs provide services to assist the import of consumer goods and the distribution of domestically manufactured items.

An online article titled 'The Coming Wave of Service Provider Convergence', at www.eyefortransport.com, states:

> global logistics is a $179 billion market. But contract manufacturing generates $170 billion. And outsourced technology represents a $300 billion market! All of these markets are maturing, as 20–30 per cent growth

rates from the 1990s have fallen to 5–15 per cent today. Increasingly, as other outsourcing markets mature alongside logistics, we will see convergence.

If this forecast proves correct, then the largest LSP will expand through M&A activity outside their current area of expertise to provide a complete range of logistics services.

Improving an LSP business

LSPs develop their business to address the market in a manner that helps to differentiate them from competitors. When analysing an LSP business approach, there is a three-step process, as shown in Figure 5.4 below.

While the role of a pure 'box shifter' is diminishing, the *Third-Party Logistics Study* (Capgemini/Georgia Institute of Technology 2009) reports that shippers 'continue to outsource logistics activities that are transactional, operational and repetitive and less frequently strategic, customer facing and IT intensive'. This is not to diminish the importance of the operational functions, since efficient and timely execution is vital to business performance; but it illustrates the effort required by LSPs to be seen as more than operational and transaction-level contractors.

The study identified the main problems with LSPs from the shippers' viewpoint as follows.

- LSPs lack business capability to be entrusted with more responsibility.
- There is low satisfaction with IT services provided by LSPs.
- There is a lack of continuous and ongoing improvements by LSPs to reduce their costs and improve service.
- LSPs need to actually achieve the service offerings promised.
- Unrealised commitments occur at service level, that is, over-promising and under-achieving.

Suggestions for improvement within LSPs, from shippers in the study noted above and from the authors' experience, are as follows.

- Understand the shipper's business in terms of its aims and objectives and how logistics services can assist in furthering the objectives. The brand company's approach to its supply chains will indicate the approach for the LSP in providing services.
- Build specific industry and/or regional expertise.
- Provide IT expertise concerning international trade compliance and logistics.
- Provide analysis of total landed costs for shippers.

Figure 5.4 **Segmenting LSP business approach**

	Asset based	or	Non-asset based
Step 1:	e.g. 3PL Distribution Co		e.g. Freight forwarder

	Business segment
Step 2:	Geographic areas
	Mode: air, sea, road, rail
	Speciality: intermodal, express, refrigerated/chilled, reverse
	Throughput: warehouse, DC (dedicated customers or common usage)

	Standard services	or	Customised services
Step 3:	**Standard services**	or	**Customised services**
	Target industries: regional/global		**Target industries:** regional/global
	Specific industry relationships		Industry knowledge
	Specific industry IT applications		Supply chain innovation
			IT development capability
			Industry based added value services
	General industry: regional/global		**General industry:** regional/global
	General IT applications		Conceptual knowledge
	Utilise operational assets		Supply chain innovation
			IT development capability
			Added value services—modelling and simulation; optimisation

- Share assets with other LSPs to gain and increase asset utilisation and lower costs.
- Provide inventory financing for shippers through all steps of the supply chain—this could result in LSPs owning the inventory and therefore increasing their assets (and risks). Conversely, they could structure a separate finance division.

LSPs noted that the improvements that shippers could make were as follows.

- Publish their operational plans and schedules in time for LSPs to respond to changes—this could extend to the LSP being a part of the S&OP process.
- Be willing to team up with their LSPs to re-engineer operational processes.

A consumer-goods brand company and LSPs generate profits from different approaches; therefore their views will differ on what is 'best'. The brand company focus is market and product innovation, brand marketing and sales through building customer relationships. It makes money from new product introductions—'big wins' and promotions. The objective is therefore flexibility to respond to the market and a continuous reduction of costs through outsourcing supply chain operational processes.

Due to short-term transport and materials-handling capacity constraints, LSPs are unlikely to quickly respond to 'big wins' in the market by their clients. In part, this has been self-imposed through actions to reduce unit costs. There has been a move towards fewer but larger units, especially trucks and ships and in distribution to centralise (where feasible) within countries and regions, to provide a 'hub and spoke' network. But fewer transport units and centralised distribution make for less flexibility.

The challenge is therefore to position a larger LSP business that will rise above the current perceptions of shippers. At the core of the decision about which business model to adopt lies the question of business identity and purpose: 'What is the role of the LSP business in the shipper's supply chains?', and the question, 'How can operational excellence and customer integration be achieved that provides a return on invested capital?'

Outsourcing decisions and using LSPs

The operational flow through supply chains can consist totally of activities undertaken by LSPs. It is possible for a business to own the rights to products designed under contract and have those products manufactured, distributed and sold by contracted services organisations—the extreme of this being the 'virtual organisation', as shown in Figure 5.5.

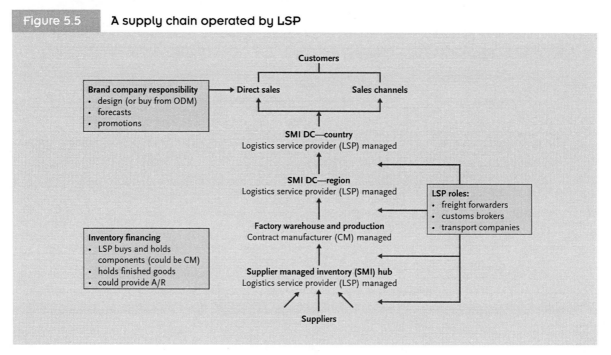

Figure 5.5   **A supply chain operated by LSP**

Understanding the customer's business allows meaningful discussion to occur concerning how goods will be moved and at what speed. Air freight is a valid freight option if the value-to-weight ratio of the component or final product is high. For example, mobile smartphones have an air-freight component of approximately 1 per cent of the retail price. Air freight has also been justified for a $60 automotive part sent from Korea to Australia, based on the savings in inventory and financing.

There are various international distribution options and each option will have different time and cost elements; therefore the challenge is to match these (and other) options to the shipper's business needs, as shown in Figure 5.6.

| Figure 5.6 | International distribution options |

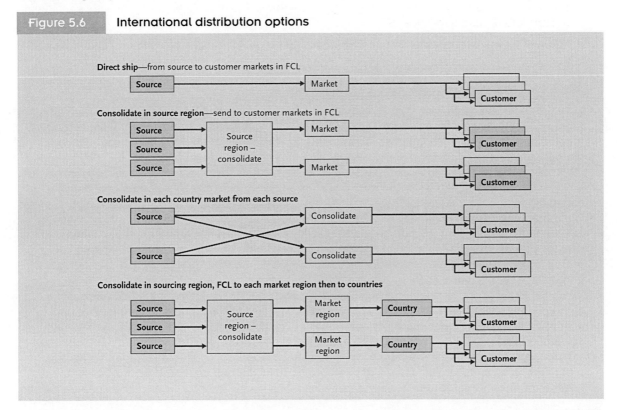

For example, the majority of retail fashion businesses have a business model that requires outsourcing production to low cost countries (LCC) such as China, Vietnam and Bangladesh and using LSPs to ship and distribute. While this approach is the generally accepted 'wisdom', it can cause low supply-chain effectiveness with increased costs. It is only by analysing and understanding the shipper's business that the potential challenges can be identified and an improved logistics service offered.

Major retail chains are gaining pricing power in the supply chains of developed economies and in so doing can demand to buy at the 'factory gate price' or 'free on board' (FOB) basis and for the retailer to contract for transport services from the supplier's facilities to the distribution centres (or wherever the customer wants the product delivered). This practice is also increasing for international purchases and will likely become standard practice for retailers that have a focus on private (or own) label products.

The result will be large retailers negotiating major logistics contracts with a small number of large LSPs that have the capability to support this size of business. As the most common selection process continues to emphasise price and quality at the level of operational logistics, it could put added pricing pressures on LSP companies.

Value of outsourcing

The business value of outsourcing should be more than costs. Some of the additional considerations, which cannot always be accurately quantified, as follows.

- Creating an external customer relationship between the LSP and the shipper can offer an improved level of flexibility and therefore responsiveness to demands of the shipper's customers.
- Outsourcing arrangements lead to improved asset utilisation. It is in the LSP's interest to maximise its return on investment, whereas if the same investment is in a product company's in-house logistics operation, it can be treated as a sunk cost.
- Contracting with LSPs transfers some of the risks associated with logistics operations; these include the occupational health and safety risk of injury from moving machinery and material handling, employment, compliance, industrial disputes and other risks. Shippers cannot negate all responsibility as 'chain of responsibility' legislation in some countries requires the shipper to have visibility of contractor's and their subcontractor's operational standards.

Figure 5.7 below identifies the effect an LSP may have on each approach of a client to gain competitive advantage.

Additional considerations by the shipper are as follows.

- How will the relationship with the LSP be managed and who will own the relationship? It is a mistake to assume that when a shipper contracts an LSP, it is a 'set and forget' solution. The relationship needs to be actively managed by both parties to ensure the forecasted savings, service levels and efficiencies materialise.
- LSPs may own assets, such as aircraft, trucks, distribution centres, factories, airports and seaports, to expedite the movement of products between suppliers and customers' locations. However, to provide higher utilisation of the assets, LSPs will want to move customers' products through those facilities, even if it is not the most effective routing.
- LSPs can provide increased flexibility through an ability to increase or decrease throughput; however, if demand increases, the LSP may increase their labour force by engaging temporary staff through labour hire agencies. The downside of this is the potential for quality problems through the use of potentially untrained or poorly trained staff.
- What is the impact on the rapport between management and the workforce at a brand company after entering into a business contract with an LSP? This has been a critique of outsourcing (and offshoring)—the loss of jobs and expertise. Employers can blame this on the inflexibility of labour agreements and employees. Trades unions argue that the reduction in costs is achieved by reducing salaries, worsening working conditions and removing job security. It is not uncommon for staff retrenched in the outsourcing process to be re-employed by the LSP under different terms and conditions, to do the same job.

Collaboration

While the term 'strategic partnership' is widely used by LSPs and their clients, it is a misnomer. The term 'partnership' requires shared risk and reward but, in practice, relationships between LSPs and their clients appear to be standard supplier–customer contracts. This difference between the language used and the actual situation provides for a gap between a stated desire for collaboration between the parties and the real ability for companies to work collaboratively.

A supposition of supply chains is that between parties collaboration is a matter of self-interest. But collaboration in the LSP context can mean very different things to the LSP and its clients. For the

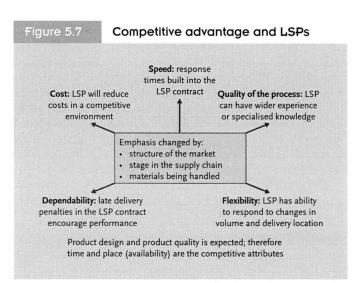

Figure 5.7 **Competitive advantage and LSPs**

Speed: response times built into the LSP contract

Cost: LSP will reduce costs in a competitive environment

Quality of the process: LSP can have wider experience or specialised knowledge

Emphasis changed by:
- structure of the market
- stage in the supply chain
- materials being handled

Dependability: late delivery penalties in the LSP contract encourage performance

Flexibility: LSP has ability to respond to changes in volume and delivery location

Product design and product quality is expected; therefore time and place (availability) are the competitive attributes

LSP it may mean the prospect of a longer term contractual arrangement, which requires investment in people, equipment and systems. From the client's perspective, the question underlying any discussion of collaboration is 'How well does the LSP understand our business/processes/customer requirements?' It appears that product companies consider that LSPs should not get too close, because that can result in a 'lock-in' of the contract.

Because the LSP can become a beneficiary from collaboration between parties in a supply chain, it is an advantage if they facilitate discussions about the types of relationships required, developing collaborative processes and the effective use of technology. This will not be easy, as shippers generally do not view LSPs as having this role. If an LSP wishes to succeed in portraying its business as a collaborator in a venture, it must have business managers with the skill set required to influence changes in attitudes held by customers.

Measuring performance

Typically, a set of performance measures will be provided by the client, but instead, the LSP should devise the performance measures (often called **key performance indicators (KPI)**) they consider are applicable, based on their review of the customer's business. The essential factor about KPIs is that they are *key*, not the many measures expected under too many contracts that have not been thought through concerning service delivery and cost.

If the relationship is to maximise the value of the client's supply chains, it needs to be managed in a systematic way. This means the LSP needs to devise a way of measuring the performance and improvements offered and having a set process for how the data is collected and information assessed and communicated.

The article, 'Measuring Performance in Services' (*McKinsey Quarterly*, 2006) identifies three aspects of measuring performance in a service environment:

1. Service companies need to compare themselves against their own performance rather than against poorly defined external measures.
2. Service companies must look deeper than their financial costs in order to discover and monitor the root causes of those expenses. Data collection is usually driven by the requirements of financial cost reporting, which often fails to shed light on ways of improving performance.
3. Service companies must structure broad cost-measurement systems to report and compare all expenses across the functional silos common to service delivery organisations. The goal is to improve the service companies' grasp of the cross-functional trade-offs that must be made to rein in total costs.

The article also identifies why a service company's achievements against metrics are not uniform across the business units:

- There are differences among jobs and groups, such as regional variations in labour costs and local geographies.
- The workload mix will differ between operations for different clients.
- There are differences in the use of capital (whether equipment is owned or leased by the company or owned by the client).
- The more types of services that are offered, the more variability there is in the agreements.
- Each client has unique aspects that are difficult to measure in terms of environment, equipment and infrastructure. An LSP will experience differences between managing a big, automated warehouse and a small, simple one.
- Size is a major reason for the wide variances in performance among customer accounts and business units.
- Large accounts should benefit from 'economies of scale', but in general they are more complex and that increases costs.
- Data is rarely defined or collected uniformly across an organisation's environments.

For these reasons and to have ownership of the measures, it is preferable for an LSP to identify and construct the applicable KPI and then negotiate these with the customer. The first step is to tabulate the applicable measures used by the client—what are they currently measuring and why. Then identify whether (and why) a KPI should be:

- a process-based metric that measures things such as 'perfect order' or 'perfect delivery', or
- an outcome-based metric that measures cost, service and quality.

Examples of process-based KPIs are:

- number of orders delivered by day
- orders in backlog by day
- delivery errors by month
- inventory accuracy by month
- distribution costs per case/pallet.

The mechanics of performance measurement can be as simple as fortnightly working meetings and monthly KPI discussions or it could mean having an employee of the client working at the LSP, so that misunderstandings and errors can be quickly addressed. Examples of these can relate to:

- consolidating large infrequent orders, which lead to consignee problems concerning receiving on time, or
- not making key information about the product or process available on time, leading to production delays at contract manufacturers.

What is important is that success of the relationship relies on there being a clear communication and agreement about how the relationship will be managed. This must be with some synergy and a sense of adding value, by the product company, rather than that of 'working a rented mule'.

Selling logistics services

Historically logistics services were sold on the basis of 'rate cards'; while occasionally necessary, selling on price is not advised as being of long-term benefit for a LSP business.

Significant buying decisions in companies are rarely made by a single person; there is a network of people with their own personal and business requirements and they are at different levels in the organisation. So, the five phases of the sales cycle are as follows.

1. Contact the prospect.
2. Qualify.
3. Investigate.
4. Propose.
5. Close.

The 'qualify' and 'investigate' phases are two very important steps, as selling logistics services becomes a more specialised example of services marketing.

The step that follows contacting the pre-assessed prospect is '*qualify* the authority to buy'; the level of sign-off for a major services purchase is often higher than initially considered by the sales person. The challenge will be to sell at all levels through the business and to use the prospect's business objectives and terms—do not discuss how good the new forklift trucks are!

The group of people involved in the prospect's buying process can be considered under five headings:

1. Economic—calculates whether the business can afford to buy the proposal when measured against alternative projects and their financial return
2. Technical—determines how adequately the proposal will meet the organisation's requirements
3. Recommender—has the trust of the final decision maker, but is often difficult to identify
4. Coach—provides the information needed to win the sale; they want to help because they consider the proposal the best on offer
5. Informer—provides information from the hidden agenda, but their observations may not always be accurate.

An essential part of qualifying is to ask the difficult questions, even if the prospect's staff are not comfortable (people do not like saying no)—it is better to walk away at the beginning than after many months of sales work. Therefore, qualify whether the prospect is willing to spend the money: this qualifier is important, not only concerning the LSP income, but whether the prospect is realistic about the cost to make the contract work.

If the prospect has been qualified, factors that require understanding and discussion in the context of quoting for new (or extended) business are:

- the value of utilising existing assets
- the synergies from investing in standard solutions
- the level of engagement expected with the client's customers.

As part of the *investigation* (questioning and listening) process, an awareness of the risks associated with accepting a given contract needs to be developed. Some of the key risks include:

- the client going out of business or being acquired
- the potential of lengthening time needed for the client to pay invoices
- the contract being terminated but capital has been invested in equipment
- a change to the client's or their customer's requirements
- a change in market conditions, such as fuel price and currency fluctuations
- the client not receiving the contracted level of service, but being locked into a contract with substantial exit penalties.

Building risk into the costing model is as vital to the proposal as accounting for all the direct costs associated with doing business.

Performance-based logistics

In recent years, the concept of **performance-based logistics (PBL)**—also known as performance-based contracts (PBC), availability-based contracts and 'power by the hour'—has been gaining attention, but slow adoption. PBL was developed to 'buy performance not the product' and commenced with maintenance agreements contracted by aerospace and defence organisations as an improved way of managing contracts against those based on time and materials (T&M) clauses.

The LSP that proposes or enters into a PBL contract will be expected to be more self-reliant—if the performance is not met, then no, or reduced payment is received or penalties are applied. This means the LSP must invest resources to:

- design the service network of distribution centres and other stocking locations to balance the allocation of capital and resources. This requires modelling, simulation and optimisation expertise
- develop business intelligence to gain improved visibility in the supply chains and in sensing changes in demand
- provide inventory or service parts optimisation to manage the risk of 'out of stock' and non-performance of the contract against over-investment
- acquire decision-support tools that assist with 'what-if' questions
- develop risk management expertise and tools that assist with pricing the expected performance requirements.

PBL contracts will be a challenge to design and execute, requiring both the client and the LSP to learn a new way of doing businesses. For LSPs that invest resources in the process, there is a potential to move away from price as the major buying criteria, being replaced by performance capability. This approach has the potential to increase profit margins for the LSP and provide improved services for the client.

Chapter questions

Operational

1. What parameters would you use to make a decision to outsource a logistics operation?
2. Which elements of a logistics operation would you contract to an LSP and which would you retain? Explain the rationale for your decision.
3. Consider a business you are familiar with. What are the risks specific to this business associated with outsourcing? What are the risks to this business associated with a decision to retain a particular function in-house?
4. Consider the different type of LSPs discussed in this chapter. Select one that you are not familiar with. What could be the KPIs relevant to assessing their performance?
5. How can the value added generated by a lead logistics provider (or 4PL) be measured?

⑥ Reflect on the ways in which an organisation can manage its relationship with an LSP it engages. What are the key information inputs that an LSP requires of a client's organisation? Could you add value by providing it in a different format or timeframe?

⑦ A food manufacturer supplies a major retailer. The supplier contracts an external warehouse and transport company to provide the following services: receive and process the retailer's orders, pick, pack and despatch the orders and deliver them to the retailer's distribution centre. Although the external company is contracted to the food manufacturer, they have daily interfaces with the customer at the ordering and delivery stages, so who is the supplier in the transactions and why?

Planning

⑧ Discuss the process you would use to establish a relationship with an LSP and the measurement process you would use.

⑨ From the perspective of the LSP, what leverage points do you have available in managing the relationship with a customer and the measurement process?

⑩ Analyse vulnerabilities of the supply chain as a result of the decision to engage an LSP. How could these be mitigated? From an LSP perspective, how could you present value added solutions to your customer in response to the risks identified?

⑪ What are the risks associated with taking on a contract for an LSP and how can these risks be mitigated?

Management

⑫ Compare and contrast outsourcing operational capability and outsourcing management. What are the consequences of this distinction?

⑬ Discuss the strategic aspect of the outsourcing decision and the impact it can have on supply chains.

⑭ Discuss the importance (or otherwise) of having an alignment of vision, values and objectives between the outsourcing company and their LSP.

⑮ Compare and contrast the strategic implications of the decision to vertically integrate against the decision to outsource.

References and links

Capgemini/Georgia Institute of Technology, *Third-Party Logistics Study*, www.tli.gatech.edu, 2009.

'The Coming Wave of Service Provider Convergence', www.eyefortransport.com.

IBM Global Business Services, 'Building Value in Logistics Outsourcing', www.ibm.com, 2006.

'Measuring Performance in Services', *McKinsey Quarterly*, January 2006, www.mckinsey.com.

Virum, H., 'Third-party Logistics Development in Europe', *Logistics and Transportation Review*, vol. 29, no. 4, 1993.

International trade logistics

Links to other chapters

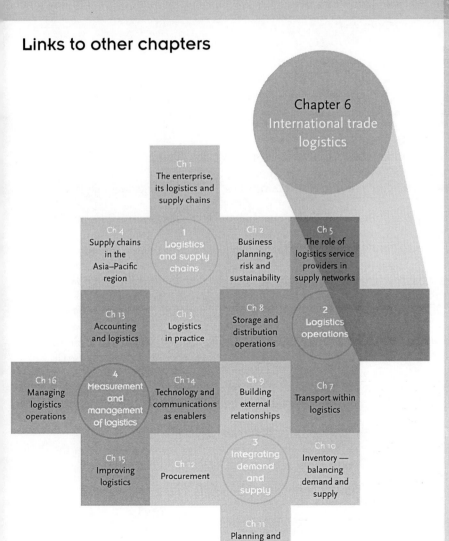

Chapter 6
International trade
logistics

Ch 1
The enterprise,
its logistics and
supply chains

Ch 4
Supply chains
in the
Asia–Pacific
region

1
Logistics
and supply
chains

Ch 2
Business
planning,
risk and
sustainability

Ch 5
The role of
logistics service
providers in
supply networks

Ch 13
Accounting
and logistics

Ch 3
Logistics
in practice

Ch 8
Storage and
distribution
operations

2
Logistics
operations

Ch 16
Managing
logistics
operations

4
Measurement
and
management
of logistics

Ch 14
Technology and
communications
as enablers

Ch 9
Building
external
relationships

Ch 7
Transport within
logistics

Ch 15
Improving
logistics

Ch 12
Procurement

3
Integrating
demand
and
supply

Ch 10
Inventory —
balancing
demand and
supply

Ch 11
Planning and
scheduling the
enterprise

Learning outcomes

On completion of this chapter you will be able to:

- understand the role of international trade logistics and the necessity for compliance with country regulations

- comprehend the elements of international trade logistics

- recognise the link between global trade, lead times and variation on management decisions

- note the facilitators of international trade logistics

- note the role of governments in international trade logistics

- recognise the factors in international trade management that must be incorporated into a supply network model.

Key terms

These terms are used in the text. Develop your own notebook by downloading information on each term.

international trade logistics (ITL)	World Trade Organization (WTO)	Doha Round
global commerce management (GCM)	United Nations Conference on Trade and Development (UNCTAD)	Certificate of Origin
governance, risk and compliance (GRC)		Free Trade Zone (FTZ)
		Export Processing Zone (EPZ)
global trade management (GTM)	transpacific	bond store
procure to pay	harmonised commodity description and coding system (HS)	Asia–Pacific Economic Cooperation (APEC)
quote to cash		member economies
globalisation	World Customs Organization (WCO)	Organisation for Economic Cooperation and Development (OECD)
multinational corporation (MNC)	Regional Trade Agreement (RTA)	
world trade	Free Trade Agreement (FTA)	
cross-border trade		

Introduction

In this chapter we will discuss the range of factors that logisticians need to understand when companies undertake trade activities across national borders. Even if the organisation has a separate trade department, the necessary interaction with inbound and outbound logistics, and the increasing cost of doing things incorrectly, make knowledge of international trade management a necessity.

Globalisation and world trade

Melbourne's *The Age* newspaper reported on 12 March 2009 that economists had forecast China's exports for February 2009 to increase by 1 per cent February 2008. This would happen because Chinese New Year did not occur in February 2009 and therefore there were more trading days. However, the actual result was a decline of 25.7 per cent!

But should this decline have been expected? Extended supply chains require that orders must be placed at least six to nine months in advance of their requirement to be on the shelf at retail shops in a distant country.

The number of container TEUs (twenty-foot equivalent units) entering US ports in the peak import month of October 2008 was 1.36 million, with the majority from China. That was only slightly down from the 2007 peak of 1.48 million TEU, recorded in September 2007, the all-time record.

So the decline in the receipt of full containers between October 2007 and October 2008 was only 8.1 per cent—in a major world recession. But the orders had been placed at least in May 2008, when the world economy was still looking good. The response in August 2008, when the global financial crisis was evident, was to substantially reduce orders for delivery in February 2009—resulting in the decline of more than 25 per cent in exports from China.

This is an example of the level of variation that is introduced into supply chains as they become longer; lead times can become too long for people to respond rationally when unexpected changes occur in demand patterns.

The additional complexity and risks in global supply chains can increase costs and affect the cash flow position of brand companies; this will require more working capital to fund increased inventories to cover the longer order cycles and their uncertainties. The situation can be made worse by:

- senior management failing to understand the complexity in global supply chains
- not employing people with the range of skills required to implement and manage the logistics of international trade
- poor selection, implemention and integration of information systems to assist logistics and international trade.

Cross-border trade

Increasingly, logisticians need to master the vagaries of international supply chains. While global supply chains offer many benefits, they also open a Pandora's box of risks that add to the challenges of domestic supply.

Of the costs to design, produce and deliver a garment into a retail store, about one-sixth of the retail price is the cost to manufacture, but that is the cost most executives consider when deciding from which country and supplier the garment will be purchased. The remaining costs are payments to logistics service providers (LSPs), internal costs and overheads associated with design, procurement and logistics. But these elements typically receive less attention in the final buying decision. Likewise, in a selling situation, how informed are the decision makers concerning the total logistics costs within the proposed sales contract?

The study and activity of logistics in an international environment is called **international trade logistics (ITL)**; it is also called **global commerce management (GCM)**. A definition used by Blinco Systems (2004) is: 'Management of asset and non-asset sourcing, manufacturing and distribution across international borders to meet the demand requirements of the organisation's customers', as illustrated in Figure 6.1 below.

ITL incorporates the increasingly important role of trade **governance, risk and compliance (GRC)**, which has become critical since 2001 following the 9/11 World Trade Center attack in New York. This is due to the requirement of countries for detailed and accurate documentation concerning cargoes; the outcome of non-compliance can be high penalties and delays in the movement of goods.

An integral part of ITL is **global trade management (GTM)**, which defines the nature and flow of documentation (electronic and physical) in the ITL environment. A definition of GTM provided by Tradebeam Inc (2009) is: 'Managing the global transaction life cycle across order, logistics and settlement activities to significantly improve operating efficiencies and cash flows'.

To indicate the integration of GTM and logistics, terms of GTM used in articles and conference presentations are **procure to pay** to describe the inbound supply chain and **quote to cash** to describe the outbound supply chain.

Complexity in international trade logistics

The complexity of ITL occurs because an enterprise does not have one supply chain, but multiple supply chains, operating as a network that can resemble a spider's web. An example of complexity for a business is shown in Figure 6.2.

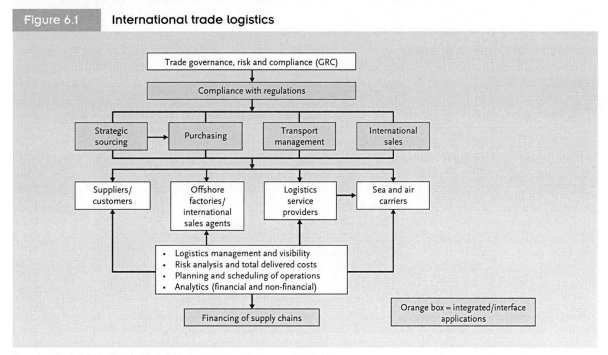

Figure 6.1 International trade logistics

Source: Adapted from *Supply Chain Digest*, August 2008, www.scdigest.com.

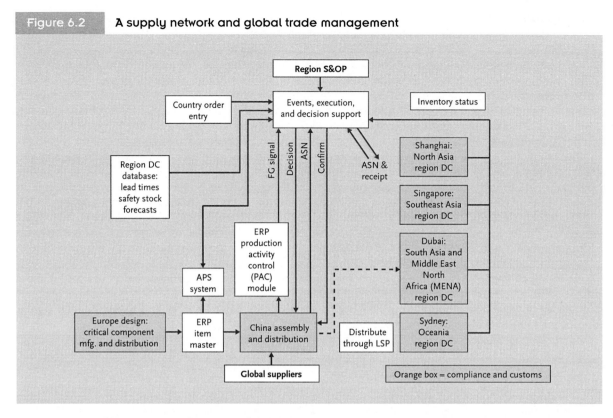

Figure 6.2   A supply network and global trade management

Every step of buying and selling in a global setting has distance (physical and cultural) and time being synonymous with ITL. The longer the distance, the less control can be exercised in the supply chains.

Elements of international trade logistics

International trade developments

International trade refers to exports of goods and services by a firm to a foreign-based buyer. Wild et al. (2003) noted that 'the purchase, sale or exchange of goods and services across national borders is called international trade'. The purpose of international trade is to provide a nation with commodities it lacks in exchange for those that it produces in abundance. When such transactions are linked with other economic policies, it tends to improve a nation's standard of living. Much of modern history concerning international relations refers to efforts that promote freer trade among nations.

The terms '**globalisation**', 'international trade' and 'international business' are commonly used when discussing trade in goods (called merchandise trade) and services across the borders of countries. These terms originated in the study of economics and therefore tend to concentrate on the aspects of business and government policy.

The classical economists Adam Smith, David Ricardo and John Stuart Mill provided the theoretical justification for international trade. Ricardo in particular promoted the concept of relative or comparative (not absolute) costs as the underpinning of international trade, through his theory of comparative advantage. This stated that countries should concentrate their efforts on providing goods that have a comparative advantage over other countries and import those goods where a comparative advantage does not exist.

Comparative advantage will be achieved on the basis of one or more factors (that can change), which are: natural resources, technology, capital, management capability and the price and availability of labour. Additional factors, which can also change over time, are political, social, cultural and the economic environment.

The theory of comparative advantage has been exploited by **multinational corporations (MNC)**, which began in the 17th century with the formation of the Dutch East India Company, the Dutch West India Company and the British East India Company. Each was a trading company focused on using the comparative advantage of the crops grown and cloth manufactured in the part of world for which they had a monopoly. They generated very high profits through sales in their home countries, neighbouring countries and colonies.

This approach expanded in the late 19th century as companies with a global vision identified that it was preferable to establish production facilities in countries as subsidiaries and have a sourcing policy whereby the facilities supplied each other as a network that linked production to markets.

This situation has grown to a level where, as Miesel et al. (2002) stated:

> The expanding global reach of MNCs largely explains the dramatic growth of world trade since World War II. In many developed market economies, MNCs account for well over three-quarters of their home country trade flows. In the United States, for instance, the goods trade associated with MNCs constituted 64 per cent and 39 per cent of exports and imports, respectively, in 1998.

This concentration of internal MNC trade as a major component of **world trade** has continued and may have increased.

In addition to the growth of MNCs in **cross-border trade**, increases in global trade since the 1950s have occurred due to two factors:

1. liberalisation of trade:
   a. reduced tariffs paid on imported goods
   b. elimination of import quotas on products.
2. business drivers:
   a. increase sales volume to cover fixed costs (many so-called variable costs in a business are actually fixed—see Chapter 13)
   b. rise of outsourcing, 'offshoring' and 'near-shoring' as a means of companies reducing their manufacturing costs
   c. IT applications and technologies available in most countries.

Global trade volumes

Global import and export merchandise trade was valued by the **World Trade Organization (WTO)** at nearly US$12 trillion in 2008, growing from US$3 trillion in 1990, some 75 times higher than in the mid-1960s. While the 2008 economic crisis slowed world trade, the projections are that trade will grow to more than US$70 trillion by 2025.

World exports to Asian countries increased from 20.8 per cent in 1998 to 26.2 per cent in 2006, with much of the increase being inter-region trade flows (Dr Gene Huang, Chief Economist at FedEx).

In Oceania for 2008–09, Australia had a total trade in goods and services of $560 billion. In the same financial year, New Zealand had a total trade in goods and services of NZ$81 billion. Import and export figures for that year in Australia and New Zealand are shown in Tables 6.1 and 6.2, below and overleaf.

Table 6.1 Australian trade in goods and services 2008–09

Exports	A$b	Imports	A$b
Minerals	52	Minerals and fuels	31
Fuels, including natural gas	77	Agriculture	13
Agriculture	32	Manufactures	160
Manufactures	44		
To	%	From	%
East Asia	53	East Asia	31
ASEAN	9	ASEAN	20
India	7	Americas	15
Pacific	5	Pacific	5
Asia–Pacific countries in top 10	7	Asia–Pacific countries in top 10	7

Source: Based on Department of Foreign Affairs and Trade, www.dfat.gov.au.

Table 6.2 New Zealand trade in goods and services 2008–09

Exports	$NZb	Imports	$NZb
Agriculture	20	Minerals and fuels	6
Manufacturers	5	Machinery and equipment	16
Total	40		41
To	**%**	**From**	**%**
Australia	23	Australia	18
Asia, excluding Japan	21	Asia, excluding Japan	33
Asia–Pacific countries in top 10	7	Asia–Pacific countries in top 10	7

Source: Based on New Zealand Trade and Enterprise, www.investmentnz.govt.nz.

Region transport capacity

The **United Nations Conference on Trade and Development (UNCTAD)** (www.unctad.org) estimates that merchant ships contribute about US$380 billion in freight income within the global economy, equivalent to about 5 per cent of total world trade.

Over the past 40 years, total seaborne trade has quadrupled from just over 8000 billion tonne-miles in 1968, to more than 32 000 billion tonne-miles in 2008. Asian ports now handle about 50 per cent of the world's container volume. The size of container ships on different voyages for 2009 is shown in Table 6.3.

What explains the different sizes of vessels on the Asia–Europe trade route in comparison to the **transpacific** trade route? The distance between ports is:

* Shanghai to Los Angeles = 5708 nautical miles
* Shanghai to Rotterdam = 10 519 nautical miles.

For reference, shipping distances within the region are:

* Shanghai to Sydney = 4632 nautical miles
* Shanghai to Auckland = 5142 nautical miles
* Shanghai to Dubai = 5667 nautical miles.

Table 6.3 Container ship size by voyage

TEU per ship	Transpacific vessels	Asia–Europe vessels	Transatlantic vessels
4–4.5k	72		27
4.5–5k	65		48
5–5.5k	67		23
>8000		203	
Sub total	204	203	98
% of total	55%	53%	70%

Source: The Shippers' Voice—a joint venture of SV2 Ltd, MDS Transmodal Ltd and Mission MKG LLP, www.shippersvoice.com.

Between 2000 and 2007, the value of world trade grew by 12 per cent, but total freight costs increased by about half this figure, demonstrating the falling unit costs of transport, including those of ocean freight. Analysis carried out by UNCTAD suggests that the ratio of total freight costs to import values represent, on average, less than 6 per cent of the retail price for consumer goods. For example, transport costs account for 2 per cent of the retail price of a television and 1.2 per cent for a kilogram of coffee.

An argument for continued low freight costs into the future is the additional tonnage that has been constructed to handle the forecast of increases in world trade and the increased size of container ships, which provide a lower unit cost to transport. However, if freight rates continue to remain low, an outcome is likely to be a continuing consolidation of shipping companies through acquisition or companies exiting the business and a potential increase of monopolies and cartels.

In 2009, the top 10 container shipping companies controlled more than 58 per cent of the total containers in circulation, as shown in Figure 6.3 opposite.

A 2009 study by Drewry Shipping Consultants provides an example of the inputs required to undertake a global supply network plan. It stated that as recently as early 2008, there was widespread concern over a growing shortage of capacity in the container terminal sector relative to demand, which caused periodic

| Figure 6.3 | Largest container shipping lines 2009 |

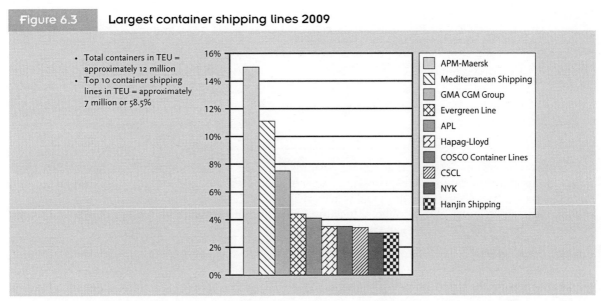

- Total containers in TEU = approximately 12 million
- Top 10 container shipping lines in TEU = approximately 7 million or 58.5%

Legend:
- APM-Maersk
- Mediterranean Shipping
- GMA CGM Group
- Evergreen Line
- APL
- Hapag-Lloyd
- COSCO Container Lines
- CSCL
- NYK
- Hanjin Shipping

Source: Based on *Alphaliner Weekly Newsletter* 15, 6–12 April 2009, p.2, www.alphaliner.com.

bottlenecks in supply chains. However, with the advent of the global financial crisis, container terminal capacity will be under much less pressure until at least 2013 as the world's container trades grow more slowly than originally forecast. Based on their analysis, Drewry states that actual capacity added on a shipping route is about one-third of that originally proposed and it arrives four years later than planned. This is another area of unknowns when forward planning a supply network.

There is a similar situation when planning air freight capacity. An example is the air freight operators that serve Hong Kong International Airport, which can be full to North America and Europe but carry little cargo back to Hong Kong. The viability of the operation relies on the rates that carriers can charge for the outbound leg. The situation becomes critical during the peak shipping season for Asia, from September through to December and at the end of each quarter, when companies try to meet their revenue targets by delivering orders by air.

Taking advantage of shipping and air space availability and favourable return freight rates makes it viable for companies in Australia and New Zealand that have unit labour costs less than 10 to 12 per cent of the selling price, to competitively sell products into Asia.

Facilitators of international trade logistics

Customs

In general, the role of customs is to protect the community in their country by controlling who and what crosses the borders into that country. In Australia the Australian Customs and Border Protection Service is charged with this responsibility and works closely with Australian Federal Police, the Australian Quarantine and Inspection Service and other government and international organisations to detect and deter unlawful movement of goods and people across the border. As such, customs perform the border clearance function, which includes processing import–export documentation that uses the **harmonised system (HS)** (discussed later in this chapter) as the basis for calculation of customs tariffs and excise.

Other countries in the region have government agencies performing the customs duty. Table 6.4 overleaf lists some of them. Most of these agencies present a range of import–export-related information on their websites.

Customs brokers

The International Federation of Customs Brokers Associations (IFCBA) defines a customs broker as 'a firm which consolidates critical business information that allows importers to clear their goods through Customs safely, securely and quickly'.

Table 6.4 Customs agencies in the Asia–Pacific region

Country	Name of agency	Website
New Zealand	New Zealand Customs	www.customs.govt.nz
China	China Customs	www.customs.gov.cn
India	Central Board of Excise and Customs India	www.cbec.gov.in/cae1-english.htm
Thailand	Customs Department of the Kingdom of Thailand	www.customs.go.th/Customs-Eng/indexEng.jsp
Singapore	Singapore Customs	www.customs.gov.sg/topNav/hom/

Customs brokers offer services that include customs clearance, customs securities, customs valuation of goods, documentation requirements, legislation advice, duty rates and tariff classification, refunds of duty and sales tax, sales tax rulings and tariff and valuation advice applications.

Specialist services may also be offered, including bounties and anti-dumping assessments, quotas and permits to import, tariff concession and by-law applications.

Freight forwarders

The role of a freight forwarder is to buy large quantities of space from companies that own ships, aircraft and trucks and then consolidate customers' shipments so the space is fully utilised. They are essentially a 'buy low and sell high' broker of cargo space.

Freight forwarders offer a range of services for clients in addition to air and sea freight consolidation, including door-to-door goods movement, transport feasibility cost studies, incoterm analysis and transit insurance.

It is common for freight forwarders to offer both freight forwarding and customs broking capabilities. Some may also offer additional specialist services including: international order monitoring, international order assembly, Administrative Appeals Tribunal applications, quarantine regulations compliance and international trade finance.

Most reputable forwarders are affiliated with an industry association, such as the Australian Federation of International Forwarders (AFIF) or the Customs Brokers and Forwarders Council of Australia (CBFCA).

Incoterms

The International Chamber of Commerce developed Incoterms—a set of internationally accepted trading terms that defines the transfer of transactional costs, risk and responsibilities between buyer and seller. They closely correspond to the UN Convention of Contracts for the International Sale of Goods, a treaty offering a uniform international sales law. Incoterms have been updated for 2010 and are divided by mode of transport.

Maritime and inland waterway transport only:
    FAS—free alongside ship (named port of shipment)
    FOB—free on board (named port of shipment)
    CFR—cost and freight (named port of destination)
    CIF—cost, insurance and freight (named port of destination)
    DES—delivered ex-ship (named port of destination)
    DEQ—delivered ex-quay (named port of destination).

Any mode of transport:
    EXW—ex-works (named place)
    FCA—free carrier (named place)
    CPT—carriage paid to (named place of destination)
    CIP—carriage and insurance paid to (named place of destination)
    DAF—delivered at frontier (named place)
    DDU—delivered duty unpaid (named place of destination)
    DDP—delivered duty paid (named place of destination).

While these terms are international in use, when trading with the United States, they are only used for imports. For exports from the United States, trading terms are based on the Revised American Foreign Trade Definitions (RAFTD). In particular, differences apply to the terms FOB and CIF.

Harmonisation system

The **harmonised commodity description and coding system (HS)**, also referred to as the harmonised tariff system (HTS), is the international standard for classifying traded items. The HS is developed and maintained by the **World Customs Organization (WCO)** and over 200 countries use the HS, equating to more than 98 per cent of world trade.

The HS is a six-digit record nomenclature that equates to a particular item and cannot be altered in any way, in order to ensure the integrity of the harmonisation. Participating countries may extend a harmonised system number to eight or 10 digits for customs or export purposes.

HS is used as a foundation for customs tariffs; collection of international trade statistics; rules of origin; collection of internal taxes; transport tariffs and statistics; monitoring of controlled goods (for example wastes, narcotics and endangered species); and customs controls and procedures, including security and compliance. It is also the basis for international trade negotiations.

Role of government in international trade

Governments play a role in regulating imports and promoting exports, which is done by applying tariffs and quotas to imports and offering subsidies and grants to stimulate exports.

In essence this is equivalent to a 'make or buy' decision, but on the scale of a country rather than an individual business. Governments take account of resources and skills in the country, employment levels, manufacturing costs and the balance of trade.

International trade is subject to a range of regulations and controls exercised through governments, which address areas such as trade agreements, arms trade, wildlife trade and antidumping regulations.

Trade agreements

Regional Trade Agreements (RTA) and **Free Trade Agreements (FTA)** between countries provide for a reduction and, in some instances, elimination of tariffs on exports and imports between parties to the agreement.

Agreements frequently cover aspects concerning goods, services, investment, intellectual property, e-commerce, temporary movement of business people and economic cooperation. They may also address measures relating to customs procedures and cooperation, phytosanitary measures, technical regulations and conformity, assessment procedures and competition policy.

As multilateral trade agreements, such as the current **Doha Round** of the WTO Agreement, take a long time to negotiate, region groupings and individual countries have resorted to negotiating FTAs with some of their main trading links.

As an example of a major agreement, in January 2010 the ASEAN-5 (Malaysia, Singapore, the Philippines, Thailand and Indonesia) and Brunei signed an FTA with China, creating the world's third-largest trade bloc. The agreement eliminates tariffs on 90 per cent of goods traded between the South-East Asian countries and China and is expected to substantially increase trade volumes between them. Four other states, Laos, Cambodia, Vietnam and Myanmar (Burma), are due to join the FTA in 2015.

However, a business must undertake specific research to determine which current or future FTA or RTA is the more appropriate and advantageous to use, in relation to the timing of market entry or when and from where to switch suppliers.

In order to benefit from the terms of a FTA, a business needs to register as an exporter to the particular country or region in question and ensure correct documentation accompanies each shipment, which includes the appropriate **Certificate of Origin**. Suppliers of materials for the product must also understand the relevant protocols and include the appropriate documentation with their shipments. Some countries, for example the United States, have specific requirements in terms of the time to provide the documents; the repercussions of not adhering to these can be costly.

Free Trade Zones

As a part of governments' role in promoting trade, an initiative adopted in some countries has been to allow **free trade zones (FTZs)** and **Export Processing Zones (EPZs)** to be established. The FTZ concept was developed from the **bond stores** that are administered by the tax offices of various countries.

An FTZ is an area within a country set aside and not subject to tariffs and quotas for companies to establish import or export operations and so attract new business and foreign investments.

An organisation can therefore transit or hold inventory for a period of time, without the need to pay otherwise applicable duties and excises. Additionally, a FTZ may be a means of quarantining inventory that exceeds the permitted quota applying at its ultimate destination.

It is common for them to be located in key nodes of international trade routes and to provide substantial infrastructure for its users. FTZs tend to have good-quality access routes to various modes of transport, flexible warehousing capabilities that can be scaled up or down on demand and extensive IT infrastructure. They may also provide various consulting services to support the businesses using the zone.

Some of the FTZs in the Asia–Pacific region are:

- Batam Free Trade Zone, Indonesia (www.batam.go.id/home/eng/index.php)
- Inspira Pharma and Biotech park, India (www.inspirainfra.com)
- Port Klang Free Zone, Malaysia (www.pkfz.com/content/profile/invest.html).
- Singapore: Port of Singapore, Jurong Port, Sembawang Wharves, Pasir Panjang Wharves, and Airport Logistics Park of Singapore (ALPS).

International trade organisations

Governments can play an active or passive role in supporting organisations that have an objective to reduce barriers to world trade.

The World Trade Organization (WTO) was established in 1995, building on the earlier General Agreement on Tariffs and Trade (GATT). The WTO administers a system of rules for international trade, aimed at liberalising and expanding trade under agreed and enforceable rules for reciprocal benefit. Information about the WTO and Australia can be found at www.dfat.gov.au/trade/negotiations.

The forum **Asia–Pacific Economic Cooperation (APEC)** was established in 1989 to 'enhance economic growth and prosperity for the region and to strengthen the Asia–Pacific community, facilitating economic growth, cooperation, trade and investment in the Asia–Pacific region'.

It is the only inter-governmental grouping in the world operating on the basis of non-binding commitments, open dialogue and equal respect for the views of all participants. Unlike the WTO or other multilateral trade bodies, APEC has no treaty obligations required of its participants. Decisions made within APEC are reached by consensus and commitments are undertaken on a voluntary basis.

APEC has 21 members—referred to as **member economies**—which account for approximately 40 per cent of the world's population, 54 per cent of world GDP and about 43 per cent of world trade.

The **Organisation for Economic Co-operation and Development (OECD)** was established in 1961 in Paris to bring together the governments of countries committed to democracy and the market economy. Members from within the region are Australia, Japan, Korea and New Zealand. The main role of the OECD from a trade viewpoint is the analysis and reporting of member countries' performance and economic outlook.

Country performance in logistics services

Companies that are heavily involved in international trade will plan their supply network using network modelling tools. There is no 'best practice' to consider, as the changing situation in the region requires the modelling to be an ongoing process, to ensure that the enterprise benefits from the most effective and efficient supply chains.

Countries in the region are at different stages of development concerning their logistics services capability (see Chapter 4) and this must be considered as part of supply chain planning. Income is not the only determinant of a country's logistics infrastructure and services capability; even in low-income countries, logistics service providers can improve the quality of their operations. However, countries with low logistics performance indicator (LPI) scores tend to have longer goods movement delays, therefore higher inventories must be planned.

When commencing the planning of a supply chain strategy for the Asia–Pacific region, a logistician should consider where each trading country ranks and the main features of logistics services within the respective logistics groups, as shown in Table 6.5.

Table 6.5 Logistics services by country group

Countries are listed in each column in order of their logistics productivity index (LPI) score

	Developed logistics services	Developing logistics services	Emerging logistics services
	Singapore Japan Hong Kong SAR, China Australia Taiwan New Zealand South Korea	China Malaysia Thailand Philippines India Vietnam Indonesia Bangladesh Mauritius Pakistan	Laos Papua New Guinea (PNG) Maldives Cambodia Myanmar (Burma) Solomon Islands Sri Lanka Fiji Nepal Bhutan (no LPI score) North Korea (no LPI score) Other Pacific nations (no LPI score)
Logistics infrastructure and services features			
1 Trade-related infrastructure	Few bottlenecks except possibly rail. Supports collaboration	Capacity bottlenecks and constraints	Poor
2 Quality and supply of logistics services	Good with industry leaders. Competitive market. Acceptance of outsourcing by prospective clients. Equipment technology implemented in larger organisations	A weak or emerging market for LSP. Increasing competition and consolidation of service suppliers, but some entrenched business practices. Variable distribution channels—from traditional to advanced. Varying implementation of equipment technology	Small and family-based material-handling businesses with low development. Government involvement. Absence of LSP sector. Manual handling
3 Customs	Superior structure and operations	Some constraints	Major constraints
4 Integration of border management services	Few problems	Ranging from few constraints to major constraints	Can be a problem
5 Regional facilitation and transit	Good	Can be a problem	Major issues
6 Data automation	Integration and exchange of data. High internet adoption	Varying levels of implementation and integration. Medium internet adoption	Limited. Low internet adoption
7 Educated and trained labour	Good supply; requires continuous skills upgrading	Limited access to capabilities. More reactive processes	Low capability. Expediting focus

Source: Adapted from World Bank, *LPI Report*, www.worldbank.org, 2010.

From the top of 'Emerging logistics' to the top of 'Developing logistics' implies two to four additional days for moving goods between the port and company warehouses; physical inspection can take 25 per cent longer.

In addition to modelling the physical movements in the network, the working capital requirements need to be modelled using inventory planning models. As feasible improvements in customer service and inventory holding are modelled for the physical aspects, so the financial results can be seen in reduced working capital requirements.

Finally, ensure that the organisation is able to manage the international trade logistics processes. The *Global Sourcing Benchmark Report* (2003) notes, 'Enterprises were particularly challenged to identify and qualify foreign sources, collaborate with offshore suppliers and formalise sourcing strategies across sites and geographies. The study also suggests that companies do not have sufficient information and tools to calculate and manage landed costs effectively.'

Chapter questions

Operational

1. In a business that you are familiar with, who is responsible for inbound and outbound logistics? What coordination is in place to ensure that documentation is correct for both imports and exports?
2. What are some advantages and risks presented by global outsourcing, and how could the risks be minimised?
3. What is a foreign trade zone (FTZ)? Explain why a logistician would consider using the services of an FTZ in moving products.

Planning

4. In the current global economic climate, finance for working capital is harder to obtain. What effect may this have on international business relationships?
5. Select three Incoterms as the basis for an agreement with a supplier and a customer. Discuss the impact the choices have on the operating costs and cash cycle of a business. How could this situation be improved?
6. Governance, risk and compliance (GRC) has become an important element in international trade. Identify what steps are required to implement a GRC process in a business that has commenced exporting.
7. Explain the difference between a tariff and a quota. What approach would you consider for each in the planning of exports and imports?

Management

8. What are the key challenges concerning international trade for a senior supply chain executive of a global enterprise? What order of importance would you place on this list, and why? Select the number one challenge on the list and identify the steps required to understand, analyse, scope for improvement and implement change.
9. How will the decision about what Incoterms trade terms to use affect the structure of a logistics strategy?
10. Should responsibility for international trade logistics and international sales be separate or within one part of the organisation structure? If in one part of the organisation, should it be within supply chain or marketing, and why?

References and links

'Balancing supply cost, performance and risks in an uncertain economy', Global Sourcing Benchmark Report, June 2003, www.aberdeen.com.

'China exports fall', *The Age*, 12 March 2009.

Blinco Systems, 'Global commerce management', Toronto, Canada, 2004, www.blinco.com.

Drewry Shipping Consultants, 'Annual review of global container terminal operators', 2009, www.drewry.co.uk.

Miesel, V., Higinbotham, H. & Yi, C., 'International transfer pricing: practical solutions for intercompany pricing', *International Tax Journal*, 22 September 2002.

Tradebeam Inc, 'Global trade management', September 2009, www.tradebeam.com.

Wild J.J. Wild K.L. & Han J.C.Y., *International Business* edn 2, Prentice Hall, 2003.

World Bank, *Globalization, Growth and Poverty*, 2002, www.worldbank.org.

Links

Asia–Pacific Economic Cooperation (APEC) forum: www.apec.org

Asia Pacific Research and Training Network on Trade: www.unescap.org/tid/artnet

Asia Pacific Trade and Investment Agreement Database: www.unescap.org/tid/aptiad

Austrade recommends a process for businesses interested in exporting: www.austrade.gov.au

Australian Customs and Border Protection Service: www.customs.gov.au

Australian Federation of International Forwarders: www.afif.asn.au

Australian Institute of Export also provides a view of preparing for export: www.aiex.com.au

Customs Brokers and Forwarders Council of Australia: www.cbfca.com.au

Department of Foreign Affairs and Trade for Australian trade policy: www.dfat.gov.au/publications/

Global Facilitation Partnership for Transport and Trade: gfptt.org

Information about the economy of New Zealand: www.investmentnz.govt.nz

Information and data on international merchandise trade statistics, UN Comtrade: comtrade.un.org

Information for importers and exporters relating to quarantine requirements, Australian Quarantine and Inspection Service: www.daff.gov.au/aqis

Information for importers and exporters relating to quarantine requirements, MAFBNZ Clearance Service: www.maf.govt.nz/quarantine

International Federation of Customs Brokers Associations (IFCBA): www.ifcba.org

International Trade Resources, Foreign Trade Database, Global Trade Resources: www.cybex.in/International-Trade-Resources/Default.aspx

NSW Business Chamber, which operates Australian Business International Trade Services: www.nswbusinesschamber.com.au

Organisation for Economic Co-operation and Development (OECD): www.oecd.org

Statistics on Australia's trade and investment relationship with the APEC region and each APEC member. Also a comprehensive analysis of intra-and inter-regional trade for each APEC member: www.dfat.gov.au/publications/stats-pubs/apec_region.html

Tips on importing goods to Australia: www.australia.gov.au/topics/economy-money-and-tax/importing-goods-to-australia

United Nations Conference on Trade and Development: www.unctad.org

World Bank: www.worldbank.org

World Customs Organization: www.wcoomd.org

World Trade Organization (WTO): www.wto.org

Transport within logistics

Learning outcomes

On completion of this chapter you will be able to:

- consider the advantages and limitations of different types of transport
- understand the role of transport in supply chains
- scope the extent of transport economics
- understand the range of variables when pricing transport
- recognise the approaches to selection of carriers and measuring performance

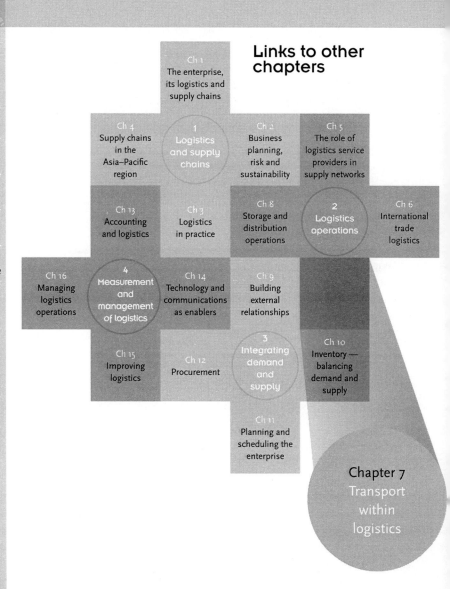

Links to other chapters

Ch 1
The enterprise, its logistics and supply chains

Ch 4
Supply chains in the Asia–Pacific region

1
Logistics and supply chains

Ch 2
Business planning, risk and sustainability

Ch 5
The role of logistics service providers in supply networks

Ch 13
Accounting and logistics

Ch 3
Logistics in practice

Ch 8
Storage and distribution operations

2
Logistics operations

Ch 6
International trade logistics

Ch 16
Managing logistics operations

4
Measurement and management of logistics

Ch 14
Technology and communications as enablers

Ch 9
Building external relationships

Ch 15
Improving logistics

Ch 12
Procurement

3
Integrating demand and supply

Ch 10
Inventory — balancing demand and supply

Ch 11
Planning and scheduling the enterprise

Chapter 7
Transport within logistics

Key terms

These terms are used in the text. Develop your own notebook by downloading information on each term.

transport mode	FEU	transport management system
just in time (JIT)	Panamax	(TMS)
cycle time	supply network	transport economics
intermodal	chain of responsibility	transport pricing
TEU	network optimisation	commodity

Introduction

This chapter provides an overview of transport and its role in supply chains. The types of transport and the associated transport planning are outlined. The scope of transport economics is considered, which includes efficiency, costs and pricing.

Modes of transport

The decision about choice of **transport mode** has a distinct effect on the speed and efficiency of moving goods. The criteria that affect the decision include:

* nature of goods (fragility or perishability)
* flexibility of routing
* urgency (service-level agreement requirements, such as a **just in time (JIT)** operation or threat of idling production)
* transit time
* reliability
* costs.

These considerations are based on the balance between value adding and cost adding through a retail supply chain, as shown in Figure 7.1 below.

It is important to consider the impact that choice of transport mode(s) has on the cost of holding inventory. In particular, some of the slower modes of transport, while offering a lower transport cost, can cause the safety stock and in-transit inventory cost to increase. The end-to-end cost of the solution in a supply chain can be lowered by using more expensive modes of transport, which affords a lower inventory holding, with a faster **cycle time**.

The advantages and limitations of each mode are summarised in Table 7.1. overleaf.

| Figure 7.1 | Transport and adding value |

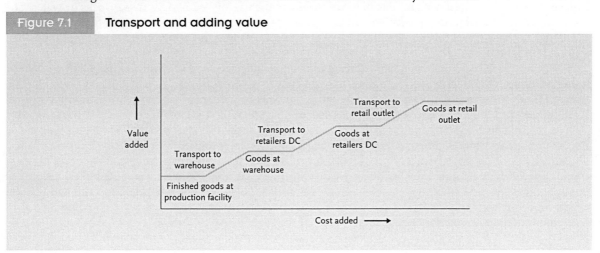

Source: Supply-Linq, www.supply-linq.com.au.

Table 7.1   Transport mode advantages and disadvantages

Mode	Advantages	Limitations	Applications
Road	Routing flexibility Ability to backload Highly competitive market Trunk routes and local deliveries	Limited capacity per vehicle Environmental impact Safety (driver fatigue, large trucks passing through small towns)	Finished goods and commodities (e.g. apparel, electronics, furniture, grain, livestock)
Rail	High capacity	Quality and standard of infrastructure Low routing flexibility Limited competition in the sector Inability to backload Slow speed	Commoditised high-volume low-value raw materials (e.g. coal, grain, cement) Containers in countries with developed infrastructure
Air	Speed Safety of product Flexibility International access	Cost	High-value low-volume finished goods (e.g. electronics, pharmaceuticals, internet shopping, deliveries)
Sea	High capacity Low cost International access	Slow speed	High-volume low-value raw materials Containerised goods
Pipeline	Low operating cost Efficiency	High infrastructure cost Slow speed Inflexible routing Only suitable for particular products	Liquid commodities (crude oil, gas, petrol, minerals in slurry form)

Intermodal transport

Intermodal freight handling is a solution to the challenge of transferring goods between modes of transport. This involves the use of containers to transport goods and transferring them between multiple modes of transport (rail, ship, air and truck), without handling the physical goods when changing modes.

Rodrigue et al. (2005) stated that intermodal transport is 'the movements of passengers or freight from one mode of transport to another, commonly taking place at a terminal specifically designed for such a purpose'.

Intermodal transport originated in the 1780s, when the earliest wooden containers, called 'loose boxes', were used for shipping coal on the Bridgewater Canal in England, and 'road' transport was still horse drawn. Iron containers were introduced in 1841 to move coal from the vale of Neath to Swansea Docks in Wales. The early 1900s saw the adoption of covered containers, used for the movement of furniture between road and rail. The key challenge of this era was the lack of standards, limiting the value of intermodal solutions that require standardisation.

It was not until 1956 that containers started to change freight transport, with the use of 58 containers loaded aboard a refitted oil tanker that sailed between Newark (New York) and Houston (Texas) in the United States. The US Department of Defense began using standard containers for military use during the Korean War; these were 8 ft × 8 ft (2.4 m × 2.4 m) cross-section in units 10 ft (3 m) long.

The International Organization for Standardization (ISO) adopted this standard in the late 1960s, ensuring interchange ability between different modes of transport worldwide, giving birth to the term 'ISO container'.

Containers of 20 ft (6.1 m) and 40 ft length are the standard in ocean freight. The width of these containers is 8 ft (2.4 m) and the height is 8.5 ft (2.6 m), with container measurements typically stated in imperial measures. The common term for a 20 ft container is **TEU** (twenty-foot equivalent unit) and **FEU** for a forty-foot equivalent unit.

Some variations on the standard container are:

◉ refrigerated intermodal containers used for perishables
◉ specialised 30 ft (9.1 m) containers for the plastics industry

* pallecons (a metal pallet-like base with a container built on top of it) for chemicals
* 'tanktainers', consisting of a tank for liquids fitted inside a standard container frame
* air-freight containers, which are shaped to optimise the space utilisation inside the fuselage of an aircraft
* a range of non-stackable open box containers
* specialised containers used in Europe, which include containerised coal carriers and 'bin-liners'— containers designed for the efficient road/rail transport of rubbish from cities to recycling and dump sites.

Other lengths of cargo containers that can be used in domestic situations are 10 ft, 30 ft, 45 ft, 48 ft and 53 ft. These containers are also available as half height (approximately 4.3 ft) or as high cube (9.5 ft), to accommodate additional volumes of lightweight products.

TEUs are carried by container ships, typically stacked up to seven units high; rail can allow for double stacking on selected routes, while trailer trucks can carry up to four TEU. Limitations on container ships on global shipping routes are governed by International Maritime Organization regulations. **Panamax** vessels fit in a classification system that also includes the smaller Suezmax and larger Malaccamax classifications.

Panamax ships can measure up to 294.13 m long × 32.31 m wide × 57.91 m above the waterline and up to 12.04 m under the waterline. Ships that are outside the Panamax measurements are called Post-Panamax vessels, which include container ships capable of carrying more than about 5000 containers. These should be capable of navigating the Panama Canal when new locks are operational from 2014.

In the Asia–Pacific region, transport plays an important role, as world consumer goods manufacturing consolidates in East and South-East Asia. To provide an indication of this importance, seven global container terminal operators are headquartered in Asia; they are:

* COSCO Pacific (China)
* Evergreen (Taiwan)
* Hanjin Shipping (China)
* Hutchinson Port Holdings (Hong Kong)
* International Container Terminal Services Inc (ICTSI) (Philippines)
* NYK/Ceres (Japan)
* PSA International (Singapore).

To improve their overall performance, major shipping companies are investing in port operations (that is, vertical integration) to gain priority berthing, maintain dedicated berths and improve crane productivity. Drewry (2004) noted that nearly 40 per cent of world container throughput was owned or part-owned by shipping companies.

The role of transport in supply chains

Transport planning

Transport is a significant component of the cost structure of most businesses trading in goods; therefore transport decisions require a degree of planning. Historically, transport planning has been based on the rational planning model. This involved defining goals and objectives, identifying problems, generating alternatives, evaluating alternatives and developing the plan.

However, the changing global and regional demand requirements and future global legislation concerning transport requires a broader approach. Key concerns of the newer approaches to transport planning are:

* the design of **supply networks** and the specific routing and scheduling within them
* managing demand loads and the effective use of assets
* environmental considerations.

Additionally, safety considerations play an important part in the work of a transport planner. In some countries, including Australia, **chain of responsibility** legislation, which apportions responsibility for transport accidents and injuries to all parties in a supply chain, has raised the profile of the challenges for transport participants. This legislation considers road vehicle speed, driver fatigue management, safe loading practices and similar issues. This is a developing area for which the current information can be found online at www.chainofresponsibility.com.au.

Incorporated within the chain of responsibility approach is managing fatigue at work. Drivers on long intercity trips, or who have to deliver goods to customers at times specified by customers, may have to work long or inconvenient hours. Employees may therefore be required to work at times to suit the needs of the business, resulting in work patterns of rotating shifts, 12-hour shifts or other work structures.

For managers and supervisors in transport planning and operations this involves the added responsibility of ensuring that employees are not fatigued and are able to undertake their duties without endangering themselves, their colleagues or the public. An understanding of the causes of fatigue, and of how to minimise its effects, is therefore a requirement of transport managers in road and rail and of managers in ports.

Transport may represent the single largest component of material movement costs within supply chains. It provides the links between nodes (where cargo changes either mode or form) and bridges these gaps between geographically separated parts of a supply chain. The inbound element of the transport task is the gateway to all the processes that follow in the logistics system, while the outbound component is the link to the customer base of the goods-providing organisation. These are illustrated in Figure 7.2.

| Figure 7.2 | A supply chain identifying the transport links |

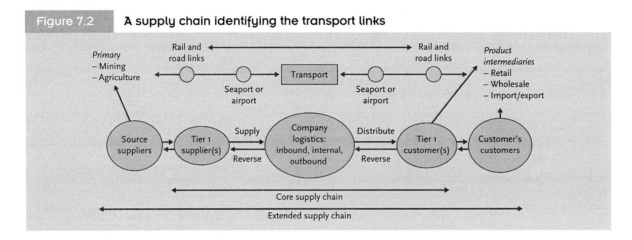

Transport management

Managing transport in an effective and efficient manner is a core requirement of a goods-providing enterprise's ability to facilitate its procurement, manufacturing and customer service expectations.

Transport is an inherent part of the supply network for a goods company and the overall plan for transport use should be a part of the logistics strategy. The physical performance of transport operations will be undertaken by either the in-house transport department or an external logistics service provider (LSP). Domestic transport can be contracted with the provider of the service—road, rail, sea, inland waterway, air and the hybrid courier, express and parcel (CEP). International transport space will often be booked through a freight forwarder. The decision to keep transport functions in-house or to outsource is strategic and is discussed in Chapters 2 and 5.

The inherent risk associated with transport is non-delivery at each stage of the goods movement to the final end user. This needs to be actively managed by transport managers of both the carrier (the transport provider) and their customer. The non-delivery risk can be disaggregated into two key causes:

1. shipment delay—this may be caused by infrastructure disruption, operational error in scheduling, change to the route or industrial action
2. shipment destruction—this may be a result of involvement in an accident, sabotage, exposure to weather or an adverse substance.

Transport management is a complex discipline. Managers must balance the requirements of customers with the needs of the business under a range of transport and occupational health and safety (OH&S) regulations and profitability targets, often with limited information and conflicting priorities of the various links within multiple supply chains. Transport managers must be aware of two logistical trade-offs when making transport decisions, as noted by Chopra and Meindl (2007):

- the trade-off between transport and inventory cost—this is important in the design of a transport network and should be based on the decisions relating to inventory aggregation policy and the choice of transport mode
- the trade-off between transport cost and customer responsiveness. For example, a 1500-metre train can carry as much freight as 100 semitrailer trucks, but while the cost of rail may be cheaper, the mode may not be as responsive.

An example of the transport-to-inventory trade-off is the decision by Australian importers that have a reach across the eastern seaboard; the freight costs from Asia to the main Australian ports are very similar, but there is a time factor as ships traverse the coast. The decision is therefore whether to hold a lower total volume of imports at one central location and deliver to all sales points, or deliver the allocation of containers to each State capital and hold inventory in each State. This will require a higher level of total inventory to be held.

Network optimisation

A substantial area for improving supply chains is concerned with **network optimisation**—the science of maximising operational efficiency, given the geographical constraints of the network within which a business operates. Key challenges of network optimisation are the quality of historical data and assumptions relating to future demand requirements.

Network optimisation seeks to answer the broad question, 'What is the ideal configuration of the supply network?', and then establish the 'ideal' location and capacity of each link in the network. For example, the network of a national retail chain will require distribution centres (DCs) that have proximity to supplier's warehouses (especially if buying FOB) and to retail stores. On the other hand, a global food manufacturing company may have the main warehouse located adjacent to each factory and consolidation centres within proximity to the major retailers' distribution centres, or it may deliver direct from the factories—each presenting different opportunities and challenges.

The network efficiencies are affected by:

- how well the movements can be planned and how well the vehicles/vessels/containers can be used
- technology solutions to assist network design, such as **transport management systems (TMS)**—discussed in Chapter 14
- route planning for distribution.

For an example of route planning efficiency, consider a scenario where a truck goes from a DC at point A to a retail store at Point B. It goes out with a full load and returns back empty to the DC. Only 50 per cent of the trip has a paid load.

Now consider if the same truck went with a full load from a DC at point A to the retail store at point B. The empty truck then travels to a supplier's DC at point C, where it picks up a full load destined for the DC at point A. In this example 66 per cent of the trip is now paid, thus reducing the inefficiency of the network through better route planning.

Twenty years ago a company may have reviewed and restructured its distribution network on a five-year cycle. Challenges that companies face today require a review of the whole supply network on a more frequent basis—at least annually.

Transport economics

Transport economics is the discipline of allocating resources within the transport sector and maximising the commercial and operational efficiency of a transport operation. Transport has a dependent and derived demand, which means it is created in response to the demands by customers or consumers for products to be transported. As such, it operates within constraints, such as peak demands and flow speeds limitations of specific modes. This section will focus on the cost structures and efficiency drivers in relation to transport.

Drivers of transport economics

While each mode of transport seeks to exploit the strengths that are inherent in the nature of that mode, there are five key drivers in transport economics, regardless of the modal choice:

1. *Density of product*—the relationship between weight and volume of the product. Freight rates are normally linked to weight of the parcel of freight. However, if that was always the case, carriers would

be disadvantaged if they were to move a truckload of potato chips, compared to a truckload of cans of baked beans. To counter this effect, carriers have developed 'cubic rates' based on an assumption that a certain volume of space will represent a certain weight of product. If the density of the product results in the actual weight occupying that space being lower, the customer is charged for the assumed amount of weight.

For example, a carrier may state that 1.2 m × 1.2 m × 1 m (a pallet footprint stacked 1 m high) is equivalent to 1 tonne of product. If presented with a pallet of low-density product with the same dimensions that only weighs 600 kg, the customer will be charged for 1 tonne of freight. This is an important consideration as it can substantially affect transport costs. Consequently, if a truck can take 20 pallets on a single layer, it is nominally a 20 tonne payload; however, carrying the lighter product means that only 12 tonne in weight is carried, but the equivalent of 20 tonne freight cost is paid.

2. *Stowability/stackability*—describes the ability to place one pallet of product directly on top of another. Stowability is affected by a number of factors:
   a. vertical strength of the packaging (a function of packaging quality and pallet configuration)
   b. weight of the products to be stacked
   c. possible movement during transport and nature of the products (fragility, value, size and shape).
3. *Handling*—is there a requirement for specialist equipment to handle the load? An example is the equipment required to handle steel or concrete pipes against that for pallets.
4. *Liability*—as the product moves through its supply chain, the ownership and possession plus liability transfer between various organisations. It is important that all parties are clear about responsibility and liability for the product at any given point in the chain. To clarifying this issue, the International Chamber of Commerce developed Incoterms—a set of internationally accepted trading terms defining transfer transaction costs, risk and responsibilities between buyer and seller that reflect current transport practices. Incoterms are discussed in Chapter 6.
5. *Market*—the transport lane volume and balance are important factors in determining the carrier's ability to find a backload that will amortise the costs of the return trip. An example in Australia is the lower backhaul rates that companies pay from Perth and Adelaide to the more populous east coast cities.

Efficiency theory

Can an enterprise achieve efficiency through economies of scale or scope? The original thinking revolved around the idea that 'big is good'. Specifically, it suggested that the economy of scale could be exploited by producing goods in larger batches and so reducing the unit cost. Conversely, 'economy of scope' relies on effective grouping of like tasks, to increase the range of product available and so gain synergies in selling and distribution. The failure of centrally managed economies illustrated that economies of scale have their limitations, especially when not linked to market demand. Economies of scope are best limited to products that are designed for quick changeovers and short production runs.

In the context of services in general and transport in particular, this translates into the 'economy of distance' (scale) and 'rule of efficiency' (scope), as shown in Figure 7.3.

'Rule of efficiency' is the term used to denote efficiencies gained in transport operations through:

Figure 7.3	Scale and scope criteria	
	Scale	Scope
Product	The more that is made, the cheaper it is per unit	The more that like tasks are grouped together, the better the effectiveness at meeting customer needs
Transport	The further a vehicle travels, the cheaper it is per km	The more loaded in the vehicle, the cheaper it is to transport, per unit

* minimising handling at points of transfer between modes
* consolidating and break-bulk activities at freight terminals
* maximising capacity of the transport vehicle, based on the use of space in the vehicle or container; that is, the size of shipment or 'parcel of freight' is large enough that it provides economic benefit. It costs almost the same to run a truck between points A and B whether it is full or partly full. The costs of purchasing or leasing the truck, registration, insurance, paying the driver's wages, etc. are all fixed

* avoiding travelling empty whenever possible; it wastes fuel, uses non-productive labour and depreciates the capital value.

'Economy of distance' is also known as the 'tapering principle' and refers to the decreasing cost per unit as the distance increases. Most of the cost, regardless of mode of transport, is associated with starting and stopping. Once the truck, plane or vessel is moving, the cost is comparatively low—the fewer the stops, the lower the total costs per unit. This principle is also observed in the 'internal routing' through manufacturing and warehousing processes. The fewer 'touch points' and less manual handling, the cheaper the process becomes on a per unit basis.

Cost groups

Business costs in general, and transport costs in particular, are divided into four categories: variable, fixed, joint and common costs, as shown in Figure 7.4.

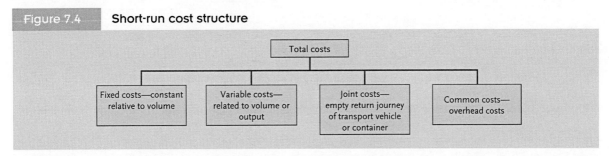

Figure 7.4 **Short-run cost structure**

A quite typical approach states that these costs are applicable in the short run (say, up to 12 months) but in the long run they are all variable. Another view says that, especially for international companies, many costs that appear to be variable (maintaining brand equity, IT) are in fact fixed.

Variable costs, sometimes referred to as direct or marginal costs, are inherent in operating a transport service. Examples of such costs are labour and fuel. The only way of eliminating these costs is by cancelling the service. These costs are normally measured as cost per distance or unit of weight ($/km or $/tonne) and are the minimum a carrier must charge in order to remain in business.

In contrast, fixed or indirect costs are unaffected by the operational variable such as shipment volume. In fact, these costs do not change even when the company is closed for holidays or other reasons. Examples of such costs are the cost of owning or leasing vehicles, terminals and other operating equipment. These costs must be covered by a contribution above the variable cost on a per transaction basis.

Joint costs are created as a consequence of operational decisions that need to be recovered. For example, a road service from A to B is offered. This creates a cost of returning the vehicle from B to A. The carrier must either allocate this cost to the original customer that has booked the shipment from A to B or find a back-loading or return journey opportunity, to at least cover the variable costs. The same can occur with a sea or air freight container when there is an imbalance between the origin and destination cargo profile; for example, Australia and New Zealand import consumer and capital goods, but export minerals and agricultural products; therefore, inbound containers may be returned empty, which creates its own handling challenges and costs.

The last group of costs is common costs or overheads (called 'burden' in the United States). These typically administrative costs, such as company management and office facilities, are incurred on behalf of all parts of the business.

Transport pricing

The decision about which approach to use concerning **transport pricing**, or the pricing of transport services, will be conditioned by business factors, such as:

* the cost and value component of the **commodities** to be transferred—taking account of product characteristics such as the propensity of the product to be damaged, lost or stolen, volume and frequency of traffic and special handling or equipment requirements

⚙ operating conditions—distance, traffic density and compatibility with other cartage tasks performed by the carrier

⚙ economics of the customer's industry—demand for the product and competition with other carriers.

The criteria under which pricing is established are:

1. route related
   a. interstate (or province)
   b. intra-state
   c. export
   d. import
2. distance related
   a. distance to travel
   b. group multiple deliveries
3. volume related
   a. full truck load (FTL) or full container load (FCL)

   b. less than truck load (LTL) or less than container load (LCL)
   c. incentive rates—volume-related discount
4. miscellaneous
   a. assorted freight or freight all kinds (FAK)
   b. container use
   c. commodity prices
   d. regulated rates
   e. minimum charges
   f. fuel and other surcharges.

There are four basic pricing approaches used by carriers:

⚙ cost of service
   o marginal cost
   o variable cost
⚙ value of service
   o price

⚙ fully allocated pricing
   o average cost
   o fully allocated cost
⚙ risk-based contribution margin.

The *cost of service* approach is used for low-value products that have a low gross margin, for which a high cost of freight would be prohibitive. Cost of service is designed to recover the variable costs incurred by the carrier and as such is a short-term approach, not sustainable over the long term. This approach often involves an element of cross-subsidisation of one product by others being carried concurrently.

The *value of service* approach is based on extracting the value that the market will stand, allowing for a maximisation of profit by the carrier.

Somewhere between these two approaches is the *fully allocated pricing* model, which is the absorption pricing structure covering all variable and fixed costs, a nominated percentage of overhead and joint costs; plus the carrier's profit margin.

The *risk-based contribution margin* pricing model is useful when pricing period contracts, as it considers the risks associated with the contract, in relation to the price charged. It also allows the price to be established without having artificial amounts of overhead charged to the contract on a 'per hour' or 'per km' basis. To calculate the price or total contract fee:

Selected price per unit, weighted for risk − Variable costs per unit = Contribution margin per unit

Contribution margin per unit × Total units = Contract contribution to the enterprise profit

Contribution to the profit from all contracts − Enterprise fixed costs = Total profit.

In addition to risk, there are other factors to be considered in establishing the price, including:

⚙ comparisons with and impacts on other contracts
⚙ the strategic nature of the contract—relation to development plans for the type of transport service
⚙ the effects on cash flow—the fewer days of accounts receivable, the lower the finance risk
⚙ economies of scale and scope—improved use of equipment and reduction in unit costs or opportunities to enter additional areas associated with the transport service.

Carrier selection and performance

Carrier selection is a specific procurement decision made after the mode of transport has been selected. Similarly to the modal choice, this decision is based on a range of criteria, essentially relating to:

- the carrier's capability
- geographical presence
- commercial competitive position
- equipment availability.

While the mode decision presents a set number of options, the carrier selection can be a very different experience depending on the mode(s) chosen. Road transport offers a wide range of providers for general freight, although the choice is more limited for specialist services such as chemical tankers; however, rail typically provides few options over a defined route.

The traditional approach to carrier selection has been to award a short-term contract following tenders and then regularly test the market. However, the total cost associated with this process is high, so businesses need to consider options. This is discussed in Chapter 12.

Prior to discussions with service providers or carriers, strategic decisions must be made about the level of commitment to a particular carrier—will the company award the entire transport task to a single carrier or split it between different carriers? Both of these options offer benefits and limitations. Working with a single carrier can lead to a closer business relationship, where synergies are discovered and exploited. Alternatively, splitting the task between carriers can provide competitiveness in both the rates and service levels.

Operational factors affecting carrier selection can be grouped into cost-, service- and flexibility-related categories. The cost category factors include:

- What is the end-to-end total cost of working with this carrier?
- How willing is the carrier to develop a pricing arrangement that aligns with the potential client's business model?

The service category concerns the level of:

- operations service
  - o performance
  - o low damage/ loss incidence
- customer service
  - o accuracy of billing
  - o claim investigation and processing
  - o ability to 'track and trace' the goods
  - o performance reporting.

The flexibility category addresses the carrier's responsiveness to:

- changes in requirements
- equipment availability
- scheduling flexibility.

While contract negotiations are an important component of establishing a relationship, equally important are managing performance and building the relationship.

Measuring transport performance

Analysis of transport performance plays a crucial role in managing the transport task. Establishing the trends enables early intervention and ensures that profitability of the product and of the carrier is protected.

Good-quality data about customer requirements and performance levels achieved by the carrier is essential. This includes despatch and delivery dates (and in some instances times) and damage or loss information from the receiver. The data is consolidated to form the transport metrics and includes:

- order turnaround time
- on-time delivery (discussed in Chapter 9)
- loss or damage rates
- inventory accuracy.

The customer organisation may weight these metrics equally or differently.

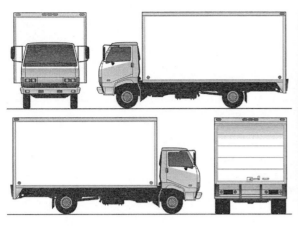

Delivery truck

Single-axle covered truck

Prime mover and trailer

Curtain trailer,
side- loading

Road train

B-double

Single-axle truck
(South Asia)

Three-wheel delivery vehicle
(South-East Asia)

Chapter questions

Operational

1. Consider the capacity constraints of key ports in East and South-East Asia, particularly at peak times, such as in the lead-up to Christmas. What impact do these constraints have on the consideration of supply chains in countries importing the manufactured products?

2. What are the key considerations for a transport manager, given the geographical and cultural specifics in your country?

3. How does understanding a carrier's cost structure strengthen the negotiating position of the buyer?

4. Use the following table to rate various modes of transport against the range of criteria affecting the mode selection. Use a scale of 1–10 (1 = best; 10 = worst).

Mode	Route flexibility	Cost	Transit time	Reliability	Product safety
Road					
Rail					
Air					
Sea					

Planning

5. How can procurement teams negotiating contracts with international freight forwarders best identify the trade-off between the supplier's margin and the limited seasonal capacity of international freight?

6. Which Incoterm would ensure maximum control of inbound transport by a manufacturing enterprise?

7. How is the value of benefits offered by intermodal transport captured by an enterprise?

8. Outline the benefits of measuring transport performance for both the customer organisation and the carrier.

Management

9. List the elements in the process of establishing a transport tender for road transport. Estimate the labour-hour commitment for each of these for a medium-size road transport operator. Evaluate the cost of this process.

10. What are the implications of implementing a 'chain of responsibility program', including fatigue management, within a transport operation? Consider the concurrent challenges of providing innovative added-value services for clients.

11. In the text, Chopra and Meindl state that there is a trade-off between transport and inventory cost. An Australian example is provided. Identify which option you prefer for an electronic consumer good retailing at $100 and state your reasons for the selection.

12. The text provides examples of cost, service and flexibility factors to consider when making a carrier selection. Identify additional factors you might consider.

References and links

Annual Review of Global Container Terminal Operators, Drewry Publishing, 2004, www.drewry.co.uk.

Australian chain of responsibility legislation, www.chainofresponsibility.com.au.

Bureau of Infrastructure, Transport and Regional Economics (BITRE), *Australian Transport Statistics*, Department of Infrastructure, Transport, Regional Development and Local Government, BITRE, Canberra, June 2008.

Chopra, S. & Meindl, P., *Supply Chain Management—Strategy, Planning and Operation*, 3rd edn, Pearson Higher Education, 2007.

International Chamber of Commerce, www.iccwbo.org.

International Maritime Organization, www.imo.org.

Rodrigue, J.P., Slack, B. & Comtois, C., *Intermodal Transportation*, 21 February 2005, people.hofstra.edu/geotrans/eng/ch3en/conc3en/ch3c5en.html.

Storage and distribution operations

Links to other chapters

Chapter 8
Storage and distribution operations

Ch 1
The enterprise, its logistics and supply chains

1
Logistics and supply chains

Ch 4
Supply chains in the Asia–Pacific region

Ch 2
Business planning, risk and sustainability

Ch 5
The role of logistics service providers in supply networks

Ch 13
Accounting and logistics

Ch 3
Logistics in practice

2
Logistics operations

Ch 6
International trade logistics

Ch 16
Managing logistics operations

4
Measurement and management of logistics

Ch 14
Technology and communications as enablers

Ch 9
Building external relationships

Ch 7
Transport within logistics

Ch 15
Improving logistics

Ch 12
Procurement

3
Integrating demand and supply

Ch 10
Inventory — balancing demand and supply

Ch 11
Planning and scheduling the enterprise

On completion of this chapter you will be able to:

- understand the key distinctions between the terms 'warehouse', 'distribution centre' and 'stores'

- appreciate the roles of warehousing and distribution operations

- understand warehousing processes

- understand the dynamics of choosing the location for a warehouse

- appreciate the importance of facility design

- appreciate the protective role of packaging

- understand the building-blocks levels of packaging

- understand the measures used to assess the performance of a warehousing or distribution operation.

Key terms

These terms are used in the text. Develop your own notebook by downloading information on each term.

distribution	stores	cluster picking
warehouse (WH)	service levels	zone picking
inbound	store ready merchandising	batch picking
outbound	(SRM)	pick to paper
general merchandise (GM)	velocity	pick to light
high-rise automated	centre of gravity	radio frequency (RF) picking
temperature controlled	location decisions	barcode
retailer	just in time (JIT)	pick to voice
commodity	centralised	autopick
bulk	decentralised	kitting
container	facility design	protective packaging
postponement	unit load	stock keeping unit (SKU)
distribution centre (DC)	picking operations	returnable plastic crate (RPC)
cross-dock	discrete order picking	

Introduction

This chapter will discuss the role of **distribution** in supply chains. In doing so we will consider the evolution of warehousing and distribution centres and discuss a number of distribution operational models in contemporary supply chains.

Types of warehousing

The role of a **warehouse (WH)** is to provide a buffer between **inbound** shipments from the supplying facilities or factories and **outbound** orders destined for customers. Customers usually order in patterns that are not compatible with the capabilities of suppliers, so the amount of storage required in warehouses depends on the difference between the patterns of outbound orders and incoming deliveries.

Warehouses are designed and built for specific purposes. The most common types are:

- **general merchandise (GM)**—the most common type and is capable of handling a broad range of goods that do not require highly specialised equipment. Multi-user is a variant, whereby goods owned by multiple owners are handled in the same facility
- **high-rise automated**—typically for fast moving consumer goods (FMCG) and consumer packaged goods (CPG) operations in developed countries that are designed to respond quickly to customer orders at low operating costs
- **temperature controlled**—serving cool supply chains and designed to serve the food industry for such items as vegetables, fruit and frozen foods. It can also be used for pharmaceuticals
- **retailer**—can be a mix of the above types and built to serve the internal needs of a general retailer
- **commodity**—storing and handling discrete products that are strapped in standard unit loads, such as timber, cotton and wool
- **bulk**—for products that flow, such as fertilisers, chemicals and liquids. Bulk warehouses can provide break-bulk and product mixing services.

As developed countries in the region increase their imports of finished products, warehouses (which are often managed by an LSP) are required to provide an expanding range of services for complex global supply chains, for example:

- un-stuffing ocean **containers** and loading to rail or truck for distribution to inland cities and towns
- storing goods for long periods in bonded warehouses or free trade zones (FTZ), where duty is not paid until the goods are distributed

* holding products in a form to which 'adding value' services can be provided as customer orders are received and before distribution. This comes under the heading of **postponement**. The services can range from price ticketing and labelling to the final assembly of electronic sub-assemblies into products
* sorting, packaging and delivery services for retail store orders
* adding value processes, such as kitting sub-assemblies for delivery to production facilities.

While the underlying reason for having warehousing facilities has not changed, the emphasis has moved from a focus on storage to a focus on the speed of transactions. The aim is to turn inventory into sales by storing minimal amounts for a minimum of time. This has been caused by:

* the development of time-based strategies by manufacturers in FMCG and CPG industries
* the time-sensitive demands of major retailers
* the development of technology for warehouses
* the trend in developed countries to international sourcing for finished goods
* the trend in developing countries to international sourcing for components and sub-assemblies that will go into the final assembly of a product.

Warehouse or distribution centre

The terms 'warehouse' and **distribution centre (DC)** have come to be used interchangeably; however, a warehouse and a distribution centre are not necessarily one and the same.

Warehousing is operational in nature and by its name is focused inwardly on storing product. The warehousing process can be described as a sequence of:

* receiving (inbound)
* put-away and storage
* inventory control
* picking/packing of goods
* despatch (outbound).

A distribution centre is a means to an end—satisfying customers' requirements through distribution. As a consequence, it is not necessary that it holds inventory, although it may hold some for short periods of time. Therefore, the distribution process can be described as a sequence of:

* receiving (inbound)
* processing
* despatch (outbound).

A DC that has the facility to transform an inbound load of goods into a number of outbound orders without the items being stocked is called a **cross-dock** facility.

The main differences between a warehouse and a distribution centre are summarised in Table 8.1.

Table 8.1   Differences between warehouses and distribution centres

Activity	Warehouse	Distribution centre
Storage	Fast-selling items <50% of total inventory. Stock turns <8 times	Fast-selling items >70% of total inventory. Stock turns >8 times
Order handling	Receive, store, pick and distribute >90% of the items	Cross-dock >50% of the items
Communications mode	Batch data collection	Real-time data collection

The process sequence for a warehouse and distribution centre is illustrated in Figure 8.1 overleaf.

Although the functions of a warehouse and a distribution centre are different, the term 'warehouse' will be generally used in this chapter to describe the role of holding and moving stock.

The term **stores** is also used; this refers to the concept of storing materials and internal items, and specifically to the inbound storage of:

| Figure 8.1 | Warehouse and distribution centre processes |

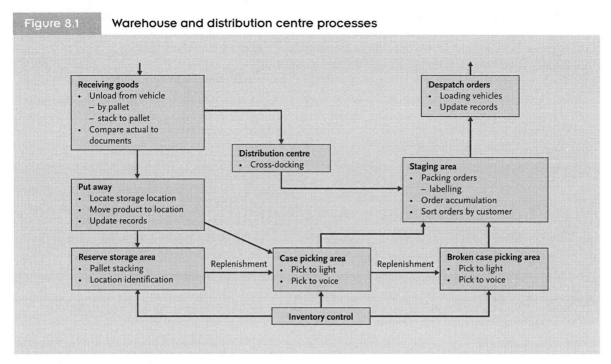

Source: Adapted from a diagram by Shaun Hodges.

* materials for manufacturing
* maintenance service parts
* the intermediate storage of materials (work in progress (WIP)) between stages of production
* finished goods awaiting despatch to another site.

The term store is also applied to bulk storage sites. In this case although there is not a building, the processes and consideration of inventory to the business are just as important.

Why are warehousing and distribution important?

Warehousing is an element of supply chains that has a direct interface with the customer. Outputs from the warehousing process provide inputs to the customer's processes—be they manufacturing, retail or warehousing. Any errors in despatch become very apparent at the customer site; consequently, warehousing plays a prime role in managing customer **service levels**.

The reasons for the importance of warehousing are as follows.

1. Goods are held in either a delivery centre or warehouse within a reasonable delivery range of customers to enhance the customer service experience.

    The 'reasonable' delivery range depends on the geography, physical infrastructure and demographic structure of the country or region. Island-based nations such as Indonesia, the Philippines, Papua New Guinea (PNG) and the Pacific island states are governed by the transport challenges of inter-island movement. Countries with a lower standard of physical infrastructure will require more delivery centres to compensate for the slow traffic movement and countries with dispersed populations may also require additional delivery centres (this is dependent on the standard of infrastructure).

2. It is a cost-sensitive process. Specifically, in developed countries in the region, such as Australia, New Zealand and Japan, which rely on local labour and where the cost of labour is comparatively high, inefficient processes can affect the competitiveness of the enterprise. From the regional perspective, even though some countries offer lower costs of labour, they may have limited expanses of space for building, high utility costs or other limitations, which result in cost sensitivities of their own.

Receiving countries that have encouraged high levels of imports of finished goods, such as Australia and New Zealand, are developing a trend towards offshore warehousing—that is, holding product until as late in the delivery process as possible, then sending the order to the most convenient distribution centre in relation to demand and packed (either in the export country or on arrival in the receiving country) in a manner that is ready for display at a retail store. This is called **store ready merchandising (SRM)**.

3. The relationship with inventory management. As the scope of the task grows (number of SKU, number of sites, etc.) the complexity of inventory management grows with it. In product-based companies, inventory frequently represents a major proportion of the assets shown in the balance sheet and funding inventory is often provided by debt finance.

Inventory represents a substantial risk, particularly if the product is subject to obsolescence, expiry or damage. The starting point for inventory control is 'receiving', with its role being to ensure the integrity and correct quantity of the stock entering the warehouse. Together with the put-away and storage component of the warehouse process, this ensures the business can answer three inventory control questions:

* What items of stock do we hold?
* How much of each item do we have?
* Where are the items?

A business that can answer these questions is more able to respond to customer orders in an efficient and effective manner, which is the process of picking, followed by packing and despatching to the destination.

Companies that recognise the criticality of inventory are continuously exploring ways to minimise their inventory holding costs. This is with a view to releasing capital for more productive uses, while at the same time increasing **velocity** of the products through the supply chains. Inventory management practices are discussed in Chapter 10.

Key decisions in distribution

Location of a facility

Decisions about the location of a warehouse or distribution centre are made initially at a macro level concerning where in a country or State/province a facility should be located; this is followed by the exact location. Decisions about geographical positioning of the site can have an impact on the efficiency of all the supply chains affecting the business. The decisions may be influenced by a number of parameters:

* *Lowest cost calculations*, such as the **centre of gravity** of the supply network—for example, if 80 per cent of the business is around location A and 20 per cent is around location B, there may be a case to have a single warehouse that services the entire market. There are mathematical models and simulation applications that can assist with **location decisions**. While the centre of gravity model is commonly used in Europe and the United States, it needs to be used judiciously, as this model delivers a good result in densely populated countries with intensive infrastructure. As such, it can work well in China and India, but it may not be recommended for countries such as Australia, where it could place warehouses in the middle of a desert!
* *Service-level requirements*—short lead-time expectations by the customers or **just in time (JIT)** contractual obligations may force decisions about the site location.
* *Feature of the product*—products are commonly described as being in one of two categories—weight gaining or weight losing. Weight gaining products increase in weight as they travel through their supply chain. For instance, soft drink starts as powder or condensed syrup; this is mixed with water and packaging is added, thus increasing the weight. In this scenario, the distribution site should be as close to the point of consumption as possible, to minimise the cost of transport.

Conversely, mining products shrink though their supply chain; a tonne of mined iron ore may result in a 65 per cent conversion to steel and subsequent weight reductions at each stage of processing. Similarly, agricultural products 'shrink' as they go through the process of adding value. In this situation, it would appear that as much value adding as possible should be done close to the site of origin, so the least possible volume of product is transported. However, import duties levied by developing countries typically favour raw materials, with nil or minimum duty applied, so that value adding can be done using local labour. For this reason, iron ore and wheat are more likely to be shipped than steel and flour.

- *Access to infrastructure*—a requirement to have easy access to ports, freeways, rail terminals, etc. may dictate the location, as may the traffic flow situation in city locations.
- **Centralised** *vs* **decentralised** *approach*—this is based on a mix of the business strategy in relation to centralisation of operations and response to the trade-off between the costs of storage and transport against the lead times for the items. This decision will affect the determination of the number of warehouses in the country or region.
- *Ownership and operation*—the issues relating to the decision to own or contract out the management and/or operations of distribution. The location of logistics service providers' current facilities may govern the decision if distribution is contracted to an LSP.

Facility design and picking operations

FACILITY DESIGN

The factors to be considered in the **facility design**, or layout design, and material-handling process selected for a distribution operation are the bridge between the logistics strategy and logistics operations management. These factors are discussed below.

- **Unit load** *utilisation.* Use the most appropriate unit loads that will minimise the number of movements, enable easier handling, provide efficient loading and unloading and minimise the risk of damage. Typical unit loads are the traditional pallet, pallets with attachments to contain goods, standard drums, bulk bags and ISO containers.
- *Space utilisation.* Minimise costs associated with the land and its buildings. Only hold the inventory actually required in achieving the defined customer service levels; minimise gangways and 'dead' space. Australia is an example of a land-rich country with spread-out cities that allow the luxury of using single-storey expansive warehouses. However, more densely populated cities in Asia need to be resourceful with space utilisation. This has led to the development of technologies that assist with vertical warehousing, such as mezzanine flooring with gravity feed to lower levels, vertical carousels and goods-handling escalators.
- *Slow-moving items.* One of the issues in warehouse design is the handling and picking of slow-moving items. Even when managed, these items will occupy the largest percentage of a facility's floor space and a disproportionate amount of labour time to handle them. In many warehouses, the medium and slow-moving items can account for as much as 80 per cent of the total SKU. The challenge is the floor space used and how it can be reduced. Work zones of fast-moving and slow-moving items can be created by profiling the inventory items by size and velocity.
- *Movement minimisation.* The underlying design parameters are to locate together the most popular lines where there is the highest turnover and separate picking stock and reserve stock. For small parts, the use of carousels can provide savings by optimising the floor space required and using otherwise wasted overhead space. In countries with higher labour costs, these costs are reduced by automatically bringing every item to the operator and eliminating wasted walking and searching time.
- *Control.* Both visual and system-based processes are used to track product location and movement and establish cycle stock-take procedures.
- Safety and security. The safety element applies to employees who are working around unguarded mechanical equipment, while security applies to minimising the risk of damage and pilferage (stealing), depending on the value of the products.
- *Environmental.* It is necessary to adhere to laws concerning noise, truck movements, night operations, fumes and waste-liquid discharges. To improve their sustainability, some warehouses use the rainwater run-off from the roof and install roof-top photovoltaic panels to provide a proportion of their electricity needs.
- *Storing vs picking.* The conventional design of warehouses depends on whether the predominant requirement is for storage or picking, as these two functions have opposing requirements. Techniques that maximise space utilisation tend to complicate picking and make it less efficient, while large storage areas increase distance and reduce picking efficiency. The ideal picking situation requires small stocks of items in dedicated, close locations, but this does not assist the efficiency of storage. Automation of handling, picking and packing can minimise these opposing requirements; however, automation is expensive to

implement and operate. The matrix identifying storage requirements and picking activity is summarised in Figure 8.2.

A major assumption associated with warehouse design is that cross aisles are straight and must always meet picking aisles at right angles; also, that picking aisles are straight and are oriented in the same direction. However, although this is the most common structure inside warehouses, it is not the only feasible design. Cross aisles can improve efficiency for workers when travelling to and from some of the picking locations and a design that resembles the skeleton of a fish (called fishbone) has been found to be effective in some situations.

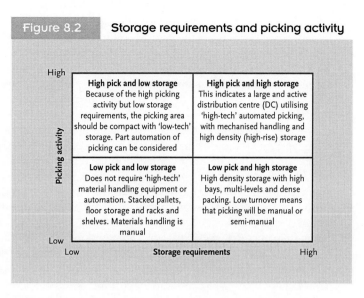

Figure 8.2 Storage requirements and picking activity

	Low pick ← Storage requirements → High

High pick and low storage
Because of the high picking activity but low storage requirements, the picking area should be compact with 'low-tech' storage. Part automation of picking can be considered

High pick and high storage
This indicates a large and active distribution centre (DC) utilising 'high-tech' automated picking, with mechanised handling and high density (high-rise) storage

Low pick and low storage
Does not require 'high-tech' material handling equipment or automation. Stacked pallets, floor storage and racks and shelves. Materials handling is manual

Low pick and high storage
High density storage with high bays, multi-levels and dense packing. Low turnover means that picking will be manual or semi-manual

Designing a warehouse layout requires skill and knowledge, and a poor design can be an impediment to successful warehouse operations for years into the future. Remember that for a new warehouse, design of the access perimeters is required; this must take into account the width of roads and truck parking areas, the turning circle required for the length of trucks and loading bay heights and angles.

Picking operations

Picking operations are the most complex and resource-intensive process in a warehouse and, due to the output being visible to the customer, are very noticeable. In picking operations, travel time and accuracy are key drivers of performance.

There is a range of choices for the picking process, depending on:

- the volume of orders
- whether the product is picked by pallet/layer/case/split case pick
- value of the items
- requirement for the stock picking to be by line item or by customer
- picking staff capabilities.

Some of the most common picking methodologies that can be used individually or in combination are outlined below.

- **Discrete order picking** is employed by companies with lower volumes or for high volume, but less than a full pallet, picks of a single SKU.
- **Cluster picking** works where there are few line items per order and product sizes are small.
- **Zone picking** requires technology like conveyors, scanners and RFID/barcode labels to enable many employees to simultaneously pick portions of a single order.
- **Batch picking**, also known as wave picking, is useful where a number of similar orders for a number of customers are being picked over a short time. An example of this might be orders of biscuits for a supermarket chain before a promotion starts. The DC will release a batch of orders by geographical area or by retail stores of similar size.

The decision concerning which pick methodology to use should be based on the specific requirements of the business; therefore, it is important to evaluate order profiles, the SKU range, order volume and business plans.

The technologies available to use with the picking methods are as follows.

- **Pick to paper** is the original picking methodology in which a warehouse employee is given a pre-printed list of the items to pick for an order. It is expected that the order in which the line items are listed is the same as the picking locations. This method is prone to error concerning what is actually being picked, from what location and how much of the item has been picked. It also presents some inventory control challenges, with a potentially long lag between the order-picking activity and system reconciliation.

- **Pick to light** requires the installation of specific equipment. At each location in the warehouse there is an electronic pick shelf-front with an LED display and a button. Conveyor belts go past every location and software directs the tote bins on the conveyor belts at switch points to coordinate orders and locations.

  The site is divided into zones. The digital number display at the picking location signals how many units of an item must be picked into the tote on the conveyor belt. Once picked, the operator confirms the pick by pressing the button. Accuracy relies on the picker being trained to count correctly.

  A limitation is that only one picker can work in each zone, so if the demand suddenly expands, the site has limited ability to quickly increase its output. A later generation of pick to light systems has been introduced which enables two pickers to work in the same zone, by installing two lights/displays with different colours.

- **Radio frequency (RF) picking** is a paperless picking process in which the warehouse operator's tasks are managed by a small portable terminal carried by the employee or attached to a fork truck. The system directs picking staff to the required location, where they scan the location **barcode** to confirm the correct location. The operator then scans every unit (often a full carton or shipper) as they pick the order until picking is complete from that location and they are directed to the next location. The benefit of this system is that the operator never loses count and provided the right stock is in the right location, the picking accuracy is very high. There are also no restrictions concerning how many operators can pick at the same time—the only limit is the number of RF devices that are available.

- **Pick to voice** is similar to RF picking, except that the operator is prompted by a headset instead of by a screen. This system relies on a 'check digit' that is assigned to each location, so that instead of scanning it themselves into the location, the operator repeats a random number written on the side of the location to confirm the correct location. A major advantage of this system is that it can be configured to operate in any language to suit the employees in the warehouse.

- **Autopick** is based on a carousel machine which efficiently picks products that fit a certain criteria. The machine ejects the unit(s) into a tray or tote that is moving on the conveyer belt. This process is suitable for fast moving small size items, such as some pharmaceutical lines or SIM cards.

- **Kitting** is a value-add picking process, whereby an SKU is 'manufactured' by collating a number of smaller items. The most common applications of this process in distribution are for exhibition 'show bags', promotional and sample kits and PR material. Kitting is also the term used for picking a kit of parts in the stores, to be assembled as a product in manufacturing.

The important consideration for design decisions is that no one material handling technology, racking system or software application is 'the solution'. Warehouse operations commence with order profiling and determining common pack size and velocity characteristics; from that, order picking, packing and consolidation methodologies can be designed to meet the needs of the facility.

Equipment and technology

It is important to remember that both the equipment and technology used in distribution are a 'means to an end'—their purpose is to enable the business processes. As such, decisions should be based on what the business and the customers require, whether relating to the choice of a warehouse management system, yard management system, order picking application or any other aspect of the distribution process. Aspects of technology in a supply chain environment are discussed in Chapter 14.

Packaging and unitisation

Protective packaging

When we consider the term 'packaging', our thoughts are usually about the product's container or wrapping. From a marketing perspective, packaging improves the product presentation, but from a logistics perspective, packaging is concerned with the **protective packaging** and is a function of product handling.

Protective packaging is the outer packaging for a pack of items that is typically removed before the item is displayed for sale. For bulkier items that can be delivered to the home, such as white goods (for the kitchen) and brown goods (for the home), the protective packaging may be used for each item (for example a refrigerator or television).

The objective of protective packaging is to improve the vertical strength of the item when held in stock and to reduce in-transit damage when being transported.

In recent years the trend (often through legislation) has been towards more environmentally friendly packaging, with the introduction in many industries of returnable packaging such as crates or cages and shelf-friendly packaging. This has eliminated superfluous levels of packaging and material handling.

According to the report *Asian Environmental Packaging Laws—A Compliance Guide*, Asian countries have introduced new legislation, modified existing laws and enacted changes to policy that will impact the way packaging is produced, used and recovered. For example, the Chinese Government has enacted more than 16 new laws and amendments in the 18 months since January 2008 that regulate package materials, production and packaging waste disposal.

In Australia, the National Packaging Covenant (NPC) is a voluntary initiative by government and industry to reduce the environmental effects of packaging on the environment. After a decade it is starting to produce some results, such as the number of retailers that have withdrawn the use of free plastic carry bags for consumers. Importantly, there is legislation to support this initiative through the National Environment Protection (Used Packaging Materials) Measure.

Unit loads

The retail unit is the basic unit of identifying inventory items for sale and is referred to as a **stock keeping unit (SKU)**. Even though a company may have the same basic product, it can be packaged in multiple pack sizes (500 g, 1 kg, 2 kg) with each pack size recognised as a separate SKU. So, a company selling pens may sell red and blue pens as separate items; each will be an SKU and when a red and blue pen are packed as a twin pack, that becomes another SKU.

SKUs used in retail can be packaged in the following ways:

* *Inner*—an inner is usually formed by wrapping plastic or thin cardboard over a group of retail units, for example a 6-pack of soft drink cans.
* *Outer/shipper/carton*—these are usually cardboard boxes, which form the protective or secondary packaging. A shipper will contain a number of inners; for example a shipper of headache tablets, which is made up of 20 inners, each containing 10 retail units. Multiple shippers are typically stacked on a pallet and can be shrink-wrapped for security and damage reduction. Shippers are a substantial contributor to the reverse logistics process, whereby cardboard or plastic packaging is recycled.
* **Returnable plastic crates (RPC)**—these are used for loose items such as vegetables, milk, bread and mixed pharmaceutical or computer parts orders. The advantage of this style of packaging is that it eliminates the need to recycle the packaging material. While some businesses elect to own their own crates, others choose to hire the equipment from asset owning companies. Both are valid choices and should be considered in the context of the specific business situation.

Minimising the range of protective packaging used for a product family of SKUs can force the standardisation of pack sizes, which leads to better space utilisation and higher operational efficiencies in the warehouse.

The building blocks of packaging are illustrated in Figure 8.3 overleaf.

After the order is picked, it must be packed in a unit load suitable for the delivery mode and distance, such as those described below.

Pallet—sometimes referred to as a skid, this is a piece of supporting equipment, commonly made from wood, plastic (often recycled), metal or cardboard. The purpose of a pallet is to stabilise the cartons of product in storage or transit environments. A pallet also provides material-handling efficiency by allowing a number of cartons to be lifted in a single move. It is common to secure the stock on a pallet by means of shrink-wrapping it or strapping it to the pallet.

Palletising stock also allows a business to reduce industrial injury from manual handling by staff; it does,

Figure 8.3 The building blocks of packaging

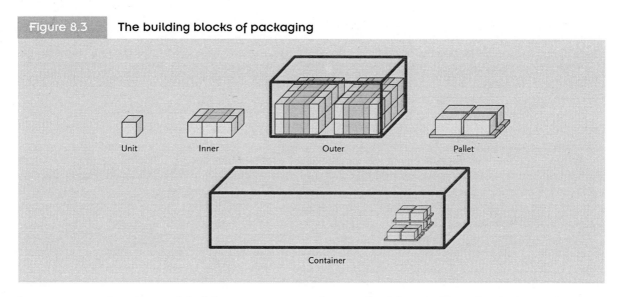

however, mean there is a need for lifting equipment such as a pallet lift or a pallet jack, which comes with its own set of costs.

As a result, while the use of pallets is a common practice in countries with high labour costs, it is not necessarily common practice in other countries of the region. The comparatively low cost of labour and lower safety standards in developing countries means that it is more efficient to pay labourers to hand stack or unpack a container one carton at a time.

Unfortunately, there is no universal size for a pallet. The International Organisation for Standardisation (ISO) sanctions six pallet dimensions, which address the most common pallet sizes used internationally. These are listed in Table 8.2.

Table 8.2 ISO-approved pallet sizes

Dimension (W × L) (in mm)	Where most used
1219 × 1016	North America
1000 × 1200	Europe and Asia
1165 × 1165	Australia
1067 × 1067	North America, Europe and Asia
1100 × 1100	Asia
800 × 1200	Europe

European containers are often about two inches (50.8 mm) wider than the ISO standard, to accommodate the euro-pallet standard. There are also multiple additional sizes used around the world.

Importantly, there is no general standard for the height of pallet loads—this is determined by the individual companies in a supply chain, based on the nature of the product. For example, a pallet of potato chips can be stacked 2.5 m tall, as the product has a very low density, but a pallet of baked beans may be limited to 1.2 m high, as the product has high density and the pallet becomes too heavy and unsafe to handle.

Another limiting factor may be the warehouse configuration of the customer. For example, retail chains can configure their pallet locations in distribution centres to be 1.4 m high and consequently their suppliers need to limit the height of their pallets to the same height.

Pallets are commonly a rented asset provided by specialist companies. They charge the businesses using their pallets on a 'per pallet per day' basis, with charges varying, depending on the volume of pallets used. Consequently, it is important that a company is aware of how many pallets they are responsible for on any given day and are able to reconcile the charges when presented.

While there are options for how the record of pallets is transferred between user companies (dockets, cards, etc), the essence is that when a pallet load of product is moved from the possession of one company to another, the pallet(s) needs to be either transferred from one company's account to the other, or an empty pallet must be given in return. This is to prevent the supplier being charged for a pallet they are no longer using. Fundamentally, it is a system of debits and credits, which works much like a bank account except that the currency is pallets, rather than money.

Australia and New Zealand import many products manufactured in the Asia–Pacific region. However, the two countries have specific rules relating to quarantine. Therefore, to avoid goods being detained and fumigated on account of using wooden pallets, it is preferable at the time of ordering to specify plastic or metal pallets rather than wood, or in fact no pallets at all.

Container—this is the largest denomination of unit load used for long haul transport, with the most common variety being the intermodal enclosed weatherproof metal container. As the term intermodal implies, one of the advantages is that the container can be transferred between different modes of transport (marine, road or rail) without the need to handle the product. Containers and intermodal transport are discussed in Chapter 7.

Performance measurement

Product companies and LSP can measure the performance of the warehouse using DIFOT—delivery in full, on time for each order. However, few have the overriding supply chain performance measure of DIFOTA—that is, the capability to deliver in full, on time, with accuracy of documents. This is discussed in Chapter 15.

The common corporate measure of performance is warehouse costs as a percentage of sales. The most common measurements concerned with daily operations in a warehouse include the:

* orders/lines/SKU per labour hour
* picking accuracy
* lead time from order to despatch—order turnaround time
* vehicle turnaround time
* processing cost per order.

To assist in the improvement of these activities, some companies in North America are re-introducing the use of industrial engineering time standards. These establish the standard time to complete a task and the actual time taken is compared to arrive at an efficiency rating.

Within a warehouse, the three elements of effectiveness that should be measured are:

* use of storage space
* effectiveness of stock rotation—first in, first out
* lot or batch tracing (if required for the products or by country law).

Even as supply chains are redesigned to reflect changing trade and business relationships, the role of warehousing remains important for the success of enterprises. This is because warehousing will continue to serve customer needs through the capability to:

* meet customer time requirements for deliveries
* mix product lines from different sources
* balance the output from manufacturers with the demands of customers.

And it will be done in an efficient and cost-effective manner.

Wine storage

Bulk-stack warehouse

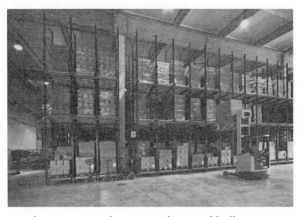

Warehouse scene showing picking and bulk-storage locations, pallet jacks and a forklift

Multiple roller conveyers

Extended forklift

Steel rolls

Industrial drum. One of many varieties

Bulk bags; for bulk quantities of industrial solids such as chips, granules and beads

Delivery cage similar to those used by postal organisations; retail roller cages are an adaptation of this

Returnable plastic crates

Pallet jack and pallet

Stacked pallet

Loading iron ore onto a marine vessel

Drive-on loading pallets to a truck using a manually operated pallet jack. Contrast this with side-loading using a forklift

An airline loading containerised cargo. Note the shape of the container, aimed at optimising space utilisation

Pallecon

Break-bulk steel

Chapter questions

Operational

1. Identify additional KPIs that can be used in a warehouse environment. Explain why they have been selected. What value will they have to informing customer service?
2. Propose a selection of approaches aimed at reducing the operational cost of warehousing across a range of products.
3. Consider the packaging (display and protective) used for products in a particular industry or company. What benefits does this particular packaging format offer in relation to the product that it contains? What are some of the challenges that this packaging solution presents?
4. Reflect on the layout of a warehouse or distribution centre that you are aware of.
   a. Define the layout.
   b. Is it optimal for the customer demands and the processes and procedures performed?
   c. What advantages does this layout offer and what challenges does it present?

Planning

5. Compare and contrast the KPIs used in a warehouse and a distribution centre. How do these measurements assist in meeting the objectives of both facilities?
6. Discuss the impact of the lack of international standardisation of pallet sizes used in international trade.
7. Discuss the relationship between the warehouse design and the inventory policy of an enterprise. Provide examples.

Management

8. Reflect on the logistics trade-off between cost and service level in the context of the warehouse location.
9. Compare different modelling techniques used in warehouse optimisation.
10. Discuss the strategic role of warehousing in supporting and improving customer service levels. Provide examples.

Exercise 1

A successful online grocery retailer is Tesco.com in the United Kingdom. In 1996 it began by pioneering a 'store-based' network strategy to support the online business. This strategy relied on the use of the existing network of stores to process and pick customers' orders placed online. Tesco used a pick-to-paper process, with staff picking off the customer order printouts. The orders were then delivered by a fleet of Tesco vehicles to the consumers.

This contrasts with the 'warehouse' supply network strategy pursued by most of Tesco's competitors. This is a capital-intensive strategy reliant on investment in new warehouses and systems to support the online operation.

1. Draw the supply chains for both of the approaches explained above. Are 'economies of scale' available with either of the approaches?
2. Does this exercise identify why most of Tesco's competitors selected the warehouse model? Identify potential reasons for a competitor to move from a warehouse model to an store-based model.

Exercise 2

Global Express Corporation
Developed by: Kerry Hammond

Global Express is a multinational logistics services company with a core business of courier, express, parcel (CEP) and freight services. It is considering a new hub to service its customers in the western Pacific region. It plans to use a 'leading edge' operation and provide a fast reliable service that connects with its operations in North America and Europe.

The company has asked the key local managers to develop a factor rating method to determine the best location.

1. Using the table below and the loading for key areas (1 is low and 5 is high) select a location and explain why that location is preferred.

No	Critical success factor	Candidate country ratings			
		Taipei	Shanghai	Tokyo	Manila
Technology					
1	Rate of technology change	4	4	5	2
2	Acceptance of logistics technology	4	3	5	1
Level of education					
3	Number of skilled workers	4	3	4	2
4	Availability of logistics competence	3	3	4	1
5	National education rate	3	3	4	2
Political and legal aspects					
6	Stability of government	3	4	3	2
7	Trade restrictions	4	4	4	3
Social and cultural aspects					
8	Similarity in language	4	4	5	3
9	Work ethic	4	5	5	4
Economic factors					
10	Availability of land	2	5	1	5
11	Interest rates	3	3	3	4
12	Inflation	4	4	5	3
13	Tax rates	3	3	4	3
Total rating points					

Through research and personal knowledge, assess the loadings to apply in a CEP scenario. Incorporate these loadings into your final calculation:

Technology, social and cultural aspects	20%
Education, political and legal aspects	30%
Economic factors	50%
Your preferred location is:	

2 Comment on your personal ratings of the table.

References and links

'Asian Environmental Packaging Laws—A Compliance Guide', www.reportbuyer.com

Australian National Packaging Covenant (NPC), www.packagingcovenant.org.au

International Organisation for Standardisation (ISO), www.iso.org

Integrating demand and supply

Building external relationships

Learning outcomes

On completion of this chapter you will be able to:

- understand the different approaches to customer service

- recognise the range of business relationships available and that all are equally valid

- structure a customer base to segment customer service

- approach customer service based on the premise that 100 per cent service is uneconomic for a business, therefore problems will occur

- consider the basis for a customer service organisation.

Links to other chapters

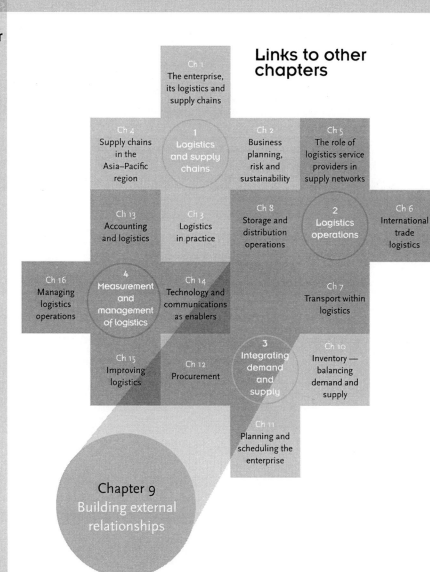

Ch 1
The enterprise, its logistics and supply chains

Ch 4
Supply chains in the Asia–Pacific region

1
Logistics and supply chains

Ch 2
Business planning, risk and sustainability

Ch 5
The role of logistics service providers in supply networks

Ch 13
Accounting and logistics

Ch 3
Logistics in practice

Ch 8
Storage and distribution operations

2
Logistics operations

Ch 6
International trade logistics

Ch 16
Managing logistics operations

4
Measurement and management of logistics

Ch 14
Technology and communications as enablers

Ch 7
Transport within logistics

Ch 15
Improving logistics

Ch 12
Procurement

3
Integrating demand and supply

Ch 10
Inventory — balancing demand and supply

Ch 11
Planning and scheduling the enterprise

Chapter 9
Building external relationships

Key terms

These terms are used in the text. Develop your own notebook by downloading information on each term.

customer service	moment of truth	customer relationship
segmentation	vendor managed inventory (VMI)	management (CRM)
business relationships	preventative maintenance	supplier relationship
consumer complaints	available to promise (ATP)	management (SRM)

Introduction

This chapter gives an overview of **customer service** provided by companies in the goods and services sectors. It recognises that the same level of service will not be provided for all customers and therefore considers **segmentation** of the customer base. Finally, some principles are discussed concerning implementation of a customer service focus within an organisation.

Business type and customer service

An enterprise that just sells product is open to increased competition from other enterprises that are able to provide a similar product cheaper or faster. A business that also provides additional services for its customers can gain a competitive advantage because services are harder to copy.

Enterprises can incorporate value-added services to complement the basic offering. The type and level of service provided to customers will depend on which of the four support models an organisation employs, as illustrated in Table 9.1.

Table 9.1 Support models

Support model	Type and level of service provided	Structural location of customer service
Customer service for products	The customer service department is charged with setting the service expectations and managing customer perceptions. The post-delivery service manages the reverse logistics of the goods or equipment no longer required due to quality, warranty claims, end of life and other causes.	Logistics or sales
Product service	Ongoing support of industrial/ capital goods and long life consumer goods. These services can extend the product by giving the end user more confidence to buy the product, knowing there are maintenance and other services available.	Separate group or within logistics; responsible for ordering and storing service parts
Customer service for services	The post-sales services for customers that support the ongoing operation of the service provided; examples are: telephone, insurance, travel and vehicle breakdown organisations.	Sales
Logistics services	Response provided by an LSP to meet contract requirements and address client problems through an escalation process.	Sales

The function of liaising with customers concerning the company's products and services can operate under a variety of titles. In this book, it will be called customer service.

A range of relationships

Given the different approaches from the buyer to the seller and from the seller to the buyer, **business relationships** will develop particular attributes that have similarities and therefore can be grouped into types. Figure 9.1 illustrates a range of relationships.

It is important to note that each of the relationship types has an equal standing; no relationship type is by definition 'better' than others. This is because it depends on the circumstances existing at the time and the number of alternative relationship types which are actually available to the parties.

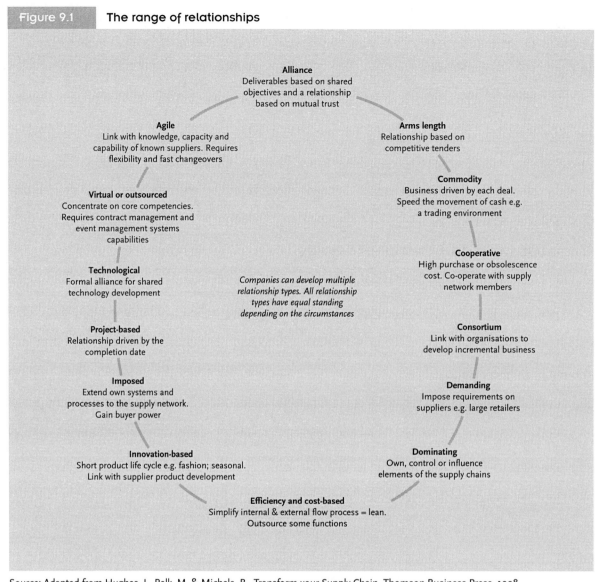

Figure 9.1   The range of relationships

Alliance
Deliverables based on shared objectives and a relationship based on mutual trust

Agile
Link with knowledge, capacity and capability of known suppliers. Requires flexibility and fast changeovers

Arms length
Relationship based on competitive tenders

Virtual or outsourced
Concentrate on core competencies. Requires contract management and event management systems capabilities

Commodity
Business driven by each deal. Speed the movement of cash e.g. a trading environment

Technological
Formal alliance for shared technology development

Companies can develop multiple relationship types. All relationship types have equal standing depending on the circumstances

Cooperative
High purchase or obsolescence cost. Co-operate with supply network members

Project-based
Relationship driven by the completion date

Consortium
Link with organisations to develop incremental business

Imposed
Extend own systems and processes to the supply network. Gain buyer power

Demanding
Impose requirements on suppliers e.g. large retailers

Innovation-based
Short product life cycle e.g. fashion; seasonal. Link with supplier product development

Dominating
Own, control or influence elements of the supply chains

Efficiency and cost-based
Simplify internal & external flow process = lean. Outsource some functions

Source: Adapted from Hughes, J., Ralk, M. & Michels, B., Transform your Supply Chain, Thomson Business Press, 1998.

For example, consider two different business relationships. The first involves an enterprise supplying a relatively expensive, low-sales-volume product that is purchased at infrequent intervals. Examples may include car sales and off-the-plan real estate sales. Customers are able to request a range of options, with some options on long lead times (the assemble-to-order model). For a successful relationship in this situation, the seller will need to structure their interactions with the customer based on features of the cooperate type of relationship.

The reason for this structure is that because of the high variability of demand, customer service issues are likely to arise. These will be caused by the inability to supply, due to possible high levels of error in the forecasts and the long lead times of some options. There will also be internal cost issues that the supplier company will have to resolve concerning:

- potentially high inventory levels (for example purchasing options that do not sell)
- expediting costs for parts that are not in stock
- the write-off of obsolete parts no longer required, due to product design changes.

The second example is a supplier of consumer packaged goods (CPG) to major supermarket retailers. The relationship will be a 'demanding' type, because each of the purchases are a low percentage of the retailer's total buy, with low risk for the buyer. However, the sale could be a high percentage of the supplier's business, with low margins and a high 'cost to serve'. Because of the power exerted by the retailer in this supply chain, the seller will need to structure the relationship such that it can efficiently supply the customer on their terms.

Customer service segmentation

Once there is an agreement to undertake a buy and sell transaction, there are three factors that guide the future relationship between a buyer and seller:

1. *Relationships are holistic.* While the relationship between the buyer and the seller appears to be focused on the point in time when a sale is transacted, the total experience also involves logistics, financial and information issues. This ideally requires an understanding by both parties of the total business systems of the buyer and seller and establishing the relationship around this.
2. *All customers are not the same.* If a comprehensive relationship requires an extensive range of understanding by the buyer and supplier of each other's business, then time and resources will only allow a few relationships to be comprehensive. Additionally, the range of customers requires different services. Therefore, customers must be segmented, based on a reasonable business criterion.
3. *Customers define service differently from suppliers.* Customers should be involved in defining the service they require. However, that does not mean the customer is always right—the supplier needs an understanding of the customer's business to guide the agreement concerning service requirements. The customer's overriding requirement is that their order is a 'perfect order'. That means it is the initial order delivered on time, not an order that has to be modified because:
   - sufficient stock is not available
   - the range of SKUs is not available or
   - deliveries cannot be made on certain days or times.
   Remember that the customer is unlikely to be impressed by the supplier's internal performance measures.

Due to the higher value of business per customer, the commercial/industrial environment is more likely to segment customers by the type and level of services provided (and their price or cost). Segmentation can be based on various factors, including:

- the 'importance' of the customer (how much they spend or strategic importance)
- the response time required following a service call from a customer
- the 'cost to serve'
- the distribution channel used
- the type of product purchased.

An example of differentiating the design and delivery of customer service by category, based on the revenue from 1650 customers of a company, is shown in Table 9.2.

Table 9.2   Establishing categories of customers

Customer category	Customers	% of accounts	% of revenue
A	Top 50	3	67
B	Next 200	15	24
C	Next 450	28	9
D	Bottom 950	54	1

Customer service experience

As individuals, we experience good and bad customer service on an ongoing basis, so we have an understanding of what we would like to have incorporated into 'good' customer service.

There has been a range of books and articles over the past 20 years exhorting organisations to 'exceed customer expectations'. However, people in the community, as both commercial customers and domestic consumers, have had enough experience of poor customer service that they would be happy if supplying organisations could focus on 'meeting the customer's current expectations of minimum acceptable competence'.

It is theoretically impossible to have 100 per cent customer service for delivery of product (discussed in Chapter 10). At high customer service levels, an enterprise experiences increasing costs (such as the cost of holding inventory) without a commensurate increase in sales. Therefore an organisation will try and opt for a balance (although often not calculated) where sales are maximised at the 'optimum' cost level.

If customer service is not to be maintained at a 100 per cent level, the customer service function should operate with the understanding that, as things will go wrong, the department should be staffed with people who are capable and trained to resolve the inevitable challenges.

Customer service organisation focus

Customer service within an organisation needs to be structured with recognition of a number of aspects:

1. Develop a customer service culture for the organisation.
2. Understand the services your customers require—do not assume.
3. Have a holistic view of the services offered, their interrelationships, and understand that trade-offs with functional aspects of the business are accepted.
4. Establish customer service standards.
5. Measure customer service performance against the standards and through audits with customers.

Each of these elements is discussed below.

1. Develop a customer service culture for the organisation

We are all individually aware that when we are unsatisfied with the service received from a supplier, we do not always complain. Numerous studies in America and Europe concerning **consumer complaints** indicate that only about four consumers in every 100 actually complain about the product or service they have purchased. Even worse for businesses, those who do not complain tell up to 13 family members, friends and acquaintances about their negative experince. However, on the positive side, consumers who have a satisfactory resolution of their complaint tell about five people.

An influential book about customer service in an environment with a direct customer interface was written by Jan Carlzon, the CEO of Scandinavian Airline Systems (SAS). *Moments of Truth* (1989), is about the turnaround of the airline into a successful business. His underlying philosophy concerning serving consumers is based upon his four perceived 'truths' about the people working in a service organisation:

1. Everyone needs to know and feel they are needed.
2. Giving a person the freedom to take responsibility releases resources that would otherwise remain concealed.
3. An individual without information cannot take responsibility; an individual who is given information cannot help but take responsibility.
4. Everyone wants to be treated as an individual.

He stated that managers of SAS had been conditioned to think the airline was the sum of its physical assets—the airline fleet, maintenance bases and administrative processes. But he identified that the paying customers provide the money for wages and invoices of the business; moreover, their perception was not about the physical assets, but about the contacts between themselves and airline employees.

He considered that if there are 10 million passengers in a year and each has contact with an average of five 'front line' employees (who are unlikely to be managers) each time they fly, this totals 50 million '**moments of truth**'. Each 'moment' lasts but a short amount of time; this is when a perception of the company is formed and a decision made whether to buy a seat with the airline on the next occasion requiring travel by air.

This situation can also apply within retail stores, banks, entertainment locations and other businesses where a physical or virtual relationship with consumers exists.

More than 20 years after Carlzon's book was published, a major airline in the Asia–Pacific region received bad publicity because the check-in counter staff were not given the authority to allow people with wheelchairs or guide dogs onto its aircraft. Instead, non-standard situations (which were not clearly identified) were to be referred to 'management' for resolution, although management were not available for late night and early morning consultation!

This illustrates that each new generation of management in a consumer-based organisation must be trained in the basics of customer service and that the customer service culture must be displayed every day by the CEO and senior management. This is achieved through 'management by walking around' (MBWA)—understanding first-hand the challenges that staff have in doing their job. If this is not done, then all the advertising by the business will be for nothing.

Is the customer service situation similar in business-to-business relationships? Well, no, because each party has professional staff members to deal with relationship issues—suppliers have sales personnel and customers have purchasing staff. In retail there are the merchandise buyers who monitor supplier performance and should provide assistance if the expected performance standards deteriorate. But even so, there are multiple 'moment of truth' experiences, when a person establishes a perception of a customer or supplier that may influence a future decision concerning selling or purchasing products and services.

Do organisations know how many 'moments of truth' they have in a year? Think about relations with the customers who actually pay the company's accounts. And what about suppliers—how many 'moments of truth' are encountered?

2. Understand the services your customers require

The reality for suppliers is that the customer's perception of service is formed by comparing what they actually receive against what they were initially offered. However, understanding the value that customers assign to different elements of the service package offered by a supplier is difficult.

In a consumer environment, responses to surveys can provide a reasonable approximation of reality, because the questions are aimed at the individual who owns and uses the product.

In a commercial or industrial environment, the 'customer' can be many people. For example, in the case of product services it will include:

* the engineer who initially specified the equipment
* the purchasing specialist who undertook the commercial negotiations to buy the equipment
* the operations person who uses the equipment
* the maintenance person who approves the support visits
* the accounts staff who authorise payments under the maintenance contract.

All have their own views concerning the importance of and the value they assign to the different parts of the service offering. Gathering that intelligence is vital for the suppliers of customer services and should be a part of the sales representatives' role.

Some markets appear to be solely driven by price and sales staff will tend to focus on price above all else. A business relationship built on price means that the seller can be seen as trading off a low price against other factors. An example of this is reliable delivery, especially when the price has recently been reduced and then a problem occurs with deliveries.

To help limit discussions about price in a business-to-business relationship, a part of the logistics role is to promote the service elements that support the product and, together with sales staff, negotiate an agreement with the customer which incorporates the logistics factors used between the parties.

Examples include:

* When does the clock start concerning receipt of an order—when the goods arrive, when the goods are put away and are available, or when they have passed a QA test and are released for sale?
* What are the acceptable trade-offs in the relationship: 'if we do this, will you do that?'

How do we find out whether customers are satisfied with our service? The three ways to determine this are:

1. formal customer research (best conducted by an independent research firm), which requires time, effort and money
2. informal sales force survey
3. informal customer feedback.

The informal sales force survey is of value if the sales representatives are able to question the range of people in the buying organisation who will have an opinion, as discussed above. It is also helpful if the sales representatives are knowledgeable about their organisation's logistics capability and can incorporate questions which reflect the feedback required.

The third method—informal customer feedback through the customer service department—is low cost, but typically not well utilised. This could be because systems need to be in place that enables the customer service staff to transform the informal feedback into structured knowledge that can be reported and acted upon.

3. A holistic view of customer service

Consider customer service from two viewpoints. One is the interaction with customers and/or consumers by the people working in the customer service group, department or unit. The second view is of the processes, procedures and systems established by the organisation to support the services that underpin the product and/ or services the organisation provides. This is illustrated in Figure 9.2.

The interaction between these two views of customer service can result in quite different customer experiences of the service provided. Consider your response if the supplier's customer service department has good systems, but staff do not have a customer service ethos—'I am just doing my job'— compared with your response to

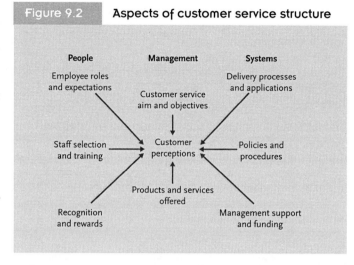

Figure 9.2   Aspects of customer service structure

a supplier with well trained and knowledgeable customer service staff, but with poorly designed associated systems.

In developed countries, the perceived high cost structure of businesses has prompted management in many large companies to outsource the provision of answering customer service contacts to call centres in lower-cost countries. This situation provides multiple challenges, because the call centre staff must be trained to respond in a foreign language to customers from a different cultural background and the associated systems must be a 'fail proof' design. This is because the call centre staff will most likely have strict limits placed on their authority to act and are less able to use the 'work-arounds' that staff located in the home country could implement.

CUSTOMER EXPERIENCE

Because the provision of a service is so dependent on the people delivering it at a particular point in time, the service experienced by a customer or consumer when contacting a supplier (or indeed an internal department) can vary, whether it concerns a product or a service.

What do we expect as a customer of a company when we contact them to buy, to enquire, to book maintenance, dispute an account or for any other reason?

1. *Empathy*. Staff we contact should be courteous, attentive to the issues and willing to be helpful.
2. *Knowledge*. The staff need to be knowledgeable about the products and the business and understand their company's systems, so they can be prompt in their dealings with callers. Remember that the customer is not always right in their assumptions about a situation—it takes people with knowledge and empathy to teach the customer and learn from the supplier.
3. *Dependability*. Customers want what was promised. Whether it's furnishings for the home, parts for the business or services to be performed, we want to believe the first promise made about such factors as the deliverables and the date and time of delivery. Logistics is essentially about *availability* and the logistics systems, plans and processes must be geared to achieving availability for customers, internal operations and suppliers. These are the essential aspects of this book.

These requirements are also applicable when the seller contacts the buyer, because buying and selling are two sides of the same coin and both should be focused on gaining a value-for-money transaction (or period contract) that allows the potential for repeat business.

Each of the above is a simple principle; however, very many organisations have difficulty in implementing them. But what are the essentials required to achieve the goals of these principles?

Empathy is the ability to put oneself in another person's situation and thereby understand their reactions. This requires the hiring and training of people who can express empathy in difficult situations, because it requires a person to remain calm and focused on the issues to resolve misunderstanding and errors. It especially requires a person to know when they should be quiet and just listen.

Empathy requires an ability to actually identify what the customer's expectations are and to define potential solutions. Listen to the caller and, if needed, break down the request into actions. The actions need to be agreed and a timeline for action and resolution established.

Suppose you are a member of staff who has contact with a customer, but you do not work in customer service. A core part of the job if there is a problem or concern is to 'own the problem', including activating the escalation process; this may require liaison with others in the organisation in order to resolve the situation.

Management needs a process in place to record these situations and provide credit for initiative and attention to customers. Remember, the customer does not care who you are or what your role is in the organisation; they just want their need resolved.

The follow-up process is vital. Therefore, if a contact with the customer has been agreed to occur at a specific time, then the contact must be made. That contact may have been arranged to be with a knowledgeable person who can address the customer's concern, but it is up to the internal 'owner' of the problem to confirm that the contact was actually made and that the customer is satisfied with the progress.

This approach to customer service is the essence of a customer service-focused enterprise and it requires a policy decision by management to delegate authority for making decisions that address customers' needs and to correct adverse situations. Staff should not have to always refer their solutions to higher levels for approval; instead, staff must be trained to understand what a reasonable solution may be. In this way, customer service becomes part of the culture of the organisation.

Knowledge is required in three areas: the organisation, the products and services and the customers. Informed organisations have a process whereby all staff members are provided with an overview of these three important factors of the business. Staff whose jobs involve regular customer or supplier interface must receive detailed updates, provided to them in the most 'user friendly' manner so that the information may be retrieved as required.

The most detail will be about products and services, providing:

- pricing
- delivery details
- performance data
- configuration (what goes with what), plus, if required,
- maintenance and support capability.

Information about products and services should be correct and concise and provided to customers and suppliers in a clear and unambiguous manner. This is easier said than done, as proficient skills in technical writing and graphic design are required for this process.

Knowledge is also about IT systems, which must be designed from the user's viewpoint. However many different types of enquiry are encountered, there will always be one approach or element the designers forgot when developing an IT solution. Systems must therefore not be too prescriptive in design, but structured for ease of drilling through layers of information and data, thus enabling the linking of selected data.

When thinking of systems design, an example scenario could be that a customer representative has checked your company's website but was unable to obtain the necessary information and has telephoned with a sales enquiry. What is the best approach?

1. The customer service team member checks the customer's company details and then asks about the enquiry.

2. The team member addresses the enquiry and, if it eventuates into an order, only then checks the customer's company details.

If you consider that the second approach is preferable, you are correct. Not only is the focus immediately on the customer's enquiry, but the data gathered can be entered into the knowledge database, because it is initially not customer specific. This means, for example, that even if the prospective customer decides not to place an order, such matters as underlying customer demand (rather than sales) data is being collected for future analysis.

Dependability is also required. Logistics within an enterprise is not just concerned with the decisions and actions needed to ensure an order is delivered, but also with the decisions and actions taken prior to an order, to ensure there is availability of products and services.

Customer service concerning an order will therefore commence when the customer:

* recognises a need to place an order
* is alerted by a supplier's sales staff
* is alerted through the supplier managed inventory (SMI) system (also called **vendor managed inventory (VMI)**).

Customer service will be completed when the product is delivered against the order; this includes the provision of any on-site assistance the customer requires and providing reverse logistics services for any products. While this defines the life cycle of an order, customer service is a 'whole-of-life' relationship with a customer.

Customer expectations regarding deliveries are established within an industry, so that delivery in one day may be expected in one particular industry, while three weeks may be acceptable in another. The role of logistics is to provide the expected level of service at optimum cost, taking into account the following:

* the company's business strategy
* supply chain influences concerning availability, cost of materials and logistics services. There are trade-offs to consider:
  o the availability and location of inbound materials, production resources and distribution facilities, with reference to the desired customer service level
  o reduced profit margins against ever higher levels of customer service demanded by some customers—quicker delivery may require higher inventory
  o decisions concerning whether to produce or buy products and whether to provide product service internally or through an external party—the decision can affect customer service-level decisions and gross margins
* the internal organisation structure.

4. Establish customer service standards

Customer service activities can be grouped into several categories through the order cycle and these categories can be the basis for establishing operating standards of performance. Examples of categories upon which to base service standards are:

* convenience of placing an order—direct, through a sales representative or via a website:
  o information-sharing capability
  o ease of informing customers of specification changes and approval of customer initiated changes
  o ease of using the product return and recall process
* order status enquiry; response capability, direct or via a website
* consistency and reliability of delivery to customers; taking account of any LSP capabilities used and customer initiated constraints:
  o order cycle times
  o order size constraints (minimum order size, container capacity and weight restrictions)
  o delivery times and flexibility within customer prescribed limitations
* using invoicing procedures and accuracy of invoices
* documentation requirements flexibility (printed or computer).

Employees at each level must know what the business targets are and be trained to convert the targets into actions. An accurate feedback system is essential as it enables teams to determine whether their actions are achieving the desired goals. This is even more important for staff who can affect customers' perceptions of the organisation but who do not have direct contact with the customer and are thus not able to receive an immediate feedback—for example, the warehouse and DC teams.

5. Measure customer service performance

Companies must measure their success in terms of the promises made to customers and not adopt a 'tick the box' approach, as a result of which they merely record having met output requirements for this day or this period. The 'tick the box' approach is overly evident in centralised organisations, where standards are established at head office and then filtered down via middle managers for staff to follow. However, in decentralised companies, where responsibility for customer service has been devolved to the knowledgeable staff, this approach is unlikely to achieve lasting results.

Overall fulfilment measures are necessary to identify that customer service is being achieved. The measures (or metrics) will therefore not reflect the activities of just one department, group or team, but will incorporate the activities of all staff who have customer responsibilities; for example, the warehouse performance measures noted in Chapter 8.

A factor to be considered in establishing the list of measures is the ease of collecting data and transforming it into useful information so that action to improve operations can be undertaken. The measurements listed in Table 9.3 reflect the possible range for an organisation.

Table 9.3 Possible customer service measurements

Service group measure	Element measure
Order availability	Product group availability
	Cases and units available
	Line item (SKU) availability
Order cycle time	Order entry completion time
	Order processing time
	Total order cycle time
Response time to enquiries	Answering telephones calls; responding to email and fax enquiries
	Order status
	Order confirmation
	Order shortages
	Product substitution
	Order tracking
	Back-order status
Error rates	Order errors
	Pick and pack errors
	Shipping label errors
	Delivery errors
	Invoice errors
Customer requests	Expedited orders
	Expedited transport and delivery
	Special packaging and labelling
Product problems	Damaged goods
	Delivery refusal, eg. of time slot
	Returned goods—credit note issued
	Customer claims
	Customer complaints

Being more than a supplier of products

Customer service can have a legitimate role in developing a business through the provision of additional services, as customers define their future needs.

By the nature of the business, enterprises in the product services sector are able to provide additional services that are typically based in an after-sales environment and comprise:

- **preventative maintenance**
- repairs
- supply of service parts
- retrofitting of upgraded modules
- refurbishment and disposal with recycling
- services on competitors' equipment located at the customer's premises.

These services are not to be seen as an 'add-on' to selling products, but as an integral part of the product value proposition. This ensures that the customer service element of the business can be developed and managed by people who are identified as 'winners' and staffed by talented people.

The Boston Consulting Group undertook a study in 2009 of 50 manufacturers of industrial machinery in America that also supplied after-sales services. The study identified that, on average, the service elements of the businesses accounted for 30 per cent of revenue and a gross margin of 24 per cent, with the top quartile of businesses having services at 47 per cent of revenue and gross margins of 36 per cent.

To achieve these results requires that a customer service business culture is developed within the supplying business—not an easy transition to make for an organisation used to only selling products. Along with the change in culture is the requirement to develop standardised service products and to segment customers based on service requirements.

In the product service sector, the elements of customer service at each stage of the business relationship can be identified, with relevant elements being applicable to other industry sectors, as shown in Table 9.4.

Table 9.4   Customer service elements at different stages

Pre-sales	Order receipt	Delivery	Whole-of-life relationship—value-adding services
Provide written statement of customer service policy, including standards for service performance (freely available to customers and internally)	Know the inventory available and **available to promise (ATP)** situation, together with the product substitutions available	Provide product tracking and tracing	Ensure supply of service parts
Identify the services available	Ensure order convenience	Provide installation, commissioning, warranty and parts	Provide preventative maintenance contracts
Structure the customer services capability	Provide order entry information	Identify training needs of customer's staff	Provide repairs and parts replacement
Identify the decision flexibility (knowledge required and authority provided)	Identify transaction steps in the order cycle	Replace faulty items	Provide retrofit of upgrade modules
Create a recognition and rewards process for service initiatives	Expedite orders to ensure the organisation's effectiveness Monitor system accuracy audit process		Provide • refurbishment of equipment units • disposal and recycling • services for competitors' equipment • consulting services • financing and insurance

Relationship management

Customer relationship management (CRM) and **supplier relationship management (SRM)** are IT approaches to integrating data and information, with the objective to better relate with customers and suppliers through an enhanced information capability.

At the retail level, an organisation will be involved with consumer transactions that are a one-time purchase, without any built-in expectation of a repeat purchase (although repeat purchases will be encouraged through advertising and promotions).

In a business-to-business environment there is often an expectation of a repeat purchase, so the customer's or seller's details are recorded in the following ways:

- credit check as a due diligence review so that undertaking business transactions will not deliver unwanted surprises
- purchase orders and invoices issued (and recorded) by each party.

Thereafter, the relationship can develop to whatever level the parties decide is mutually beneficial.

CRM requires that all data concerned with sales and the post-sales events be collected and analysed, to establish patterns and trends across all markets and customer segments. SRM differs due to the requirement for IT integration with individual suppliers, based on the significance and complexity of the buying transactions. These applications are discussed in Chapter 14.

Chapter questions

Operational

1. You work in an open office environment and walk past the customer service department. All the customer service team are either busy or absent from their desks. A telephone rings at one of the unattended desks.
   a. What should be the maximum number of rings before the call is answered?
   b. If the maximum number of rings has occurred, should you pick up the telephone, even though you are not a member of the customer service team? Explain why or why not.
   c. If you do answer the call, do you tell the customer 'It's not my job' and leave them on hold while you try to contact a team member, or do you transfer the call to a busy customer service team member?
   d. If you have answered the call, should you own the problem, even though you are not a member of the customer service team?
2. Do the four 'truths' of customer service in a service environment (noted in this chapter) also apply within organisations that supply goods and services to commercial organisations in a business-to-business relationship? If not, why not?
3. Figure 9.1 and the subsequent text discuss different relationships in supply chains. Select any two and identify, for each, the main elements of customer service that could be provided by the enterprise.

Planning

4. Using the answer to question 3, what planning response, logistics response and system capability will be required to address the customer service requirements?
5. The section 'Customer service segmentation' identifies five criteria for segmentation. Identify the planning priorities required to address each criterion.
6. Table 9.3 identifies 26 possible customer service measures. A focused organisation requires no more than 10 measures within customer service. Select your top 10 and justify why each measure was selected.
7. Identify the main elements required of a CRM and an SRM application. Justify the need for each main function.

Management

8. If a business only has a limited set of options for prospective customers to select and effective systems are developed to assist delivery of those options, should staff be restricted in using their initiative, so that a consistent service is provided to all customers? Provide justification for your response.
9. What is required to achieve a customer service excellence position where both the people and systems capability are ranked by customers as 'high'?
10. Figure 9.1 identifies 14 different types of relationships in supply chains. Structure the criteria you would use to identify the type of relationship existing between an enterprise and any one customer or supplier in the supply chains.
11. When sales executives are negotiating a contract with a prospective customer, should a logistics specialist attend the meeting or should the sales executive be briefed by the logistics department? Provide reasons for your selection.
12. India and the Philippines are two countries in the Asia–Pacific region that have developed a call centre sector. Should a company that sells industrial supplies and equipment to business customers, contract out their customer service operations to a call centre company located in another country? Justify the reasons for your selection.

References and links

Hughes, J., Ralk, M. & Michels, B., *Transform Your Supply Chain*, Thomson Business Press, London, 1998.

Carlzon, J., *Moments of Truth*, Harper Row Publishers, New York, 1989.

'Achieving Excellence in After-Sales Services', September 2009, Boston Consulting Group, www.bcg.com.

10

Inventory—balancing demand and supply

Learning outcomes

On completion of this chapter you will be able to:

- understand the effect of incorrect management decisions on the performance of a business
- identify the different groups of inventory items
- understand why inventory is held at company and off-site locations
- understand the cost of holding inventory
- comprehend the basics of inventory management, including policy, planning and control
- identify the different approaches to inventory optimisation.

Links to other chapters

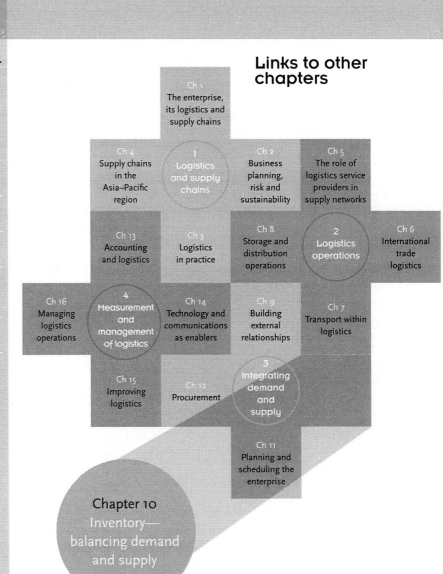

Ch 1
The enterprise, its logistics and supply chains

Ch 4
Supply chains in the Asia–Pacific region

1
Logistics and supply chains

Ch 2
Business planning, risk and sustainability

Ch 5
The role of logistics service providers in supply networks

Ch 13
Accounting and logistics

Ch 3
Logistics in practice

Ch 8
Storage and distribution operations

2
Logistics operations

Ch 6
International trade logistics

Ch 16
Managing logistics operations

4
Measurement and management of logistics

Ch 14
Technology and communications as enablers

Ch 9
Building external relationships

Ch 7
Transport within logistics

Ch 15
Improving logistics

Ch 12
Procurement

3
Integrating demand and supply

Ch 11
Planning and scheduling the enterprise

Chapter 10
Inventory—balancing demand and supply

Key terms

These terms are used in the text. Develop your own notebook by downloading information on each term.

seasonality
availability
stock keeping unit (SKU)
demand and supply
inventory carrying cost
opportunity cost
inventory management

return on investment (ROI)
return on assets (ROA)
inventory turn rate (ITR)
variability
mean, median and mode
standard deviation
normal distribution

cost of goods sold (COGS)
service parts
radio frequency identification
    device (RFID)
inventory optimisation

Introduction

This chapter will introduce the reader to what we consider to be the most critical topic in the logistician's knowledge bank. An understanding of inventory management, incorporating policy, planning and control, is fundamental to the success of supply chains in a global, regional and local economy. Get this wrong, together with planning as discussed in Chapter 11, and all the effort put into transport, distribution and other responsibilities will not be worth very much.

Using inventory in business

Types of inventory

Inventory is the totality of unique items held by a company. It is therefore more than finished goods; it also covers items known by different names, as shown in Table 10.1.

Table 10.1 Types of inventory

Description	Inventory term	Driver of demand
Products for sale Refurbished goods for sale	Finished goods (FG)	Customer and consumer demand for finished goods
Parts to service products that have been sold	Service parts (also called spare parts)	Customer and consumer demand for service parts
Partly made goods Sub-assemblies	Work in progress (also work in process) (WIP)	FG inventory requirements
Purchased items for production: • component parts • packaging materials	Raw materials (RM)	Materials and components required to commence production
Items used to assist production	Consumables	Available as required
Items used in the general business	Office supplies Technical (or laboratory) supplies	Available as required
Items used in maintenance	Maintenance, repair & overhaul (MRO)	Mean time between failure (MTBF) and Available as required

Management decisions that affect inventory

Inventory 'guru' Hal Mather referred in his presentations to 'the INSANE approach to inventory'. By this he meant the decisions that senior management can make which have unplanned consequences and may lead to subsequent poor business decisions. The INSANE approach is shown in Table 10.2.

Examples of other decisions that can adversely affect the effective management of inventory are:

- sales target decisions
  o extreme sales objectives—such as 'double sales in the next 12 months', which requires a pre-build of inventory for the sales promotion effort

o periodic sales targets—typically monthly or quarterly, which force the enterprise into extra efforts to meet output and sales targets by the end of the period, only to have excess inventory in the first week of the new period. From a customer service viewpoint, the 30th day of one month is no different to the 1st day of the next month, so long as the customers' orders are satisfied in full and on time

● sales promotions decisions

o promotions not communicated in the company; the result being that a sales manager in a distant State or province can contact the distribution centre demanding to know where the inventory is to support the new promotion that has just commenced in their State—of course, planning and the DC were not informed of the promotion

o logistically ineffective promotions, such as 'buy 12, get one free', when the packaging or unit load for distribution does not allow for multiples of 13 items; shortages of items can be the result

● advertising decisions

o created **seasonality**—whereby advertising creates artificial peaks in consumer demand that may require increased quantities of finished goods to be stored months prior to the 'season' of high consumer demand (Mother's Day, Christmas and Chinese New Year are examples)

o erratic advertising—increases consumer demand when the advertising happens, but sales decrease substantially when the advertising stops (and a competitor is advertising); this can cause shortages and excesses of inventory because demand is erratic

● accounting decisions

o payment terms—can affect when a customer orders goods so they are able to obtain the longest period for payment of the invoice; this can harm the effectiveness of supply chains, due to customer orders 'bunching' at certain time periods, requiring higher inventory

o payment discount structure—causes customers to modify their order pattern to gain the maximum payment discount. Again, 'bunching' of customer orders can occur if sufficient customers take advantage of the early payment discount structure.

Table 10.2 INSANE approach to inventory

Instruction from senior management	Result
'Reduce inventory by 10%' (or any other specific, but not calculated, amount)	Because this edict affects all products equally, customer service will suffer
'Improve customer service'	Requires more inventory investment, affecting the profitability of the business; unless inventory planning, internal control processes and business relationships are changed
and 'Improve the net earnings'	Among other actions, may require a reduction in inventory investment to improve the profit margin; again affecting customer service

Logisticians and inventory

Logistics is the science and art of providing **availability**. If you go to a supermarket shelf and the required product is not available, then logisticians and the supply chains have failed in their objective—the product is not available. So, the management of inventory is a critical capability of a logistician.

In commerce, inventory is the list of items purchased and made by a business but not yet sold. This list will provide information concerning the amount and value of each unique item (the **stock keeping unit** or **SKU**) held in inventory and the total value of all items. But is this sufficient for managing the balance between **demand and supply** of the item?

In response to this question, businesses may wish to hold sufficient inventory of finished products to satisfy the majority of customer demands most of the time; however, it will be at a substantial cost, which can affect the working capital requirements of the business.

A fundamental part of the logistician's role is to optimise the amount of inventory in the organisation. This requires logisticians to thoroughly understand inventory management principles and the quantitative analysis required to provide leadership in optimising inventory for the business.

This also applies to logistics professionals employed within a logistics service provider (LSP) which provides distribution services for clients. A major objective of the business should be to provide value-added services, through assisting clients to optimise the inventory held within their supply chains.

The value of inventory

There are three business reasons for holding inventory:

1. Inventory is held to decouple, or provide a buffer, between the demand and supply for an item. This is because the amount and variability of demands from external customers, consumers or internal sources is unlikely to be the same as the amount and rate of supply of materials through an organisation's supply chains.
2. Inventory is used as part of the broader business strategy. There are three types of inventory identified within this category:
   a. *Anticipation inventory.* This is when inventory is built in advance of a peak demand. It can be for seasonal demand, for public and religious holidays, or to overcome potential shortages caused by the planned shutting of a factory for maintenance, extended holiday periods or supplies of a material becoming restricted.
   b. *Hedging inventory.* Companies that purchase traded commodities, such as natural fibres, grains and metals, can buy additional physical materials when the global price is considered to be low (although this may not be a correct assumption).
   However, instead of investing in physical goods, the company can decide to 'lock in' the future price of the material through trading contracts for future purchases on the international commodity exchanges. Examples are the Sydney Futures Exchange, London Metals Exchange and Chicago Board of Trade.
   c. *In-transit or transport inventory.* The extent of globalisation has resulted in a substantial increase in the distance travelled by materials, parts, components, semi-finished goods and finished products. This can be between suppliers and the brand owner's facilities, or their outsourced manufacturers, original design manufacturers (ODM), logistics service providers (LSP) and agents. If the items are purchased by the brand owner and they arrange transport, the inventory value becomes part of the company's assets and therefore is designated as in-transit inventory.
3. To improve the chances of meeting the in-full and on-time expectation of customers and to minimise the likelihood of logistics operations' plans not being achieved, two types of inventory are defined and calculated for each SKU in the inventory list:
   a. *Cycle inventory.* This is the amount of inventory to be held for an SKU at the mid-point through the replenishment cycle (half the order quantity), based on a selection of the most appropriate order policy, as discussed in Chapter 11.
   b. *Fluctuation inventory.* This is the inventory that is held in excess of the cycle inventory to overcome the uncertainty associated with unplanned events. This calculated level of inventory is called either safety stock, reserve stock or buffer stock and is illustrated in Figure 10.1.

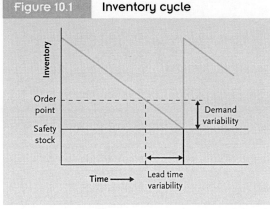

Figure 10.1   **Inventory cycle**

The illustration shows that inventory is depleted through the replenishment period towards the order point, which has been established to allow sufficient time for the replenishment order to arrive.

However, if there is an unplanned increase in demand and/or a longer lead time for the item through the replenishment period, then the safety stock will be used to satisfy the needs of customers. This approach accepts that 50 per cent of the time the safety stock will not be required, because, 'on average', the demand for finished goods is below the forecast.

Conversely, the absence of safety inventory will mean that when an unplanned event occurs, there is a shortage of inventory at the warehouse or distribution centre, triggering a back-order on the supplying unit.

This could require the expediting of an emergency production order at the supplying facility (whether owned by the business or by a supplier), which upsets the manufacturing plan as other products are pushed back in the production queue.

Safety stock can be reduced at links in a supply chain if the lead time is reduced; shorter lead times reduce uncertainty, so demand can be forecast over a shorter horizon and supply occurs at shorter intervals. This, together with the necessary improvement in the accuracy of inventory records, will result in an overall lower inventory. Improvements in logistics and supply chains are discussed in Chapter 15.

An alternative to holding safety stock is to plan for safety capacity and safety labour. This will require additional equipment capacity to be available and trained labour to be on call, either through overtime or additional shifts, or by calling on temporary labour (which can be from labour hire companies). Planning is discussed in Chapter 11.

Cost of holding inventory

To cover for unplanned events, holding a calculated 'safety stock' allows an organisation to reduce its total operational costs, due to fewer disruptions. However, there is a cost incurred from holding inventory. The total cost of an item includes the material costs, the manufacturing costs, the costs incurred in buying and transporting the SKU and, finally, the costs in holding the item at a store or warehouse.

The **inventory carrying (or holding) costs** as a percentage of the cost of goods sold (COGS) are shown in Table 10.3. In addition, some companies make a charge for the additional money borrowed to finance the inventory held. This is called the **opportunity cost** and reflects the income that could have been earned if the money had been used for new product development or new ventures.

As an easy to remember figure based on Table 10.3, an inventory carrying costs at 24 per cent per annum can be used. That is 2 per cent per month of the inventory value at COGS—the cost for items to sit in the warehouse!

Table 10.3   Inventory carrying costs

Cost category	Expenditure	Cost as % of COGS
Capital	Cost to borrow money to purchase the materials	10–15% depending on the credit market rates
Inventory servicing	Insurance premiums	1–3%
	Government (central, State/province and local) taxes and charges	1–2%
	Administration costs	2–4%
Storage space	Company owned, rented or public warehouse space	2–4%
Inventory risk	Obsolescence of items in inventory	1–2%
	Damage to inventory	1–2%
	Shrinkage of inventory value through stealing Reduction in inventory value through age, e.g. 'use by date' Reduction in inventory value through reduction in potency, e.g. chemicals	2–4%
	Per annum cost	20–36%

Inventory locations

Where the inventory belonging to an enterprise is located will be governed by the customer service policies approved by senior management (see Chapter 9). This objective is then conditioned by the actual customer demand characteristics and the pattern of supply.

The number of warehouses and distribution centres supported by the brand owning company, or by an LSP on its behalf, will be governed as much by the geography and infrastructure conditions as by quantitative analysis and modelling. For example:

- In Indonesia, Papua New Guinea and the Philippines, with their multiple islands and the need to book shipping space, there is a requirement to have more outlying storage space than in a compatible country that comprises one land mass.

- In India, a radius of about 450 km from a warehouse will enable a 24-hour lead time, due to infrastructure challenges. The result could be a national network of about 30 warehouses or DCs, if relying on the road network.
- In eastern Australia, the linear nature of cities and towns that are predominately within 200 km of the coastline has resulted in a more centralised distribution pattern, with fewer distribution centres for the distances involved.

The more distribution centres or warehouses in a network, the higher the safety stock of inventory. This is due to the increased amount of uncertainty that will occur concerning customer demand at each inventory location. The calculation of additional safety stock inventory for each new location is called the square root rule.

If an organisation is deciding whether to add an additional warehouse or DC, the increase in safety stock required will be equal to the square root of the new total of locations, divided by the square root of the number of existing locations.

As an example, an organisation has three DCs and is considering opening an additional DC. The following assumptions are made:

- The demand from each location approximates a normal distribution.
- Each location has approximately the same level of demand.

$$\text{New safety stock} = \frac{\sqrt{4} \times \text{Current safety stock}}{\sqrt{3}}$$

The projected increase in inventory will be 1.156 × current safety stock, calculated for each category/class classification; these will be discussed later in this chapter.

This is an acceptable approach for calculations used in the decision process concerning an additional facility. If the decision is made to proceed, the actual safety stock will naturally change to suit the final composition of SKU held at the facility.

> ### REVIEW OF INVENTORIES
> In this first part of the discussion about inventory we have considered the following business aspects:
>
> - the different types of inventory—name them
> - the INSANE approach and other actions that some management can have towards inventory—name them
> - the role of logisticians in effectively managing inventory—what is it?
> - the value of inventory—why hold goods in storage?
> - the cost of holding inventory—what cost rate will you use and why?
> - the additional safety stock of a decision concerning an increase in storage locations—what is the additional safety stock required?

Managing inventory

Inventory management is the overall term used to address three aspects of interest to logistics professionals:

1. *Inventory policy*—measured at the aggregate (or cumulative) level, it is the decision about how much money the organisation is prepared to invest in inventory and the inventory locations.
2. *Inventory planning*—measured at the product or family group level, and based on the parameters provided by the inventory policy, it is the inventory planned to be held at each location, by time period.
3. *Inventory control*—measured at the SKU level, it is the process used, through accurate record keeping, to identify the actual amount held in inventory and ascertain reasons for discrepancies against the inventory plan.

A discussion of the first two aspects follows. Inventory control is discussed later in this chapter.

Inventory policy

Senior management is responsible for aggregate level decisions concerning the total investment in inventory by the enterprise at each stage through its inbound, internal and outbound logistics. They should also consider the trade-off between:

- the investment in inventory
- customer service level objectives
- effectiveness of inventory planning and
- efficiency of operations which handle and move the inventory.

The investor in a business (whether a private or public enterprise) expects a return on their investment; this is called the **return on investment (ROI)** rate. Decisions about the ROI are made by the CEO and board of directors. Managers who are responsible for a division of the business or strategic business unit (SBU) are typically provided with a share of the assets and expected to earn a **return on assets (ROA)**.

Under accounting conventions, inventory is considered an asset in the balance sheet and therefore a measure of performance for inventory is required. This is called the **inventory turns rate (ITR)**; the higher the ITR, the more effectively the inventory within a product group of line is being used.

The inventory turns rate (ITR) for finished goods is measured as:

$$\text{ITR} = \frac{\text{Cost of goods sold (COGS) value for a period of time and annualised}}{\text{Inventory investment at the end of the period of time}}$$

An example of ITR calculation is shown in Table 10.4.

The inventory value at the end of Qtr 1 (March) is \$5.0 million. It is expected that by the end of Qtr 2 (June), inventory will have increased to \$6.0 million.

ITR for Qtr 1 was: $\dfrac{(2.2 + 2.5 + 3.1)}{5.0} \times 4 \text{ quarters} = \dfrac{31.2}{5.0} = 6.24 \text{ turns}$

ITR for Qtr 2 is planned as: $\dfrac{(3.4 + 3.8 + 4.2)}{6.0} \times 4 \text{ quarters} = \dfrac{45.6}{6.0} = 7.6 \text{ turns}$

Table 10.4 ITR calculation

Cost of sales ($m)					
Actual			Forecast		
Jan	Feb	Mar	April	May	June
2.2	2.5	3.1	3.4	3.8	4.2

Figures of about six stock turns per year and higher should be expected within companies that sell consumer products. Note that six turns means the inventory is sitting in stores and warehouses for two months, taking up space and costing money!

Inventory can also be expressed as 'days of sales' (\$ value of inventor ÷ 365).

Another measure of finished goods inventory is the time period covered. It is the period (often expressed in weeks) that the expected sales are covered by inventory. This calculation protects the higher-volume items that have more predictable sales, but does less to protect the low-volume, but more erratic, selling items.

$$\text{Weeks cover} = \frac{\text{Inventory invested at the end of a period of time}}{\text{Average weekly COGS}}$$

Weeks cover for Qtr 2 (above) is planned as:

$$\frac{6.0}{(3.4 + 3.8 + 4.2)} \,/\, 13 \text{ wks} = \frac{6.0}{0.89} = 6.74 \text{ weeks}$$

Similar measurements are used for work in progress (WIP) and raw material (RM) inventories.

These measures are generally satisfactory at the business policy level, where aggregate and product family or group measures can be converted to financial measures and ratios for establishing the business budget. However, inventory turns and period cover are of little value at the inventory planning level, where greater detail is required.

Inventory planning

The maximum amount of inventory held for an SKU is the cycle inventory plus the fluctuation (safety stock) inventory. The amount of the cycle inventory is based on the forecast of customer demand over the lead time.

Forecasts of future events will never be 'correct' as they are based on the most likely scenario; therefore, the calculation of safety stock commences with identifying the forecast error. Using the term 'error' does not signify a mistake; this is a statistical term to identify the difference between planned and actual situations.

The range of forecast errors will enable a logistician to see different patterns occurring. Therefore, multiple SKU with similar patterns can be collated together in a category for common decisions to be made about planning and the level of control required.

Understanding and responding to **variability** in supply chains is one of the critical challenges for a logistician. Management of variability involves considering and responding to changes in demand, inventory, output capability and supplies from one period to another.

Analysing variability requires the use of high school mathematics, although many aspects of quantitative analysis are now contained in computer applications. However, it is dangerous to rely on the 'correct' answer from a computer unless you understand the underlying mathematics and know the limitations of each quantitative technique.

Initially, you need to be comfortable with the terms **mean**, **median** and **mode** as related to a set of numbers, together with **standard deviation** and the structure of the **normal distribution**. A text on statistics or an internet search can help with any gaps in your knowledge.

ABC analysis

Within inventory planning, making groups from the list of SKU into categories for planning purposes is called an ABC analysis. The principle underpinning ABC is the observation by the Swiss-based Italian economist Vilfredo Pareto that relatively few items dominate the results in a situation. His observation, later called the Pareto Principle, or the 80/20 rule, states that 80 per cent of the influence in a situation will be exerted by 20 per cent of the elements involved. For example, approximately 80 per cent of sales are to approximately 20 per cent of the customer base.

For finished goods inventory in fast moving consumer goods (FMCG) and consumer packaged goods (CPG) companies, the ABC analysis of finished goods is typically based on the annual sales volume at **cost of goods sold (COGS)** value. To determine the ABC ranking for each line item (SKU):

- Multiply the annual sales volume of each SKU by its cost to manufacture or buy (COGS), to obtain the annual value per SKU.
- Rank all the SKUs by annual value, from highest to lowest.
- Identify the inventory investment for all SKUs.
- Divide the annual value for each SKU by the inventory investment for all SKU, to obtain each SKU item's percentage of the inventory investment.

The resulting ABC categories are shown in Table 10.5. The subsequent ABC chart is shown in Figure 10.2.

Depending on the business and type of products, additional decision criteria may be used to place an SKU in its final category. These include:

- total cost of the SKU
- cost of a stock-out for the SKU
- product range integrity—the assertion by the sales department that, to enable the sale of fast moving items, particular slow-moving items within a product group must be available—these assumptions must be evaluated
- shelf life and batch control requirements
- special storage requirements for finished products or materials
- engineering or technical design complexity

Table 10.5 ABC categories

Category	% of sales at GOGS value	% of SKU
A	70–80%	15–20%
B	10–15%	20–40%
C	10–15%	40–65%

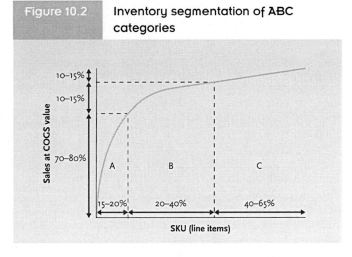

Figure 10.2 Inventory segmentation of ABC categories

- physical size of the final product
- high risks in obtaining materials or components and the risk of pilferage
- availability of specialist internal resources for the SKU to be produced.

The ABC categories for finished product inventory items enable decisions to be made concerning the amount of inventory per SKU, the locations where inventory will be held and the control system to be used. ABC analysis can also be undertaken for purchased parts and components, manufactured items and sub-assemblies.

An extended ABC classification of inventory

The limitation of using ABC categories is that all items within a category will be treated the same, even though the demand pattern for items may vary. Using a client example, the annual sales pattern for a company's category A products is illustrated in Figure 10.3 and the annual sales situation for this company's category A products is shown in Table 10.6.

To overcome the limitation of grouping products with similar total sales together, Tom Rafferty of Supply Chain STO P/L has developed the coefficient of variation for management (CoVM©). This utilises the variability of sales by each SKU, allowing the ABC categories to be extended from categories A to F.

The extended category A to F breakdown of a typical SKU list within a FMCG or CPG organisation is shown in Table 10.7.

The coefficient of variation (CoV) is calculated by dividing the standard deviation of sales for an SKU by its mean (average) sales. The CoV cut-off is identified by class within each category, as shown in Table 10.8.

As an example of how a category of SKU can include multiple classes, Table 10.6 is repeated in Table 10.9, but showing the CoV.

This indicates that products Red and Blue are in class a, Green and Black are in class b, Grey is in class c, Yellow in class d and Pink in class e.

The output from the analysis is therefore five active Pareto categories of inventory, A to E (with category F classified as the dead stock), each with five CoV classes, structured as Aa, Ab, Ac etc. and totalling 25 category/classes. The CoVM© matrix of category/classes is shown in Figure 10.4.

Under this structure, it is more likely that, for example, cells Aa, Ba and Ca (and Ab, Bb, Cb), have similar patterns and therefore can be managed similarly.

Figure 10.5 shows the numbers from Table 10.7 structured into a matrix format.

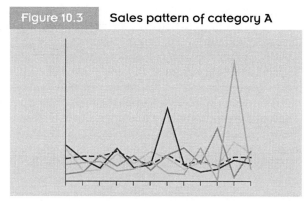

Figure 10.3   Sales pattern of category A

Source: Tom Rafferty, Supply Chain STO P/L.

Table 10.6   Category A situation

SKU	Annual sales in units	Sales mean	Standard deviation of sales
Red	13 923	1 160	165
Blue	14 414	1 201	300
Green	14 267	1 189	381
Black	13 990	1 166	554
Grey	14 601	1 217	756
Yellow	14 286	1 191	1 155
Pink	14 576	1 215	1 217

Source: Tom Rafferty, Supply Chain STO P/L.

Table 10.7   Category A to F breakdown

Category	Description of demand	% of sales at COGS value	% of SKU
A	Steady	5	1
B	Variable	65	5
C	Erratic	15	5
D	Irregular	5	10
E	Lumpy	10	72
F	Dead	0	3

Source: Tom Rafferty, Supply Chain STO P/L.

Table 10.8   CoV cut-off by class

Class	CoV cut-off
a	Less than or equal to 0.25
b	Greater than 0.25 and less than 0.50
c	Greater than 0.50 and less than 0.75
d	Greater than 0.75 and less than 1.00
e	Greater than 1.00

Source: Tom Rafferty, Supply Chain STO P/L.

Table 10.9   Category A sales situation

SKU	Annual sales in units	Sales mean	Standard sales deviation	CoV
Red	13 923	1 160	165	0.1 422
Blue	14 414	1 201	300	0.2 498
Green	14 267	1 189	381	0.3 204
Black	13 990	1 166	554	0.4 751
Grey	14 601	1 217	756	0.6 212
Yellow	14 286	1 191	1 155	0.9 698
Pink	14 576	1 215	1 217	1.00

Source: Tom Rafferty, Supply Chain STO P/L.

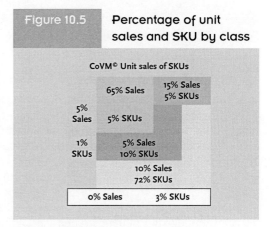

Figure 10.4   CoVM© matrix

Source: Tom Rafferty, Supply Chain STO P/L.

This matrix can now be shown as a description for the pattern of demand by category, as shown in Figure 10.6.

Safety stock calculation

Having completed the ABC/CoVM analysis for each item, the next task is to calculate the amount of safety stock for each SKU, depending on the level of customer service that is defined for each class within a category. As an example, consider product 102; the analysis is calculated in Table 10.10.

Standard deviation (∂) = Variance squared/periods
$$= 1086/10$$
$$= 108.6$$

Now calculate the square root (shown as symbol √) of the variance = 10.42 (rounded to 11). Note that the most accurate approach is to use the number of periods minus one; our intention, however, is to illustrate the broad principles.

A forecast of 100 (and the assumption that 100 are manufactured or supplied at the commencement of each period), means there is insufficient inventory available at the end of periods 6 and 9. Safety stock is therefore required to provide a cover against this possibility.

The safety factor against each level of service required can be identified; this must be applied against the standard deviation to calculate the amount of safety stock held, as shown in Table 10.11.

In this example, the opening inventory for product 102 at each period needs to be 111 units (cycle inventory of 100 + one standard deviation of 11), to provide an 84 per cent customer service level.

By having one ∂ amount of safety stock, there will be sufficient inventory to cover the 2 out of every 10 ordering occasions that were identified when it is most likely there will be insufficient inventory to meet the sales demand.

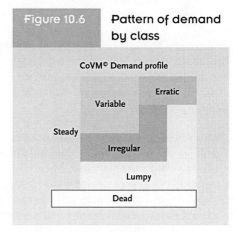

Figure 10.5   Percentage of unit sales and SKU by class

Source: Tom Rafferty, Supply Chain STO P/L.

Figure 10.6   Pattern of demand by class

Source: Tom Rafferty, Supply Chain STO P/L.

To provide a 98 per cent customer service level and ensure that the chance of a stock-out will only occur on 2 in every 100 ordering occasions, will require two ∂ of safety stock (20.52 units). For a 99.8 per cent customer service level, three ∂ of safety stock (30.78 units) are required and a 99.99 per cent

Table 10.10   Analysis of product 102 (A)

Sales period	Forecast	Actual sales	Variance ('error')	Cumulative variance	Variance squared
1	100	100	0	0	0
2	100	87	−13	−13	169
3	100	112	+12	−1	144
4	100	94	−6	−7	36
5	100	107	+7	0	49
6	100	110	+10	+10	100
7	100	82	−18	−8	324
8	100	108	+8	0	64
9	100	110	+10	+10	100
10	100	90	−10	0	100
	1000	1000			
Mean sales		100			
Total variance (ignore + / −)			82		
Total variance squared					1086

customer service level will require four ∂ of safety stock (41.04 units). Statistically, a 100 per cent customer service level can never be obtained, although it will get close—but at a very high cost in the total amount of inventory held.

In too many companies, the dominant culture is to avoid a stock-out of an inventory item, as stock-outs give rise to enquiries and 'witch hunts'. Put yourself in the place of the logistics manager when the CEO visits the sales offices and distribution centre in a distant State or province. The CEO is met by the sales manager and told that the No 2 selling SKU is out of stock and 'I cannot sell from the back of an empty truck'. That the replenishment stock is arriving in the afternoon, in time for loading that evening's delivery vehicles (as a fast moving line should), is of no consequence as the CEO shouts threats of dismissal over the mobile phone to the logistics manager.

This type of situation gives rise to the approach that 'if a little extra inventory is safe, a lot of extra inventory will result in an easier life'. However, given the increased inventory (and other) costs incurred to achieve a higher level of customer service, it requires that logisticians have a clear understanding of the service and cost implications when making (and explaining to senior management) service level decisions, such as whether to have 95 per cent or 98 per cent service level for a particular SKU.

Management of each category

The actions required by a logistician for each category is based on the pattern of demand by category, as shown in Figure 10.6. The actions are identified in Figure 10.7.

Table 10.11   Inventory safety factor

Service level (% of order occurrences without a stock-out)	Safety factor as a multiplier of the standard deviation
50.00%	0.00
75.00%	0.67
84.13%	1.00
90.00%	1.28
95.00%	1.65
98.00%	2.05
99.00%	2.33
99.86%	3.00
99.99%	4.00

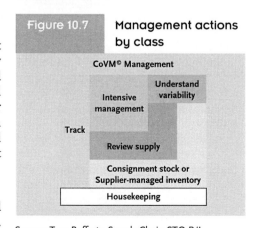

Figure 10.7   Management actions by class

Source: Tom Rafferty, Supply Chain STO P/L.

The group of SKU in class a shows a STEADY demand with little variation, regardless of the volume sold or used; the situation can therefore be TRACKED. Forecasts are likely to be close to the actual sales, with a low variability of demand (and hopefully, supply). If the items are 'make to stock' (MTS), a high service level will not result in a high safety stock.

Inventory is managed through using the tracking signal. This is calculated for an SKU by dividing the cumulative variation for the number of periods under review by the standard deviation; a control limit is established by class. For items in the STEADY category, the acceptable tracking signal will be about 4. If the tracking signal is within these limits, the forecast for that SKU is in control.

For product 102 (STEADY class) in period 20, the tracking signal is calculated in Table 10.12.

Table 10.12 Analysis of product 102 (B)

Sales period	Forecast	Actual sales	Variance ('error')	Cumulative variance	Variance squared
11	100	115	+15	15	225
12	100	92	−8	−7	64
13	100	96	−4	−11	16
14	100	109	+9	−2	81
15	100	120	+20	18	400
16	100	105	+5	23	25
17	100	112	−12	11	144
18	100	84	−16	−5	256
19	100	88	−12	−17	144
20	100	96	−4	−21	16
	1000				
Total variance (ignore + / −)					
Total variance squared					1371
Cumulative variance				21	

Standard deviation ∂ =
Variance squared/periods = 1371/10 = 137.1.
Square root $\sqrt{}$ of the period variance = $\sqrt{137.1}$ = 11.71
Therefore, the tracking signal for period 20 = Cumulative variance/∂ = 21/11.71 = 1.8

The tracking signal for STEADY category items should be less than about 4; a tracking signal of 1.8 indicates that product 102 is in control.

The VARIABLE category of SKU requires intensive management. Forecast error is likely to be more varied; therefore, use a tracking signal of more than 7.0 for an SKU as the trigger for a review. Also, use differing customer service levels or safety factors (which provide different safety stock requirements). This applies especially in category/class Ac and Bc.

The ERRATIC category of SKU can contain individual SKU items which have substantial sales, but the sales levels may vary dramatically. This can provide a challenge for logistics professionals, because the timing of a large sale may not be communicated. The solution is to work with the sales department to understand the causes of variability for items in this group. Often, the sale of these products is to a small number of customers, so together with the sales representative, visit the customer and find out about their business and discover why their buying pattern is erratic—it may be due to restrictions concerning order quantities that have been established by the selling organisation!

The categories named IRREGULAR, LUMPY and DEAD make up the slow and obsolete (SLOB) stock that is sitting in large quantities on warehouse shelves, gathering dust and costing money!

A slow-moving item is defined as an SKU that has not registered any demand (or sales) for six of the preceding 12 months. Slow-moving items cannot be forecast using the standard methodology applied to faster-moving items, as this method is based on the ability to apply *time series-based forecasting* techniques for an SKU.

The IRREGULAR category of SKUs is usually purchased by customers in small quantities on an irregular basis. Note that the number of SKUs in this group is similar to the total of the previous three groups, yet constitutes only about 10 per cent of sales. As a group, the items may be achieving between two and four stock turns per year, which is not satisfactory.

The 'ideal' decision would be to eliminate these SKUs. However, the sales department could state that 'customers demand a full range of product'. This statement requires analysing by logistics professionals. For example, companies supplying products into large retailers within some countries of the Oceania sub-region (Australia and New Zealand) are experiencing retailers de-listing suppliers' brands and introducing an increasing range of their own private labels (or home brands).

If the sales department is correct, then logistics should consider different ways of supplying the product lines. Outsourcing production to a smaller company may be a solution—a small product line in a large company can become a large product line in a small company. If the item is imported, often with minimum order quantities, then the product's gross margin and customer service level should be reviewed, to ensure the item is viable within the sales catalogue.

The LUMPY group of SKUs can contain up to 70 per cent of all the SKUs, yet only total about 5 per cent of the sales value—rarely ever more than 7 per cent.

Trying to eliminate this group of products in the FMCG and CPG sectors is a major challenge and will be contested by marketing and sales. Experience by the authors shows that if logistics managers are able to have some of this group eliminated, the SKU will be replaced with 'new and exciting' products within 18 months. Product elimination process therefore needs to be an inherent part of the inventory management process, but it rarely is.

The DEAD group of SKUs is made up of those items which have not sold anything in the past 12 months. If they are not 'insurance' service parts, the SKUs should be eliminated from the catalogue.

The concept of CoVM© can also be applied across a wide range of functions where there is a time series with variability, such as accounts receivable and service/maintenance areas.

Value of inventory items

An item for sale can remain in inventory for extended periods before a demand is triggered. The logistics professional must therefore know whether holding the part in inventory is earning a return for the business. The calculation for this is the gross margin return on inventory investment (GMROII):

$$\frac{\text{Gross margin} \times \text{Inventory turns}}{1 - \text{Gross margin}}$$

For example, a product has a gross margin of 56 per cent and inventory turns of 1.7 turns per year.

$$\text{GMROII} = \frac{0.56 \times 1.7}{1 - 0.56} = \$2.16 \text{ gross margin per \$ of inventory investment}$$

Considering the costs associated with holding inventory, an enterprise should expect to receive about three dollars for each dollar invested in inventory. For a higher return on the inventory investment, a product either needs to sell faster, with frequent replenishment (higher stock turns) or earn a higher gross margin, to compensate for lower stock turns.

In the example above, if negotiations with the supplier cannot reduce the re-order quantity or reduce the lead time for the item, then increasing the price to obtain a higher gross margin must be considered. Of course, the final decision will depend on current market conditions, but even if the current price remains, the company has on record the 'inventory holding loss' it is making on the item.

The GMROII should be used in retailing and service parts to calculate the return on investment from each SKU that is for sale.

Service parts

The majority of **service parts** fit into the LUMPY category of SKUs and managing service parts inventory is a dedicated endeavour. Service parts are either for sale to customers as part of the company's business—mainly in the automotive, defence and industrial equipment industries—or they are used within a company's own facilities as service parts for operational equipment.

An example of internal use is the support function within a country's military forces, or a large mine site that may hold over 30 000 different service parts, requiring the inventory and purchasing review of more than 100 part numbers per day!

Planning service parts

To plan service parts requires segmentation to identify the criticality of each part, as shown in Table 10.13.

Table 10.13   Critical service parts analysis

		Supply risk			Low
	LT > 90 days Single source	LT > 30 days Single source	LT < 30 days Single source	LT < 30 days Multiple sources	LT < 7 days
Catastrophic failure (kill people or affect ongoing business viability)	Aa	Ab	Ac	Ad	Ae
Operational failure (severely affect the services or service)	Ba	Bb	Bc	Bd	Be
Operational impairment (reduce performance of staff)	Ca	Cb	Cc	Cd	Ce
Non-critical item (OOS will not cause significant problems)	Da	Db	Dc	Dd	De

(CRITICALITY: High → Low)

Where applicable, the supply risk will be augmented by an analysis concerning the risk (probability) of failure for the more critical parts, using the 'mean time between failure' (MTBF), calculated by the design technical staff. Service levels will be established; for example:

- 99+ per cent for 'catastrophic failure' parts
- 98 per cent for 'operational failure'—'immediate' parts
- 95 per cent for 'operational impairment' parts
- 84 per cent for 'non-service/non-critical' parts.

In addition, the action required is identified for the occasions when an 'out of stock' occurs in each section of the matrix.

Insurance service parts

These are parts for retail sale that have ceased production or importation; the seller therefore orders a final batch prior to the production dies and moulds being destroyed. These service parts are an insurance against being out of stock for the economic life of the finished product and are known as 'life of type' (LOT) or 'all-time buy' (ATB) items. Insurance items are often held in inventory as higher assemblies, such as only holding replacement gearboxes rather than each of the component parts.

The overriding challenge with insurance items is to get them written off by the finance department when a part has reached the end of its economic life. Finance does not like to do that (especially when the write-off value is in the millions of dollars), because inventory is an asset and writing off inventory affects the value of the business, as recorded in the balance sheet.

Calculating safety stock for slow-moving items

Safety stock for SLOB items can be calculated, but it requires the use of different distributions from the normal distribution that is used for faster-moving items.

The most common is the Poisson probability distribution, which recognises the ordering pattern of small, infrequent demands, where the quantity of items in an order is fairly constant. The safety stock is calculated in Table 10.14.

Calculate $f \times \sqrt{a}$, where:
f = service factor (similar to the standard deviation)
a = average number of orders during the lead time

For example, during the supply lead time for a service part, the average number of orders is 40, each requiring 1 unit. If the item has a service level of 98 per cent (f=2.1), the safety stock is calculated as:

2.1 × √ 40
2.1 × 6.32 × 1
= 13.28, say, 14 units

Table 10.14   Poisson probability distribution

Service level %	f
75	0.7
80	0.8
85	1.0
90	1.3
95	1.7
98	2.1
99	2.3
99.9	3.1

In this situation, the standard deviation is equal to the square root of the mean (average) demand. However, where the ∂ of demand does not closely align to the $\sqrt{}$ mean, then the Poisson technique is not appropriate. In this situation, it may be preferable to use the Laplace or Croston probability distributions (calculation details can be found in statistics textbooks and on internet sites).

In recent years, developments have occurred that enable desktop computers to run multiple iterations of an intermittent demand profile. This provides a statistically robust solution concerning the inventory required to cover likely demands over the replenishment period. An example is the Smart-Willemain technique from Smart Software.

A valid inventory management technique, in organisations that stock service parts for use on their own imported equipment, is to join with other organisations that are using the same equipment in the city or country. The objective is to hold service parts inventory for the critical and expensive parts at a single location and so reduce total inventory. When a member company requires a part, they draw it from the central stock and then order a replacement part, identifying their billing (invoice) address but using the central location as the delivery address.

In general, the inventory for items purchased for production is only that which is available against planned production. The exception is items that are low value consumables which may be ordered and controlled through a 'two-bin' system. The process is that each bin (which may be an electronic record) is equal to the amount consumed over the lead time. When a bin is empty, that is the signal to order an amount equal to a bin quantity; this will arrive as the second bin becomes empty.

Safety stock inventory and lead time variability

In the discussion so far, the focus has been on planning sufficient inventory to account for variations in demand (sales). However, the additional aspect of variability to be covered by safety stock is the length and variability of the lead time for a finished SKU and its materials.

If the long or variable lead time is a problem, the logistician needs to work with the supplier to identify and rectify problems. However, when lead times remain a problem, safety stock is required.

The first calculation is where the lead time to receive the item is more than the interval between placing orders. In that time period, there is a likelihood that actual demand will differ from that forecast.

If the interval between placing orders is one month, but the time to receive the order is two months (which is not unusual in an importing situation), the calculated standard deviation must be uplifted by a multiplier. The multiplier to be used is shown in Table 10.15 opposite.

The second calculation is the variation in the lead time between the planned and actual times, which can occur when moving materials around the region. The calculation of variation is shown in Table 10.16 below.

The calculation of safety stock to allow for variation in lead time is:

∂ = Variance squared/periods = 229/10 = 22.9
$\sqrt{}$ of the period variance = $\sqrt{22.9}$ = 4.78 (rounded to 5)

Therefore, to cover for an 84 per cent customer service level will require holding approximately 5 days of sales as safety stock, in addition to that allowed for the variation in demand and for the variation in demand between the order and delivery intervals.

Consider the safety stock requirements to meet an availability expectation to provide a 98 per cent service level for an imported SKU in the VARIABLE segment. This will result in a total safety stock that could be more than double the calculated safety stock required to cover just the demand variability. For this reason alone, a logistician's knowledge is required to first minimise the variability in the system and then use inventory principles to implement an inventory holding policy.

Table 10.15   Uplift for standard deviation

When interval between placing an order is 1 period and lead time period for the order is:	Standard deviation is multiplied by:
2	1.63
3	2.16
4	2.64
5	3.09
6	3.51
7	3.91
8	4.29
9	4.66
10	5.01

Table 10.16   Analysis of variation for an example imported item

Sales period	Forecast lead time (days)	Actual lead time (days)	Variance ('error')	Cumulative variance	Variance squared
1	60	70	10	10	100
2	60	62	2	12	4
3	60	57	−3	9	9
4	60	66	6	15	36
5	60	61	1	16	1
6	60	59	−1	15	1
7	60	67	7	22	49
8	60	64	4	26	16
9	60	58	−2	24	4
10	60	63	3	27	9
		627			
Mean lead time		62.7			
Total variance (ignore + / −)					
Total variance squared					229

Inventory control

While holding inventory in a store or warehouse may be an essential part of successful businesses, it must be remembered that the items are going nowhere—it is transport at zero km per hour. The objective is for inventory to quickly become an integral part of the distribution process.

The two fundamentals required to achieve inventory control are:

- location accuracy
- SKU accuracy.

The topic of location within warehouses is discussed in Chapter 8. Obviously, however, every location must be identified, so that it can be matched with the correct SKU quantity.

The accuracy of SKU volumes in the warehouse is obtained through counting. Just as the teller in a bank counts your money when it is received and again counts the money (usually more than once) when giving you cash, so the warehouse is the company's bank and stock should be treated in the same way.

The annual stocktake that is still required by some external auditors is insufficient as a control tool. To maintain inventory accuracy, control in the warehouse must be exercised on a daily basis. In addition to counting SKU as they arrive and depart, the core control technique is cycle counting.

Establishing the cycle counting process requires the same extended ABC/CoVM categories discussed earlier.

The counting regime will be established within each enterprise to suit its business, but, as a general rule, A and B items should all be counted every month, C and D items within three months and E and F items within six months. Because of the 80/20 rule, there will be few items in the A and B categories and many in the E and F categories, so not too many items will need to be counted each day.

Assume that a warehouse has 800 SKUs:

- A and B items @ say, 15 per cent = 120
- C and D items @ say, 25 per cent = 200
- E and F items @ say, 60 per cent = 480

The daily count will therefore be:

- A and B items 120/20 working days = 6
- C and D items 200/60 working days = 3–4
- E and F items 480/120 working days = 4
- Total = 14

The items chosen for counting will be randomly selected (inventory modules within ERP systems can usually do this). As part of the internal discipline, the count should be undertaken by a senior supervisor, so that inventory accuracy is seen as an integral part of their job and not the role of a clerk. The supervisor should receive the list of items for count on arrival at work; within the time of counting, no items are picked or moved.

On completion of the cycle count, the actual and computed totals are compared and if there is a difference for an item, a recount should be done (remember, this is the organisation's bank). If the second count shows a difference, the responsible manager has to make a decision whether to authorise another recount or report the difference to the finance department for a decision concerning an adjustment to the accounts.

To continue with the discipline of inventory record accuracy, an additional inventory count of an item is required when:

- the computed total for an item is at its re-order point
- the inventory level for an item shows zero in the IT system
- goods are required to be put away at a location and it is found that another SKU is stored at the location
- goods are required to be moved from a location and that location is found to be empty
- the number of movement transactions for an SKU within the period exceeds a specific number; this is because a high number of transactions can hide cumulative errors.

If these necessary procedures are not already in place, then the implementation process will take some time. The steps required are as follows:

- Senior management changes the performance measurement system to include inventory record accuracy.
- Responsibilities for the performance are allocated.
- An education program is commenced for the warehouse team(s). This program must influence the employees to understand why inventory accuracy is necessary and be aware of their role in helping the facility meet its performance targets.
- The team(s) conduct a review of the goods movement transaction processes.
- The stock location plan (to optimise the utilisation of storage space) is reviewed by the team(s).
- A review of the stock rotation procedures is undertaken by the team(s).

* All employees involved in counting stock and correcting any errors are trained.
* The operating manual, containing multiple illustrations to describe the processes is written.

As the use of **radio frequency identification devices (RFID)**, attached at the pallet or shipper level, becomes more common in DCs and warehouses, the counting regime will change. There will be a capability for a whole-of-facility count or spot counts of a storage location using a mobile RFID reader. RFID is discussed in Chapter 14.

REVIEW OF INVENTORY MANAGEMENT

The second part of the chapter has been concerned with managing inventory and the essentials of inventory policy, planning and control. The main points have been:

* For policy, identify the stock turns measure for internal improvement and as a competitive measure. Consider the annual accounts of some public companies and calculate their approximate stock turn figure.
* In planning, the concept of ABC and the extended classification is the important base from which to commence a structured planning system. How can inventory classification be used within a planning system?
* For service parts, the approach is different, due to the criticality of some parts, but the slow movement of many. Should the planning and control for service parts be different from other SKU?
* Within planning of inventory is the need for safety stock to cover for lead time variation in addition to the safety stock to cover for demand variation. Is this sufficient justification for action to reduce lead times?

Inventory optimisation

Inventory optimisation is a planning technique that is gaining acceptance in CPG and FMCG businesses, and in organisations with high service parts; this is due to the increasing inventory levels required by longer lead times within the extended supply chains. Optimal inventory is defined by Carter McNabb, a partner at GRA Pty Ltd, as 'the minimum amount of inventory required to achieve availability targets at the lowest total cost'. This is shown in Figure 10.8.

Carter explains that inventory optimisation techniques attempt to optimise the complex

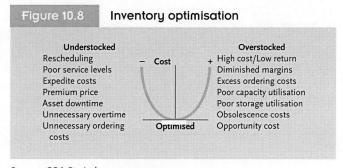

Figure 10.8　Inventory optimisation

Source: GRA Pty Ltd, www.gra.net.au.

relationships between costs, capacities, target service levels and variability/risk (for example forecast error and supplier delivery performance) for each item in each location of a business, across all its supply chains in the network. There are different techniques available and it is important to understand which technique is appropriate for a particular situation.

At a fundamental level, there are two tiers of inventory optimisation—strategic and operational/tactical.

Strategic inventory optimisation

Strategic inventory optimisation focuses on the policy and structure of supply chains and, therefore, the maximum review frequency tends to be annually or when a major change to a supply chain is being considered.

Operational/tactical inventory optimisation

Operational/tactical inventory optimisation deals with the recurring operational processes of demand and supply planning, which may occur daily, weekly or monthly. This optimisation aims to keep inventories optimally balanced for the specified service level as various factors change. For example, inventories should adjust dynamically in response to changing demand patterns and risk factors (such as forecast error and supplier performance).

For operational/tactical inventory optimisation to be truly effective, it must be genuinely integrated with demand planning and the replenishment planning processes. For example, if forecast accuracy improves, safety stocks should automatically decrease; this leads to an automatic decrease or deferral of replenishment requirements.

This means that static inventory policies such as 'weeks of cover or supply' are not applicable, as they are not responsive to changes in supply chain variability and risk, and service level targets or costs.

Following are some of the prevailing inventory optimisation techniques and their application.

INVENTORY DEPLOYMENT OPTIMISATION (IDO) AND NETWORK FLOW OPTIMISATION (NFO)

These techniques determine where to store or produce inventory and how inventory should flow from the source of supply to consumption. These decisions are best made with knowledge of the total supply chain for an item and are often made in the context of strategic supply chain planning. For example, where products should be stored will depend on various factors, including:

* demand profiles
* the number of sites (which can also be a variable in the analysis)
* the carrying cost at each site
* procurement and/or production costs at each site
* the function, capacity and capability of each site
* production, storage and transport capacities and constraints for each node in the supply chain
* the relative value of the inventory and profit margin versus transport costs (for example a cement distributor is likely to have more sites holding inventory to minimise the number of deliveries)
* fixed and variable costs by resource, network node and channel
* customer service levels
* supplier and customer lead times
* supply chain variability and risk profiles.

MULTI-ECHELON OPTIMISATION (MEO)

MEO can be applied in environments where product and/or component substitution is possible. The computer manufacturing and assembly industry is a good example of an ideal MEO environment, as it has many interchangeable components and redundant stocking across a large, distributed supplier base.

In traditional inventory optimisation techniques, inventory levels for both finished goods and bill of material (BOM) components are established on an item-by-item basis, based on service level, variability and cost optimisation techniques. For example, an aim to achieve a service level of 95 per cent for a finished item, with three interchangeable component items stocked at 95 per cent, provides an actual service level of 99.9 per cent+; so inventories are excessive relative to service level requirements. The same is true if three warehouses stock the same product (provided that all warehouses can deliver to the customer).

MEO techniques factor in substitution possibilities across the manufacturing and distribution network and set optimal stock levels based on service level targets across the interchangeable inventory population. In environments where the substitution potential is high, MEO techniques can deliver inventory reductions of 10–30 per cent above traditional techniques.

SERVICE-LEVEL OPTIMISATION (SLO)

SLO is a technique that determines the optimal service-level policy for a given set of constraints. As stated previously, the traditional method uses service level as the constraint (that is, the lowest possible inventory for a given service level). Using this method, it often takes 50 per cent more safety stock to increase service levels from 95 to 99 per cent, as an additional standard deviation of supply chain variability must be carried.

As a result, the significant increase in inventory and carrying costs for a relatively small increase in service level can erode profit margins. SLO provides an alternative approach that sets service level policies at the point where profit margins are maximised, based on the trade-off between profit margin, revenue realisation and inventory related costs. SLO can also be used to determine the ideal set of service level policies by item, given an aggregate inventory budget constraint. For example, if there is a $5 million inventory holding constraint, SLO can determine the mix of service level policies that maximises total fill rate to customers.

This technique may also assign higher service levels to faster-moving, lower-value items and lower service levels to slower-moving but higher-value items.

MARGINAL ANALYSIS AND OPTIMAL SERVICE PARTS

Marginal analysis is used primarily in maintenance repair and overhaul (MRO) environments. It seeks to determine the cost optimal mix of rotable, repairable items and service spares to deliver maximum asset availability (for example for aircraft, power generators) against a given budget. Conceptually, this technique shares some similarities with MEO and SLO, but the mathematical approaches are different, given the unique characteristics of MRO environments (for example very slow-moving items, repair cycle turnaround time, etc.). The savings available from this approach are from an example shown in Figure 10.9.

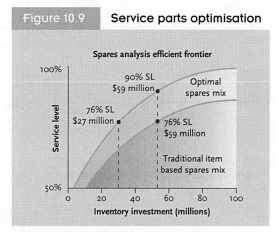

Figure 10.9   Service parts optimisation

Source: GRA Pty Ltd www.gra.net.au.

Constraint-based optimisation

This technique is used to determine inventory strategies, given the presence of significant critical constraints which are common in assembly production, commodity scheduling and material processing environments. Examples of these environments include grain processing and distribution, petroleum processing and distribution, process manufacturing (for example float glass production, dairy product manufacturing) and commodity export shipping (for example coal export scheduling across an interconnected rail and port system).

Benefits resulting from the effective application of inventory optimisation include:

* 20–40 per cent inventory investment reduction
* increased service levels ranging up to 99.9 per cent
* significant working capital improvement
* compressed cash-to-cash cycles
* improved return on capital employed/net assets
* improved debt to equity ratios
* improved capacity and fixed asset utilisation
* improved relationships with suppliers and customers
* integration of business goals and operational practices.

Chapter review

This chapter has provided an insight into the breadth of application that can be implemented by logisticians to better manage inventory across a range of enterprises. For logisticians, managing inventory is more than reducing the costs associated with holding inventory; it is understanding the hidden costs to the business that excessive inventory can cause. Examples are distribution problems which can be 'covered up', low delivery performance by suppliers and reduced flexibility of the business to change products as markets and customer demands change.

As noted in the introduction to the chapter, inventory management is a critical item in the logisticians' knowledge bank and, even though it is about understanding and manipulating numbers, the benefits make it well worth understanding the underlying concepts and techniques.

Chapter questions

Operational

1. Table 10.1 indicates that consumables, office supplies, some MRO items and laboratory supplies have a driver of demand that is 'available as required'. What inventory planning and control technique should be used for these items and how would you implement it?
2. There are five types of inventory. Identify the basis for calculating the volume of each type.
3. It is proposed in the chapter that an inventory carrying cost of 24 per cent per annum should be used as a reasonable figure in lieu of a calculated figure. If an item is expected to be held at the warehouse for the next three months, what 'no cost' discount could sales give to a customer for an immediate sale? Should sales be credited towards their quota with the full price or the discounted price? What part of the business should be 'charged' the value of the discount?

Planning

4. A company sells imported vehicles. One of the value propositions the marketing department uses to justify consumers purchasing the cars is 'excellent service support'. Therefore, the internal response is that all demands for service parts will be met from inventory held in the country.

   The company decides to release a new model range into the market and service parts are purchased to support the expected sales. Later analysis identifies that of the total service parts purchased, 1600 SKUs at a purchased value of $635 000 were never required.

   What are the challenges of trying to sell the parts back to the manufacturing company (at a substantial discount), or, at some time in the future, writing off the value?

5. You are the planning manager for a country sales division of a consumer electronics company. A new product is to be introduced that adheres to a car windscreen and provides a signal when a police radar unit is detected. The product launch is planned for Fathers' Day in September and will have heavy television, print and social networking promotion. Sales over the three-week campaign are forecast to be 300 000 units, but then will reduce to about 1000 per week until the next campaign for Christmas. Production from the contract manufacturer will commence at 40 000 per month, rising steadily to 400 000 per month over a period of seven months. Your division has been informed that it will be allocated between 20 per cent and 30 per cent of production in any one month. Lead time from the manufacturer to your division's DC is six weeks; two weeks is allowed for delivery of orders to retail outlets, which order on a weekly basis and pay in 90 days. Sales for the Fathers' Day campaign are 350 000 units. The landed value of each item is $50; the gross margin is 50 per cent and the transfer cost is $35, payable to head office within 45 days of month end.

   a. How much capital could the division invest in inventory prior to the launch?
   b. Will any inventory remain after the launch period? If so, how much?
   c. If the allocation of production continues, how much inventory will be on hand prior to the Christmas selling season commencing December 1?
   d. Discuss the value and costs of seasonal promotions.

Management

6. The central distribution centre of an MNC selling into the CPG market has the following inventory status:

   48 per cent of all SKUs at the location
   = 24 per cent of the total inventory volume, of which
   = 4 per cent of the annual sales value

   Do these figures indicate a good inventory policy? Discuss.

7 A supplier of CPG has the following financial situation:

Sales revenue	$10.0m
Cost of goods sold (COGS)	$8.0m (material purchases = $6.0m)
Gross profit	$2.0m
Taxes + bank interest	$1.0m
Net profit	$1.0m

Inventory investment: $1.6m = 1.6 years of net profit
Inventory turns: 6.0m / 1.6m = 3.75 turns per year
Objective: To increase net profit, reduce inventory by 50 per cent.
Is this a valid objective? Why or why not?

8 The INSANE approach to inventory is alive and well in business. As a logistics manager, present to management an alternative approach to inventory management that incorporates the techniques discussed in the chapter.

References and links

GRA Pty Ltd, www.gra.net.au
Supply Chain STO P/L, www.sto.au.com

Planning and scheduling the enterprise

On completion of this chapter you will be able to:

- understand the 'one plan' approach to planning a business
- be a constructive part of a sales and operations planning (S&OP) implementation
- scope the extent of a demand plan
- consider how to structure a collaborative approach through planning with customers and suppliers
- understand the significance of the capacity plan
- follow the steps through planning the master plan/schedule, the materials requirements plan (MRP) and the capacity plan.

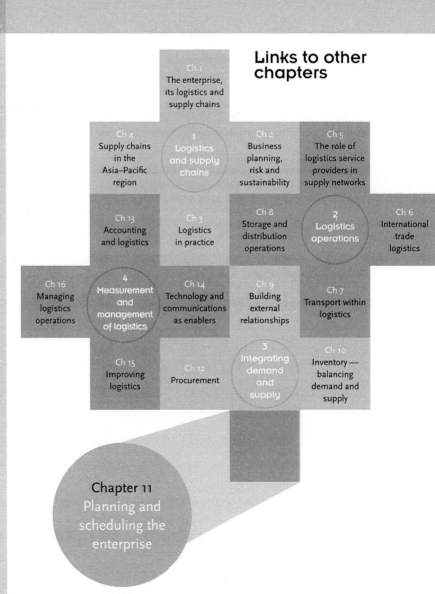

Links to other chapters

Ch 1
The enterprise, its logistics and supply chains

Ch 4
Supply chains in the Asia–Pacific region

1
Logistics and supply chains

Ch 2
Business planning, risk and sustainability

Ch 5
The role of logistics service providers in supply networks

Ch 13
Accounting and logistics

Ch 3
Logistics in practice

Ch 8
Storage and distribution operations

2
Logistics operations

Ch 6
International trade logistics

Ch 16
Managing logistics operations

4
Measurement and management of logistics

Ch 14
Technology and communications as enablers

Ch 9
Building external relationships

Ch 7
Transport within logistics

Ch 15
Improving logistics

Ch 12
Procurement

3
Integrating demand and supply

Ch 10
Inventory — balancing demand and supply

Chapter 11
Planning and scheduling the enterprise

Key terms

These terms are used in the text. Develop your own notebook by downloading information on each term.

business plan
sales and operations planning
   (S&OP)
demand plan
capacity plan
sales and inventory optimisation
   planning (SIOP)
integrated business planning
   (IBP)
master planner
forecast
master schedule
market research
demand shaping
demand sensing
demand planning
aggregate forecast
Delphi method

forecast 'error'
time series
trend
cycle
seasonality
randomness
smoothed weighted moving
   average
forecast accuracy
mean absolute percentage error
   (MAPE)
back-orders
rough cut capacity planning
   (RCCP)
collaborative planning,
   forecasting and
   replenishment (CPFR)

efficient consumer response
   (ECR)
stock keeping unit (SKU)
software as a service (SaaS)
consignment stock
vendor managed inventory (VMI)
MRP
ERP
dependent demand
advanced planning and
   scheduling (APS)
infinite capacity
theory of constraints (TOC)
economic order quantity (EOQ)
distribution requirements
   planning (DRP)

Introduction

The theme of this chapter is that planning is central to a successful business. Without it, the staff become reactive to events. While this looks good as a 'can do' attitude, running around to put out fires is an ineffective and expensive way to operate. Planning should be based on the 'one plan' approach, which identifies how each planning step is linked and is an integral part of supply chains.

Business planning

The cornerstone of a successful planning and scheduling process is the 'one plan' approach, which emphasises that to be truly effective, an organisation must have only one plan. It is therefore essential that all affected divisions, groups, functions and departments have input to and understand the output decisions of the plan.

The discussion throughout this chapter will follow the structure of the 'one plan' approach, which is illustrated in Figure 11.1.

Business plan

As discussed in Chapter 2, the **business plan** is developed to provide a focal point for thinking about and planning the future of the business. It requires senior executives to understand the context in which they operate and so be able to respond more rationally to the inevitable competitive and economic pressures they experience.

The business plan provides the framework around which the subsequent planning and scheduling processes will function. The core planning process, which takes account of current opportunities, is **sales and operations planning (S&OP)**.

Sales and operations plan

Although S&OP is a management activity, many staff across disciplines are involved in its development and ongoing administration; therefore, knowledge of what it is, how it works and the roles people have in the process is of value.

Sales and operations planning was developed about 30 years ago to overcome the problem inherent in many organisations, where each function plans its own activities with minimal reference to other parts of the business. S&OP is not complex, nor reliant on sophisticated software applications, but has failed in many

Figure 11.1   'One plan' approach

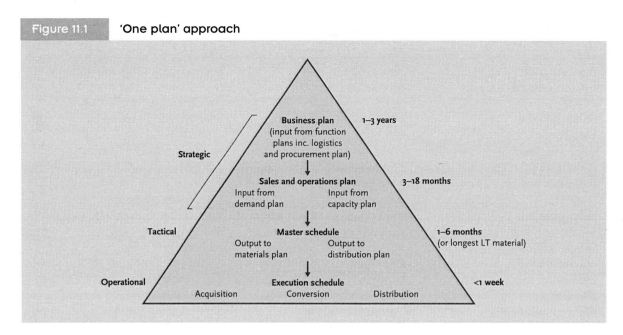

implementations because it relies on the ability of people to work as a team to implement a change in the way the business is managed.

When implemented correctly, and after about six months' experience of the process, it becomes what we call the *hub* of the business. When this happens, the result can be significant; as one CEO said, 'At last I know how the business actually operates—before I was dealing with a queue of executives, all pushing their own points of view'.

Within S&OP, the term 'operations' is used to incorporate logistics, procurement, production planning and technical/engineering—that is, the functions that work to supply products for sales.

While this discussion is concerned with businesses that make products, the principles and process are just as applicable to companies that import product, contract out all their operations or sell services. Logistics professionals will recognise that S&OP and its main elements—the **demand plan** and the **capacity plan**—can be used throughout a supply chain and are as applicable in planning a coal loading terminal or a shipping container park as planning a product business.

In recent times, some consultants and academics have tried to 'improve' S&OP by calling it **sales and inventory optimisation planning (SIOP)** or **integrated business planning (IBP)**. In this book we continue to call it S&OP and focus on the principles.

S&OP in the business

S&OP is a structured planning process, based on a monthly cycle, with the objective to improve the balance between market demands, company resources and the supply of materials and services.

A sequence of steps is followed within each monthly period (preferably a four-week cycle of 13 periods per year) as shown in Figure 11.2.

The S&OP process is owned by the senior manager of the organisation, be it the CEO, general manager, division manager or country manager, and they provide a written S&OP policy document.

The critical elements of the policy are as follows.

- The S&OP meeting dates are established in advance to avoid schedule conflicts.
- A formal agenda for each of the S&OP meetings in the month is circulated by the **master planner** at least two days in advance of each meeting.
- The meetings will last for one hour (one of the S&OP performance measures), although the initial three meetings may take longer. Allow 5–10 minutes for the past period review ('How did we perform against the previous periods S&OP?'); the balance of the time is used to consider the new plan.

Figure 11.2 S&OP process

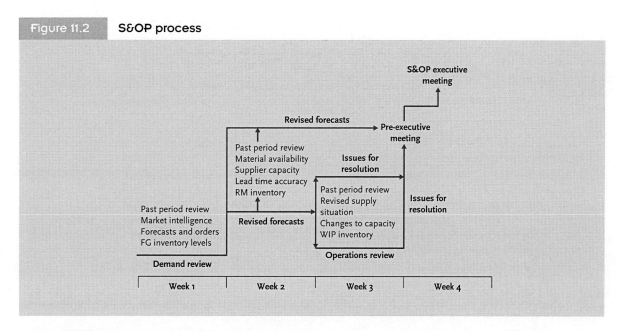

- The S&OP executive meeting is rescheduled if the senior manager is unable to chair the meeting—no substitutes are allowed, as it can become a habit and the process will fail.
- All invited executives will attend the S&OP executive meeting, with no substitutes allowed, except when unavoidable (for example sickness); attendance is part of each executive's performance measurement.
- The master planner (or equivalent title) is the presenter of the plans, trade-offs and issues.

Each review meeting is hosted by supply chain/logistics with the master planner as coordinator. Operations, marketing/sales and finance attend. To be effective, the S&OP process requires factual input from all parts of the business—so accuracy and timeliness of data is very relevant.

To ensure the process does not become focused on individual products (and drowned in data), S&OP operates through 'aggregate families' of products as follows.

- The number of product families varies between 5 and 15 (preferably a range of 6–12).
- Families are based on the capacity and capabilities of manufacturing and distribution resources, as output governs what the business can sell.
- In some circumstances, for example supplying automotive assemblers, families may reflect the major customers, models or brands.
- Families are expressed in a unit of measure that correlates with the constraint resource. The plans are reviewed by product family using the common unit of measure; this provides a consistent communication base across all functions.
- **Forecasts** by product line or group are summarised by market segment/territory and business/division total. The product line/group's forecasts are linked to the S&OP families.
- Production items are summarised within an S&OP family.
- A simulation of capacity requirements should ideally be available to enable the impact of alternative plans to be modelled against constraints in the business.

The S&OP has two parts that are considered at each step throughout the process:

1. A review of recent performance (past period review) against the agreed S&OP, notes the allowed variances:
   a. sales plan variation: variances for S&OP families of more than +/– 5 per cent can cause problems for operations.
   b. operations plan variation: for each S&OP family there are accepted variances established for inventory, order backlog and lead-time.

At the S&OP executive meeting, the organisation's executive team will approve the S&OP; therefore, the organisation as a whole must identify how to rectify any notable variances against the plan. This reduces the 'finger pointing' and recriminations so prevalent in businesses that are planned in isolation.

2. The input of future customer requirements against the most likely internal capacity constraints and capabilities that have been established is considered with respect to corporate objectives.

It is important to recognise that S&OP is not:

* the business plan: S&OP provides structure for planning current opportunities, while the business plan reflects future opportunities
* a budget review: budgets are financially driven, established for a 12-month period at a point in time. S&OP has a different timescale and its figures may well diverge from the budget because it is based on the latest inputs concerning demand and supply
* a monthly or weekly operations meeting: S&OP is a formal process of near-term planning meetings within each month, requiring attendance by all interested parties and driven on behalf of the most senior executive by the master planner of the organisation.

The S&OP provides inputs for the **master schedule**, which in turn is the driver for supplier, production and delivery plans and schedules. In an ideal supply chain, these schedules can be used by suppliers as input to their S&OP process and those suppliers will do the same for their suppliers and so on. If this occurs, uncertainty is reduced, allowing organisations along the supply chains to:

* reduce inventories
* reduce order quantities
* reduce lead times.

Inputs to the S&OP

DEMAND PLAN

The demand plan is one of the inputs to the S&OP. Demand is the measure of what customers and consumers want to buy, while sales represents what they are sold. But sales figures reflect the past, and future demands will not always be similar to historical sales; therefore, a business needs to know:

* what customers and consumers would like to buy
* how to mould buyer perceptions, such that the products people want are represented by what the company has to offer
* how the future plans will meet profitability goals.

To build this knowledge, four marketing techniques are brought together under the heading of demand management. The techniques are:

1. **market research**—this is used to gain an improved understanding of consumer attributes that drive behaviour when buying
2. **demand shaping**—these are incentive programs that are designed to increase customer and consumer demand for the products on offer and so allow the company to meet its financial targets. They include product promotions, price reductions, commercial buyer (or trade) incentives and sales force incentives. New product releases and current product upgrade releases also help to shape demand. However, these techniques present a danger of increasing variation through the supply chains if implemented in an uncoordinated manner
3. **demand sensing**—for consumer products, this is identifying buying trends through using the buying data generated within each sales channel. Whenever possible, this is best obtained from scanned barcode data captured as the product is purchased through the point of sale (POS)
4. **demand planning**—calculate the best estimate of market demand and profitability, taking account of market research, demand shaping and demand sensing data. This also incorporates the organisation's ability to supply the products or services, through encompassing the associated risks

Because there are many sources of uncertainty in supply networks and these sources will change, demand planning connects with the following methodologies to assist in managing the availability and location of products:

- demand forecasting (or sales forecasting)
- supply planning
  a. master schedule, which includes:
    i. prioritising of sales orders and customers by their requirements
    ii. allocation of product to customers based on:
      1. customer priority
      2. region priority
      3. promotion priority
      4. percentage of available inventory
  b. materials requirements planning (MRP)
  c. distribution requirements planning (DRP)
  d. scheduling of production and distribution.

Forecasts

Demand characteristics change over the life cycle of the product, which follows the pattern of introduction, growth, maturity and decline. To limit the decline phase, companies can affect demand through product re-launch, promotions and other events designed to stimulate market demand; features are also added to extend the product's life. These actions are most common in the food and beverage, apparel, cosmetics, consumer electronics and automotive sectors.

However, these activities can introduce additional variability in the demand, which increases uncertainty within the supply chains, as shown in Figure 11.3.

Forecasts of future demand (how much customers and consumers would like to buy) and sales (how much the company will be able to sell) are fraught with uncertainties, but must be calculated to ensure the business is less wrong than if it did nothing.

Based on experience of working with sales forecasts, some points to note are:

1. Forecasts of sales are for what is called 'independent demand' items. That is, demand for one item has relatively little effect on the demand for another; they are independent.
2. Forecasts should not be developed in isolation—they are one of the elements within demand management, which, in turn, is an input that supports decision making within the S&OP.
3. Forecasts are about the future and therefore provide answers that will not be correct—calculate the forecast 'error' to understand the actions that must be taken to minimise the effect of being 'wrong'.
4. The further out the forecast horizon is, the less accurate the forecast. To reduce the volume of calculations and improve accuracy, forecast in increasing periods of time, from weeks in the near future, to months and then quarters.
5. There are two approaches to forecasting:

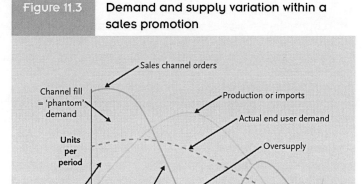

Figure 11.3 **Demand and supply variation within a sales promotion**

a. The **aggregate forecast** is a top-down approach by which the sales department develops national, State or province sales by **stock keeping unit (SKU)** and then planners use quantitative methods to break down the aggregate quantity to a forecast of SKU by location. The aggregate forecast relies on sales managers and planners understanding the value for the business of 'accurate' forecasts.

b. The use of IT application algorithms is a bottom-up approach that forecasts each SKU by location, then totals the forecast by SKU for each State or province and then consolidates to the national sales. This requires the purchase of forecasting software, having trained planners and the management of large quantities of data.

Forecasting aims for accuracy; whatever methodology is used it should involve an interdisciplinary team from sales, marketing and supply chain/logistics, working as a panel of experts, and using a formal approach to arrive at a consensus of opinion. This approach is called the **Delphi method**.

To achieve improved accuracy of forecasts, the sales analyst must interpret risks to the company's supply chains from **forecast 'error'** and other uncertainties that can affect product life cycles, such as:

- relationships with customers
- impacts of competitor actions
- changes in technology
- changes in regulations.

The analyst therefore needs to spend as much time analysing the forecast as they do in initially establishing the forecast.

When developing the period forecasts, it is assumed that features of historical patterns will continue into the future. The historical data for a period of time (a data set) is called a **time series**. A time series will enable four measures of the data set—**trend**, **cycle**, **seasonality** and **randomness**—that provide the base information to enable forecasts about the future.

The most common forecasting models involve various forms of weighted and smoothing methods that minimise the influence of older data and short-term variations in the data. Experience has shown that the most common forecasting approach is applying the **smoothed weighted moving average** to the data.

Complexity associated with developing the forecast means that having one sales number per month attached to a product or item is too simplistic; for example sales of product 'x' for June is forecast at 1000 units, but it is unlikely that the actual sales will reflect this. Future sales should therefore be shown as a range, identifying both optimistic and pessimistic forecasts, with probabilities that reflect the likelihood of them occurring.

Forecast based on ranges can help the operations side, because it means that supplies of long lead time items can be purchased at the optimistic forecast level, while easy to obtain items can be purchased at the pessimistic forecast level, but with provisional orders in place to increase purchases at short notice.

Specialist computer applications are used for forecasting by companies that supply many SKU into retailers, businesses in seasonal fashion sectors and organisations with the need to manage high volumes of service parts, such as mining companies and the defence force.

Companies without the need for dedicated applications can use the forecasting capability built into ERP systems, which may be supported by internally developed spreadsheets. At the basic level, forecasting methods are provided within Microsoft Excel.

Accuracy of demand

The biggest challenge for a demand planner is minimising the inaccuracy of a forecast. If demand is underestimated, potential sales revenue may be lost; or sales can only be maintained through expediting products or materials and incurring higher costs in logistics activities.

However, if the demand is overestimated, the company has additional inventory that will take time to reduce and therefore incur holding costs. In both situations, the company has not allocated its resources effectively, which affects the profitability of the business.

Forecast accuracy is measured by each inventory category/class that was discussed in Chapter 10. The forecast error is the statistical term used to measure the difference between the actual and the forecast. A common measure of the 'error' is the **mean absolute percentage error (MAPE)**. Logisticians define the MAPE as the difference between forecast and actual sales divided by actual sales.

Table 11.1 illustrates the MAPE calculation for 10 products in the STEADY group for one period.

Given that forecasts consider the future, what accuracy should be expected from the forecasts? A MAPE of 10–15 per cent for the STEADY group of SKU can be considered good, while the range of 20–30 per cent is not unusual in other inventory groups. The objective is to reduce the MAPE (become more accurate) through investment in training and systems.

While MAPE provides an indication of the forecast accuracy for all SKU in a category/ class, the tracking signal is calculated for individual SKU, as discussed in Chapter 10.

Measuring the accuracy of forecasts is critical, as forecasts and the subsequent demand plan have a direct impact on the effectiveness of supply chains. As all supply chain measures are interrelated, this raises the question of where responsibility for the forecasts will reside. Companies need to resolve this question, based on the requirements of the business and the balance between quantitative forecasts and collaborative approaches in forecasting. Organisation structures and responsibilities are discussed in Chapter 16.

Table 11.1   MAPE calculation

Products	Forecast	Actual sales	Variance ('error') Show positive only	Percentage 'error'
1	100	120	20	16.7
2	100	87	13	14.9
3	100	112	12	10.7
4	100	94	6	6.4
5	100	117	17	14.5
6	100	120	20	16.7
7	100	82	18	21.9
8	100	117	17	14.5
9	100	91	9	9.9
10	100	110	10	9.1
Total	1000	1050		135.3/10
MAPE				13.5%

Capacity planning

Capacity can be difficult to quantify. For example, consider a family-owned business, making and selling branded consumer goods; it has a policy that purchased capital equipment will have a life of about five years—approximately reflecting an economic cycle. To gain a lower cost of ownership, the company makes its capital purchases in periods of economic slowdown, to negotiate a lower buy price. To gain a further discount of between 8 and 13 per cent, equipment is purchased without a manufacturer's warranty—the machines will always be set to run faster than the manufacturer's recommended speed, therefore invalidating any warranty. How will capacity be calculated?

There are nine ways to measure capacity and each is valid; this is shown in Figure 11.4.

In the example of the family-owned business, we could identify the standing, rated, productive, demonstrated and budgeted capacity for the same piece of equipment. So, the first thing to do when discussing capacity is to define which measure of capacity is being used.

Capacity is under constant change, due to events such as product-mix changes, improvement to processes and equipment, labour skills and transport mode availability. Therefore, to enable the correct balancing of demand and supply in the S&OP process, planners need to evaluate the capacity plan with the same regularity as the demand plan.

Is the capacity of an enterprise finite (fixed)? Of course, this will depend on the nature of the business. Enterprises using large and inflexible equipment, such as a steel mill, or requiring difficult to employ skills, will have a constrained capacity and will find it difficult to increase output above a given level. The option of contracting out the work is often not practical, due to the requirement for specific equipment or skills.

When more generic equipment and skills are used, more variation in capacity is available through acquiring additional

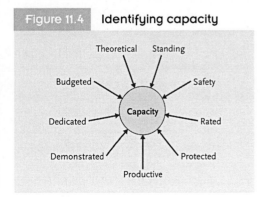

Figure 11.4   Identifying capacity

equipment, working short-term overtime, recruiting staff (or contracting through a labour-hire company) and contracting out the work.

The flexibility of the operation is therefore based on the lead time to change (or flex) the operation and the total cost to change. Automotive assembly lines may have a flex time of up to six months, with a substantial cost to change their output of cars per day.

As the load on a facility increases, the options available to accommodate new customer orders are reduced. To overcome the pressure, planners may increase the lead time and/or split orders and batches to try and get some of the orders through the facility. But increasing lead times can be dangerous and splitting orders requires more downtime in equipment changeovers, so capacity is reduced.

In a buoyant market, the lead time effect can drag an enterprise into a cycle of missed delivery dates, as shown in Figure 11.5.

If delivery dates are missed and planners increase the lead time, **back-orders** will increase, because customers will order more to cover for the increased lead time. As this situation gets worse, through a continual increase in lead time and back-orders, the directors of the company may well authorise construction of a new facility.

When the new facility commences operations, the capacity has increased and the lead time has been reduced. Therefore, customers have no need to place an order and so the lead time progressively falls to the original level and the new facility is closed—real demand has not changed!

This situation is not hypothetical; it has occurred on more than one occasion, with severe effects on the affected businesses and their people.

| Figure 11.5 | Effect of increasing the lead time |

Delivery date missed

Each step makes the situation worse

Increase planned lead time

Orders released earlier

Production input increased

Load on work centres increased

A cycle of missed delivery dates

Queue time increased

Actual lead time increased

Missed delivery date

Management of lead times is another of the important elements in the planning of supply chains. When considering capacity, be aware of operational problems, such as:

- unreliability of equipment
- continuing quality problems
- ongoing skills shortages
- lack of training and therefore flexibility of staff and
- inconsistencies with outputs from the computer-based planning and scheduling system.

In ERP systems, there is usually a module called **rough cut capacity planning (RCCP)**. As the term suggests, the application is not designed to consider detailed capacity planning; it is the base from which to consider the capacity available within the planning periods, equal to the longest lead time of purchased items. It is typically linked to the master planning module, but can be modified to also reflect the needs of S&OP.

Review of S&OP

From this discussion has developed an understanding that capacity, lead times and capacity constraints in an organisation and its supply chains are interrelated and vital to the successful functioning of the business.

The first section of the chapter has introduced sales and operations planning. The main points to note are:

- The 'one plan' diagram in Figure 11.1 is the guide through the planning and scheduling process.
- The business plan and logistics plan are discussed in Chapter 2.
- The sales and operations plan is the *hub* of the business—the senior management group must sign off to signal there is 'one plan' that all are expected to achieve.

- S&OP is a process that must be built into the business culture to be successful and followed every period.
- Be clear about what S&OP is not.

The second sections has discussed the inputs to the S&OP, with the main points being as follows.

- There are four elements of demand management.
- Forecasts are always wrong—the objective is to reduce the forecast 'error'.
- For improved accuracy, generate forecasts as an expert group.
- Recognise the nine measures of capacity and know what is being used as the measure.
- Consider the challenges in providing accurate lead times.

Master planning

If the S&OP is the *hub* of the organisation, then the master plan/schedule is the *heart*, because its role is to manage individual SKUs through the veins of the company's processes.

Each month, the **master schedule** takes the agreed S&OP plan as its primary input. The aim is that the aggregate planned outputs are used to balance the order requirements from sales and customers, together with some level of stability for importing, manufacturing and distribution. Planned safety inventory is used to compensate for the occasions when actual demand exceeds the capability to produce or supply imports.

To assist with having a stable master schedule, companies can divide the planning horizon into 'freedom to change' steps—the closer to the present time, the more restrictive are the rules concerning schedule changes.

An 'unstable' master schedule exists when there is inadequate safety stock and the company is changing short-term schedules to provide customer orders, which is very expensive. This can be a sign of an inadequate forecasting system and a failure to measure and act on the forecast error.

The master schedule is a key link in the organisation's supply chains, interfacing with applications in sales, distribution planning, production planning and capacity planning. It is the input for the **materials requirements planning (MRP)** module of the **enterprise resources planning (ERP)** system in a manufacturing or assembly operation.

A product-based organisation can be structured to address broad market segments of engineer to order (ETO), make to order (MTO), assemble to order (ATO) and make to stock (MTS), as discussed in Chapter 1. Each requires a different approach to structuring the bills of material (BOM), used for calculating the **dependent demand** items that need to be made or purchased.

For companies that operate an ATO repetitive flow (or just in time) system, the S&OP and master schedule processes also remain fundamental to the success of the business. It is only after the master planning stage that planning and scheduling processes differ from those in other operational structures.

Some of the decisions made at the master planning level concerning short-term operational challenges for individual SKUs are shown in Figure 11.6.

Output from the master planning process must provide the customer service department with information concerning availability and lead times, based on the following criteria:

| Figure 11.6 | Master planning decisions |

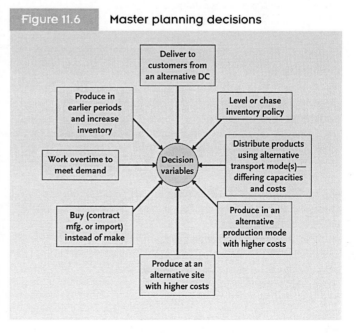

- available in stock (AIS)
  - o the item is available for delivery within a defined geographic area
- available to promise (ATP)
  - o the item is scheduled within the current production or import plan
- capable to promise (CTP)
  - o the product can be planned if there is sufficient demand
  - o product, components or materials are available within a defined lead time.
  - o there is available production or storage capacity and capability
- capable to deliver (CTD)
  - o the following are available and acceptable for planning a product, if required
    - – transport mode and schedules
    - – transport lead time and variability
    - – transport nodes capacity and schedules.

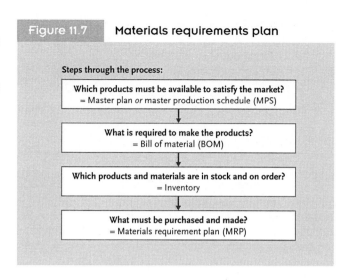

Figure 11.7   Materials requirements plan

Steps through the process:

> **Which products must be available to satisfy the market?**
> = Master plan *or* master production schedule (MPS)

> **What is required to make the products?**
> = Bill of material (BOM)

> **Which products and materials are in stock and on order?**
> = Inventory

> **What must be purchased and made?**
> = Materials requirement plan (MRP)

Materials plans

The master plan/schedule provides input to the materials requirements plan (MRP), which establishes plans for availability of customer orders, production work orders and materials acquisition requirements from suppliers (that is, the call-up against purchasing contracts).

The questions to be answered in the planning sequence are shown in Figure 11.7. While the questions are relatively simple, the complexity is in the high number of iterations required; this is why MRP is built into ERP systems.

A fundamental weakness of the standard MRP process is that only ERP systems which contain **advanced planning and scheduling (APS)** modules are able to plan material and capacity requirements concurrently. In other situations, only when materials requirements have been planned can the required (and detailed) capacity resources be evaluated.

The basic software application presumes there is **infinite capacity** available; therefore, if the plan indicates that capacity is required in excess of the nominated amount available, the plan must cycle back for the MRP to re-plan materials. But there is typically insufficient time and people for this to occur.

Constraints

To overcome this planning 'loop', the use of an element in the **theory of constraints (TOC)** is valid. The theory states that operations (a supply chain, a distribution sequence or a production line) are governed by the constraint in the system.

To assist in making the system more effective and reducing variability, the constraint in the system is identified and schedules developed that are based on its capability, as illustrated in Figure 11.8.

The constraint (in this case it is a production work station that has the lowest output) is called the capacity constrained resource (CCR) or the drum and its beat dictates the throughput; therefore it must be utilised to the maximum.

The release of materials or orders to all parts of the operation (the rope) should be at the same rate as for the drum, because that is all the system can use. To ensure that the drum is protected and does not lose any time

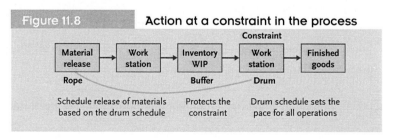

Figure 11.8   Action at a constraint in the process

| Material release | → | Work station | → | Inventory WIP | → | Work station | → | Finished goods |

Constraint (above Work station, second one)

Rope — Buffer — Drum

Schedule release of materials based on the drum schedule | Protects the constraint | Drum schedule sets the pace for all operations (which cannot be recovered because it is fully utilised), a buffer of inventory or orders is kept behind the drum. Goldratt & Fox (1986) refer to this as the drum-buffer-rope (DBR) sequence.

Advanced planning and scheduling (APS) modules of enterprise resource planning (ERP) systems may include the TOC concept; however, within the basic MRP process the records and knowledge in an organisation can identify the constraint and its maximum throughput. The required MRP output can be evaluated against the known constraint in the system. If there is sufficient capacity for the planned throughput, then the MRP suggested work can be accepted, because there will be sufficient capacity in the remaining steps through the process.

To further understand the theory of constraints, read *The Goal* by Goldratt and Cox. Written as a novel, it is one of the most enlightening and enjoyable books concerning business management.

To help ensure the plan is achieved, the structure of the flow should be that more capacity is available closer to the customer. Therefore, in a production flow situation, the finishing and packing operation should have additional safety capacity, to allow the output of multiple SKU and time for product changeovers. This means that selected equipment will be idle at planned occasions (under-utilised), which is difficult for accountants to accept and is discussed in Chapter 13.

How much to order?

In an organisation where the management of logistics operations has a high visibility, the lot size for items needs to be dynamic, being automatically re-calculated each time the item is required, on criteria other than just cost. The main criteria in calculating the lot size is the capacity at the bottleneck operation in the system. Here, the cost of an hour of downtime is equal to the net value of throughput for the hour over the total facility. For all non-bottleneck operations, the cost of any downtime is zero, as these resources have excess capacity.

The traditional approach, is to calculate the 'economic' lot size, which means that trade-offs are calculated between production and procurement costs and the cost of holding inventory to the cost of a stock-out. This is the **economic order quantity (EOQ)**, which attempts to minimise the total preparation (the ordering and set-up) costs and the inventory holding costs.

The EOQ concept was initially discussed in an article written in 1913 by Ford Whitman Harris in the American magazine *Factory: the magazine of management*. He noted that the calculation was based on a number of assumptions, the validity of which can be challenged. They are:

* The rate of demand for the item remains constant.
* The order lead time for the items is fixed.
* The cost to order the item remains constant.
* The purchase price of the item remains constant.
* The delivery of the total order is made at one time.

Many academic articles have been written to promote and extend the EOQ formula as the main approach to calculating lot sizes; however, the underlying assumptions in EOQ may well limit its use to budget planning and calculating the lot sizes of indirect items.

Distribution planning

Companies may have a complex distribution network of central, branch and satellite warehouses. For example, products move from a central distribution point to State- or province-based warehouses (owned or distributors') to area distributors and then to retailers. To manage this network and provide the expected level of customer service, the product brand company must have knowledge concerning the availability of items through the final distribution part of a product's supply chain.

Distribution requirements planning (DRP) can be a computer application, or module within an ERP system, that plans the cumulative replenishment requirements within a distribution network. To meet projected inventory 'out of stock' situations, it calculates expected inventory levels over time periods and generates warehouse transfers (or purchase orders) with the appropriate time offsets that account for the distribution lead time.

Linked to the DRP can be a transport allocation module which collates information about contracted transport service providers' capabilities, by geographical region. This will identify the maximum and minimum transport capacity available before it becomes necessary to hire transport at short-term spot rates.

If the DRP application is required and implemented, it can be an important input for the system, because it defines the cumulative requirements for finished goods over defined time periods, which become inputs to the master plan/schedule. This is shown in Figure 11.9.

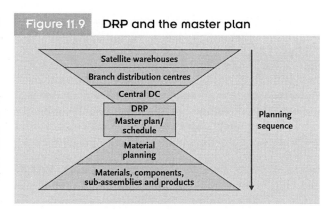

Figure 11.9   DRP and the master plan

Collaborative approach with customers and suppliers

Communication with customers is vital. They cannot all have delivery on the same date, so who has the priority and why? The outputs from S&OP can be used to help improve external collaboration between the supplier and customer, which addresses the perceived unpredictability and complaints of inaccuracy.

Collaborative planning, forecasting and replenishment (CPFR)

The technique of **CPFR** commenced in the early 1990s with a large and powerful supplier (Procter & Gamble) and a large and powerful retailer (Wal-Mart) in America recognising that variable ordering patterns, high inventories and low customer service were expensive for both companies. They commenced development of a process for joint demand forecasting, coordinated distribution of goods to the retailer's warehouses and shared information concerning meeting the plan. This was the beginning of **efficient consumer response (ECR)**.

The four elements of ECR are:

- efficient assortment—rationalise the SKUs on offer to improve the performance of supply chains but still meet consumer requirements
- efficient replenishment—ensure that processes are efficient to minimise replenishment costs
- efficient product introduction—introduce new consumer products only after the impact on supply chains has been analysed
- efficient promotions—evaluate the impact of retail promotions on the supply chains prior to the event.

The CPFR concept was developed from the core elements of ECR to include:

- a formalised process for sales and order forecasting
- a formalised process for handling exceptions in the forecasting process
- systems to transfer point of sale (POS) data from the retailer to suppliers
- structured feedback systems to report on the process and improvements.

CPFR has been adopted by some retailers and suppliers, mainly in America and Western Europe, with a few examples in the Asia–Pacific region. However, the principles are applicable across many customer/supplier interfaces and therefore should be considered without the influence of retail.

The CPFR process is divided into seven stages, as shown in Figure 11.10 opposite.

When establishing a CPFR agreement with a major retailer, or other type of customer, there could be a situation of multiple SKU/location data collection points. When this occurs, the volume of data means that planners from both parties are unable to manually compare forecasts and order plans to identify the exceptions. They will therefore rely on computer applications to compare the figures of each company, based on parameters established in the collaboration plan. This recognises that using different algorithms for forecasting and planning within each company will mean there is unlikely to be an exact match, so an acceptable margin of difference is allowed.

The advent of hosted internet-based services (called **software-as-a-service** or **SaaS**) means that the CPFR plan can be managed by the two parties over the internet on a per transaction cost basis, without a high initial investment in computer applications. CPFR, like other planning approaches, is for companies with management that understand the principles and believe in the process. A half-hearted and undisciplined implementation will lead to failure, recriminations and possible dismissal of the innocents!

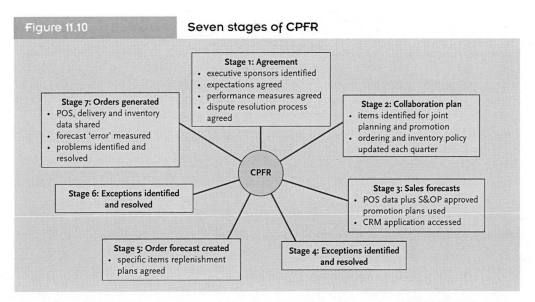

Figure 11.10 — Seven stages of CPFR

Stage 1: Agreement
- executive sponsors identified
- expectations agreed
- performance measures agreed
- dispute resolution process agreed

Stage 2: Collaboration plan
- items identified for joint planning and promotion
- ordering and inventory policy updated each quarter

Stage 3: Sales forecasts
- POS data plus S&OP approved promotion plans used
- CRM application accessed

Stage 4: Exceptions identified and resolved

Stage 5: Order forecast created
- specific items replenishment plans agreed

Stage 6: Exceptions identified and resolved

Stage 7: Orders generated
- POS, delivery and inventory data shared
- forecast 'error' measured
- problems identified and resolved

CPFR

Source: Adapted from Andraski, J. & Haedick, J., 'CPFR: Time for the Breakthrough', *Supply Chain Management Review*, May–June 2003 (www.scmr.com).

Consignment stock and vendor managed inventory (VMI)

This is another approach to reducing uncertainty in the forecasting process through the parties working together. The supplier agrees to place an amount of inventory of selected SKU at the customer's premises, with usage or sales recorded as they occur and typically reconciled at the end of each month. Payment is made based on the amount actually used or sold.

The concept began in manufacturing, where it is called **consignment stock**, and was later introduced into retailing under the term **vendor managed inventory (VMI)**.

The advantage from the customer's point of view is that inventory they do not own is available for use. From the supplier's point of view, the advantage is that they have 'locked in' the customer to at least purchasing the amount held on consignment, hopefully at an additional margin, which represents the cost of holding the additional inventory on the balance sheet.

The disadvantage of this approach is that the customer must provide the storage or shelf space for the products; they may be paying a higher price for the certainty of having stock available; and they are 'locked in' to the supplier for a period of time until the product is used or sold.

Collaboration, like 'partnerships', is considered a 'good thing', but remember that companies do things for their reasons, not yours. Collaboration is a term used for improved processes; therefore, it should be based on data and information supplied and analysed by both parties, recognising the costs and benefits of the outcomes.

Chapter review

The hidden strength of supply chains and logistics is not just the capability to move and store product and materials, but the ability to plan and schedule the movements and storage. The main planning activities of a product-based business, with reference to its supply chains, are summarised in Figure 11.11.

Figure 11.11 — Supply chain and logistics planning activities

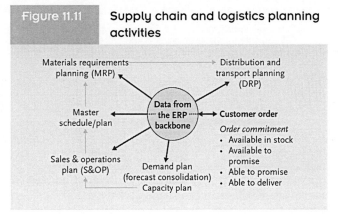

Materials requirements planning (MRP)

Distribution and transport planning (DRP)

Master schedule/plan

Data from the ERP backbone

Customer order

Order commitment
- Available in stock
- Available to promise
- Able to promise
- Able to deliver

Sales & operations plan (S&OP)

Demand plan (forecast consolidation)

Capacity plan

Logistics is therefore a 'thinking' discipline as much as a physical requirement. This requires logistics professionals to have a blend of analytical and line management skills that enables them both to understand the planning process and to execute the agreed plans.

An example is the master planner, a person who is the main planning link between all elements of the business. The role of master planner includes the following responsibilities:

- facilitate the S&OP process, including demand and capacity planning
- evaluate the impact of new product introductions and run-out plans for products
- provide the lead time criteria for incoming orders and match actual requirements with the master schedule
- evaluate the business impact of material and production delays
- be the 'font of knowledge' for all the difficult questions about how the business is actually progressing.

Whatever the title for the role, it should be viewed as a stepping stone to logistics manager and supply chain director positions.

Chapter questions

Operational

1. What are the likely effects on logistics operations at a brand company's distribution service provider (3PL) from the implementation of a 'one-plan' approach within the brand company? Identify the effects at each stage of the storage and delivery process.
2. Why should logistics operations support the S&OP process?
3. Forecast accuracy is important for a business—why?
4. Figure 11.4 shows nine measures of capacity. What would be the most likely capacity measures used for a finished goods distribution warehouse? Discuss why.
5. Flexibility of an operation relates to the time taken to change capacity. Identify the factors to consider for changing the capacity of a general warehouse and an automated storage and retrieval system (AS/RS) DC.

Planning

6. The 'one plan' approach requires a good planning team. What responsibilities may a master planner have in addition to those identified at the end of the chapter?
7. Output for customer service from the master planning process addresses AIS, ATP, CTP and CTD. How will customer service use each of the information sets when dealing with customers?
8. Consider any process and identify the constraint. What action would you take to reduce the delay effect of the constraint?

Management

9. Establish an implementation plan and timeline for introducing the S&OP concept into any type of business.
10. What actions would you take to ensure the S&OP process did not become a budget review or an operations meeting?
11. As an account manager within an LSP, how would you seek to influence a client to implement S&OP at their business? Would you seek to be a part of the monthly S&OP executive meeting? Why or why not?
12. The demand plan identifies four marketing techniques. Should the demand plan be solely the responsibility of marketing? Justify why or why not.
13. A collaborative approach can provide benefits for the businesses in the relationship. Identify the type of costs that may be incurred to implement a collaborative approach.

Exercise 1

A company sells its consumer products through retail outlets. At a particular retailer it regularly sells 1000 cases per order. The retailer's buy price is $10 per case and the retail sale price is the equivalent of $20 per case, providing a gross margin of 100 per cent to the retailer.

To assist an increase in sales, the supplier makes a special promotion offer to the retailer. If they buy 10 000 cases, the buy price will be $8 per case. With a 'special' retail sale price of $18 per case, the retailer's gross margin will be increased to 120% and sales will increase.

This is good for the consumer, because the product price will be less. The sales representative will gain, because they will have achieved their sales quota and may receive a high sales commission. The buyer at the retailer will be pleased because they have gained an additional 20 per cent in gross margin. This process is called investment buying and it appears that all parties will gain. However, it also includes the additional supply chain costs, as follows.

Logistics costs
- overtime
- express freight on 'rush' supplies
- hiring of additional short-term staff
- costs of holding inventory to account for the increased production order
- use of short-term storage and double handling costs within the warehouse.

Administration costs
- entering and tracking of changing prices
- order entry detail changes
- higher incidence of disputed invoices—what were sale items as opposed to regular items.

1. What steps should be taken to minimise the supply chain costs for promotions?
2. The measurement of success has been based on the gross margin. What can be the effect on net profit?

Exercise 2

A CPG company decided to expand the business into a new segment of the market and therefore has developed a new product range. As a new segment, there is not a forecast of sales based on a known history.

New production equipment was purchased, packaging designed, materials developed and purchased and a promotion campaign developed. Everyone was excited about the prospects for the new product until time for the meeting to plan production and distribution (S&OP was not established in this company).

The sales forecasts developed by marketing were impressive, but a point of concern arose at the planning meeting—to sell the forecast would require *every* person (man, woman and child) in the country to consume one of the new products every week!

The forecaster had accepted multiple inputs from knowledgeable people and obtained market research information about the likely acceptance of the product, but was so immersed in figures and trend lines that the basic 'reality check' question was not asked—until it was too late.

a. If you were responsible for expanding a business into a new segment of the market, how would you ensure that reality ruled?
b. What are the key risks associated with such an expansion into a new business sector?
c. How can planning and scheduling skills help in management these risks?
d. What are the key considerations from a planning point of view at a time when an organisation is launching into a new market segment? How are these different to those of marketing, production or logistics operations?
e. What forecasting tools would you use to assist in the scenario detailed in this exercise?

References and links

The American Institute of Business Forecasting and Planning provides information and online education in aspects of forecasting and S&OP: www.ibf.org

A useful resource concerned with forecasting accuracy and safety stock planning: www.demandplanning.net

APICS provides information on all aspects of resource planning and interested professionals can study for the internationally recognised CPIM qualification: www.apics.org

Collaborative Planning, Forecasting and Replenishment (CPFR) in America: www.cpfr.org

Andraski, J. & Haedicke, J., 'CPFR: Time for the Breakthrough', *Supply Chain Management Review*, May–June 2003.

Goldratt, E. & Cox, J., *The Goal*, North River Press, New York, 1984.

Goldratt, E.M. & Fox, R.E., *The Race*, North River Press, New York, 1986.

Whitman Harris,F., *Factory: the Magazine of Management*, 1913.

12

Procurement

Learning outcomes

On completion of this chapter you will be able to:

- comprehend the range of responsibilities and activities that comprise procurement and the roles of procurement professionals

- understand the sequence of stages through procurement and the important steps within each stage

- recognise the various software applications that are available within procurement and the challenges posed by their implementation.

Links to other chapters

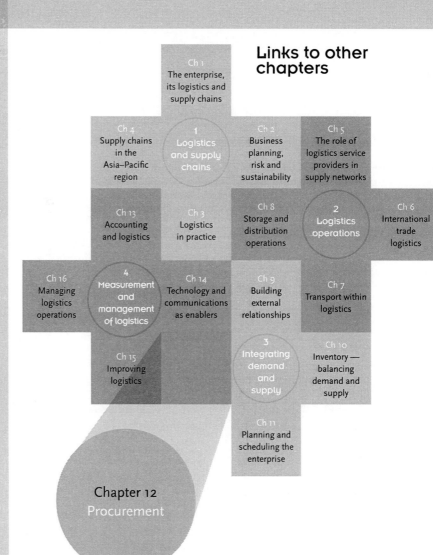

Ch 1
The enterprise, its logistics and supply chains

Ch 4
Supply chains in the Asia–Pacific region

1
Logistics and supply chains

Ch 2
Business planning, risk and sustainability

Ch 5
The role of logistics service providers in supply networks

Ch 13
Accounting and logistics

Ch 3
Logistics in practice

Ch 8
Storage and distribution operations

2
Logistics operations

Ch 6
International trade logistics

Ch 16
Managing logistics operations

4
Measurement and management of logistics

Ch 14
Technology and communications as enablers

Ch 9
Building external relationships

Ch 7
Transport within logistics

Ch 15
Improving logistics

3
Integrating demand and supply

Ch 10
Inventory — balancing demand and supply

Ch 11
Planning and scheduling the enterprise

Chapter 12
Procurement

Key terms

These terms are used in the text. Develop your own notebook by downloading information on each term.

procurement	supply risk	PEST analysis
supply	monopoly	Porter 5-force analysis
purchasing	cartel	supplier capability
acquisition	make vs buy	supplier research
supply market	spend analysis	supplier visits
sourcing	category management	request for information (RFI)
contracts management	product life cycle	request for price (RFP)
whole of life	sourcing plan	request for quotation (RFQ)
offshoring	procurement risk	statement of work (SOW)
public–private partnership (PPP)	vendor managed inventory (VMI)	supply market analysis
transfer pricing	early supplier involvement (ESI)	
maverick spend		

Introduction

We all buy things and services, from insurance to mobile phone agreements, and are therefore often engaged in making decisions that result in a purchase. The essence of our personal purchasing decision lies in the evaluation of value against price and conditions (delivery and warranties). But does this knowledge prove to be sufficient for the professional, who buys for business, government or for other organisations?

This chapter considers the fundamentals of procurement, which can be applied across all organisations; however, the emphasis will be placed on enterprises that operate within product supply chains, where procurement is a fundamental part of the business.

Procurement in the organisation

Like many areas within the context of supply chains, a number of terms are often used interchangeably when discussing this area, causing some confusion about meanings. In the context of a relationship between a buyer and seller, the most common terms used to describe the total process are:

- procurement
- supply
- purchasing
- acquisition.

Each of the terms is valid and we should not become too emotional about which is correct. In the UK, and in many Commonwealth countries, the professional body is the Chartered Institute of Purchasing and Supply (CIPS). In the USA, the leading association is the Institute for Supply Management (ISM). Cousins et al. (2008) describes purchasing—the most common term used in Europe—as dealing with the daily buying activities of an organisation. Acquisition is a term used by the military that covers all aspects of acquiring weapons systems and supplies. In the civilian context, acquisition is used to signify the calling up of items against an agreed contract with a supplier.

Procurement is the term used in this book, as it is the term most commonly employed in the Asia–Pacific region. A standard definition is not available, but Professor Guy Callender, Professor of Strategic Procurement at Curtin University in Western Australia, considers that procurement themes include:

- **supply market** and **sourcing** intelligence
- risk management
- knowledge management
- management of relationships with suppliers and internal customers
- alignment of corporate and procurement strategy
- 'whole-of-life' contract planning, including development and management of goods and services contracts

* financing supply chains; cash flow and working capital requirements of supply chains and through the buying cycle
* development and implementation of procurement innovations
* advising and managing outsourcing and **offshoring** decisions (including **public–private partnerships (PPP)** by governments)
* supplier development.

What is bought?

In the past, purchasing was associated with buying physical items for production or operations. As organisations have sought to bring their total expenditure under control, the range has broadened to include such items as:

* indirect materials (materials that do not go into products)
  o sales promotion and advertising
  o office furniture and fittings
  o travel and accommodation
* services
  o professional services: consulting, auditing, legal, insurance and consulting
  o labour and equipment hiring services
  o operating services: catering, telecommunications, printing, security, IT services
  o facilities management: cleaning, utilities, maintenance
  o logistics service providers (LSP), freight forwarding and distribution being the most common.

Ideally, no area of external spending should be excluded from procurement oversight; however, the number of organisations which include all the above categories within a formal procurement oversight remains low.

Factors affecting procurement

As global trade has increased, so procurement has become a core part of some organisations, while gaining visibility in others. The factors causing this situation are:

* increasing percentage of corporate income spent with suppliers
* outsourcing of major functions
* mix between materials/services and labour costs continues to move in favour of materials/services
* increased expenditure on non-production costs such as marketing, sales, promotion, IT and after-sales service
* buying packages of items (products plus services) from suppliers, which are more complex purchases than individual items
* global sourcing, with cross-border challenges of:
  o duties and tariffs
  o local content rules
  o **transfer pricing** between divisions/subsidiaries of a business
  o taxation rules
  o economic changes and natural disasters in supplying countries
  o apparent attractiveness of sourcing from low cost countries (LCC)
* longer-term contracts that must be managed
* increasing length and complexity of supply chains
  o time to market pressures, with decreases in the planning time allowed
  o inbound inventory location decisions.

An objective of procurement should be that more than 80 per cent of the total external spend of the organisation is within the procurement system, although not necessarily performed by the procurement function. Money that is spent outside the organisation's oversight is called 'maverick' or 'rogue' spend. An ongoing task is to limit **maverick spending** through education of employees and controls at the system level to disallow non-compliant spending.

As procurement is a cross-organisation function, procurement teams for product groups should include members representing other business functions, with procurement providing the leadership role.

In the past 20 years, there have been multiple articles and conference presentations concerning 'partnerships' between buyers and sellers; however, few use the dictionary definition, which is 'a sharing of risk and reward'. While there must be examples of this sharing actually occurring, the authors have asked more than 1000 post-graduate students over recent years to provide substantiated examples that meet the definition and only one has been forthcoming.

Suppliers are typically independent of the buying organisation and exist for their own reasons. Therefore, procurement professionals must understand what the success factors of suppliers are and negotiate a business relationship which best suits the interests of both parties.

The terms 'supplier' and 'vendor' are used interchangeably to describe the organisation with which the buyer is conducting business, but 'supplier' is preferred as it means 'provider of what is needed'.

Procurement professionals

The responsibilities identified by this role require professionals of high calibre. A survey titled *Procurement Strategies*, conducted by Aberdeen Research (2009), questioned 220 chief procurement officers (CPO), or similar titled executives, concerning the capabilities they required of staff undertaking major procurement activities. Over two-thirds of respondents stated they needed a skill set comprised of the following attributes.

1. The fundamentals of sourcing, including:
   a. investigation and analysis of products and services within supply categories
   b. ability to undertake research of the supply market for different products and services
   c. knowledge of the inputs required for **supply risk** analysis
   d. knowledge of financial and business analysis processes
   e. understanding of marketing and sales principles
2. Purchasing process skills, including development of negotiation plans and understanding of the sales process and tactics, including negotiating and working with **monopolies** and **cartels**
3. Contract management fundamentals, including comprehension of the legal framework and development of balanced contracts
4. Knowledge of six sigma, lean and other improvement techniques, together with the ability to understand the motivation for suppliers' improvement activities
5. Collaborative leadership expertise with larger and broader groups of stakeholders, which requires a wide set of business and personal skills.

Procurement sequence

There are four stages to the procurement process, as depicted in Figure 12.1.

Within each of the responsibilities, there a number of activities; these will be discussed in this chapter.

Participate in the business strategy review

An outcome from the business strategy review (see Chapter 2) is the identification of business needs, in part concerning the capability to be supplied from external sources. Hence, it is important that procurement participates in the business strategy review to gain an 'early warning' of how it can contribute to achieving the business strategy.

Defining business needs is a critical task in the procurement process; for example, determining whether to employ staff or hire contractors; or perform

Figure 12.1   **Procurement responsibilities**

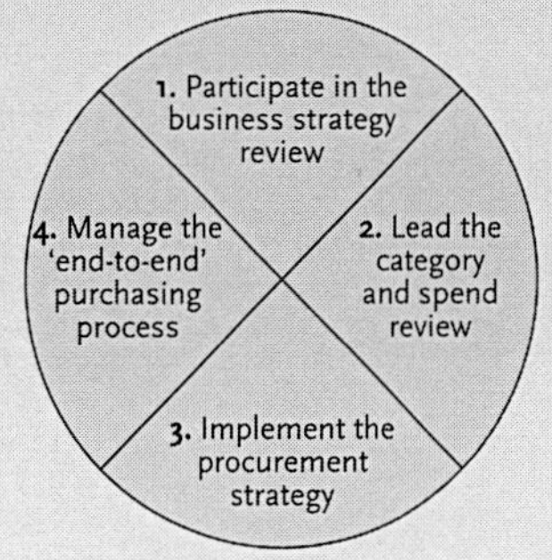

1. Participate in the business strategy review
2. Lead the category and spend review
3. Implement the procurement strategy
4. Manage the 'end-to-end' purchasing process

the function within the business or buy from suppliers ('**make vs buy**'). Identifying business needs ensures that the role and responsibility of each stakeholder in the procurement process is defined and approved. This avoids conflict of priorities and miscommunication and helps to promote trust and confidence of the procurement team.

Lead the category and spend management review

Commencing with the **spend analysis**, it is valuable to understand where money is spent in the organisation within broad categories of expenditure, as shown using the cost map in Figure 12.2.

Category management

When there are many items and services to buy, it is preferable to segregate the large categories identified in Figure 12.2 into manageable groups; this allows for a set of business rules to be applied to each category. This is similar to the approach taken in retail where similar products are grouped together when buying goods for resale.

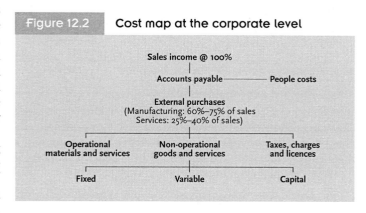

Figure 12.2   Cost map at the corporate level

Within each of the major spending areas of an organisation, categories can be structured, as shown in Figure 12.3.

As an example of the structure, within the process group named 'facilities', there can be a category called 'industrial supplies', which then has a sub-category of 'safety glasses'.

Categories of spend will vary to suit the business needs of an individual organisation within different industries. For example, organisations in the health or food industry will categorise a fluid transfer pumping system differently to an organisation that provides a waste water maintenance management service. To assist the process, there are internationally recognised standards used for category formats, such as the United Nations Standard Product and Service Code (UNSPSC) and the NATO coding structure. These are mainly used in large engineering operations, such as mines and power generation, as well as in defence and defence industries.

Sub-categories are assessed and weighted, based on their potential financial and reputation impact on the organisation. For example, sub-categories in the marketing process group expenditure could be:

- high impact: product advertising
- medium impact: market research
- low impact: promotional 'give-aways'.

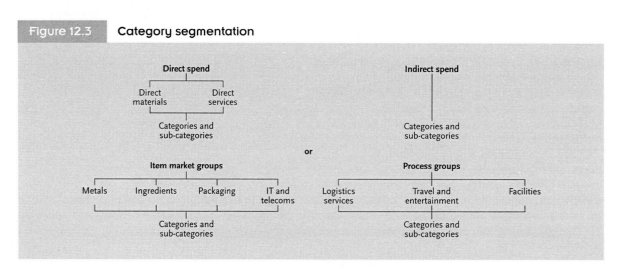

Figure 12.3   Category segmentation

As an example of applying sub-categories within procurement decisions, a major telecommunications company reserves its high impact items for global sourcing, the medium impact items for regional sourcing and the low-impact items for country sourcing. However, as the **product life cycle (PLC)** of telecommunication technologies goes through rapid transformation, this approach could change.

Only the sub-categories with a high impact would be considered for a complete **sourcing plan**, with the horizon being three to five years. Those with a medium impact will have an abridged sourcing plan that considers the next 12–18 month period and those with a low impact will have a tactical negotiating plan.

The analysis required for a full sourcing plan will consist of elements such as:

* current supply market situation
  o availability and capacity
  o technology developments
  o expansion plans and new entrants
  o current situation
  o trend for orders and inventories
* external influences and risks
  o corporate
  o product/service
  o buying
* current suppliers in the market, with details of ownership, capacity utilisation, profitability, cost/price structure
* influence of buyer or supplier: power and dependencies in the supply chain(s)
* major buyers for the item: identifying their strengths in the supply market
* historical price movements: their causes, plus expected pricing trends
* competitor activity: use of the item and potential trends and changes
* organisation's internal requirements: for the item plus any trends and changes.

Spend analysis

A sourcing plan for a category or sub-category will require an initial analysis of the procurement spend. During this process, 'intelligence' needs to be derived from the data that is collected in order to better understand how procurement can achieve outcomes that satisfy the business needs. One approach is to use the risk–spend positioning matrix in Figure 12.4.

This matrix brings into perspective the scale of spending in relation to risks in the supply market from where the goods and services are sourced. A higher level of **procurement risk** indicates the more restricted opportunities in that supply market.

Figure 12.4 **Risk–spend positioning**

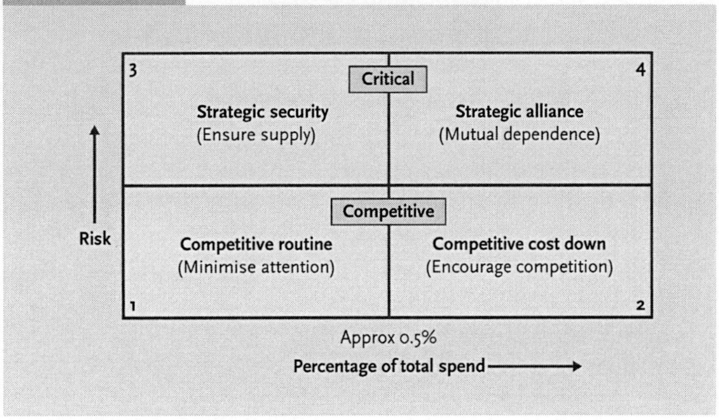

Source: Adapted from Kraljic (1983).

Quadrant 1—Competitive routine. The amount spent on an item is a low percentage of the total and there are low risks in doing business. The objective is to make buying a routine process. Therefore, simplify all processes so that minimal attention is required; for example, the use of electronic-based processes like online buying, e-auction and a strategy of **outsourcing** or **vendor managed inventory (VMI)**. An example is office stationery.

Quadrant 2—Competitive cost-down. Higher percentages are spent, but the risks remain low. Competition between suppliers to reduce costs can be encouraged if the buyer has commodity expertise and knowledge of the market, such that global sourcing can be undertaken. Examples are glass windscreens and windows used in a vehicle assembly operation.

Quadrant 3—Strategic security. The risks associated with the buy are high, yet the percentage spent is low. There are limited alternatives for the item, with service parts and capital equipment as examples. Purchase price is not as important as security of supply; therefore, develop a close relationship with suppliers and focus on removing any bottlenecks in the supply chain and other impediments to doing business. An example of a possible approach would be to develop potential suppliers through an **early supplier involvement (ESI)** program, to ensure that limited or restrictive supply market conditions are avoided or removed.

Quadrant 4—Strategic alliance. This involves items which are critical to success of the enterprise. Risks are high, but the percentage of annual spend is also high. The objective is to develop a long-term relationship based on a mutual dependence between the parties. Work closely with suppliers to improve the total performance of the relationship and consider developing a strategic alliance. An example in this category would be a production material such as garlic, used in garlic bread. While this is an everyday commodity when consumed in a household, for specialist bread manufacturers it is a business-critical spend. Risks are the:

○ availability of reliable suppliers
○ timing of supply, affected by the use of fertiliser, with its price and use being impacted by the price of oil and
○ location of supply sources to minimise in-transit risks of the garlic becoming stale.

Categories that are prioritised and being reviewed may influence the approach taken to the lower impact categories. For example, based on the risk-spend positioning matrix in Figure 12.4, the procurement of pumps for a waste water treatment plant are likely to be in the strategic security quadrant, while lubricating oil falls within the competitive cost down quadrant. If the enterprise is reviewing the types of pumps to use, as part of an equipment standardisation strategy, lubricating oil could be incorporated into the strategic security quadrant.

Implement the procurement strategy

Supply market analysis

For any procurement process to be successful, it is critical to attain a good understanding of the supply market. Only then can the potential be measured concerning whether there is a suitable source of supply for the goods and services required to meet the targeted business needs. The supply market analysis allows the procurement professional to better understand current and potential suppliers and therefore structure relationships, enact policies, and define responsibilities and performance objectives that reflect the reality.

Tools for supply market analysis include:

○ **PEST analysis** (P: Political; E: Environment; S: Social and T: Technology), which provides a macro view of the supply market
○ **Porter 5-force analysis**, which provides indications on how the dynamics between the 'buyer market' and 'seller market' operate
○ supplier analysis of customers matrix, as shown in Figure 12.5.

In this analysis, the buyer needs to 'get inside the mind' of the current or potential supplier and analyse how the supplier considers the:

○ actual or potential attributes of their customer (the buyer)
○ percentage of total annual sales that are (and could be) obtained from their customer (the buyer)
○ weighted by the gross margin earned plus the 'cost to serve' (discussed in Chapters 1 and 13).

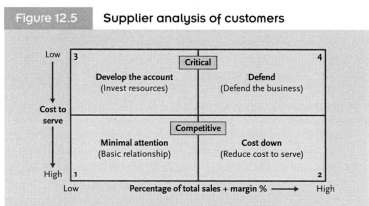

Figure 12.5   Supplier analysis of customers

Source: Adapted from Shapiro et al (1987).

Quadrant 1—Minimal attention. A low percentage of total sales, with a high cost to serve. The supplier's decision will be to either maintain a minimal relationship or cease doing business with the customer or client. Alternatively, if the customer has a product at an early stage of the product life cycle, with potentially good sales and margins, the supplier could elect to develop a relationship that moves the customer's profile to either the 'develop the account' or 'cost down' quadrants.

Quadrant 2—Cost down. While the percentage of annual sales is good, the cost to serve is high, which affects net profits. If the customer is willing, the supplier could work with them to reduce the cost to serve.

Quadrant 3—Develop the account: Although the percentage of sales is low, the cost to serve is also low and there may be a potential for increased business. The supplier can invest resources to develop the account and build a case for additional sales.

Quadrant 4—Defend. With high sales and low cost to serve, the business must be defended. The focused tactics by the supplier to hold the account are likely to be:

* provide high levels of customer service
* employ a dedicated account manager
* initiate discussions that could lead to a formal alliance.

The completion of this analysis enables a procurement professional to identify, by quadrant, the suppliers with an approach that mirrors the buyer's needs and also where there is a mismatch that may require attention.

For example, if the buyer views an item such as office stationery, to be competitive routine (see Quadrant 1 in Figure 12.4), the ideal match will be where the supplier views the account as their core business to defend (Quadrant 4 in Figure 12.5). In this situation, the supplier is more likely to provide the level of customer service under a period contract, which allows the buyer to have their required 'minimal attention'.

Conversely, challenges will occur for the buyer if they think that the supplier views the customer's account as minimal attention (Quadrant 1 in Figure 12.5), because neither the buyer nor supplier will put effort or resources into the arrangement.

Having provided a structured base from which to build relationships with suppliers, consideration can be given to developing a more sustained position in the supply market and to reducing costs. This is *not* about just reducing supplier prices and needs to be evaluated from a broader business perspective than simple cost savings.

SOURCING STRATEGY

There is an imperative for an enterprise to harness the capability of supply markets; this can be through supply market intelligence and sourcing to create and protect knowledge or intellectual capability that satisfies the business needs.

A responsive sourcing strategy can be regarded as making a procurement strategy happen and is one of the key success factors for a business. The sourcing strategy will consist of the:

* identification of targeted supply markets
* identification of potential suppliers that can or should be engaged
* resultant purchaser–supplier(s) relationship development plan
* 'end-to-end' procurement (including contract management) process.

For new physical or service items, or where there is a change of policy for established items—for example change the packaging for an item from its current material to a biodegradable material—the organisation must identify whether there is a real and justified need.

Established items, such as production components for ongoing products or office supplies, which have reached the end of their current supply contract, may be re-negotiated based on their current specifications and supplier. Alternatively, the decision to 'go to market' can be made, allowing additional suppliers to submit a proposal for supply.

DISPOSAL STRATEGY

A critical aspect of procurement that is (surprisingly) taken for granted is the cost of disposal. It is not only the disposal costs that are directly attributed to the targeted equipment; there could also be environmental management issues. Disposal cost evaluation also includes replacing ageing equipment with second-hand units, the cost of which is offset by selling the existing equipment to recover some salvageable value.

To be effective in the disposal process, procurement needs to understand the underlying cost and its structure. A spend analysis and supply market analysis process should be used to quantify the impacts of the approaches being considered when implementing a disposal strategy for an item.

SPECIFICATIONS

In the past, organisations would be expected to provide complete technical specification for suppliers to bid against; but this approach relies on staff having the latest knowledge of the item. Also, a critical aspect of self-design is that legal liability lies with the buyer when the supplied item complies with specifications, even though it does not meet the user's intentions in operation. Examples of specifications and their scope are shown in Table 12.1.

Table 12.1 Specification types

Material specification	Engineering specification	Functional specification	Production specification	Purchasing specification
Stability / quality	Measurements	Storage	Economical production • Value add	Markets available
Substitutions available	Design	Consumer Acceptance	Workability of materials	Material availability
Supplier production methodology • Batch • Continuous • Periodic	Testing capability	Performance	Compatibility with other materials needed	Supplier capability
Weight and measurements		Support		Costs
Standards available				Obsolete dates Governing laws Ownership issues—intellectual property Integration with current products

Source: Courtesy of Melissa Bayley, melissa@save-it.com.au.

In other situations, there will be interaction between the buyer and seller to develop a specification. This is where the scope of liability can become a joint responsibility. An example is when the design for a stairway in a factory may originate from the buyer. Following a review of the original design by the supplier, the design could be modified, taking into account the supplier's expertise.

The buyer has now relied on the expertise of the supplier and consequently the scope of supply (including the design) would need to recognise that the supplier has a partial liability concerning the eventual use of the stairway. The contract would identify the supplier as liable, albeit with a cap, for any safety incidents created by the design of the stairway.

An alternative approach is to provide a performance- or outcome-based specification, which states what the buyer wishes to achieve from the contract. A much-quoted example is the specification for a staff dining facility, which stated 'feed us'. On a visit to Norway, one of the authors was told that the functional (technical) specification for an offshore oil rig was 1600 pages in length and the equivalent performance-based specification (PBS) was 11 pages. The latter approach achieved a 40 per cent lower total cost.

Supplier capability statement

One of the most challenging aspects of procurement is to know where to find the 'best' supplier. It is therefore advisable to develop a standardised **supplier capability** statement document that is used to itemise the capabilities of current and prospective suppliers.

Although an organisation might have an incumbent supplier for an item or service, it does not mean they are the right supplier. The incumbent supplier may have:

- become too familiar with the 'organisational politics' of the customer
- allowed the buyer organisation to become accustomed to a 'cosy' relationship that can breed an environment of complacency
- lost motivation to bring new or innovative ideas to the business.

It is therefore necessary that a practical, ongoing system of measuring supplier capability and performance is implemented. Measures must be compatible with the business needs and a measurement regime must take account of ongoing changes in the business strategy.

Potential suppliers can present very compelling proposals for the products or services they sell. They are most likely to sell based on one or more of three 'values':

- price (value perceptions)
- technology (design, engineering, planning and scheduling)
- services (additional value).

To overcome bias in the buying decision, the requirement factors for an item should be evaluated, through **supplier research** and **supplier visits**. Undertaking supplier research enables the buyer to collect the base information about the possible suppliers, using a web search for additional business and product information. The number of potential suppliers may be limited by the size and complexity of the factors stipulated in the requirements.

Following are two examples of factors for consideration when identifying supplier capabilities:

1. Consider the share of the supplier's total business that the proposed contract is likely to absorb; a committed supplier can be good, but it also brings associated risks. For example, in countries with a concentration of large retailers, such as Australia and Singapore, small suppliers may have one customer that provides more than 50 per cent of income, with the risk to the supplier's other customers if the large supply contract is cancelled. Alternatively, there are large multinational corporations (MNC) that will not exceed 5 per cent of sales with any one customer on a global basis; therefore, potential customers in a country or region may not be supplied.
2. Examine whether the supplier has the financial strength to deliver on the contract, although this can be more difficult in the Asia–Pacific region. It is only in countries that have a strong financial reporting code and legal recourse that financial accounts of companies are available and possibly believable. In other countries, the risk of default increases, but this is due to a lack of knowledge, not that suppliers *will* actually fail. The buyer must therefore implement a procurement process that minimises the consequences if a selected supplier fails in a country with a low transparency of financial accounts.

For items, services and suppliers that are in the critical categories (see Figure 12.4), visits to suppliers by the buyer team should be mandatory, because that is where the actual situation can be assessed. The information required will depend on the occasion—enquiry, poor performance or celebration, and the country, company and its product. Enquiry and poor performance visits will mainly focus on planning and scheduling, quality issues, labour practices, equipment maintenance and pre- and post-sales support.

If the visit is to a factory, then always look over the back fence before entering the foyer—that will provide current information about operational attitudes at the supplier. Ask to visit meeting rooms. Even when all data is on computer, companies like to have good news stories concerning output and quality posted on the wall—but how current is the information? Always have the factory tour done in reverse, from despatch to incoming materials, as it is easier to pose cost and volume questions (some in ambiguous ways) while viewing the flow.

Manage the 'end-to-end' purchasing process

Flow of activities

The main steps for the purchasing and contracting sectors of procurement are shown as a flowchart in Figure 12.6.

Figure 12.6	Flow of purchasing and contracting activities

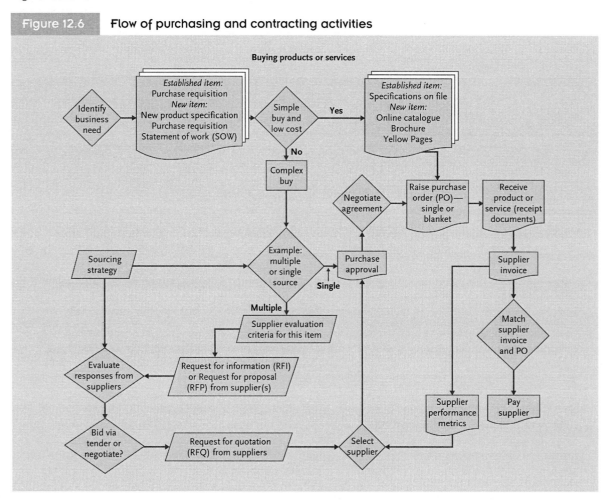

Invite bids or proposals (also called 'go to market')

As noted in the previous section, potential suppliers may be pre-qualified to ensure their suitability. Acceptable suppliers will respond to either a **request for information (RFI), proposal (RFP)** or **quotation (RFQ)**. These are collectively called RFx; their title identifies the range of information required. In addition, when services are to be supplied a **statement of work (SOW)** or statement of required outcomes may be provided. In order to obtain a fair appraisal of the responses, they should be evaluated based on a common structured scoring format.

Proposal evaluation

Each supplier proposal is to be evaluated, taking into consideration findings from the supplier capability statement. This may require additional factors in the evaluation criteria.

As an example, part of the evaluation is to conduct reference checks, especially for service contracts, such as with a logistics service provider (LSP). This is because the contract will be a relational exchange; therefore an evaluation of the cultural fit between the organisations is vital. No matter how good the price, the people who will make the contract happen are important. The deliverables of service contracts are also difficult to assess at the time of contracting and only when experience has been gained by the buyer and the service provider will a good measure be derived. Hence, during reference checks it is important to question the supplier's referees on the quality of service, staff turnover and attitude of the supplier concerning delivery of the required services.

DELIVERABLES NEGOTIATION

As each proposal is being evaluated, it will become clear which of the short-listed suppliers should be invited to participate in a negotiation process. Negotiations can include both technical and commercial requirements. Using the example of procurement for a staff dining facility, the technical requirement to be negotiated would include the types of cooking utensils if there is a mix of employees from different religious faiths. The commercial implication of such a specific requirement would probably be that separate areas would be needed in the kitchen—a common space allocation requirement for Asia-based food preparation facilities.

Negotiation criteria are prepared in advance to ensure that acceptable outcomes can be achieved. This will include meeting business needs such as 'lowest price', but not compromising other essential targets, such as 'lowest total cost'.

When negotiating acceptable outcomes it is important to consider the implication of both business and commercial and/or legal risks. For example, when negotiating a service contract to organise a public event, a business need will be to ensure the maximum number of people attend the function, but with public safety and security measures in place. A possible compromise could be selecting a service provider that is not the lowest priced but has the management systems to indemnify the buyer from legal challenges in the event of accidents.

CONTRACT FORMATION (INCLUDING THE RAISING OF A PURCHASE ORDER)

A contract is an exchange of conditional promises or an agreement which is enforceable at law. It can be as simple as a hand shake attached to a verbal agreement, a one-page purchase order or as detailed as a multi-page document with the contents varied to suit the situation. By default, buyers may rely on the supplier's terms or industry contracting standards, such as the Australian Standard AS4910, which includes standards relating to design, supply, delivery, installation and commissioning of equipment.

The terms and conditions of a contract are often a mix of standard clauses and special conditions of contract, where both parties (the buyer and the seller) through negotiation, agree to bind each other to the contractual obligations of the contract to deliver (by the seller) and to accept (by the buyer).

Some of the elements that can be jointly considered by the customer and supplier when structuring a contract are listed in Table 12.2.

Table 12.2   Contract clauses terms and conditions (T&C)

Business relationship	Operational	Transaction
Adherence to contract terms	Design responsibility	Deliverables
Contract compliance and performance	Price adjustment	Payments
Joint activities in productivity and product innovation	Compliance tracking	Alerts and reminders
Intellectual property (IP)	% of business guarantee	Taxes and duties
Supplier audit and evaluation	Material and labour cost indexing	Dispute procedure
Contract renewal process	Logistics processes incl. inventory planning process	Remediation
Contract administration	Service-level requirements	Termination
	• Acceptance, warranties & guarantees	• Administration workflow
	• Management & technical support	

The efficiency of the downstream stages of the procurement process is very much influenced by the effectiveness of implementing the earlier stages, which have been discussed through this chapter.

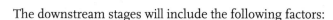

The downstream stages will include the following factors:

- scope variations management
- payment process
- purchase order expediting
- supplier performance (or feedback).

Although these factors might be 'downstream', they are still important to the success of a purchase. For example, if the change in scope (in relation to a contracted statement of work) is not well managed, cost can escalate and/or delays in delivery experienced. Hence, it is critical that as part of the management of contracts (or purchase orders), order expediting is in place to ensure that delays and cost-related risks are identified as early as possible, to minimise the effects.

Proactively managing contracts and purchase orders through order expediting will give the buyer and seller the opportunity to monitor the ongoing performance of the other party in meeting the mutually agreed contractual obligations (as set out in the contract). The monitoring process will also provide the data for future assessment by the customer of supplier performance and provide the buyer with data to carry out a supplier capability statement or to be used as input for a **supply market analysis**.

Implementing e-procurement

To improve processes, some organisations have invested in e-procurement and e-sourcing applications. Essentially, this is not an investment in a technology alone, but in a business process that is assisted by technology.

Spend management application suites are designed to gather data from the entire procurement process, as illustrated in Figure 12.1. They may include the following applications, or each sub-application can be purchased and implemented individually:

- E-sourcing applications usually address the pre-purchase activities, consisting of supplier qualification, RFx management, e-auction participation and related areas. To justify this application, an organisation must have sufficient sourcing projects on a regular basis.
- Spend analysis is an application that collects the spending transaction data from multiple systems; then matches and eliminates duplicate records and classifies the data for reporting purposes. Spend can also be analysed using a database such as MS Access or Filemaker or by using MS Excel.
- Supply base management is an application to support the supplier relationship process. It tracks a supplier capability for the supply of an item and their performance. It is used for the creation of supplier 'scorecards' and can be used to monitor and enforce supplier mandated criteria such as ethical behaviour and sustainability.
- Contract management is a central electronic repository that helps companies to store, track, monitor and update all contracts. This is especially helpful in decentralised companies, enabling the access and search of all contracts, based on predefined parameters.

These applications can also be delivered online as a 'software as a service' (SaaS) model, which allows organisations to use and pay for specific functionality that meets a particular need.

E-marketplace or internet-based business-to-business (B2B) networks tend to be used for buying low-value, high-volume goods and services, such as stationery and marketing materials, found in catalogues and supplier websites. E-auctions must be conducted using the highest integrity standards, otherwise suppliers will believe that auctions focus only on price and therefore destroy business relationships.

Higher value items will often continue to be purchased using EDI; this uses the established protocols (XML, ebXML, UBL) for point-to-point exchange of standard business forms such as purchase orders and invoices. Due to the importance of these purchases, the use of printed purchase orders that are faxed or emailed to suppliers is likely to continue.

Mobile phone applications (phone apps) are available that keep track of commodity prices, provide supplier alerts and allow approval of purchase orders (PO).

In practice, the implementation of procurement applications can present challenges:

- The new process will most likely change the 'old' process and many businesses or divisions within businesses may be unwilling, or unable, to implement standard procurement processes.
- Buyers may consider the 'trust' element in relationships developed with established suppliers is missing and be reluctant to be involved with the applications.

- Decentralised and ad hoc purchasing ('maverick' or 'rogue' spending) may not be controlled.
- Organisations may invest in e-procurement applications before implementing strategic sourcing. As strategic sourcing has the objective of reducing business complexity, it is the preferred step before investing in software applications.
- There may be a lack of senior management support for strategic sourcing activities.
- Expertise in e-procurement applications and processes may be lacking.

Whether implemented as an in-house application or through an IT service provider, process integration will have the same level of importance as the application integration. This is a substantial amount of work that companies must budget for, as it requires the development of process definitions, methods and procedures, user guidelines, training of staff and implementation of appropriate governance and compliance frameworks.

Chapter questions

Operational

1. A case has been argued that buying items from a single supplier has value for the customer. Using Figure 12.3 consider in which sector(s) buying an item from a single supplier may apply and why. What risks are associated with single supplier sourcing?
2. Purchase price variance is an accounting measure of performance that is commonly used for measuring the procurement/purchasing function. What are the benefits and deficiencies of this measure from the view of good procurement practice, as discussed in this chapter?
3. Consider the need for a procurement management system. What are the broad application requirements of such an application?
4. What metrics should be used to measure the contribution of procurement to corporate aims and objectives?
5. Total cost of ownership is a term used in procurement. What cost elements must be collected for imported products to calculate the total landed cost?
6. Supplier managed inventory (SMI), also called vendor managed inventory (VMI), is part of a contractual agreement. How would the process be implemented?

Planning

7. How may a company buying imported items ensure that suppliers adhere to accepted minimum 'human rights' standards in their employment practices?
8. Discuss the merits and drawbacks of two approaches to relationships with suppliers: regular tendering for products and services vs. developing strategic long-term relationship with selected suppliers.
9. Procurement risks are present with all purchases. Identify the elements of risk under the headings of corporate, product/service and buying risks; select two from each and identify the steps that could be taken to mitigate the risks.

Management

10. Consider how globalisation of supply is affecting the key aspects of procurement. Is procurement becoming more or less important within supply chains, and why?
11. Should procurement be a service function for the organisation or established as a services group that sells services for internal customers? What are the advantages and disadvantages of each approach?
12. Procurement has two elements—strategic initiatives and continuing operations. How may the function be organised to incorporate these elements?

Exercise

You are the procurement manager for a building fit-out company. The latest project is sourcing and fitting 7600 environmentally friendly light fittings for a hotel under construction in Melbourne, and due to commence in three months.

There are proposals from three suppliers based in the Asia–Pacific region:

- Supplier 1 proposes a light fitting referred to as model A. This is a cylindrical light fitting 15 cm high and 10 cm in diameter. The fittings are individually packed into cardboard boxes measuring 10.5 cm × 10.5 cm × 16 cm. A packaged unit weighs 500 g and costs $A3.00 ex-works (EXW) at the factory gate in Taiwan.

- Supplier 2 proposes a light fitting referred to as model B. This is a spherical light fitting 15 cm in diameter. The fittings are individually packed into cardboard boxes measuring 16 cm × 16 cm ×16 cm and require protection with 'bubble wrap' material. A packaged unit weighs 600 g and costs A$7.00 delivered duty paid (DDP) Melbourne.
- Supplier 3 proposes a light fitting referred to as model C. This is a conical light fitting 12 cm in diameter and 15 cm high. These fittings can be stacked into each other with a layer of protective insulation and packed as lots of 5 into cardboard boxes measuring 16 cm × 16 cm × 12.5 cm. A packaged box weighs 2600 g and costs A$30.00 CIF Melbourne. A 2 × TEU intermodal container measures 8 ft × 8.5 ft × 40 ft and carries about 25 tonnes or 72 cubic metres

Operational

1. How many of each type of light fittings can be transported in an intermodal container if it cannot exceed 25 tonnes?
2. Explain the transport cost implications of the different way the suppliers are quoting to you as a buyer.
3. What are the three different Incoterms used by the suppliers? Explain each of these terms.

Management

4. Develop an evaluation matrix against which you can assess the three responses by suppliers.
5. Identify the risks associated with currency fluctuations in importing materials. How can these risks be managed?
6. Which Incoterms would you prefer to use to buy the light fittings? Explain your answer.
7. What is the landed cost per unit of each model (A, B and C) of light fittings?
8. Which of the proposals will you accept? Explain your decision.

References and links

Chartered Institute of Purchasing and Supply (CIPS): www.cips.org.uk.

Chartered Institute of Purchasing and Supply Australia (CIPSA): www.cipsa.com.au

Institute for Supply Management: www.ism.ws

Cousins, P., Lamming, R. & Lawson, B., *Strategic Supply Management: Principles, Theories and Practice*, Prentice Hall, London, 2008.

'Procurement Strategies', a survey conducted by Aberdeen Research, April 2009, www.aberdeen.com.

Kraljic, P., 'Purchasing must become Supply Management', *Harvard Business Review,* September–October, 1983.

Shapiro, B.P., Rangan, V.K., Moriaty, R.T. & Ross, E.B., 'Manage Customers for Profits (not just Sales)', *Harvard Business Review*, September–October, 1987.

United Nations Standard Product and Service Code (UNSPSC): www.unspsc.org

NATO Supply Classification Code: www.nato.int

P
A
R
T

4

Measurement and management of logistics

Learning outcomes

On completion of this chapter you will be able to:

- consider the areas of financial management that are important for measuring supply chains

- recognise the limitations of traditional management accounting approaches in the management of logistics

- assess the improvements required for structuring the profit and loss account to address logistics requirements

- discuss alternative approaches to identifying and managing costs in logistics

- identify improvements to the budgeting process.

Links to other chapters

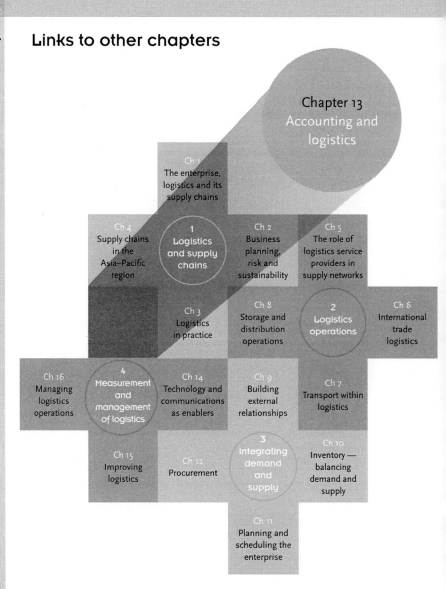

Chapter 13
Accounting and logistics

Ch 1
The enterprise, logistics and its supply chains

Ch 4
Supply chains in the Asia–Pacific region

1
Logistics and supply chains

Ch 2
Business planning, risk and sustainability

Ch 5
The role of logistics service providers in supply networks

Ch 3
Logistics in practice

Ch 8
Storage and distribution operations

2
Logistics operations

Ch 6
International trade logistics

Ch 16
Managing logistics operations

4
Measurement and management of logistics

Ch 14
Technology and communications as enablers

Ch 9
Building external relationships

Ch 7
Transport within logistics

Ch 15
Improving logistics

Ch 12
Procurement

3
Integrating demand and supply

Ch 10
Inventory — balancing demand and supply

Ch 11
Planning and scheduling the enterprise

Key terms

These terms are used in the text. Develop your own notebook by downloading information on each term.

profit and loss
balance sheet
cash flow
working capital
return on investment (ROI)
accounts receivable (AR)
accounts payable (AP)
cash-to-cash cycle time
earnings before interest and tax
   (EBIT)
strategic profit model

DuPont chart
return on equity (ROE)
return on assets (ROA)
return on capital employed
   (ROCE)
absorption costing
contribution accounting
order cycle
cost to serve (C2S)
activity-based costing (ABC)

time-driven activity-based costing
   (TDABC)
throughput accounting
constraints management
theory of constraints (TOC)
life cycle cost (LCC)
application of funds
generally accepted accounting
   principles (GAAP)
debt-to-capital ratio

Introduction

To be successful in presenting proposals to improve the supply chains of a business, logisticians must be able to talk in financial terms. An understanding of the language and role of finance, accounting and budgets is required, but this must be combined with knowledge of the challenges associated with using management (or cost) accounting reports in a logistics environment.

This chapter will discuss the role of accounting from a logistics viewpoint. It is assumed that readers have an understanding of the general principles of accounting and the terminology used.

Logistics and profitability

Two financial documents that are used in a business are the **profit and loss** statement (also called an income statement) and the **balance sheet**. Understanding and analysing these documents is one of the underlying skills of a logistician, which is necessary not only for knowing about their own company, but also in order to understand the business of many suppliers and customers.

The annual profit of a business is the outcome from activities undertaken on a daily basis. For logisticians, the important financial drivers of business continuity are **cash flow**, **working capital** and **return on investment (ROI)**.

Cash flow

Cash flow is the critical near-term measure of business viability. Is there sufficient money to continue the business? What is the cash income and expenditure plan? When will customers who have been invoiced actually pay and when will the business pay its suppliers?

In addition to the cash flow statement, a cash flow model will assist in indicating the cash situation under a number of scenarios, both revenue increasing and decreasing. In a situation where revenue may decrease and therefore costs must be reduced to remain profitable, the model will enable a projection of the potential outgoing cash reduction actions that could be performed without jeopardising the business. These actions may include stopping non-critical projects, not renewing labour hire contracts, stopping overtime work and eliminating administrative 'stuff' that is of no value to the business.

Working capital

Working capital is money that business processes consume—the longer a process takes, the more money is consumed. Working capital is money invested in the operating processes to buy, make and sell items, comprising:

- **accounts receivable (AR)**
- *plus* inventories
- *plus* cash
- *less* **accounts payable (AP)**.

This calculation identifies the short-term funds available for the business and is the lowest-cost source of finance for use to fund the day-to-day activities and other initiatives, such as reducing company debt and building new capacity.

Poor working capital performance is not just a finance problem; it is usually a symptom of failings in the operational business processes. Problems with working capital are due to inefficiencies in the way an enterprise collects money from customers, the credit management and invoice dispute resolution processes, how inventory is managed, effective sourcing and relations with suppliers.

Some large companies in retail, for example supermarkets, vehicle, furniture and white goods retailers, have low (and sometimes negative) working capital; that is, they collect money as quickly or quicker than they pay suppliers. If inventory is managed, retailers take cash from consumers at the checkout shortly after the product has been delivered by the supplier. For larger products the retailer is paid within a short period by business finance companies for the retail display of product (called floor stock). However, suppliers must wait for their money—some large companies pay their accounts between 90 and 120 days on a 30-day invoice, while 60–90 days is quite common. As a general measure, if about 10 per cent or more of accounts payables in a business are unpaid for longer than 45 days, then an organisation has a policy of using suppliers' money to at least partially finance its business.

But the effect of this policy is that supply chains can suffer. The product suppliers may be unable to fund extended credit terms that are forced upon them, so they extend payment terms to their suppliers, who are even less able to fund it. These businesses may have to pay suppliers of critical material on terms of net 7 days or even 'cash on delivery'!

Smaller suppliers in supply chains are under constant financial pressure; this can end in bankruptcy and therefore cause follow-on problems for their customers, especially those in 'just in time' (JIT) supply chains, such as automotive and electronics assembly.

The supposed financial benefits of paying suppliers slowly may be worth less than the savings customers could gain from adopting more efficient processes with their suppliers. Segmentation and analysis of customers, suppliers and inventory is a key requirement of working capital management, together with IT applications that assist in the tracking, consolidation and measurement of working capital performance.

Working capital optimisation should be 'hand in glove' with optimising the core supply chains. As both are complex and involve many business processes and people within an organisation, it is preferable that they are managed as one entity.

Cash-to-cash cycle

Companies may generate significant working capital improvements by knowing the **'cash-to-cash' cycle time**; this calculates the time that operating capital (cash) is *not* available for use by the enterprise. The model restructures the working capital calculation, based on the time it takes for cash invested in inputs to flow back into the organisation, following the sale of products. The measure is:

Inventory days of supply + Sales receivables days outstanding – Supplier payables days outstanding.

An example is shown in Table 13.1 opposite.

There is an opinion that although the conventional calculation is as shown, the payables days should be added and not subtracted. The reasoning is that when the order is placed with a supplier, it establishes an obligation to pay (cash out). The money represented in inventory plus the money to be received from customers provides the real days cash outstanding. This approach also eliminates the desire to extend the time for paying suppliers.

The cycle days must be evaluated as a trend and measured against similar businesses through a 'benchmarking' process. The organisation can then work with its major customers and critical suppliers to focus on requirements, processes and 'rules' that have the greatest impact on working capital performance.

Return on investment

Return on investment (ROI) is a calculation viewed as an operating business model that shows **earnings before interest and tax (EBIT)**. It is sometimes called the **strategic profit model** or **DuPont chart**, named after the company that developed it in the mid-1920s. The model is illustrated in Figure 13.1.

The ROI, similar to the **return on equity (ROE)**, is the percentage return that an enterprise is achieving from using the shareholders' investment. However, for operating entities, such as a division or strategic

Table 13.1 Cash-to-cash cycle

	Month commencing June 1	Month ending June 30
Balance sheet		
Accounts receivable	$15m	$14.5m
Inventory at cost	$3.5m	$3m
Accounts payable	$7m	$6.5m
Profit and loss statement		
Sales		$10m
Cost of goods sold (COGS)		$7m
Gross profit		$3m
Cash-to-cash days	**Calculation**	
Inventory days of supply	($3.5m+$3m/2) / ($7m/30 days)	14.13
Receivables days outstanding (+)	($15m+$14.5m/2) / ($10m/30 days)	44.70
Payables days outstanding (–)	($7m+$6.5m/2) / ($7m/30 days)	29.34
Cash-to-cash cycle days		29.49

Figure 13.1   Strategic profit model

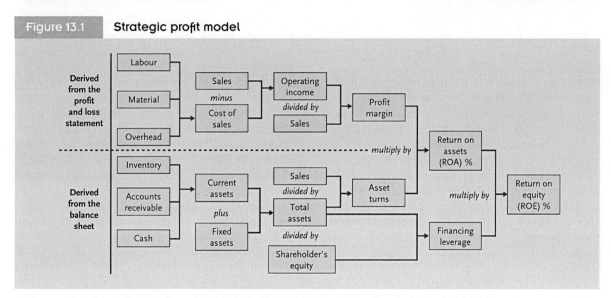

business unit (SBU), the **return on assets (ROA)** measures performance of the capital allocated to them. This can also be measured as the **return on capital employed (ROCE)**, which is similar to ROA but takes account of funding sources.

From a logistics viewpoint, the strategic profit model identifies the areas of responsibility where logistics can have the greatest impact on the ROA. This is shown in Figure 13.2.

While cash flow and working capital are common financial reports, use of the strategic profit model is less frequent, because accounting systems typically do not contain a module which incorporates the necessary ratio analysis.

Costing models

Absorption costing

The traditional accounting approach to cost allocation across a company's products and services has been to collect all the costs that cannot be directly attributed to a product or service and call them overheads (burden is the term used in America).

Figure 13.2 ROA and logistics activities

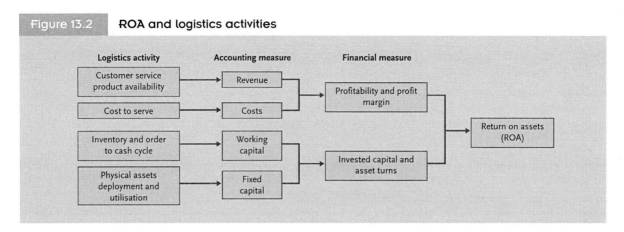

To cost a product is to identify the prime cost—which is the direct labour plus the direct materials—and add a proportion of the overhead, based on an arbitrary measure, such as labour hours, machine hours, tonnes or litres produced. By this means, the overhead is absorbed into the products and all overhead costs allocated across the products sold.

Of course, it is unlikely that the mix of product produced in the period will equate to the actual expenditure on overheads, so there is an over- or under-recovery of overheads. But try explaining to operating staff that, although they achieved excellent output and efficiencies, they lost money because there was under-absorption of overheads!

Commencing in the 1960s, the increasing use of technology and productivity improvements in manufacturing reduced the proportion of direct or prime costs (labour and materials), but increased the proportion of indirect costs. Therefore, under traditional cost allocation, large amounts of overhead were being apportioned based on small quantities of direct hours, leading to errors in pricing and product profitability.

For consumer packaged goods (CPG) companies, a challenge is that they continually introduce new products which require considerable effort to design, sell and distribute, yet the majority fail in the market. The company is therefore reliant on its established products for the majority of sales, but has a high overhead expenditure to manage new product introduction.

Using **absorption costing**, the established products are allocated an amount of these higher overheads commensurate with the labour hours or machine hours used or with volume; this means the profit margin for these established products is reduced. However, the new products receive an excess of attention, but as their volumes are low, they are allocated a small amount of overhead, so their profitability appears to be good.

The authors have witnessed a major CPG executive board seriously discussing termination of the company's major product line, even though it had been a leading selling brand for more than 50 years. Why should that be? Because the accounts showed the product was 'losing' money, due solely to the high level of overheads allocated to it!

In this case, the accounting IT system was structured to follow the standard accounting rules and conventions. This is an example of how 'systems' and technology can actually hinder the development of new ideas and approaches to managing a business.

Contribution costing

A different approach to costing products is to identify the costs that can be directly attributable—the direct labour and direct materials. If these 'prime costs' are subtracted from the selling price and multiplied by the annual volume, the answer is the *contribution* to corporate overheads made by that product. The financial success of the product can then be measured by its actual to planned contribution margin, which is directly measured, not guessed.

This approach also applies to services and, for example, has been used as the basis for managing multiple courses within a university logistics program.

Using **contribution accounting** enables 'overhead' areas, such as logistics, to be treated as entities and managed with applicable accounting measures and controls that enable the correct costs of to be identified and acted upon.

Logistics and operating costs

Consolidating costs

In developing the requirements for a supply chains and logistics accounting requirement, the main challenge is that supply chains (and the total supply network) touch many external and internal parties. The measurement of logistics costs will therefore require the consolidation of costs incurred in different areas of the business and across geographical boundaries. Traditional accounting systems find this difficult to achieve. As an illustration, the **order cycle** and the parties involved are shown in Figure 13.3.

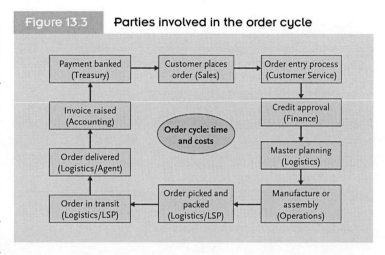

Figure 13.3　**Parties involved in the order cycle**

To understand the full extent of time and costs in the order cycle will require collection and consolidation of data from at least seven cost areas.

Cost to serve

Under traditional accounting methods, the profitability of a customer is calculated by subtracting the cost of goods sold (COGS) from the net sales value. But the outcome provides little information for decision making by logisticians, as it hides the multiplicity of costs incurred in actually serving the customer. This requires knowledge of the **cost to serve (C2S)** for identified customers.

The gross margin by each customer will differ, even if the products sold are similar, as there can be significant differences in the C2S for each customer. For example, a producer of industrial fans sells its product range to a variety of customers: mining companies for use in mine shafts; construction companies for use in high-rise buildings; defence for use on warships; and rail operators for use in passenger carriages. Although the fans may be similar by each size group, the customer requirements and buying process make the total delivered and installed costs very different in terms of service, account management, demand predictability and contract complexity.

As particular customers can demand a level of service that is different from other customers, using C2S enables the actual costs to be directly attributable for specific customers. Examples of the cost elements are:

* pre-sale costs
  o sales visits and demonstrations
  o sales calls
  o quotations (request for)
* sales costs
  o key account management time
  o promotional costs, e.g. attending customers' trade days
  o order processing costs
  o special discounts
* storage and handling costs
  o dedicated inventory holding costs
  o dedicated warehouse space
  o order size

o   special orders and their product characteristics
o   material handling costs if special handling required
o   non-standard packaging and unitisation
o   documentation costs, e.g. external quality certification
* delivery costs
o   location and access time limitations
o   delivery distance and traffic congestion
o   express transport costs
* after-sale costs
o   additional communication costs by customer service staff
o   returns of product not meeting customer requirements
o   refusal of product, due to late arrival at the customer DC
o   trade credit—the actual payment period
* for retail customers
o   in-store and cooperative promotions
o   merchandising costs.

Companies can be working under a misunderstanding by assuming that customers with a good profit margin are the customers to keep and grow. To counter this view, an example of using the C2S approach is shown for two customers, 'Alpha' and 'Beta'. Table 13.2 provides the numbers using the traditional accounting process.

Table 13.2   Example of customer results

	Alpha company	Beta company
Sales	500 000	520 000
COGS	250 000	260 000
Gross margin	250 000	260 000
Operations, sales and admin expenses @ 30% of sales	150 000	166 000
Operating profit	100 000	94 000
Profit percentage % on sales	20%	18.08%

Under this scenario, customer 'Alpha' provides the higher calculated profit. However, the actual situation is that Alpha company:

* is a long distance from the supplier and there are no other customers in the locality
* places small orders of multiple products at random times, requiring fast delivery
* pays in 65 days on a 30-day account
* expects and uses technical assistance
* wants the supplier to have a pipeline of new and modified products
* expects the sales representative to be 'on-call'.

The situation with Beta company is that it:

* is close to the supplier
* places large orders of few products at regular intervals
* pays in 42 days on a 30-day account
* accepts reasonable delivery times
* requires limited technical and sales support.

With the knowledge of each customer and calculating the C2S, it could be that Alpha company actually provides a low (or a loss) contribution and Beta company will provide a much improved real level of contribution to the business.

Knowing the C2S enables answers to be calculated against the following questions:

* What percentage of customers is unprofitable and should be discontinued?
* What percentage of customer orders incurs negative profit margins, therefore requiring modification of the product mix?
* What percentage of the product range does not make a contribution to overheads and should be discontinued?

This accounting analysis provides the basis for action to improve the profitability of low and negative profit margin customers and thus improve the viability of the business. Action steps can include the following.

* Review cost comparisons between distribution facilities and regions.
* Restructure distribution channels. Understand the complexity of supply chains that affect the customers, from source through primary and satellite distribution centre (DC) to the customer.
* Review the locations of inventory.
* Redesign customer service policies and responsibilities.
* Change sales responsibilities; for example change the account status of a customer.
* Review logistics service provider (LSP) contracts and clauses concerning delivery responsibilities.
* Renegotiate agreements/contracts with the customer.
* Review the internal administration processes.
* Review the pricing structure of products and services.
* Review the payment terms, discount policy and early payment discount structure.

In addition to showing the true costs to serve a customer, C2S can also be used to identify the real costs of serving particular markets and seasons. For example, a company may supply supermarket chains and independent buying groups, and have a 'route trade' business that sells product to small retailers directly from the driver representative's vehicle. What is the C2S for each of these groups? Another situation might be a business that experiences a high proportion of its sales in seasonal periods, with the C2S analysis able to consider the different costs of the continuing business replenishment, seasonal sales and special promotions.

Within an economy, between economies and in particular markets, a changing situation can affect the C2S for particular customers in at least the following areas:

* customer and supplier markets—geographical expansion, acquisitions, supply network changes, product range changes, changes to Incoterms used in the buying process
* customer—minimum size, operating characteristics and competence and other attributes of the relationship
* distribution—locations of DCs, outsourcing policy, unit loads.

Tracking the C2S is therefore an ongoing process, with a requirement for periodic (typically monthly) reporting. For the calculation of customer profitability, the cost to serve (C2S) information can be used as input for the **activity-based costing (ABC)** calculation.

Time-driven activity-based costing

Traditional accounting systems enable the profitability and cost variance of products (often based on full cost allocation) and the performance of functions, such as distribution, to be identified. However, as discussed, this methodology can lead to distortions in understanding costs and profitability, due to the variety of distribution channels and customers within a business.

Ideally the management (or cost) accounting system should provide the following business information:

* how total costs build as a product moves through its supply chain towards the customer
* from which customers the company's profit is derived.

Although work to develop a different management accounting system commenced in the 1960s, it was articles about activity-based costing (ABC) by Cooper and Kaplan (1988) that provided the academic support. However, subsequent problems with implementation and maintenance resulted in a review of ABC by Kaplan and Anderson (2004) which provided a simplified version called **time-driven activity-based costing (TDABC)**.

TDABC requires that *activities* in the business and their costs are identified and the *resources* associated with them; then assigning those activities to customers, products or processes. Examples of activities are:

* accepting customer orders
* delivering customer orders.

The resources will be the people, technology, equipment and money to undertake the activities. In the activity of delivering orders, the cost elements will include:

- vehicle lease costs
- fuel costs.

As the activity uses resources, the total costs associated with an activity can be assigned, based on the 'driver' which causes the costs to occur. To keep the structure at a manageable level, the number of drivers can be limited, so that many activities are triggered by the same event.

For example, a driver called 'customer orders' may be used for the activities of:

- pick customer orders
- load vehicles
- process invoices.

Activities can cut across functions, so that resource costs assigned to distribution could come from the warehouse, IT and administration; it does not matter where in the general ledger (GL) the expense is recorded.

There are three types of activity cost drivers:

- transaction: assumes that the same quantity of resources is required every time an activity is performed
- duration: used when significant variations exist in the amount of activity required for different outputs
- direct charging: for resources used each time an activity is performed. This is used only when the resources associated with performing an activity are both expensive and variable.

TDABC requires two input measures for an activity:

1. the unit cost of supplying the capacity
2. the consumption of capacity (unit times) for each activity.

Both inputs can be updated as changes in operating conditions occur.

The unit cost of supplying the capacity is calculated by taking the total costs, divided by the capacity at 80 per cent (or an appropriate percentage to allow for non-productive time). For example, if the total costs for the logistics planning office is $350,000 for 9600 nominal hours per year, the unit cost will be $350k × 0.8/9600 = $45.57 per hour. The consumption of capacity is an estimate of the time used on each occasion a resource performs an activity.

Deducting the product prime costs and the cost to serve from the price provides the customer's profitability. Consolidating the profitability of customers enables logistics to segment the customer base, as shown in Figure 13.4.

Throughput accounting

Management (or cost) accounting principles were developed in the late 19th century when direct labour costs and efficiencies were important to the success of a business. This required that a business is divided into manageable areas and their performance measured, typically in weekly or monthly periods.

In a product-based business today, the emphasis should be on the flow of materials and products, reducing the need for inventory; this approach follows logistics thinking. However, the effectiveness of the flow will be affected by constraints in the system. If these can be identified and reduced or eliminated, increased materials will flow through the whole system, resulting in higher sales but without the need for additional investment.

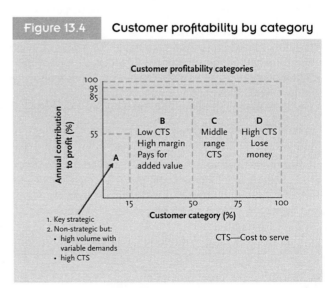

Figure 13.4 Customer profitability by category

The approach to measuring the effectiveness of the flow is called **throughput accounting** and is based on **constraints management** (or the **theory of constraints—TOC**). The basic assumption is that over the short term, all costs except materials are fixed in relation to throughput. Therefore, an increase in costs, in the form of inventory or operating costs, identifies a constraint that needs to be removed or improved, whether it is internal or external to the business.

Logistics support accounting

As more organisations move towards a 24/7 operational focus, effective physical asset management is gaining in importance and visibility. If not available, it impacts operational logistics effectiveness, service parts availability and increases operations costs.

For certain organisations, asset management is a core activity, with the main logistics challenges being asset-related. In a paper mill, an aluminium smelter, an airport, a coal loader or an airforce weapons system, the capital costs of equipment and facilities will typically represent less than 30 per cent of total life cycle asset costs. The situation with the remaining 70 per cent of total costs is as follows:

- About 50 per cent of the supportability decisions have to be made during the concept stage.
- Only 20 per cent of support decisions can be changed without considerable effort after the design and development stage.
- Only 5 per cent of support decisions can be changed without considerable effort once the capital item is producing or operational.

Planning the support required prior to purchase of capital items has a profound effect on the total life cycle costs of an asset, as there are major operational cost inputs connected with the buying of spare parts and maintaining an asset.

The **life cycle cost (LCC)** is therefore a balance of: costs, operational performance, support levels, strategic materials inventory, critical resources availability, risks and trade-offs. The objective is to minimise the LCC through an ongoing analysis of these cost drivers and this is required within a logistics accounting system.

Supply chains and logistics accounting structures

To be identified as an effective contributor to a business, supply chains and logistics require their own accounting measurements and reports that reflect the processes undertaken; currently this is not done. The result is that logisticians are being asked to defend their actions, but without the supporting numbers provided by a corporate system that has been designed for their needs and which has been approved by the finance director. To develop an accounting system for supply chains and logistics, the approach needs to recognise the particular considerations, as noted in Table 13.3 overleaf.

Recognising supply chains in the P&L statement

In traditional accounts, the profit and loss (P&L) statement gathers together all the supply side expenditure under the general heading of cost of goods sold (COGS) and sales side expenditure under sales and administration. The cost of supply chains in terms of materials purchased and expenditure on service contracts with LSPs are therefore hidden. This can result in supply chains and logistics not having the impact in the accounts that sales revenue has with senior management.

When reading the P&L statement of a business, think about an approach that can reflect the amount of exposure supply chains create for the business. A traditional and restructured P&L statement is shown in Table 13.4. The accounting terminology does not change.

By identifying the supply market spend on materials and services and the total logistics employment costs, the total investment that the business is making in its supply chains is more evident. This can assist in changing perceptions of supply chains and logistics in a product company from a cost to the company into an investment in the external supplier businesses.

This approach can be more easily understood by all employees in the enterprise. The P&L statement, balance sheet and **application of funds** statement that are used by external organisations, such as audit firms, investors, banks and tax authorities, are less relevant as a basis for identifying wealth generation and improvement inside the organisation.

Table 13.3 Considerations about accounting for supply chains and logistics

Supply chains and logistics considerations	Traditional accounting approach
Supply chains recognise the inter-dependencies with external parties.	Accounts are structured with an internal view of the organisation.
Supply chains operate horizontally across functional boundaries.	Transactions are identified and summarised by vertical, functional groups, for example manufacturing and distribution.
Logistics costs flow from suppliers and logistics service providers, across different parts of the enterprise and out to customers. The total logistics costs are required, including inventory holding costs.	Transport and warehousing charges show in the P&L statement, but inventory value is on the balance sheet and inventory holding costs are not directly identified—they are 'lost' in the financing costs within overheads.
Supply chains are dynamic, so that suppliers, facilities, inventory locations and volume, order sizes and mix can change. The value of these changes is required.	Accounting view is more static, being based on cost and price. For example 'purchase price variance' is a common measure of procurement performance, yet is only concerned with price—it provides the wrong message concerning how best to work with the suppliers. Transport costs can increase due to a change in the product mix, but this is not linked to marketing decisions.
When the product stops moving (due to internal constraints and external bottlenecks), major costs are incurred.	Product is expected to 'stop moving' on defined dates so that the inbound, outbound and WIP inventory can be accounted for and overhead costs apportioned for the period (usually a monthly 'bucket').
Time is a major creator of cost.	The effects of time lost or gained do not appear in financial statements.
The operational period is a day, therefore monthly and quarterly 'buckets' are not relevant to performance.	The operational period is a month, which generates the 'month-end rush' to produce and deliver, but without the costs of so doing being recorded, for example, high cost freighter planes waiting at airports to load 'month-end' deliveries.
Measures required for each: • inventory segment—velocity; turns; yield; cycle times • customer segment—delivery in full, on time, with accuracy (DIFOTA); cost to serve • supplier segment—outsourcing and offshoring total costs.	Financial performance metrics do not measure value and cost of each supply chain.

Although the restructured format can be implemented within current ERP systems, few companies provide the P&L statement in this manner; therefore, in the foreseeable future logisticians will be relying on the traditional accounts structure, while influencing the accountants to revise the P&L statement.

Implementing logistics accounting

The preceding sections have identified some of the main requirements for an accounting system that can support the needs of supply chain and logistics within product companies. The benefits to a business could be substantial, however, in the consideration of a supply chains and logistics accounting system, some of the challenges could include the following.

- Extracting data from the current accounting system may be difficult.
- Data is insufficient because the organisation does not collect the data in the form required.
- Finance department support and involvement in the development and implementation stages is essential for there to be any hope of success.
- The senior logistician must be able to sell the concept to finance and the organisation's management. Implementing logistics accounting means that resources must be diverted from other projects, so all stakeholders must be 'on-side'.

Table 13.4   P&L account to reflect the impact of supply chains

Traditional accounts	%	Restructured accounts	%	Explanation of restructured accounts
Sales revenue	100.0	Sales revenue	100.0	
Cost of goods sold	78.8	Supply market spend	51.4	Spending on purchased products, materials and services
Gross profit	21.2	Gross margin	48.6	Equivalent to the added value
Tax/interest	15.9	Internal spend		The cost of adding value to the supply market spend
Net profit	5.3	Employment expenditure (say 50% of 48.6) Note: the total employment costs for supply chains and logistics in an enterprise can be identified and consolidated with the supply market spend to provide the investment in supply chains	24.3	All salaries, wages and benefits (e.g. superannuation or provident fund payments, crèche, company vehicles, training, holiday pay, meals subsidy)
Shareholders' dividend	3.0	Sales and administration expenses	3.1	Internal, non-employment costs
Retained earnings	2.3	Gross profit or earnings before interest and tax (EBIT)	21.2	
		Tax and Interest payments	15.9	
		Net profit	5.3	
		Shareholders' dividend	3.0	
		Retained earnings	2.3	

- The process for data collection, analysis and reporting must be simple—'simple systems and intelligent people' should be the approach.
- Incorporate the logistics accounting outputs into the monthly financial reports to obtain continual visibility at senior levels. To enhance visibility, the logistics accounting outputs must be an input to the logistics strategy, which in turn is an input to the organisation's business plan.

On a global basis, accounting standards are an impediment to measuring the performance of supply chains, both international and domestic. There are many inhibitors, especially rules concerning treatment of costs, particularly under the **generally accepted accounting principles (GAAP)** and International Accounting Standards, which apply to financial reporting for global corporations. Until change is effected, accounting for supply chains and logistics will need to be a separate stand-alone system that consolidates into the traditional accounting system of a company.

Budgets

The annual business plan and budget cycle consume many hours of meetings and it may take three months or more to arrive at the new budget. It can be a game of poker between finance and operating managers, or it can be a reasoned set of numbers, as discussed in this section.

The board of directors and CEO are responsible for approving the business plan, which identifies the corporate aim and objectives in terms of sales, profit, investment and return on investment (ROI). The business plan will be based on past performance, current capabilities in the business and realistic future opportunities. These elements of the business plan then become the financial framework for managing the business and establishing the operating budgets.

Schultz (1984) devised a budgeting approach (which can be structured as a spreadsheet) where all the elements are linked, so that the budgeting process can be logically followed.

Step 1 is the investment plan, approved by the board of directors, as shown in Table 13.5 overleaf.

Table 13.5 Investment plan

Description	Objective	Calculation ($m)
1. Opening net worth (shareholders' equity plus retained earnings)		20.00
2. Real growth forecast	10% of $20.0	
3. Inflation growth	3% of $20.0	
4. Closing net worth	lines 2 + 3 × 1	22.60
5. Required return on equity	15% × $22.6	3.39
6. Earnings to re-invest	lines 4 − 1	2.60
7. Dividend to shareholders	lines 5 − 6	0.79

Step 2 is for senior management and operating managers to complete the profit plan, based on the traditional accounting structure, as shown in Table 13.6.

Table 13.6 Profit plan

Description	Objective	Calculation ($m)
1. Net profit objective	7% on sales	
2. Sales budget	Investment plan line 5 / Profit plan line 1 ($3.39 / 0.07)	48.23
3. Cost of goods sold (COGS).	% to be selected; say 65% × line 2 (0.65 × $48.23)	31.35
4. Gross profit	lines 2 − 3	16.88
5. Expenses: operating (including Logistics), sales, R&D and administration. Break out by each expense area	% to be selected; say 28% × line 2 (0.28 × $48.23)	13.50
6. Net profit	lines 4 − 5	3.38

Step 3 is for senior management and operating managers to complete the asset plan, as shown in Table 13.7.

Table 13.7 Asset plan

Description	Objective	Calculation ($m)
1. Sales per day	Profit plan line 2 / 360 ($48.23 / 360)	0.13
2. Cash required in days of sales	Time-phase cash flow: AR, AP and payroll; Say 10 days of sales (10 × $0.13)	1.30
3. Receivables in days of sales	Estimated collection time; say 60 days x line 1 (60 × 0.13)	7.80
4. Inventory objective	COGS (profit plan line 3) / Stockturns target ($31.35 / 3.5)	8.96
5. Current assets	lines 2 + 3 + 4	18.06
6. Fixed assets	Industry average; say $1 of fixed assets supports $4 of sales. Profit plan line 2 / line 4 ($48.23 / 4)	12.06
7. Total assets	lines 5 + 6	30.12

Step 4 is for senior management and operating managers to complete the capital plan, which is passed to the Board of Directors for approval. This concerns the **debt-to-capital ratio** and the total amount of bank debt required to finance the business, as shown in Table 13.8.

Table 13.8   Capital plan

Description	Objective	Calculation ($m)
1. Total assets	From Asset plan line 7	30.12
2. Current ratio	Calculate current assets / current liabilities. Assume ratio @ 2.5.	
3. Current liabilities	Asset plan line 5 / 2.5 ($18.06 / 2.5)	7.22
4. Total capital required	lines 1 – 3	37.34
5. Opening net worth	Business plan line 1	20.00
6. Debt required	lines 4 – 5	17.34
7. Debt /capital ratio	line 6 / line 4 × 100	46%

If the debt required and therefore the debt-to-capital ratio is not acceptable, then re-plan from the asset plan backwards, as the directors will be the last to agree to any change in the investment plan. Areas to consider for improvement are the cash requirements, collection of accounts receivables and inventory turns. Then re-plan the capital plan, where the current ratio can be reviewed.

When this financial planning process has been completed, it can be used as the basis for operational level/ department managers to structure their budgets. As an example, the distribution element of logistics could use the budget framework derived from Christopher (2005). It would be utilised to extend the sales budget by customers and their 'cost to serve', in order to identify the major expense areas as a matrix; this is shown in Table 13.9.

Table 13.9   Budget matrix

	Logistics functional area Activity 1	Logistics functional area Activity 2	Logistics functional area Activity 3	Total distribution budget by customer
Customer 1				
Customer 2				
Customer 3				
Distribution activities				
Total costs				

The aspect of concern in the budgeting process and cycle of organisations is time. When a budget has been established and then a major event occurs that requires the budget to be reviewed, how quickly can the organisation respond to the change and how long will the budget process take?

In too many companies, the planning and budget cycle can take 60 days, and some have a problem in keeping it under 90 days. As organisations become larger and more complex in structure, there is an increasing difficulty in balancing objectives and priorities and then allocating resources. However, the criterion for success in business today is promoted at conferences and in magazines as:

* customer focused
* responsive
* innovative
* flexible
* cost effective.

Then why should the annual budget cycle take so long? Applying all these adjectives to the budget cycle should provide an objective to reduce the planning and budget cycle time from the current 60 days to, say, 20 days or less.

Chapter questions

Operational

1. It is possible for a business to be profitable yet become bankrupt. Explain how this can occur.
2. Extending payment to suppliers may be considered good financial management for a business. Identify the range of problems this policy may cause.
3. As a supplier, the trading terms on your invoices are 'net 30 days; 3 per cent discount for payment within 10 days'. Identify why it is of benefit to provide a discount for early payment.
4. To accurately calculate the cost to serve requires the collection of data from multiple areas, followed by consolidation by measurement criteria such as geographic area or customer type. Select a cost type from the list provided in the chapter and identify the 'lowest-cost' manner of collecting the data.

Planning

5. Identify how cash flow, working capital and cash-to-cash cycle time could be incorporated into the sales and operations planning (S&OP) process.
6. Absorption costing remains common in companies. What outcomes may occur in a product company if the product profit margin is used as a guide to planning operations?
7. Comment on the following statements concerning LSP pricing for quotations:
   a. As the gross profit on the proposed contract contributes to the fixed overhead, the bid price can be reduced to win the contract.
   b. The contract will be priced at $'x', as that will cover variable costs.
   c. Our vehicles already pass the potential client's premises; therefore the delivery charge can be removed from the quotation.
   d. The potential client is located next to a current customer. How will distribution costs be established?

Management

8. Working capital optimisation and supply chain optimisation should be implemented as one undertaking. Discuss whether this statement is valid.
9. Consider cash flow, working capital and cash-to-cash cycle time. How would you use these three measures as a basis for managing supply chains?
10. **Transport costing and facilities investment**
    A division of a global chemical company manufactures and sells a product in the form of granules, which are delivered by the company direct to the customer. The product is produced and delivered in three forms of packaging:
    - bulk: in a specific delivery vehicle designed to blow granules directly into a holding tower at the customer site
    - 1 tonne bulk bag: for customers without the holding tower installation
    - 25 kg bags: stacked and shrink-wrapped on a pallet, for low usage customers.
    The market share for each delivery form is:
    - bulk = low
    - bulk bag = medium
    - 25 kg bag = high.
    The basis of calculating the $ per tonne transport cost for delivery is:
       Total transport costs for the financial year ÷ Total tonnes budgeted to be sold
    A proposal has been submitted to management for investment in a new automated packing line for the 25 kg bags. Comment on the value to the company of this investment.

References and links

Christopher, M., *Logistics and Supply Chain Management,* 3rd edn, Prentice Hall, 2005.

Cooper, R. & Kaplan, R., 'Measure cost right: Make the right decision', *Harvard Business Review,* Vol 96, No 103, September–October, 1988.

Kaplan, R. & Anderson, S., 'Time driven Activity based Costing', *Harvard Business Review*, November–December 2004.

Schultz, T., *Business Requirements Planning—the Journey to Excellence*, The Forum Limited, 1984.

Technology and communications as enablers

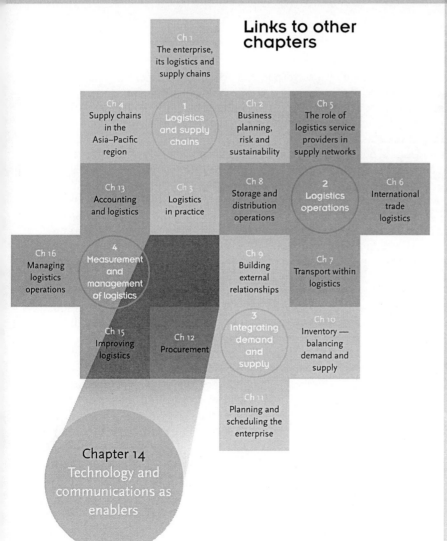

Links to other chapters

Ch 1
The enterprise, its logistics and supply chains

Ch 4
Supply chains in the Asia–Pacific region

1
Logistics and supply chains

Ch 2
Business planning, risk and sustainability

Ch 5
The role of logistics service providers in supply networks

Ch 13
Accounting and logistics

Ch 3
Logistics in practice

Ch 8
Storage and distribution operations

2
Logistics operations

Ch 6
International trade logistics

Ch 16
Managing logistics operations

4
Measurement and management of logistics

Ch 9
Building external relationships

Ch 7
Transport within logistics

Ch 15
Improving logistics

Ch 12
Procurement

3
Integrating demand and supply

Ch 10
Inventory — balancing demand and supply

Ch 11
Planning and scheduling the enterprise

Chapter 14
Technology and communications as enablers

On completion of this chapter you will be able to:

- understand the role of technology in supply chains and logistics

- recognise the distinctions between data, information and knowledge

- follow the steps required to obtain cooperation, coordination and collaboration through supply chains

- comprehend the scope of global standards

- consider the requirements for applications in supply chains and the implementation challenges

- recognise the distinction between e-business and e-commerce.

Key terms

These terms are used in the text. Develop your own notebook by downloading information on each term.

operating system	serial shipping container code (SSCC)	enterprise resources planning (ERP)
software application	electronic data interchange (EDI)	global trade management (GTM)
data	automatic identification and data collection (AIDC)	warehouse management system (WMS)
information	radio frequency identification devices (RFID)	manufacturing resources planning (MRP2)
knowledge	optical character recognition (OCR)	international trade logistics
pipeline visibility	EPCglobal	software as a service (SaaS)
information technology and communications (ITC)	International Standards Organisation (ISO)	cloud computing
cooperation		web 2.0
coordination		e-business
collaboration		e-commerce
GS1		
global trade item number (GTIN)	global location number (GLN)	

Introduction

Every move in the physical supply chain is accompanied by a corresponding action in the logical or data chain. For example, when an order is placed for a product or service, a transfer of data takes place concerning each item, its quantity and price, by each organisation. This data transaction is then accompanied by the physical picking and acceptance of the items. Similarly, at the point where goods are delivered, the customer's receiving process incorporates both the data aspect and the physical aspect.

The synchronisation of the physical and logical processes is vital to maintaining the integrity of supply chains. This chapter considers the approaches and applications in support of integrating the physical and logical realms that need to be considered.

Technology in supply chains

Technology is a collective term that refers to a range of computing and communications hardware, **operating systems** and **software applications**. A justification for the purchase of technology is to reduce costs in the supply chains. But is technology just for reducing costs or should it be identified as a means to grow and improve the business?

In a 'business to business' environment, there is often an expectation of repeat business. Therefore, customer and seller details are recorded by each party; there are due diligence reviews (for example a credit check) to ensure that undertaking business transactions will not provide unwanted surprises, and a purchase order and invoice are issued and recorded by each party to the contract. Thereafter, using this base data, the relationship can develop to whatever level the parties decide is mutually beneficial. However, this not only requires the development of relationships; it requires the development of systems.

Internet-based software applications have begun to change the way business is conducted. The future could move in the direction of mobility, with extensive use of mobile devices in sales, by customers and consumers, in the warehouse and on vehicles.

The major benefits that consumer product companies should be seeking from technology in supply chains are:

- a closer alignment of marketing and product development with logistics, providing a reduced 'time to market'
- visibility of product movement in real time
- increased velocity of material flow and the reduction of inventory along each supply chain
- reduction in the 'cost to serve'
- the consequential reduction in working capital required to operate the business.

Using technology in supply chains does have some challenges:

1. In developed countries, relationship power in consumer-linked supply chains is moving towards major retailers. Their ability to gather **data** and **information** from supply chains can result in the use of this **knowledge** to further increase their power.
2. Suppliers may not be in a financial position to implement technology demanded by larger customers. If there is a collaborative relationship, then sharing of investment costs, or the customer using its buying power to influence the total cost for suppliers, are ways to limit the problem.
3. The cost and time for specification, purchase and implementation of technology is too often underestimated by companies, which can lead to frustration by staff, annoyance by customers and suppliers and potentially cash flow and profitability concerns for the organisation.

Ultimately, technology selection and implementation must be approached as a 'change management' process, with the depth of involvement by senior management that a critical change to the business deserves.

Data and information

There is a hierarchy of value attached to words and numbers:

* *data*—the words and numbers in a technology environment
* *information*—data that is structured into something meaningful
* *knowledge*—information from a variety of sources that is assembled in a manner that enables people to make judgments about the past and the future.

For example, A0203-146539-350 is a piece of data. Unless the syntax (the order of a sequence of data) is known, it is meaningless. If it is known that the syntax is structured as Location-Item-Quantity, the data has meaning and is now Information—Location A0203, Item 146539, Quantity 350. If the daily consumption rate of the item is 200 and the lead time is two days, then the total of the information available provides knowledge on which to base a decision concerning ordering of additional items.

Using data and information

The majority of companies do not yet have timely visibility into the critical processes involved in managing their global supply chain events and relationships.

While it is nice to have information, it does come at a total cost that enterprises must evaluate against the value it provides. Full **pipeline visibility** through all links in a company's supply chains appears to be the ideal, because it enables a company to:

* view customers' consumption of the company's products
* track the delivery performance of logistics service providers (LSP)
* know the suppliers' schedules
* see when orders at suppliers will be completed
* know the performance of the supplier's suppliers in delivering materials and components against orders.

Whether operating in global or domestic supply chains, businesses are being required to exchange data and information. At each node or link point of data collection in a supply chain, there are transactions within and between organisations. Each has its feedback loop and correction activity (for when things go wrong). Data collection points occur when we:

* connect to shipping schedules and book space on a vessel or aircraft
* book a road transport vehicle or space on a vehicle
* pay freight invoices
* arrange financing of shipments, if import or export
* track goods on transport (ships, aircraft, trains and road transport)
* link to customs and insurance companies
* register delivery and receipt of shipments
* notify non-conformance of shipment
* pay for shipments
* track goods in warehouses
* locate and count inventory.

The requirement for data could increase substantially into the future, with demands from government agencies to address aspects of product recalls, carbon emission recording and health and nutrition objectives of an economy.

At the same time as this increasing requirement for exchange of data between multiple parties in supply chains, governments have enacted privacy laws that may preclude the passing of data to third parties in a contract; for example, can a buyer receive information about the supplier's delivery schedules from an LSP? Also, some governments have passed laws or regulations concerning the dissemination of data and information in the country and across borders, which may limit the effectiveness of enhanced communications.

To collect, store, integrate and distribute all the data and information is a substantial task and expense in terms of **information technology and communications (ITC)**. Initiatives are required to ensure that the data is 'clean' and accurate, that the IT applications of each organisation can incorporate the data and that it can be transmitted at fast speeds.

TOWARDS COLLABORATION

For organisations to progressively work more closely together, technology can provide the underpinning of the required three 'Cs':

1. **cooperation** of the people involved
2. **coordination** through standardisation of data
3. **collaboration** through access to the same information.

If resident data is the same in the IT systems within departments and divisions of an enterprise and between buyers and sellers, then organisations can *coordinate* their operations between suppliers and customers and internally.

If people have confidence in the data, then organisations and internal groups can *collaborate* to predict trends and provide consolidated reports.

The steps for data to become meaningful and useful to a wider scope of interested parties, from the company to the supply network and the wider knowledge network, are illustrated in Table 14.1.

Table 14.1 Moving towards a collaborative environment

Level	Degree of working together	Explanation
Knowledge network	Integration	Network is viewed as a single entity
	Collaboration	Knowledge is shared within the network
Supply network	Integration	Networked sharing of knowledge, e.g. using advanced planning and scheduling (APS) application
	Collaboration	Companies share information, e.g. using collaborative planning, forecasting and replenishment (CPFR) process
	Coordination	Data and messaging standards used across the supply network
	Cooperation	Willingness to work together and a level of trust between the parties
Company network	Integration	Centralised or networked. Share knowledge throughout the company
	Collaboration	Functions and divisions share information
	Coordination	Data and messaging standards for the company to assist sharing of data
	Cooperation	Willingness to work together across functions, e.g., the S&OP process

From a systems viewpoint of Table 14.1:

- Logistics is concerned with *coordinating* the internal and external processes to provide availability.
- Supply chains are the vehicle for *collaboration* between the internal and external entities and systems.
- Integration of supply chains can possibly occur through harnessing the knowledge of the organisations within a supply network.

However, too often we read or hear of organisations that promote their 'collaboration' with 'business partners' when they have not even achieved a predictable level of data coordination inside their own business—so beware of the hype!

Global standards for collection and transmission of item data

Need for standards

To be effective and efficient in the collection, collation and use of data requires that global standards are used, so that clear and understandable exchanges can occur within and between organisations.

To illustrate the opposing situation of not having standards, GS1 Australia (2009) identified the situation with shoes. There is no global standard for shoe sizes; therefore, the same fashion shoe for women must be manufactured in a factory as:

- size 38 for sale in Shanghai
- size 23 for sale in Tokyo
- size 5½ for sale in Sydney
- size 7 for sale in New York
- size 4½ for sale in London
- size 37.5 for sale in Paris.

The production lots must be planned and kept physically separate, because each shoe is marked with its specific size. This also means that all correspondence concerning purchase orders, import documentation, delivery and invoices must contain an identification of the correct size for the market. All this additional effort increases costs.

The identification of each shoe SKU as an item has already been standardised, together with a multitude of other items around the world. This is through use of the barcode, which is recognised as the standard identification system for a product. This system has been developed since the 1970s by member-owned organisations, which amalgamated in 2005 to become the global organisation **GS1**.

GS1 numbering system

GS1 has developed an internationally recognised and accepted standard of identification and communication for products, services, assets, shipments and locations that is global, open and can be applied to multi-sector industries. This enables the electronic reading of product and non-product descriptors through six layers in a supply chain, as shown in Table 14.2.

Table 14.2 Layers in a supply chain

Layer	Movement or storage descriptor
0	Item in its immediate protective wrapping
1	Package, or the inner carton (can also be called an outer in some organisations)
2	Transport unit, or the shipper (can be called an outer carton in some organisations—do not confuse with Layer 1)
3	Unit load, typically the pallet
4	Physical storage location
5	Movement container, e.g. 20 ft sea container (TEU) or 40 ft sea container (FEU)
6	Movement vehicle, e.g. truck, aircraft, ship, train

The basic identifier of an item is the **global trade item number (GTIN)**, which is a 14-digit identifier that denotes a family of data structures. It is used for retail and non-retail items and provides the capability for raw materials, components and finished products to be tracked through a supply chain—from the mine or farm, through each manufacturing facility, at all transport and storage locations and then to the point of sale.

The GTIN is not meaningful in itself but is a means to access a database of product-related information. There are four formats used for retail products.

For North America:
- GTIN-12.

For the rest of the world:
- GTIN-8
- GTIN-13
- GTIN-14.

The full 14-digit GTIN is maintained within a format of shorter length by completing the number with zeros justified to the left. Therefore, the full 14-digit data string for each item is entered into a company's database and stored.

The GTIN-13 is used for the majority of items and encodes a 13-digit number, as shown in Figure 14.1.

Figure 14.1   GTIN-13 data format

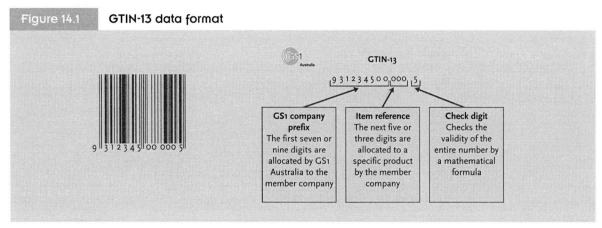

Source: GS1 Australia.

Non-retail items

The GS1-128 barcode is the standard for labelling objects used in logistics activities; that is, at the case level and other items that do not cross a point of sale.

The **serial shipping container code (SSCC)** is for the identification of transport and/or storage units. In addition, the SSCC may be required for receipt of the order into customers' facilities, as shown in Figure 14.2.

Barcodes are required on the majority of retail items and their packaging; therefore, companies in consumer packaged goods (CPG) and fast moving consumer goods (FMCG) businesses have implemented the base technology for coordinating data within the organisation and between their trading parties. Barcodes have been implemented in some other industrial sectors, but if not, a company should provide barcodes for all incoming and outgoing items to enable internal controls.

Figure 14.2   GS1-128 barcode

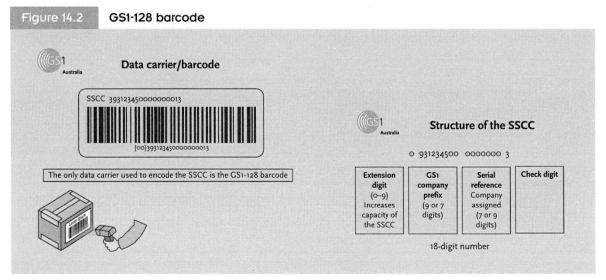

Source: GS1 Australia.

Implementing data standards in business

Achieving the higher levels of cooperation and collaboration required through the supply chains requires six phases in order to implement all global standards. Implementation is not intended to be sequential and more than one phase could be implemented concurrently.

Phase 1—Improve internal performance

The corporate adoption of the GS1 standard as a business tool should initially be to improve internal performance; this requires that barcodes encoding GTIN be used for internal tracking. The use of barcodes will have differing benefits at each stage of the internal processes, such as:

1. improved 'in-full' performance (inventory accuracy)
2. improved 'on-time' performance
3. reduced errors in documents sent to customers (accuracy rate)
4. improved 'inventory turns'
5. reduction of non-value-added time.

Phase 2—Communicate using the standard

Success achieved within the enterprise from using barcodes gives the confidence to discuss the adoption of the GS1 standard with suppliers. Customers should be approached last, when there is much higher confidence of success.

Suppliers may already have barcodes on their product packaging in order to comply with other customer requirements. The challenge is how to use this data to improve the relationship between the enterprise and its suppliers.

GS1 has a global standard (eCom) for electronic business messaging, or **electronic data interchange (EDI)**. It is defined by GS1 as the 'transfer of structured data, by agreed message standards, between computer applications with minimum human intervention'. The GS1 standard contains two options: GS1 EANCOM and GS1 XML.

This means that all the previously paper-based documents can now be stored in an electronic form, irrespective of the computer hardware and software applications, saving people's time and effort and also saving the business money.

The selection of the technology to adopt will be based on what the company's trading parties are currently using or by the choice of a powerful retailer, supplier or industry group of participants.

Phase 3—Synchronise the master data

Companies that want to track events in supply chains may encounter problems caused by discrepancies in the master data held by each party and therefore inaccurate data in transactions. These errors lead to inaccuracies in forecasts and reports that generate ongoing problems in the relationship, especially if the company personnel are overwhelmed with bad data that has not been checked.

The GS1 UK *Data Crunch Report* (2009) identified that in the UK grocery retail sector, over 80 per cent of transactions between suppliers and retailers had inconsistencies in what should have been identical data. The impact of this situation in terms of lost or late deliveries, inaccurate orders, additional transport costs and duplicated work was estimated at £700 m over five years. The situation in the Asia–Pacific region is assumed to be of a similar magnitude, where invoice discrepancies are a major cause of non value adding costs; human intervention and manual work-around processes are required to overcome the problems.

When a party updates data for each SKU, in terms of product, location and demand/supply information, all organisations with a need to know should receive the same data update directly to their databases for:

- sales and merchandising documents
- inbound and outbound material and product movements
- retailer stock control, availability and pricing
- invoice reconciliation and payment.

The GS1 global data synchronisation network (GDSN) works via a network of data pools (electronic catalogues of standardised item data) and the GS1 Global Registry (the 'yellow pages' that enable the finding and inter-operability between data pools). Within the GDSN, each trade item is identified using a unique combination of the item GTIN, the GLN of the supplier and the GLN of the country (or countries) where the item will be sold. In Australia and New Zealand this service is called GS1net.

GS1 estimates savings in supply chain costs at between 1 and 3 per cent, following a less than one-year implementation. However, as with all supply chain software, ensuring clean basic data, synchronisation of data, interfacing with other applications and implementation takes time, and GDSN is no different.

Phase 4—Use data carriers

Data carriers are various technologies used that enable a message to be transmitted and read. The barcode reader is only one of several **automatic identification and data capture (AIDC)** technologies, others being **radio frequency identification devices (RFID)** and **optical character recognition (OCR)**, as used on cheques, magnetic stripe and smart cards.

The AIDC technologies differ in the way they encode and carry data, the quantity of data held and their ease of deployment for a given task. For example, the barcode system has inherent limitations of requiring a 'line of sight' and a relatively short distance to provide a successful read. In AIDC, no one technology is inherently better than another and there are solutions for all needs. Rather than getting confused about the technologies, organisations should initially concentrate on establishing a meaningful business case for the adoption of a track and trace capability throughout their core supply chains.

Scanning a barcode with a hand-held scanner

RFID AS A DATA CARRIER

EPCglobal is an organisation within GS1, formed to establish and support the electronic product code (EPC) global standard for use in RFID tags and readers. The RFID technology was developed from independent research undertaken at the Auto-ID Center within the Massachusetts Institute of Technology (MIT) and separate standards were developed by the **International Standards Organisation (ISO)**.

The technology allows data stored in an RFID tag to be transmitted as electronic pulses. A reader gathers data from the RFID tags that are within its RF field of view, without the need to pass a scanner directly over the tags. This enables the automatic identification of items over some operating distance and it can be on a non-'line of sight' basis for 'active' tags, as the RF energy can penetrate most non-conductive materials.

Developments in RFID tags and readers that use sensors now make it possible to receive data concerning a tagged product's geographic location, temperature, humidity and any other details that may affect the product's condition or resale value.

The supplier and product ID used in the EPC RFID tag is the same as the global trade item number (GTIN) used within a barcode, but, because the EPC contains a serial number, each instance of the GTIN read can be uniquely identified.

When the term RFID is used, it relates not only to the various tags but the readers, RF operating parameters, communication settings and the software; so implementation can be complex.

The more likely implementation of the technologies for consumer products will be RFID tags at the container, pallet and shipper levels and barcodes at the item level and locations. Barcodes and RFID should therefore not be considered as individual component technologies, but as two of several technologies that can be integrated to deliver a viable, cost-effective solution.

RFID tags and readers can also be used for:

◦ product tracking within an organisation

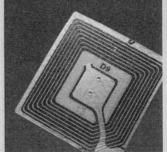

RFID chip

- facilities access control
- road toll collection
- movable assets tracking, such as within a mine site, hospital or a herd of cattle.

These remain the most successful implementations of the technologies.

Phase 5—Know the location

Linking products to a location is an important element of the base data. However, for a location to be meaningful, there must be a standard identifier attached to the location that trading parties can access and interrogate.

The location standard is called the **global location number (GLN)**, while the GTIN is used for identifying products. The GLN is the GS1-128 type and can be read with a barcode reader or an EPC RFID tag.

A GLN may be assigned to:

- legal entities, such as a registered company or division of a company
- physical entities, such as ship-from locations and ship-to destinations, which can include specific locations such as a shelf in a laboratory
- operational entities, such as buying and invoicing departments
- electronic addresses that enable parties relevant to the transaction to be identified, such as the location of the sender and recipient of electronic transactions and the LSP.

The use of a global number identifier enables more accurate information and speedy undertaking of logistics processes, including: ordering, transport, electronic messaging of transactions, inventory management, traceability and product recall.

Phase 6—Ensure traceability of product and materials

Product recalls can be initiated through a company's technical department, a consumer complaint or government direction. When this occurs, the manufacturer or importer and retailers need to access all records that pertain to the recent sales, production, landed goods and distribution for the product SKU.

This process is called traceability and to successfully manage a national recall within a short timeframe requires global standards that all parties can access and use. In a similar manner to other standards, GS1 has created the global traceability standard (GTS), to enable (if necessary) a global recall along each supply chain for the product, plus along the extended supply chains for the ingredient or material that may have been the cause of the recall.

Applications for supply chains

Requirements for supply chains and logistics software applications (sometimes called apps) can be defined in any configuration that suits the business outcomes, whether for a brand company, an exporter/importer or an LSP.

There are three levels of complexity for applications: strategic, tactical and operational. Examples of the levels are:

- integrating data in the organisation is across all three levels (**enterprise resources planning** or **ERP**)
- coordinating global product movements is tactical and operational (**global trade management** or **GTM**)
- operating a warehouse is tactical and operational (**warehouse management system** or **WMS**) and
- cooperating with colleagues and externally is operational (office application such as MS Word).

Not all companies require a full-featured ERP, GTM, WMS or any other application. These applications can be big, intrusive in daily processes, complex to configure and can take a long time and much expenditure to install.

Technology goes through a number of steps before becoming an accepted part of business; this is called the 'hype cycle', as shown in Figure 14.3.

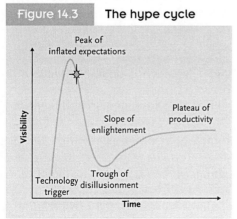

Figure 14.3 **The hype cycle**

Source: Gartner Group, July 2009.

The hype cycle works as follows.

- The technology trigger is the technology announcement or product launch that generates media attention.
- The peak of inflated expectation is the increasing unrealistic expectations with more implementation failures than successes.
- The trough of disillusionment happens when the technology is abandoned and the media lose attention.
- The slope of enlightenment occurs when businesses with a belief in the technology persevere to understand the practical applications of the technology.
- The plateau of productivity is reached as the technology becomes stable and the benefits become accepted and used within a wide or niche user community.

Some of the current ideas and technologies will come through the hype cycle and be implemented by many enterprises. However, it must be recognised there are companies today that do not use the barcodes printed on their finished product packaging for internal counting, tracking and control—a technology more than 30 years old!

ERP systems

The main application that is often encountered in business organisations is the enterprise resources planning or ERP system, which contains a range of application modules designed to integrate management plans, resources, people and money.

Typically, the finance and accounting module is a core application, but the remainder of the modules need to be specified to meet the organisation's requirements. Therefore, ERP represents an approach to data and information management rather than a specific system.

For a manufacturing company, the traditional ERP system modules are structured similar to the outline in Figure 14.4. Service areas such as HR have been omitted.

The main product planning application within ERP systems may be called **manufacturing resources planning (MRP2)** and addresses either discrete or process production methods.

Discrete ERP systems are designed for products that are in a solid form and can be disassembled into their discrete components, such as electronics, motor vehicles and furniture. A process ERP system is suited for organisations that manufacture products which are in a liquid, semi-solid or powder form—such as foods and beverages, pharmaceuticals, paints, chemicals and plastics—and which cannot be disassembled into discrete components.

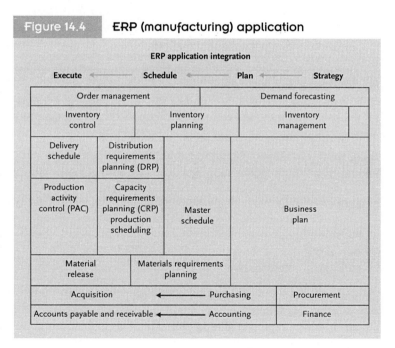

Figure 14.4   **ERP (manufacturing) application**

Interfacing and integrating applications

As time progressed and the effectiveness of well planned supply chains and logistics became more important, companies began to interface their ERP system with specialist supply network analysis and planning (SNAP) applications that address the needs of logisticians. Examples are shown in Figure 14.5 opposite.

The adoption by companies of SNAP applications has prompted suppliers of ERP systems to integrate the most popular applications into their ERP products.

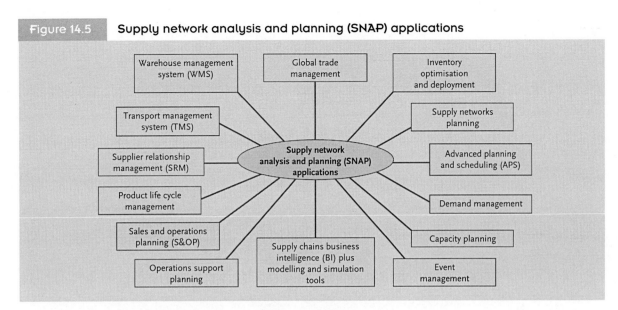

Figure 14.5   Supply network analysis and planning (SNAP) applications

The essential difference between the two types of application is:

- interfaced applications maintain their own data structure and synchronise with the ERP database
- integrated applications use the ERP database; therefore, synchronisation is not required.

The trade-off is that the interfaced application may have more functionality, but the need for data synchronisation means that it can be more expensive to support. This difference continues a long running IT industry discussion: whether it is better to:

- implement a comprehensive ERP system that contains all the capability required, even though some elements may not be totally satisfactory, or
- interface a number of 'best-of-breed' applications that are comprehensive in design and capability.

Another view is that, because companies are outsourcing functions and changing their structures to address market needs, the comprehensive ERP system, with its fixed functionality, becomes a hindrance to the changes actually occurring. Instead, the ERP system should be positioned as the transaction backbone of the organisation. It would contain an audit trail of sales orders, purchase orders and payments, plus basic accounting, production control and HR data. Information processing would, however, happen through interfaced specialist applications. This approach is illustrated in Figure 14.6 overleaf.

In this scenario, the specialist applications, whether based in-house, at a data centre or at an LSP, access the base data from the backbone, complete their tasks and send the solution back to the ERP backbone for consolidation.

When selecting or adding to ERP systems, the challenge is to identify the level of interfacing and integration required and the capability and availability to implement and manage the result.

Distribution systems

Logistics service provider (LSP) companies that provide distribution services are more likely to implement a warehouse management system (WMS) as the core application. This can be enhanced with financial and accounting, purchasing, light manufacturing or final assembly and test and transport management system (TMS) applications. For LSPs operating internationally, these modules may also be interfaced to a global trade management (GTM) application or other elements of an **international trade logistics** application.

The primary role of a WMS is to plan the operational requirements (that is, movement and storage) and resources of the warehouse (or distribution centre), as shown in Figure 14.7 overleaf.

The distribution plan is generated from customer orders and inventory data. The plan is executed through an operations control module, which is required if the warehouse does more than hand pick using pallets and paper pick lists. The operations control module operates in real time to integrate all the warehouse equipment and re-plan in response to equipment downtime.

Figure 14.6   ERP as the backbone application

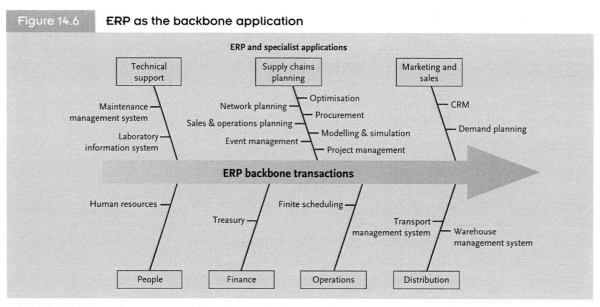

Figure 14.7   Warehouse management system (WMS)

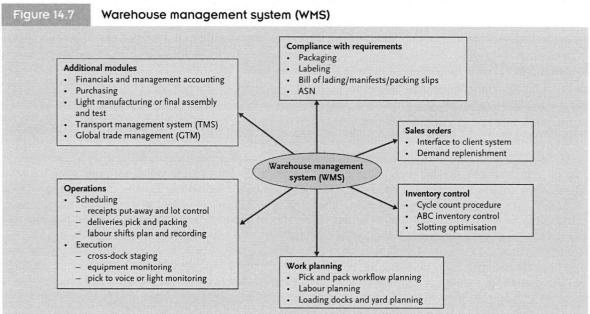

A change in the business needs of clients is requiring some LSPs that operate internationally to enhance the WMS for store ready merchandise (SRM) distribution. This is where orders destined for multiple retail outlets (or consumers) are separately assembled, ticketed and packed. The packed orders are then loaded to containers destined for the port nearest to the customer. This requires a tight linkage between orders received, warehouse operations, supplier deliveries, shipping and customs applications.

To justify a comprehensive WMS, the warehouse or DC should be a substantial size, handling a volume of orders, with multiple SKU per order and operating with extensive material handling equipment.

Developments in applications

Small and medium sized enterprises (SME) must focus on their business and generally prefer not to know about servers, networks, communication protocols and the like. They typically want a reliable and fast IT service that exists everywhere the business may operate (that is, it is ubiquitous).

This approach to accessing applications is called **software as a service (SaaS)**, whereby a service provider removes many of the technology risks, with the customer paying for usage, although it is not an entirely risk-free process. The service provider is responsible for the hardware, communication, applications, specialised content (such as the harmonised system for tariffs in a global trade management application) and data storage.

A term that is used interchangeably with SaaS is **cloud computing** (the cloud-like squiggle that network designers use to denote the internet), but they are different. Both approaches use the concept of technology residing somewhere else and users accessing applications via the 'cloud'.

Cloud computing is for a company that wishes to establish and manage its own applications network on the web, although their network operations may be maintained by an external contractor. SaaS, however, has the service provider supplying a total service package.

The ease of joining a social network highlights the potential ease of joining a network in a logistics environment. Applications that are grouped under the heading of **web 2.0** and currently used for social interaction may be modified for use in supply chains.

Supply networks ideally require 'up-to-date' data and information, so that business plans and schedules can remain current. A communication platform designed like a social network can provide the immediate data required. Confidentiality is maintained through members of a supply network only allowing selected managers within the network to be 'friends'.

Implementing applications

Implementing IT and communications (ITC) systems and critical applications, such as ERP, is not only a capital cost, but a potential threat to the business. This can occur if the purchase does not meet the required specification, or the business is not sophisticated enough to manage the implementation and ongoing operations. The time and expense of implementing (not just installing) applications is too often underestimated within companies—implementing corporate networked applications is not the same as loading Microsoft Office on a PC!

The relative time and effort to implement different applications measured against the complexity and capability of the application type is shown in Figure 14.8 below.

As supply chains become a more critical part of successful businesses, so responsibility for the effectiveness of systems in this area will increasingly fall to the supply chain or logistics manager. It has reached a stage in some companies where a supply chains systems manager has been appointed.

Whether or not that occurs, the most senior supply chain manager will need to understand and be effective in project management. When a new system goes live on the promised date, there is no second chance!

E-business and e-commerce

The discussion concerning standards and transmission of data identifies that organisations will progressively enhance their IT systems, so that electronic transmission of all transactions could become very common.

Figure 14.8	Supply chains application implementation

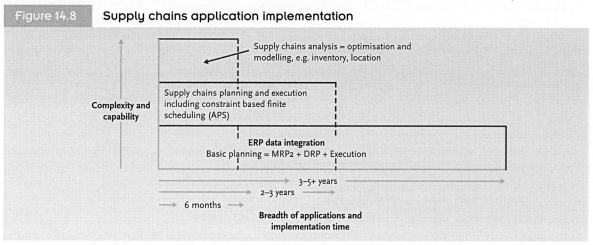

Source: Adapted from GRA Pty Ltd, www.gra.net.au

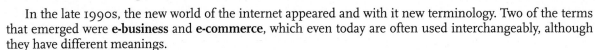

In the late 1990s, the new world of the internet appeared and with it new terminology. Two of the terms that emerged were **e-business** and **e-commerce**, which even today are often used interchangeably, although they have different meanings.

E-business describes an enterprise that operates only online and enables 'web-based self-service' to reduce the necessity for human customer service and support, although they may have warehouses or use LSPs. Amazon and eBay are examples of large e-businesses.

The types of e-business that can be encountered are:

- **B2B (business to business)**—companies doing business with each other
- **B2C (business to consumer)**—businesses selling products and services to the general public, often using 'shopping cart' software applications
- **C2C (consumer to consumer)**—these sites provide classified advertisements and auctions (for example eBay auctions) allowing individuals to purchase items using online payment systems
- **C2B (consumer to business)**—individuals post details of their project requirements and budget to a site and suppliers submit bids for selection; these sites are not yet widely evident.

E-business can also involve interactions with governments, identified as:

- G2G (government to government)—project control between layers of government
- G2B (government to business)—licences, payments
- G2C (government to citizen)—planning permissions, licences, payments
- B2G (business to government)—industry information and lobbying activities
- C2G (citizen to government)—sites such as www.fixmystreet.com where citizens provide information to government agencies.

E-commerce is the enhancement of key business processes within an organisation's structure, using the internet and other communication technologies. The business processes that are web enabled are internal communications and external 'business to business' transactions with parties; these can be financial or non-financial, such as a customer request for information.

An internal private network is called an intranet and when the private network is extended outside the business to suppliers and customers, it becomes an extranet.

Approach to e-commerce

E-commerce is becoming 'the way we do business' and will eventually lose its separate identity. Implementing e-commerce should be linked to the six phases previously described to achieve cooperation, coordination and collaboration within a company's supply chains. Some examples of e-commerce implementations are as follows.

ON THE SELLING SIDE

Transaction site: to provide product information for customers or consumers that enables the purchase of products and services, online or offline. The objective is to make it easier for customers or consumers to buy.

Services site: to provide company and product information, e-newsletters and after-sales service that builds relationships and informs long-term purchasing intentions. The objective is to generate enquiries and sales leads from current and potential customers.

Brand building site: to provide experiences for consumers (for example competitions) that support a company's brands; typically found in the CPG and FMCG sectors. This can also incorporate activities through social networking sites, such as Twitter, Facebook and MySpace.

ON THE BUYING SIDE

Portal site: a gateway to information, with links to different parts of the organisation and also to external sites. It provides information for suppliers on a range of topics such as:

- requirements to be considered as a supplier
- technical information about required supplies
- production schedules that inform current suppliers concerning deliveries.

Transaction site: to provide information for suppliers that enables the sale of their products and services to the company, both online and offline. The objective is to make it easier for suppliers to sell.

Chapter questions

Operational

1. In what ways can consumer mobile devices such as smartphones, personal digital assistants (PDA), netbooks and tablets be used in logistics activities? What limitations may exist for use in a business environment?
2. Identify how social media sites can be used in a logistics environment. What limitations may exist for use in a business environment?
3. Consider any computer-based application that you are familiar with. How user-friendly is it? What could be done to enhance its interaction with users? Do these requirements also apply to logistics applications and if so, why?
4. Figure 14.3 illustrates the 'hype cycle'. What current technologies are proceeding through their hype cycle and at what stage are they?

Planning

5. Figure 14.1 identifies that cooperation is the first step towards a collaborative relationship. Identify how to enhance the planning of supply chains through building a cooperative relationship within a company and the company's supply network.
6. The section 'Using data and information' lists links along a supply chain where data can be collected. Are there more links for specific products? In what order of priority should the links be identified as necessary for collaboration within a supply chain?
7. There are six phases for implementing data standards in business to achieve integration between enterprises. What type(s) of business would need to implement all phases and why?
8. Figure 14.5 shows a variety of supply network analysis and planning (SNAP) applications. List the applications in order of priority for implementation in a CPG or FMCG company and justify the selection.

Management

9. Will implementing 'best of breed' supply chain applications that interface rather than integrate, reduce the capability for collaboration within the organisation? Justify your reasoning.
10. Figure 14.7 shows that the core of a system for a distribution services company (3PL) is a warehouse management system; whereas for a brand company, the core application is finance and accounting. Will the system at the 3PL be called an ERP system and, if so, why?
11. Software as a service (SaaS) provides for mobile computing. Should a distribution services supplier (3PL) consider implementing all their applications using this technology? Justify why or why not.

Exercise

Some challenges facing business logistics are: the lack of visibility of movements of goods; ensuring availability of the product; costs associated with redundant logistical tasks and asset protection in transit. Implementing RFID may assist.

a. Discuss how wireless asset tracking improves visibility and productivity in supply chains. Consider examples from three different industries (for example heavy industry, retail, military, etc).
b. What is the relationship between the nature of the assets to be tracked and the viability of the implementation business case?
c. What is the justification for wireless tracking:
   a. at item and pallet level
   b. with barcodes used at item level?
d. Discuss building the business case for implementation of RFID at either item or pallet level. Outline a skeleton business case.
e. Discuss how the business case could be improved by considering indirect benefits (for example increase in sales and a reduction in stock holdings, etc).
f. What are some of the solution design and technology decisions facing a supply chain manager seeking to implement RFID?

References and links

Amazon.com: www.amazon.com
Data Crunch Report, GS1 UK, Oct 2009, www.gs1uk.org
eBay: www.ebay.com
'Understanding the Hype Cycle' Fenn, J. & Raskino, M.: www.gartner.com/pages/story.php.id.8795.s.8.jsp.
'Why Standards Count', *Link magazine*, Issue 23, GS1 Australia, 2009.

Learning outcomes

On completion of this chapter you will be able to:

- understand the need for performance management and measurement

- identify the measurement regime required within a 'one plan' approach for the business

- recognise the requirement and use for control of processes

- understand the main techniques that assist in the improvement of supply chains

- acknowledge the scope of responsibilities required of a project manager.

Links to other chapters

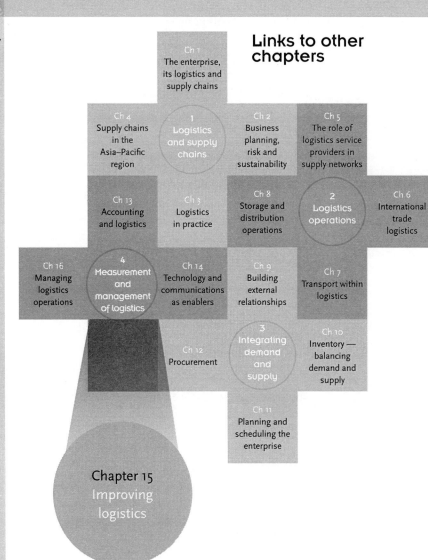

Ch 1
The enterprise, its logistics and supply chains

Ch 4
Supply chains in the Asia–Pacific region

1
Logistics and supply chains

Ch 2
Business planning, risk and sustainability

Ch 5
The role of logistics service providers in supply networks

Ch 13
Accounting and logistics

Ch 3
Logistics in practice

Ch 8
Storage and distribution operations

2
Logistics operations

Ch 6
International trade logistics

Ch 16
Managing logistics operations

4
Measurement and management of logistics

Ch 14
Technology and communications as enablers

Ch 9
Building external relationships

Ch 7
Transport within logistics

Ch 12
Procurement

3
Integrating demand and supply

Ch 10
Inventory — balancing demand and supply

Ch 11
Planning and scheduling the enterprise

Chapter 15
Improving logistics

Key terms

These terms are used in the text. Develop your own notebook by downloading information on each term.

performance management	effectiveness	constraint management
innovation	probability	business process re-engineering
flow process chart	PDCA/PDSA/DMAIC cycles	(BPR)
variability	lean	supply chain operations
control charts	agile	reference (SCOR) model
efficiency	theory of constraints (TOC)	project management

Introduction

'We behave how we are measured' is a very true phrase; the behaviours of an organisation, department, team or individual tend to be reinforced by how they are acknowledged. Measurement is the other important word here because, to use another common quotation, 'Without measurement, you are just another person with an opinion'.

This chapter considers the need for performance management and performance indicators together with continuous improvement against agreed performance targets.

Performance management

Performance management is providing the policies and processes that enable staff within the organisation to perform their work to the highest ability. For the best performance over time, the skills and contributions from individuals and teams must be recognised. This enables a culture of individual and collective responsibility for the improvement of processes.

As an indication of involvement in the improvement of performance, the *Carbon Disclosure Project Transport Report* (2010) identified that only 9 per cent of transport companies reported having current investments in new technologies or emission reduction initiatives. The Australian Bureau of Statistics (ABS) Business Characteristics Survey (2008) stated that more than half of all businesses in the wholesale trade, retail trade and manufacturing were 'innovation-active'. However, improvements to logistics, delivery and distribution methods were as low as 5 per cent in small businesses and only 7 per cent in medium-sized businesses. The first survey was international and the second was of businesses in Australia but, as the percentages quoted are similar, they could be representative of many countries in the region. This indicates that substantial change is required within organisations in order to enhance productivity in the logistics service provider (LSP) sector and in the logistics operations of product companies. A flowchart of performance management is provided in Figure 15.1 overleaf.

To support the performance management process, the organisation should have meaningful corporate aims and objectives so that staff can understand why particular improvement goals are necessary, as well as the expected outcomes. As an example, in the early 1950s, the American multinational Proctor & Gamble placed the following message on all its employees' ID cards:

Five points of business attitude
- Profit is our objective.
- No cost is sacrosanct—all must be challenged.
- No cost is necessary—we merely do not yet know how to eliminate it.
- There is always a better way.
- Change is our business.

Five points to improvement
- Improvement is every person's job.
- Use the 'elimination approach'—if it were not for what FACT, could this be eliminated?
- Use a team organisation for problem solving.
- Improvement targets are set.
- Publicity for improvements.

Figure 15.1   Performance management flow chart

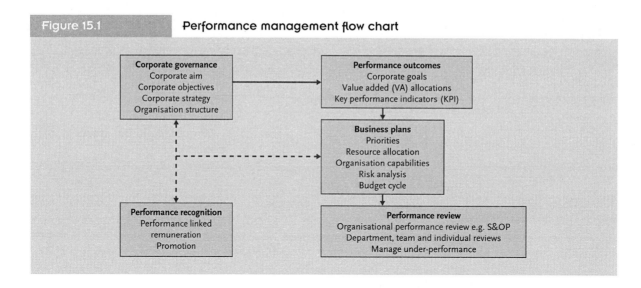

Although they were made many years ago (and P&G has since modified the principles to encompass sustainability objectives), the above statements are examples of being simple, direct and unambiguous in informing staff of a company's objectives.

An example of corporate change influencing the approach to performance improvement is PepsiCo, the beverage and food multinational, which has established 'Performance with Purpose' as its corporate mantra. One of its new operational performance indicators is the minimisation of water use.

This new objective is expected to change people's approach to processes in the business. In the past, new bottles delivered to a bottling line were cleaned with pressurised water. Now that a water minimisation performance measure has been implemented, the activity has changed so that bottles are cleaned with purified air. Would that have happened without a change in how performance is measured? We behave how we are measured.

Building a performance culture within a business starts with management. Richard Goyder, CEO of Wesfarmers Ltd, Australia's largest conglomerate business, was reported in Melbourne's *The Age* newspaper on 10 April 2010 as saying: 'To change culture, you have to change behaviour. If you can't change behaviour, you change the management.'

The ease of gaining acceptance from the workforce for methods to implement improvement will differ according to the predominant culture of the country. For example, the authors' experience of implementing performance enhancement programs in Australia indicates that they will not automatically be embraced by staff. A strong culture of performance and continuous improvement within the organisation has to be built, otherwise responses can be as follows.

- Employees consider that 'improvement' is an excuse or cover for future downsizing and retrenchments.
- Staff view the proposed change as management's 'flavour of the month' that will disappear with the next 'initiative' of the CEO.
- It is felt that managers are offloading their responsibilities onto staff and then not remunerating the employees for these added responsibilities.
- Staff consider that their external interests are of greater importance. The employees are good at their jobs, but broaden their knowledge and capabilities outside the organisation.

As improvement goals become more demanding, 'up-skilling' and learning beyond the immediate skill requirement for a job is necessary, together with an emphasis on personal development. Staff should therefore be recognised and rewarded for additional skills and learning.

In order to experience success with improvement and **innovation**, management at all levels must understand and sell to staff the aim and objectives of the organisation and how the initiatives being proposed will enable the organisation's goals to be met. To achieve this requires 'management by walking around' (MBWA), where operational managers leave their offices, computers and emails and regularly walk around the facility—it is surprising what can be learnt by talking with staff members.

Processes

Performance management commences with an understanding of the processes in the system and with identifying each of them.

Identifying processes

A process is a series of actions intended to achieve a particular output which can:

- be described and diagrammed
- have its performance measured
- be improved.

A process will have a number of tasks associated with it. For example, the process of loading a vehicle may involve tasks such as:

- obtaining the loading list
- taking a forkift to the full pallet area
- picking up the full pallets
- taking the pallets to the loading bay
- taking a hand trolley to the racking area
- picking items from their racking locations
- assembling the products at the loading bay
- checking the correct order
- loading the vehicle in predetermined order
- reporting the order completion.

The tasks can be documented using a **flow process chart**, in which each task (or activity) is allocated a symbol to identify what is happening. The process of loading a vehicle is shown in Figure 15.2.

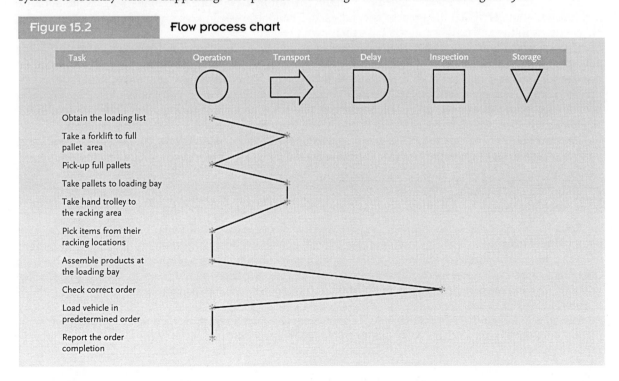

Figure 15.2   **Flow process chart**

Each activity/symbol point is linked by a line to provide an easy-to-understand picture of the task and how much non-value-adding activity is incorporated.

The quality of this process is the cumulation of performance achieved by each task in the process. If all the tasks performed in loading vehicles are performed satisfactorily within the time required, the process has quality, because it is 'in control'. The motto should therefore be: 'Manage the process, not the output'.

Variability in processes

Control is difficult to achieve because variability is ever present in a process. **Variability** describes the random events that may occur as a process is undertaken and which are always present as a natural part of any process. Individual tasks can be measured, but variations cannot be predicted; however, the total variation in a process can be measured, using probability distribution calculations. Understanding variability of processes and events, for example the timing of an ocean voyage, is a major requirement of a logistician.

The causes of variability can be described as the technology and process design elements, which are shown in Figure 15.3.

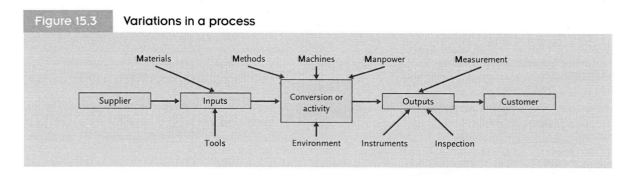

Figure 15.3   Variations in a process

The '5M' elements in a process comprise: materials, methods, machines, manpower and measurement. Each element is subject to variation, together with the environment (working conditions, such as temperature and humidity) under which the process is conducted. The tools, instruments and inspection requirements are elements in their own right and will have their own process.

Shewart (1931) first described variation in processes and made the distinction between common causes and special causes of variation. Common or system causes of variation are those that are common in occurrence, and have random outcomes, but which can be measured. About 85 per cent of the variation in a process comes from common causes. The only way to improve the process with respect to these variations is to change at least one of the 5Ms or the environment—not to pressure employees to 'do better' within the established process, which provides limited and only short-term results.

The remaining 15 per cent are the result of special or assignable causes; that is, the cause of the variation is from outside the design of the process. Examples include:

- variable capabilities of employees between different shifts
- set-up and calibration of equipment
- damage to product.

Because special causes are relatively easy to detect and assign, they can usually be removed as a factor without great expense.

A process is therefore best when it is operating with only common causes of variation, and when these are being measured by employees, using **control charts**. The role of management is to organise the process in a way that enables continuous reduction of variation in the process and to build confidence in the team's ability to perform against the defined goals.

The objective is for the process to be in statistical control or just 'in control', with results lying between the control lines of the control chart. A process that is 'out of control', with widely varying outcomes, is shown in Figure 15.4 opposite.

When the upper and lower limits have been statistically established and the process is operating between the limits, it is 'in control', as shown in Figure 15.5.

If the process is continually providing a better performance than required, the limits of variability can be narrowed so there is a new goal, as shown in Figure 15.6.

This approach allows managers to have a better understanding of how the processes they are responsible for are performing. For example: a transport manager is responsible for deliveries of goods to a city that is about 10 hours' driving time away. The actual time taken could be nine hours with a good driver, but 12 hours if the traffic is heavy. How does the manager know whether the delivery process is in control?

Records of previous journeys provide the data to calculate the upper and lower limits for the control chart. Depending on the variation from the mean, the limits could be wide apart or narrow, but this is not important. Each subsequent journey time will be recorded on the control chart to show whether it is 'in control'. A journey that is outside the control lines would be 'out of control' and subject to analysis and improvement. If journeys are consistently in control, the manager can authorise a recalculation of the control limits to bring them closer together and work with the drivers to identify changes to the 5Ms that would bring even more consistency to the times.

Figure 15.4   **'Out of control' process**

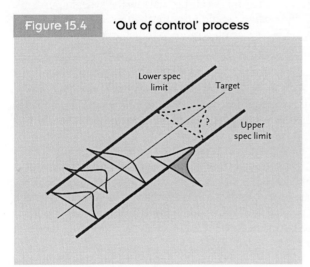

Figure 15.5   **'In control' process**

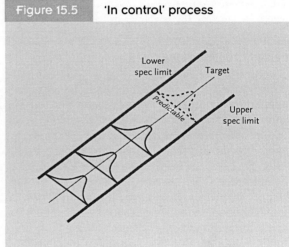

Figure 15.6   **Improvement of the process**

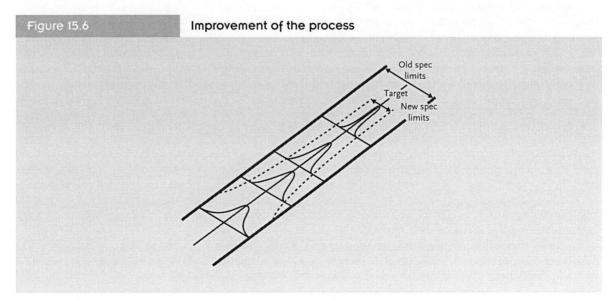

The problem for companies (and managers) without a system that measures the performance of processes is that managers often react inappropriately to events. They might assume a special cause when none exists, or that things just went wrong, when there actually was a special cause.

Using the example of vehicle journeys without measurement, it means that if a truck arrives late at a client's factory and the customer complains, the transport manager will receive a 'please explain' from senior management. But what information does the manager have to explain the situation? All the information they have is a single figure of the time that the truck took to reach the customer site, and that the truck was driven by a particular driver. This situation means that the only way to 'point the finger of blame' is at the driver, who then has to account for every minute of the trip, even though the journey time is, to a great extent, beyond their control. The manager then has to make a judgment concerning 'blame'.

As organisational reporting systems are based on short-term (weekly or monthly) reporting, with all variances requiring explanation, much time and effort can be wasted in fruitless 'witch hunts' when the variances are, to a large extent, only a system variation.

Instead, by plotting actual times on a control chart, the manager will have an indication of what may happen in the future—the trend. It is much better to inform senior management of the likely future situation and the reasons, as well as completing additional analysis to improve the process and so narrow the acceptable limits. This is proactive management through measurement. The analysis could identify changes to the system; for example, starting the trip later or earlier to miss heavy traffic; or using a more aerodynamic semitrailer or a more powerful prime mover so that time is not lost due to slowing down on hills.

Benefits of measurement

A consideration when developing and using performance measurement in the business is the cost of data collection and analysis compared to the benefits gained. For example, consider organisations that have moved or are moving to a 'design, plan, procure and sell' business model, with production, assembly and distribution contracted to logistics service providers (LSPs).

The outcome of this model is that companies can have the direct labour and operations portion of their cost of goods sold (COGS) at less than 10 per cent; purchased materials, components and services in excess of 60 per cent; and overheads at more than 30 per cent.

With this cost structure, measuring the performance of operational processes will not provide a high return. Even in the early 1990s it was publicised that if General Motors in America improved the efficiency of its direct manufacturing labour by 25 per cent in their American vehicle assembly facilities, the sale price of a mid-range vehicle would decrease by about 1.5 per cent.

Although an LSP that specialises in distribution will tend to be labour intensive, the measurements required are not labour efficiency, but delivery focused. The elements that clients are interested in are: on time delivery of goods, order accuracy, order turnaround time and inventory accuracy. These are measures of planning effectiveness rather than indications of a need for optimal labour efficiency.

As LSP companies must be responsive to the contract requirements and payment cycle of their clients, they may hire casual and contract labour that reflects the current contract situation. This has its own challenges concerning training and competency that will not be resolved by efficiency measurement of an itinerant workforce.

Efficiency and effectiveness

The terms **efficiency** and **effectiveness** are often used interchangeably when discussing logistics performance, but Darnton and Darnton (1997) argued that the terms are substantially different.

Efficiency refers to maximising the benefits, while minimising effort and expenditure. An efficient process relative to similar processes requires either fewer inputs—or produces more outputs—to achieve the same objective. It can be applied to resources such as use of time or labour and utilisation of assets and finance.

Effectiveness is a measure related to an objective of the business, rather than a measure of output; for example, timely customer service. Measuring effectiveness is achieving the required objective through plans and schedules, based on calculated inputs.

In short, while efficiency measures 'doing the right thing', effectiveness refers to 'doing things right'. For a growing company in expanding markets, efficiency is less important than being effective; however, for a stagnant company in a slowing market management typically relies on efficiency.

Principles of a performance system

AV Feigenbaum (1951) summarised the principles of a performance management system when he was director of quality for General Electric as shown in Table 15.1

Table 15.1   Principles of a performance system

Everyone serves a customer	People work within a system
All systems exhibit variability	Improvement of a system is a part of the job
Control the process, not the output	Improvement is driven by plans not events
Measure processes based on data	Improvement pays

These principles were later expanded to 14 points by the American quality 'guru', Dr W Edwards Deming, but they retained the essential focus of the approach.

A danger with a systems-based approach to statistical measurements is that managers can 'tick the box', while hiding behind a smokescreen of figures and therefore not take action. As always, there should be defined objectives within the business plan for managers to achieve. The measurements are to show how the objectives are being attained.

Corporate measure of logistics performance

The underlying driver for performance measurement of a company's supply chains is best structured as one plan, with a link between the business strategy and the actions taken to achieve the strategic outcomes. An example is shown in Figure 15.7.

This approach allows all involved in the business to understand how the actions relate to the corporate goal. To be effective, all measures must also be a part of a company-wide matrix, that shows how each measure contributes towards one of a few primary measures that are used to manage the overall business.

As the objective of logistics in a product company is availability, the primary measure of effectiveness should be 'delivery in full, on time, with accuracy' (DIFOTA). This holistic performance measure equates to achieving the perfect order and should be the objective that organisations strive towards. Its construction is shown in Figure 15.8 overleaf.

Figure 15.7   One plan approach to performance measurement

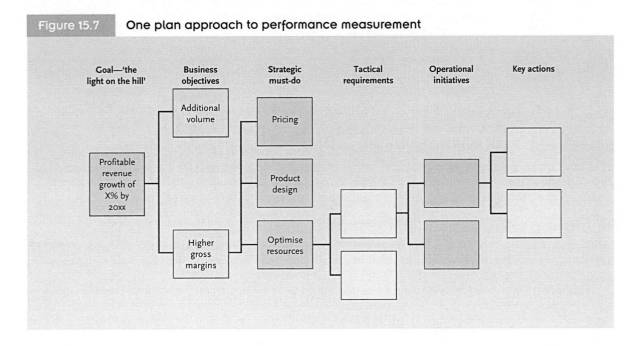

Figure 15.8   DIFOTA performance measurement

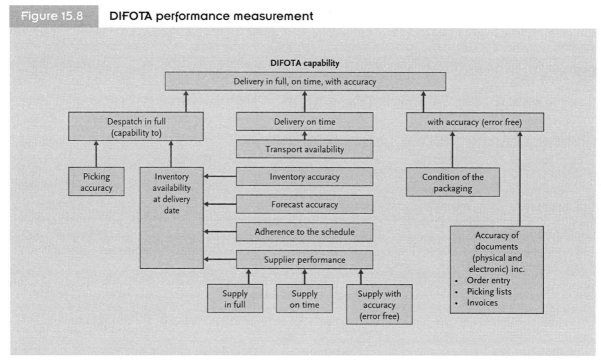

Source: With courtesy of Benchmarking Success Pty Ltd (www.benchmarkingsuccess.com).

The **probability** of achieving the perfect order is calculated through multiplication of the individual measures within each of the three groups that make up the DIFOTA scorecard. According to the database at Benchmarking Success, a 50 per cent probability is an average score; the highest observed has been about 95 per cent and some companies have scored as low as 10 per cent.

An explanation for each of the main measurements is shown in Figure 15.9 opposite.

Benchmarking Success considers that a perfect order requires at least:

* despatch in full = 99%
  o inventory availability = 95%
* deliver on time = 99%
* accuracy of documents = 99%
  o order entry = 99%
  o invoice errors = 99%

The perfect order DIFOTA objective should be at least 91%

The best in class DIFOTA objective should be at least 93%

Each step in the processes affects the overall probability; therefore, DIFOTA provides a picture across the business of the effect that each section's performance will have on the overall corporate measure. This illustrates the breadth of a logistician's oversight concerning performance in a business.

Improving performance in logistics

Improving the performance of a process is based on analysis of a situation using the 'plan, do, check, act' (**PDCA**) cycle, developed by Walter Shewart at Bell Laboratories in the mid-1930s. In the early 1990s, Deming modified the cycle to become the 'plan, do, study, act' (**PDSA**) cycle.

The concept of six sigma as a measure of performance developed from the work of Deming and is an improvement methodology that aims to reduce the variation in processes and outcomes. The term is based on a statistical measure of variance, which means that a process recording six sigma has only 3.4 defects

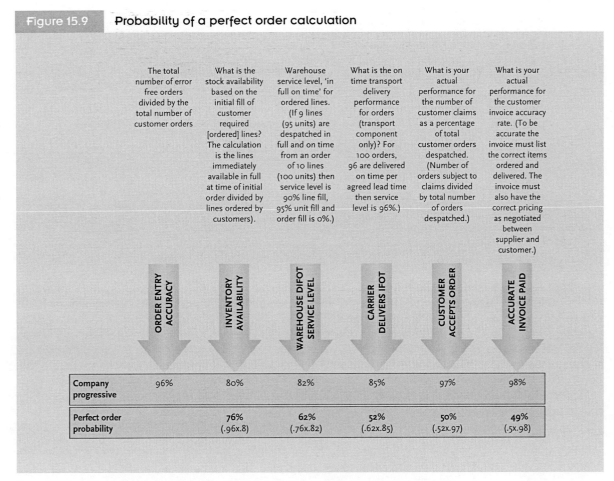

Figure 15.9 Probability of a perfect order calculation

Source: With courtesy of Benchmarking Success Pty Ltd, www.benchmarkingsuccess.com.

per million opportunities for defects to occur. Improving processes so they are six sigma compliant has required the expansion of the PDSA cycle to the 'define, measure, analyse, improve, control' (**DMAIC**) cycle.

Analysis techniques used in a cycle are not difficult to understand and use; some of the main tools are noted in Figure 15.10 overleaf.

Understanding and using these tools as the basis for process improvement provides a factual justification for proposing changes in a process. The tools can be used by operating teams to analyse improvements for their work area, with management's role to provide the training and resources.

A business could receive considerable gains from improvement and innovation across its core supply chains, both upstream and downstream. For example, a supply chain improvement project can consider how to reduce (or better still, eliminate) the month-end and quarter-end rush to gain sales orders, which is often driven by sales staff bonuses for meeting the period sales targets (or quotas). This activity can be very detrimental to effective supply chains, requiring:

- the use of premium freight
- dealers, distributors and customers carrying excess inventory
- increased but short-term manufacturing output
- increased outbound and inbound inventory
- additional demands on suppliers.

Figure 15.10	**Tools for process improvement**

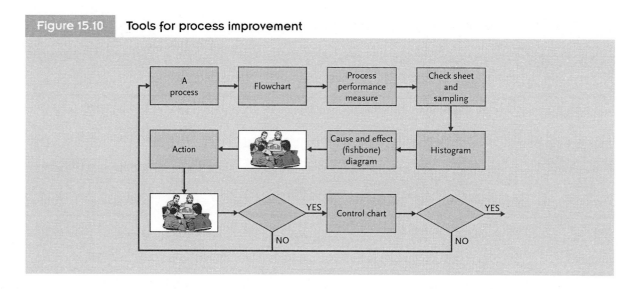

Traditional accounting systems do not identify these additional costs, but it can be assumed that such 'end of a period' orders rarely meet their profit targets.

Improving the performance of products and processes has been a feature of business activities since the earliest times. Developing supply and delivery networks, simplifying products, improving processes and increasing the speed of transport and data transmission are examples of productivity improvement that have occurred.

Examples of innovations that have influenced the development of supply chains since the 1940s are illustrated in Figure 15.11 opposite.

Lean and agile

An innovation of the 1980s was just in time (JIT), the generic name for the Toyota production system (TPS), a production process developed by the company since the early 1950s. The objective was the 'elimination of waste'. Toyota identified seven wastes:

- overproduction
- waiting
- transport/materials handling
- processing/operations
- inventory
- motion—a move does not equal work
- product defects.

If these wastes were removed then materials would arrive where required 'just in time'. Items can therefore be 'pulled' through each step of a process, using visual signals (Kanban), rather than the earlier approach governed by MRP2 planning systems of 'pushing' items into a work centre, whether they were required or not. A pull-based system leads to a more continuous flow of materials and predictable cycle times, which results in lower (or hopefully zero) inventories.

Womack, Roos & Jones (1990), documented a 10-year study comparing the processes of the world's automotive companies. The term **lean** was used to describe the Toyota approach and later to define a particular approach to improving organisations. This focuses on total system flow, removing waste from processes and continuous improvement. Lean may be summarised as follows.

- Specify what does and does not create customer *value*.
- Identify all *needed* design, order and production steps—the value stream.
- Create *flow* without interruption, detours, back-flows, waiting and scrap.

Figure 15.11   Innovations in supply chains

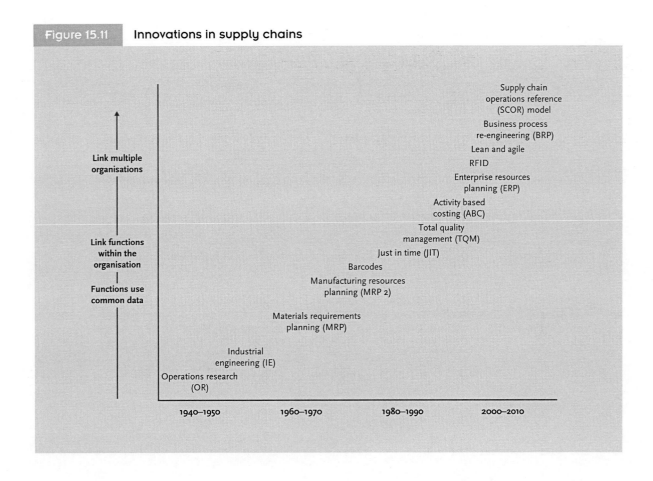

- Only make what is *pulled* by the customer—implement pull between all steps where continuous flow is possible.
- Strive for *perfection*—remove layers of waste on a continuous basis.

As with using any technique or tool to improve supply chains, lean is not the answer to all challenges. The positioning of lean and its counterpart, **agile** are illustrated in Figure 15.12 overleaf.

A lean approach tends to be more suitable for product or service companies operating in the lower right of the diagonal, where there is less variety of products or services and higher volumes of output or activity. An agile approach is more likely to fit towards the top of the diagonal, where companies are less capital intensive and therefore inherently more flexible and more reliant on their human capital. An agile approach addresses a more volatile demand, a high product mix or where production assets are shared across multiple products. Here, product availability is of a greater importance than price.

Within the diagonal, there are limits to implementing a purely lean or agile approach. Consider a capital-intensive business such as steel processing, which fits into the lower right of the diagonal.

- Equipment is large and heavy; therefore rearranging it is not realistic.
- Equipment set-up costs can be substantial.
- Some processes must be completed in large batches.
- Multiple passes of materials occur on the same equipment, such as in the rolling mill.
- Bottlenecks do exist; therefore, protective inventory is required at the bottleneck (see 'Theory of constraints' below).
- Cycle times have limits due to technical constraints, such as heating and cooling times.

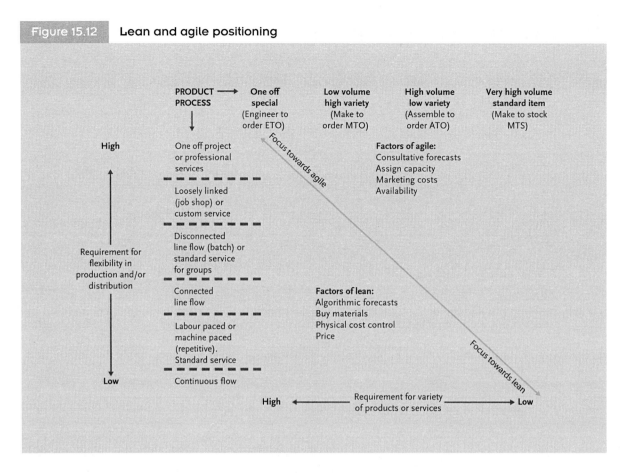

Figure 15.12   Lean and agile positioning

This example illustrates that although the situation may lend itself to implementing lean techniques, the actual circumstances may limit the applicability. Logisticians therefore need to study and understand the various improvement techniques and tools available and use the most applicable to suit the organisation's particular circumstances.

Theory of constraints

Initially introduced in Chapter 11, the foundation of the **Theory of constraints (TOC)**, also known as **constraint management**, identifies that under the traditional business approach, people work to be efficient in their area of work. However, the sum of all the individual work centre performances is not equal to the maximum output for the system or process. This is because the total throughput of the system is controlled by the capacity constrained resource (CCR)—the step in the process that has the lowest throughput, which should be planned using the drum-buffer-rope sequence shown in Figure 15.13 opposite.

Using this sequence, the CCR should not stop, because it is scheduled at its maximum throughput and whatever it produces, so will the total process. Therefore, staff must be available in the schedule to keep the CCR working through any breaks, such as meal times.

From this principle, the 'rules' of TOC were established as follows.

1. Utilisation and activation of a resource are not synonymous.
2. The CCR governs both throughput and the level of inventory.
3. An hour lost at a CCR is an hour lost for the total system.
4. The level of utilisation of a non-CCR is not determined by its own potential but by a CCR in the system.
5. An hour saved at a non-CCR is just a mirage.

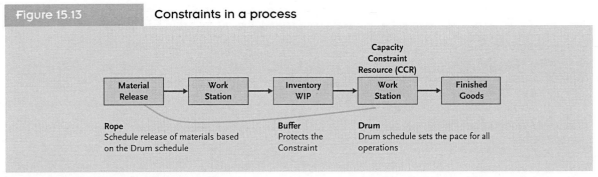

Figure 15.13   **Constraints in a process**

Source: Adapted from Goldratt EM & Fox RE (1986)

6. Lead times are the result of a schedule and cannot be predetermined.
7. Schedules should be established by simultaneously considering all the constraints.
8. Balance the flow, not capacity.
9. The batch size of an item to be processed should be variable, not fixed.
10. The batch size of an item to be transferred to another workstation may not, and many times should not, be equal to the batch size of an item that is processed.

Having identified the CCR for scheduling purposes, management can instigate a study to identify how the CCR could be modified to remove the constraint; this is continuous improvement of the most costly part of the system. When the constraint has been removed, another part of the system will then become the constraint and the process is repeated.

Business process re-engineering (BPR)

Comment over the years in the business press has argued that the commercial world is moving too fast for incremental improvement steps and that a more dramatic reshaping of business flows is required. This approach is called **business process re-engineering (BPR)**.

It is reasoned that in traditional organisations the processes typically consist of activities that are the responsibility of several functional departments (or even business units), which look after their own interests. This can lead to errors, slow cycle times and high costs, with problems compounded when the departments have different work practices or, worse still, incompatible computer systems.

BPR specialists consider that in this environment the continuous improvement approach, which is often confined to local processes, is too limiting. They argue that only quantum improvements in business performance, managed through BPR techniques and significant strategic changes in business processes, can be successful.

An example of a BPR technique is to allocate a manager as the single process owner, accountable for end-to-end processes and related activities; this will cut across typical organisation structures. Process categories can include:

- procurement (purchase to pay)
- sales (order to cash)
- accounts (account to report)
- personnel (hire to retire).

The responsibilities of the process owner are to establish the aim and objectives, performance targets, metrics and improvement targets for the total process.

Supply chain operations reference (SCOR) model

The **supply chain operations reference (SCOR) model** was introduced in the mid-1990s and is a subset of BPR that is focused on supply chains. The development of SCOR is overseen by the Supply Chain Council (SCC), a company-based member organisation.

Using SCOR enables the description of every process within inbound, internal and outbound logistics. It is a process reference framework that provides the methodology to structure and define:

- standard processes
  - o planning (plan)
  - o receiving of materials (source)
  - o production of a product or service (make)
  - o delivery of the product or service (deliver)
  - o flow of returns (return)
- standard metrics
  - o perfect delivery
  - o cash cycle time
  - o supply chain cost etc.
- standard practices: EDI, CPFR etc.

The standard processes are illustrated in Figure 15.14 below.

SCOR provides the pre-defined relationships between processes, metrics and practices, which enables the 'as is' structure of business activity and the future 'to be' state to be derived for an organisation. No part of the model is organisation specific; therefore, all parts of the model can be applied to any organisation.

| Figure 15.14 | SCOR model |

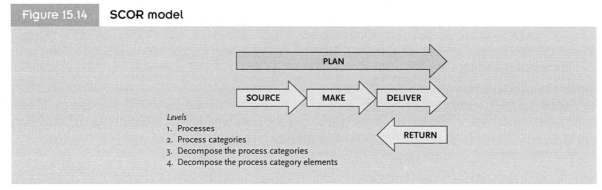

Source: Adapted from Supply Chain Council, www.supply-chain.org.

Using the techniques

The productivity techniques discussed should be viewed as complementary: more than one technique can be used. The well documented mix of techniques is 'lean six sigma', which is implemented to reduce complexity in volume output operations. Lean is used to improve processes and eliminate waste and six sigma to improve reliability of the processes through reducing variation.

The theory of constraints can be implemented as the foundation and this is referred to as TLS (meaning TOC, lean and six sigma). For a company with the resources, SCOR can be implemented first, enabling an understanding and simplification of the flow of materials, information and money through the supply chains.

The challenge can occur when, having invested substantial money and time resources in the implementation of these improvement methodologies, an internal or external crisis affects the business. The 'kneejerk' reaction is that management will change the way in which the performance management methodologies are used; from business improvement to process control with a reduction in the resources employed. This approach informs the staff that performance management is only for the good times and adds to the cynicism concerning management's motives.

Projects in logistics

A project is a scope of work required to achieve a particular outcome, be it implementing application software, reorganising a warehouse or upskilling staff through a structured training program.

Based on the scope of the project, which must be approved in advance, the amount of time, resources and money required to complete the project 'on time and on budget' can be calculated. The project plan is then developed and the project approved. As the project proceeds, the person responsible for the project (the project manager) will monitor the use of time, resources and money against the project plan.

The greatest challenge of a project is called 'scope creep'; that is, where management require small changes to the scope of the project, but does not allow more time, resources or money to cover the additional requirements, because they are small. The problem is that many small changes make for a cumulative big change and when the project is not finished 'on time, on budget', it is the project manager who carries the blame.

Project managers therefore require a unique set of capabilities. One attribute is the ability to bring all interested parties (the stakeholders) involved in the project into agreement concerning the scope of the project. Depending on the project size and complexity, this can take a long time and include many meetings, which the project manager must chair.

An example is the implementation of a new software application to assist in managing the business. The initial question is whether all application modules will be implemented or some held back until the 'core' of the application works satisfactorily. Then there is the order in which the modules will be implemented— the accountant will argue for the financials to go first, but the operations people will state that they satisfy customers' demands, while the sales people will argue that entering customer orders is vital to success. Who is right? And when the decision is made, how will those who 'lost' their claim be encouraged to remain enthusiastic about the project?

With the scope approved, the next attribute is the capability to construct a project plan. In what order will the tasks proceed, how long will they take and what are the dependencies? A task often cannot commence until a prior task has been completed. Time calculations also include identifying the critical path in the project (the tasks that govern the success of the project) and the schedules. **Project management** software is available to assist with developing and monitoring the plan, but these applications can cost from hundreds to millions of dollars, so selection of the application is a challenge in itself.

Resources include people (both employees and contractors) and equipment (including rented and materials). If special imported materials or equipment are required, allowance must be made for negotiations with potential suppliers and the lead time for delivery.

The estimation of money involves not only calculating the direct costs for each task but also allowing for contingencies—the things that can and will go wrong. Even with experience, project managers may well double the expected times and halve the expected benefits, because of the unknowns that can arise.

The next required attribute is to be able to sell the plan to management for approval and to all the interested parties. This requires 'walking the corridors' to meet people on a one-to-one basis and in small groups around the coffee machine or at the worksite. The objective is to gain acceptance or 'buy-in' for the plan before the formal meetings.

The attribute that some might consider is most required of a project manager is the ability to 'dig their heels in' and 'stare down' managers and others who engage in 'scope creep'. If the scope of the project can be maintained (or if it has to be changed, and then time, resources and money also change), the project manager can then deliver the project 'on time and on budget'.

With logisticians being given a wider range of responsibilities, gaining knowledge and qualifications in project management is recommended. The two most popular avenues are through the Project Management Institute (PMI) and through gaining certification in the PRINCE (PRojects IN Controlled Environments) project management methodology.

PRINCE provides learning manuals, and the PMI also provides the *Guide to the Project Management Body of Knowledge* (*PMBOK© Guide*), providing general information concerning the management of typical projects, based on processes described in terms of:

- inputs—that is, documents, plans, designs
- tools and techniques—that is, mechanisms applied to inputs
- outputs—that is, documents, products.

Driving improvement in supply chains is increasingly likely to be the responsibility of logisticians. The involvement by logistics organisations in change will need to increase dramatically to meet likely government-based performance targets concerning sustainability and customer demands for continuous improvement in performance.

Chapter questions

Operational

1. Review the Procter & Gamble message printed on employees' ID cards. In 10 short points or less, provide your message to employees of any company concerning the business and improvement objectives.
2. Consider a process and identify the tasks. Construct a flow process chart and identify the non-value adding activities. How would they be eliminated or reduced in time?
3. Provide some examples concerning how a logistics manager may reduce the use of energy within an enterprise.
4. How can a process be identified as being 'out of control'? What steps are required to bring it back 'into control'?
5. Based on Figure 15.10, identify the essential features of a flowchart, check sheet, histogram and cause and effect diagram.

Planning

6. The text notes that clients are most likely to measure the performance of a distribution services provider in terms of planning effectiveness. Identify how a distribution service provider (DSP/3PL) may implement and sustain an innovation program.
7. Figure 15.8 illustrates DIFOTA capability. Is this just a measure of potential performance for the enterprise or can the result be incorporated into the planning process? Justify your response.
8. What are the different system requirements to enable planning for a 'lean' and an 'agile' enterprise?
9. Would any additional requirements need to be addressed if constraint management, BPR or SCOR were implemented? Justify your response.
10. What do 'scope' and 'scope creep' mean in the context of projects?
11. Selection of the project management software can be a challenge. What are the major attributes required in a project management application?

Management

12. A distribution services provider (DSP/3PL) business has a turnover of $50m per annum. There are 50 staff members with a job title of manager or supervisor. The total manager salary cost per annum is $5m. As part of their contract, managers are expected to identify justifiable annual savings in their area totalling 5 per cent of salary. Is this sufficient for the business to prosper? Justify your response.
13. As shown in Figure 15.11, innovation in supply chains is the improvement of all activities. Consider how an innovation culture could be generated within a logistics service provider enterprise and justify your estimate of the time it would take. Accepting that in Western businesses and in rapidly expanding economies, managers are in their jobs for about two years, how would continuity of the objective be assured?
14. Figure 15.7 provides an overview of the 'one plan' approach to performance measurement in an enterprise. Identify how this would operate as a plan that all employees could view and provide input into.
15. A company decides to implement a major project in logistics. Should the logistics manager act as the project manager? Justify your response.

References and links

Australian Bureau of Statistics, 2008 Business Characteristics Survey, www.abs.gov.au.

Carbon Disclosure Project – Transport report (2010), www.cdproject.net.

Darnton, G. & Darnton, M., *Business process analysis*, International Thomson Business Press, London, 1997.

Dr Goldratt explains the theory of constraints (TOC) in a video at https://www.tocgoldratt.com/TV/video.php?id=1660.

Goldratt, E. M. & Cox, J., *The goal: a process of ongoing improvement*, North River Press, Croton-on-Hudson, NY, 1986.

'Managing Successful Projects with PRINCE2', 2009 ed, and 'Directing Successful Projects with PRINCE2', 2009 edn www.prince-officialsite.com.

Project Management Body of Knowledge (PMBOK) 4th edn, Project Management Institute (PMI), December 2008.

Project Management Insitute (PMI), www.pmi.org.

TOC tools are available at www.dbrmfg.co.nz.

Womack, J., Roos, D. & Jones, D., *The Machine that Changed the World*, Harper Perennial, 1990.

16 Managing logistics operations

Learning outcomes

On completion of this chapter you will be able to:

- recognise the differences between a business and a management model
- apply a logical approach to considering the management structure for supply chains in an organisation
- recognise the differences between leadership and management
- follow the process to employ staff
- consider aspects of managing people in a logistics environment.

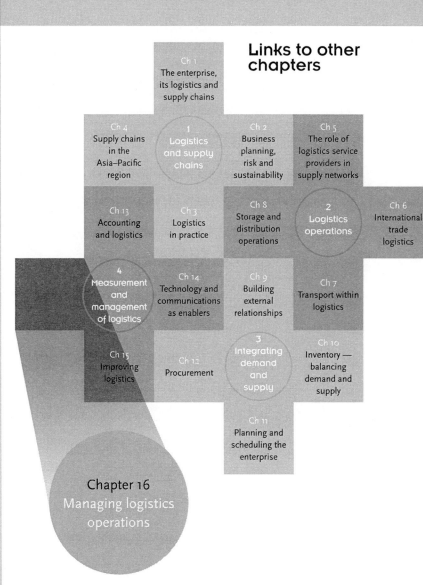

Links to other chapters

Ch 1
The enterprise, its logistics and supply chains

Ch 4
Supply chains in the Asia–Pacific region

1
Logistics and supply chains

Ch 2
Business planning, risk and sustainability

Ch 5
The role of logistics service providers in supply networks

Ch 13
Accounting and logistics

Ch 3
Logistics in practice

Ch 8
Storage and distribution operations

2
Logistics operations

Ch 6
International trade logistics

4
Measurement and management of logistics

Ch 14
Technology and communications as enablers

Ch 9
Building external relationships

Ch 7
Transport within logistics

Ch 15
Improving logistics

Ch 12
Procurement

3
Integrating demand and supply

Ch 10
Inventory — balancing demand and supply

Ch 11
Planning and scheduling the enterprise

Chapter 16
Managing logistics operations

Key terms

These terms are used in the text. Develop your own notebook by downloading information on each term.

business model
management model
strategic business unit
   (SBU)
leadership
management
cross-cultural

recruiting, selecting and
   inducting employees
job description
selection panel
referee check
job satisfaction
work performance

occupational health and safety
   (OH&S)
chain of responsibility
decision making
benchmarking

Introduction

There is not a 'right' way to structure and operate supply chains and manage logistics—strategies and organisations will change, depending on the circumstances. Management style (for example autocratic, paternalistic or inclusive) practised within an organisation is the culmination of many factors that have developed, not only within the enterprise but in the wider community.

A factor that affects management attitudes is the culture of the country in which the head office is located and its particular cultural requirements. Even though a company operates outside its national borders, its employees know they are working within, say, a Japanese, Indian, American, British or German company, and that the way things are done is particular to the business.

Supply chains and change
Business model

As discussed throughout this book, supply chains are the channels through which materials, components, parts, finished products and their associated services move from the supplier's suppliers to the customer's customers. How this is done and the parties and modes involved are a part of the **business model** of an enterprise. A supply chain is illustrated in Figure 16.1.

The structure of core supply chains has the most influence on a business model—that is, the management of relationships and operations concerning inbound, internal and outbound movements of materials and their associated services.

However, extended supply chains—upstream to the farm and mine for the base raw materials, and downstream to the end user for products—can also influence the business model over time, depending on the nature of the company's products and markets.

Figure 16.1	A supply chain

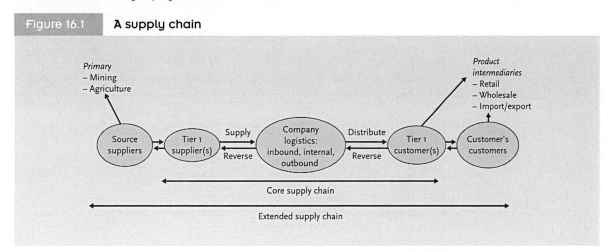

Business models within the Asia–Pacific region may not be the same as those of companies with similar products and supply chains within the Americas or Europe. Khanna and Palepu (1998) found that large diversified groups (conglomerates) in India, Chile, Brazil and Mexico have consistently outperformed 'focused' businesses (popular in developed countries) based on financial measures such as return on assets and market share.

They considered that in developing countries, capital, labour and product markets do not function to the standards of developed countries. Conglomerates overcome these deficiencies by:

* acting as an internal capital market by financing divisions and new ventures
* having their own extensive distribution and supply networks through which new products can be released
* promoting their known brand name across many products and thus removing consumer suspicion of new brands
* using the group structure to promote exports
* generating their own labour pool between divisions in countries where it is legally difficult to retrench employees
* establishing their own management and skills training schools.

Whatever the business model, changes in supply chains and logistics are a part of logistics jobs, whether in a product company or a logistics service provider (LSP). As many enterprises continue to view logistics as a cost-based rather than value-adding function, reducing costs will remain as a continuing reason for change. For those organisations that look for value addition, improvement (and change) in the performance of the supply chains can provide more benefits for the business. Change can also occur due to restructuring, merger and acquisitions (M&A) and divesting parts of the enterprise.

Management model

Enabling a business model to change without undue disruption to the current operations of the enterprise requires a **management model** that is also adaptable and responsive to change.

A management model, or 'how things are done around here', identifies how outcomes will be achieved through people (the staff). Within the management model should be recognition that the positive response of employees to change is fundamental for ongoing success. However, the approach will be different because cultures throughout the Asia–Pacific region differ. An example of different cultural responses in the region is illustrated in Table 16.1.

Table 16.1 Comparing cultures

	Chinese (China, Taiwan, Hong Kong, Singapore)	Western/Anglo-Saxon (Australia and New Zealand)
Personal control	In the hands of others	In own hands
Primary focus of life activities	Relationships Consensus building Conflict not acceptable	Task completion Problem solving Conflict acceptable
Interpersonal commitment	Family Extended family and clan Relationship based	Task specific Limited Arm's length
Personal identity gained from	Group membership	Individual achievement
Time frame for strategy	Long term	Short–medium term
Time frame for action	Short term following long term consensus decision	Long term following quick decision
Responsibility	At the top, therefore lower levels not always willing to accept responsibility	Motivation for sharing
Authority	General, throughout the organisation	Specific to task
Decision style	Bureaucratic and consensus	Immediate—'do it'
Overall orientation	Big picture	Specific, contracted, detailed

Source: Adapted from Orton T., 'Leadership across cultures in times of change', *Leadership*, Autumn 2008.

It is therefore not possible to provide a definitive description within the regional context of 'how to manage'. Instead, some suggestions and examples are provided concerning organisational structures for supply chains and logistics activities and for approaches to the management of these activities.

Organising for supply chains

When thinking about management models for supply chains, the first question to ask is 'What is to be achieved?' A basis of policy settings within an integrated management approach is outlined below.

1. Identify aspects of the end-to-end supply chains that can influence the business strategy e.g. materials supply.
2. Recognise that operational performance of the business relates to performance of the core supply chains.
3. Agree that the objective of the organisation structure for supply chains is to improve the service experience of external and internal customers.
4. Agree that management of logistics within supply chains comprises the:
   a. management of internal and external relationships
   b. availability of products and services for customers
   c. balancing of demand and supply (assisted by inventory planning IT applications).
5. Recognise that demand for products and services is managed through a systems approach

As these (or other) base policy settings are established, a number of organisational variables pertaining to supply chains will need to be reconciled with the business model. Examples of the questions to be asked are noted in Table 16.2.

Table 16.2   Supply chains organisation questions

Marketing and supply chains	Procurement and supply chains	Conversion and supply chains
Should supply chains be part of marketing and sales?	Should procurement be part of supply chains?	Should supply chains be within operations?
Can demand management be improved if it is a supply chains process?	Should procurement be split between strategic and operational elements?	Should the conversion processes be a part of supply chain organisation?
Is customer relationship management a core supply chains competence for an organisation?	Is it effective to integrate operational purchasing into supply chains?	Should a supply chain function relate directly with the business operations of contracted factories?
Should tactical marketing and sales be within supply chains?		

The answers to these questions can provide the inputs to a supply chain management model; however, there are different models, with each being valid depending on the circumstances of the enterprise. A management model to consider is focused on managing processes rather than being an operational- or functional- (that is, department-) based organisation structure. The result of this exercise could be a structure in which the activities of teams within a product business are combined to execute the supply chain processes, as illustrated in Figure 16.2 overleaf.

As supply chain processes are concerned with the management of relationships—with availability of the products and services as outputs—a senior person should be responsible for these processes throughout the organisation.

The organisation chart shown in Figure 16.2 does not imply that the person responsible for the supply chain processes must take executive control of the multiple functions that contribute to the process, however, this can happen—in which case, the dotted lines in the organisation chart will become solid.

The important factor here is that the visibility and resources associated with the senior supply chains position within the corporate hierarchy are recognised. As this is at the same level as other senior executives, it identifies this position as important for the business.

The senior supply chains position would be responsible for overall performance of the supply chain process and can work with the senior management group to influence the business strategy that takes advantage of value creation opportunities in the supply chains.

Figure 16.2 **Process relationship for supply chains**

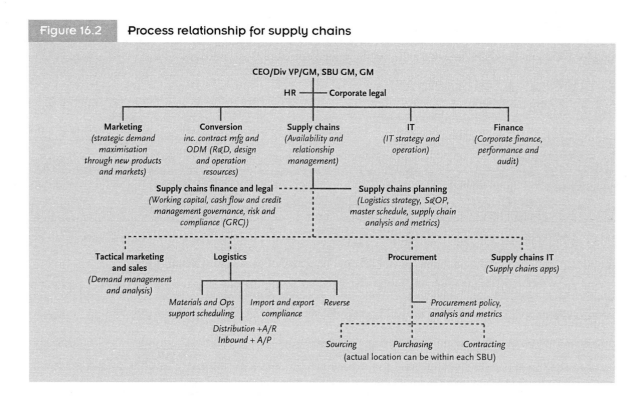

The reporting lines from the supply chains executive indicate the activities of the following six groups:

1. Supply chains planning—should be within the corporate supply chains office. It is responsible for developing strategy as it applies to supply chains and will involve the master scheduler (or similar title) driving the sales and operations planning (S&OP) process and analysts to facilitate performance of the supply chains.
2. Supply chains finance and legal—has responsibility for the finance and legal underpinnings of supply chains. A critical measure of supply chains is the measurement of working capital and cash flow and, within that, the approval of credit for customers and possible financing arrangements for selected suppliers. The legal element is an overview of the governance requirements in dealing with external parties, the management of risk within the supply chains and compliance with international and domestic laws and regulations concerned with supply chains.
3. Tactical marketing and sales—responsible for achieving short-term marketing activities and sales, based on the available supply of products; for example, retail promotions within fast moving consumer goods (FMCG) and consumer packaged goods (CPG) companies. The demand management process and input to the S&OP will be the main planning activity of this group.
4. Logistics—responsible for the movement and storage of materials and products, including reverse logistics. Associated with this is the scheduling of materials movements, ensuring that import and export of materials and products is effective and compliant with regulations. There is also the collection and payment of accounts receivable and accounts payable, incorporated into the activities of product delivery and materials receipts.
5. Procurement—management of procurement policy, analysis and metrics is a key factor of the supply chains process. The detailed sourcing, purchasing and contracting can be either centralised or located within strategic business units (SBU), subsidiaries and divisions.
6. Supply chains IT—responsible for all applications software and communications integration and interfacing that relate to the supply chains, recognising that a high proportion of data and information within companies concerns movement of product and services through the supply chains.

The size and importance of these groups will, of course, depend on the type and size of the business and the business model employed.

Another approach is the federal model, also called the strategic and staff model. Here, the central supply chains group focuses on the corporate logistics strategy, supply chains modelling and simulation and sourcing strategic commodity groups. It shares knowledge about the supply chains and best practice, but leaves operations and tactical execution to the individual **strategic business units (SBU)**, as shown in Figure 16.3. This structure was implemented by some companies as an organisation approach for procurement and has been extended to address the total supply chains requirement.

Figure 16.3   Federal organisation structure

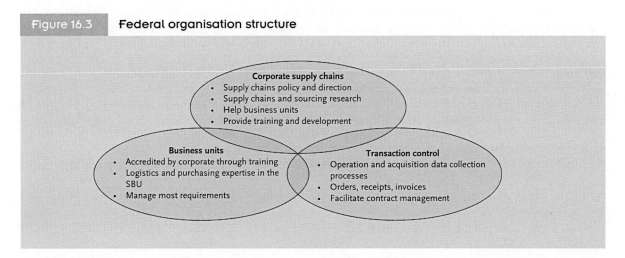

An alternative structure uses the federal model but its supply chains are based on major product markets, marketing channels or customers.

A final approach is to base the organisation structure according to whether the business is centralised or decentralised, and on the predictability of the supply network of the enterprise, as shown in Figure 16.4.

The predictability of supply chains is governed by the market in which the business operates. Where the infrastructure for movement is large and expensive, the supply chains are more predictable, such as from mines to loading ports. Compare this with companies operating in the FMCG sector, where decisions

Figure 16.4   Predictability and organisation

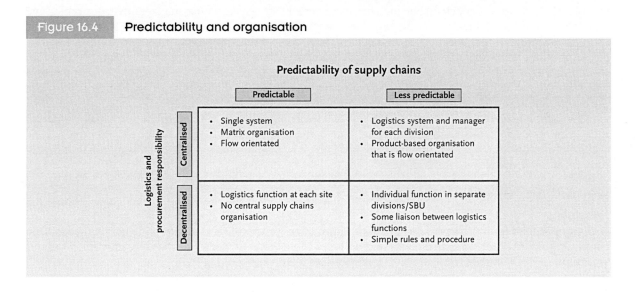

concerning supply chains must be made on a periodic basis with reference to capacity at component suppliers, contract manufacturers, logistics service providers (at both source and customer locations), sea and air ports and retail outlets.

The degree to which an organisation is centralised or de-centralised will be governed primarily by two factors:

1. the culture of the organisation; that is, the degree of autonomy and influence of business units and the willingness of senior management to mandate a policy or a process for the total business
2. the location where it is most cost and tax effective to transact and control financial transactions.

A centralised logistics organisation is best suited where the products generated from each business unit are similar and therefore require similar handling and transport services. A centralised procurement group can make decisions and exercise control over buying activities throughout the organisation, leveraging with suppliers the value of total corporate spend and enabling standard sourcing, buying processes and technology decisions.

A decentralised model is often best suited for organisations with divisions that operate as independent entities, with a high degree of autonomy and control over their logistics, sourcing and buying processes. In such environments there may be limited sharing of information between divisions.

Internal relationships—leadership and management

Whether considering the supply chain organisation within a brand name company or an LSP, the question of **leadership** and **management** needs to be considered.

In the recent past, 'managing by the numbers' has been in vogue, but in reality, management happens through people. To be effective, managers must understand the importance of people in a **cross-cultural** environment. This differs between countries but is very relevant in Australia, where in the two major cities of Melbourne and Sydney, about one-third of the workforce was born outside Australia.

Leadership, like management, has been thoroughly researched and debated at academic conferences and in journals. In essence, leadership is the ability to influence a group or individual to do what the leader wants done. Influence can be exerted through a formal appointment to a position of authority, but informal leadership can occur through a person having innate skills of influence that are recognised by others.

An example of leadership was that of a logistics masters degree student who did not excel in his studies, receiving a pass grade for the course. However, he had leadership capabilities and became the supply chain director for a multinational company. He knew what was required, but employed a team of bright undergraduates as logistics analysts—'to provide the bullets, so that I can shoot the gun' was how he explained the role. He 'sold' the supply chain and logistics management strategy to senior management, customers and suppliers and provided direction for his team, then got out of the way for them to perform.

It is unfortunate that the title of manager is now used indiscriminately in business. The essential elements of the manager's role (and this term includes supervisors who manage smaller teams) are to plan the outputs in accordance with objectives from the business plan, and to allocate resources, enabling people who report to the manager to undertake their roles at a satisfactory level of performance. Managers also have the power to reward and penalise people within established guidelines.

Although managers will only achieve their objectives through people, a manager is more likely to inherit their team of people upon appointment, rather than being able to recruit a team that meets their predefined requirements. But whether recruiting an individual or a new team, managers require training in how best to recruit and retain employees for their team.

Recruiting, selecting and inducting employees

Recruiting

Recruiting is used for two types of employment: contracting for short-term projects and employing people in continuing roles with the organisation. For both types there are both 'easy-to-fill' and 'hard-to-fill' positions, which can be at all levels, from entry-level to senior positions.

For short-term contract roles in logistics, companies will either recruit directly or contract a recruitment company to find a person who will bring identified skills and capabilities to the role. For casual work, which enables a business to balance its demand and supply requirements, the company may negotiate a contract with a labour-hire company to supply work teams.

When recruiting for continuing roles, the main difference between an 'easy-to-fill' and a 'hard-to-fill' job is the effort and expense required to make the prospective employee aware of the vacancy and the selection criteria attitude of the manager who has initiated the recruitment. In other respects, the objective is the same—to convince job candidates that being employed with the organisation is of value to their current and future career goals and that being selected for the specific job is a significant achievement.

Applicants' perceptions of the industry and the company are a key factor in employment. When a business is an 'employer of choice' in the local area, the country, the region or globally, the recruiting activity is made much easier because prospective employees have a positive attitude when applying for a job. A major challenge for companies in logistics services is that transport companies have used the term 'logistics' freely on the side of vehicles. This has resulted in people equating logistics with trucks and therefore with a male-dominated, 'blue-collar' workforce. With this perception of the whole sector, qualified and capable people may not even apply for a position, however good an individual company may be as an employer.

In commencing a recruitment activity, it is assumed that the organisation has undertaken a formal review concerning the need for the job and has eliminated the alternatives. The steps are as follows.

- Review the **job description** (if an established role) or develop a new job description. The most important element is the outcomes—what the person is required to achieve.
- Develop the selection criteria, preferably within the job description. The criteria should focus on four elements:
  o job-related skills
  o qualifications
  o abilities (skills, capacity to perform the role, competence)
  o aptitudes (ability, talent, capability for learning)
    – As logistics is a service role, applicants will need to demonstrate a service ethos and have the aptitude to act in this manner when unsupervised and responding under pressure with clients and customers.
- Define the recruitment process (advertising in newspapers, professional publications, on the internet, through a network of contacts or a recruitment services firm on a local, national or international basis) and the cost.
- Obtain approval to recruit, based on the job description, selection criteria and recruitment process.
- Appoint a **selection panel**, if required for the position. Depending on the organisation, the panel could comprise the responsible manager, a senior staff member, a manager from a different area and a representative of the personnel department.

Following completion of the advertising process, the prospective candidates need to be screened against the selection criteria to ensure they comply with the essential criteria. Online advertisements can attract a large number of unsuitable applicants, because responding to internet-based job advertisements only requires a few clicks on the keyboard. The time allowed for screening online applicants should be included in the recruitment cost.

Selection

From the screening process, a shortlist of applicants will be identified. At this stage, all unsuccessful applicants should be advised, as this demonstrates a professional approach to the recruitment process and improves the perception of the organisation.

There could be a period of discussion among the selection panel if there are insufficient applicants that meet the main selection criteria. Will the selection criteria be relaxed to enable a shortlist to be interviewed or is the recruitment to be repeated, perhaps using a different process to promote the position?

Interviewing

Training is required for managers to prepare them for meeting applicants in an interview situation. A manager needs to know:

- how an interview should be set up and conducted
- how to structure interview questions, based on the selection criteria
- how to put a candidate at ease
- how to question the candidate, to ensure they will like the work if they are offered the job
- how the candidate is likely to fit into the team and the organisation
- how a manager can 'get to know' the real person in an interview, given that the selection criteria only covers the job-related skills, qualifications, abilities and aptitudes.

Within the interview, the recruiter (manager) must control the process and keep the discussion focused on the specific job. While the manager will promote favourable aspects of the company and the job, there is a need to control any negative aspects discussed, so as not to build the wrong perceptions. As part of the interview, there can be a requirement for the candidates to give a presentation or complete aptitude tests.

At the end of each interview the selection panel should review the discussion, identifying strong and weak aspects of the candidate. At the completion of all interviews, the results can be compared and a favoured candidate selected; or, if all interviews were unsatisfactory, the recruitment process can be suspended in order to review the job description, selection criteria and recruitment process.

If there is a favoured candidate, **referee checks** should be conducted and, if these are satisfactory, the candidate recommended to the next level of management for appointment. It is then important to advise the unsuccessful candidates and wish them well in their career—this is a part of building good perceptions of the company. If the job is considered 'hard to fill', negotiations concerning salary and benefits can be conducted following a verbal offer of the job. When conditions of employment are finalised, a written contract of employment is issued.

Inducting

A new employee joining a team in the workplace is a signal for changes in the team's dynamics, especially in the initial period when both the current and new team members get to know each other. It is therefore important that the induction period is a planned event and more than a walk-around to meet the team members.

The new employee must integrate into the team and the company culture quickly or they may leave or rapidly become underperforming. If that happens, it is the manager's record that is blemished. Examples of some of the questions the manager should ask themselves concerning a new employee are:

- how to assist the new team member to feel a part of the team and wanted
- how best to motivate the new team member
- how to integrate their goals with the team's objectives.

Often, new employees are on a probation period of between three and six months. Whatever the period, the induction plan should be structured for that period, to ensure the new employee completes their probation with a good record and also feels positive about their choice of employer.

Managing people

Managing performance

The two performance outcomes for an individual, a work group or an organisation are:

1. performance effectiveness—whether the task goals are being attained
2. performance efficiency—how well the resources are being utilised.

For a manager, these outcomes apply not only to their team and to the individuals within the team, but also to the manager. They are held accountable for the performance of their team by the group of managers to which the manager belongs, and also by higher-level managers.

There are three elements that together can make for consistently high performance levels of individuals; however, the importance of each element to the others remains under academic debate. The elements are:

- **Job satisfaction** leads to improved **work performance**.
- Improved work performance leads to an increase in job satisfaction.
- Improved rewards (in the eye of the receiver) lead to both improved work performance and increased job satisfaction.

The elements must be overlaid with the effects of relationship drivers for both managers and staff. This will differ within each country of the Asia–Pacific region and is illustrated in Figure 16.5 below.

The level of job satisfaction felt by an individual can influence the amount of absenteeism from work; therefore, even though a person's performance is good when they are working, their absenteeism can cause disruption with work schedules and colleagues' work patterns. Low job satisfaction can also affect labour turnover, or can trigger the decision by a person to terminate their employment. Again, even if work performance is good, high labour turnover can be disruptive to work schedules and expensive in terms of recruitment and training.

Job satisfaction and work performance can be considered as two separate but interrelated outcomes for individuals and work groups, and they are affected by the allocation of rewards. The equity comparison by an individual concerning the allocation of rewards is not only within the immediate group, but also relative to the (known or imagined) rewards that senior executives are receiving, against their perceived (as opposed to actual) performance.

To improve the performance of people, a manager needs to understand and respond to the values and attitudes of their team. This is dependent on the size and organisational complexity of the enterprise. However, in all organisations, 'management by walking around' (MBWA) should be employed as the easiest way to understand the values and attitudes of the people in the team. It can be surprising to learn that people who pick orders or drive a forklift truck may also run a weekend business, volunteer for a charity or coach in a sporting club. Their knowledge and management capabilities are invaluable when responding to work situations that require a quick resolution.

Likewise, an 'open door' policy should be followed that allows team members to have private discussions with the manager and know that these will remain private. In both of these approaches, the manager should allow employees to voice their concerns or recognise when team members are remaining quiet, in the trust that the manager will resolve an 'obvious' problem.

While trying to be a 'good' manager, decisions concerning individuals in their teams can be affected by the manager's perceptions of people. Such preconceptions can be held by anyone, but it is important for the manager to recognise their own attitudes, as they can affect both individual and team performance. Factors that managers should be aware of include:

Figure 16.5 **Drivers of relationships and work performance**

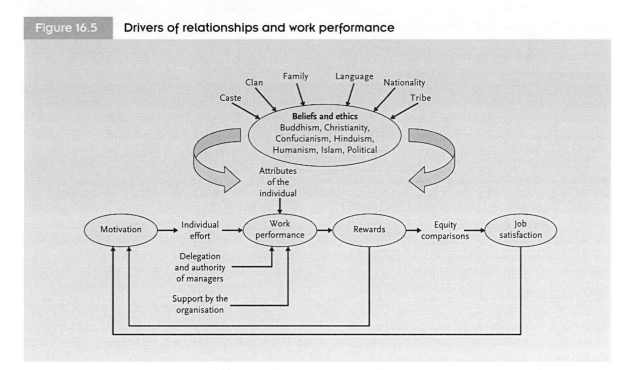

- stereotyping; that is, holding ill-informed views about age, gender and ethnicity
- using one (good or bad) attribute of a person to form an overall view of their performance
- assuming that the needs and wants of people in the team are the same as the manager's and having a lower performance expectation of those who do not hold the same views
- creating a situation (that is, a job design or job review) that confirms a manager's prior expectation of a person or group.

Performance can also be affected by change. This is often related to major changes, such as the introduction of a new computer system; however, change (or continuous improvement) should be happening on an ongoing basis. The role of managers in this situation is to develop an acceptance of change and of improving performance as normal, while applying consistency in the routine of daily events, such as picking orders in a warehouse.

Organisations and their management should be committed to effective performance management through regular personal discussion, feedback and genuine two-way performance reviews with all staff members at least once per year. Performance management will involve:

- recognising and acknowledging excellent performance by employees (groups and individuals) to provide motivation and encourage additional achievements
- ensuring that incentive awards are aligned to the performance objectives of the organisation
- analysing and identifying the cause of poor performance and implementing the appropriate corrective action.

Occupational health and safety

Maslow (1954) structured his theory concerning the hierarchy of needs to identify both higher-order needs, which he called self-actualisation and esteem, and lower-order needs, which include social (the need to receive affection and have a feeling of belonging), safety (the need for security, protection and stability on a daily basis) and physiological needs (the basic need for food, water, sex etc.).

Safety is one of the lower-order needs that must be satisfied before a person can think of or desire the higher-order needs. If performance in an organisation and its teams is to be improved, the **occupational health and safety (OH&S)** of all employees is first required.

Governments enact legislation to improve the health and safety culture within the community and individual organisations, with penalties for breaches. However, the continuous emphasis on safe working conditions must be driven by managers within an enterprise because they believe it is the correct thing to do, not because there is a legal requirement.

An example is the concept of **chain of responsibility**. Consider a large retailer that has power in the market and demands delivery conditions which it knows will require truck drivers to spend excessive hours at the wheel of a vehicle. The logistics service provider accepts the contract, knowing that it will sub-contract to a small transport company that does not have power in the market. The small company employs a driver who needs a job and will do as they are told. The driver falls asleep at the wheel and crashes the truck, causing fatalities. Is the driver responsible? Without 'chain of responsibility' legislation, which holds that all persons in the decision chain are responsible for the outcomes of contract agreements, the driver alone would be responsible.

The question is, why does it require legislation to stop unsafe practices? To answer this question requires managers and supervisors to question their own beliefs about their responsibility to people in a community.

There should be consideration not only of health and safety on a daily basis within the workplace, but also of the role managers play when emergencies occur. Do managers 'lead from the front' or are staff trained to undertake specific emergency duties, with the manager's job being to ensure that the training and resources are available and functioning?

Making decisions

People do not always think clearly, and when faced with a potential loss, gain or 'lucky break' they can function emotionally. Also, over a long period of time, if these seemingly unpredictable emotions are repeated, they become supposedly predictable and the decision maker is able to provide apparently rational explanations.

Managers in logistics can experience the same behaviour patterns when making decisions and because they relate to many different people, both within and outside the organisation, they must endeavour to understand why they are making particular decisions. Some of the challenges faced when making decisions include:

- the 'bandwagon' effect—a manager can believe the decision is correct because 'everyone else' is doing it. Decisions about buying technology can be influenced by this effect
- emotional bias—a person can believe in things that make them feel good and ignore those that leave a bad feeling. The outcome can be that a manager is not objective in their decisions; they do not recognise when things are going wrong because they do not want to. This can apply in decisions about relocating or dismissing staff
- expectation bias—a personal belief that a decision is correct, with little real evidence to support it, and without analysis, measurement or testing of the conclusion
- loss aversion—as losses can affect a manager's future more than gains, there is a tendency when making decisions to place a higher value and emotional attachment to avoiding a loss than making a gain
- selective effect—decisions that lead to micro management of profitable operations, because that is perceived to be 'safe', but which allow poor performing operations to continue in the belief that they will 'come good' in time
- sunk costs influence—in a bad situation, decisions are influenced by the amount of losses already incurred
- peer pressure—acting in a particular manner to gain approval of peers or making decisions in the same way as peers. This can become the corporate 'way'.

Human behaviour means that managers will make mistakes, have biases and distortions when making decisions; therefore being aware and accessing unbiased advace is recommended to improve **decision making**.

Benchmarking performance

Performance and decisions can be measured against the performance of other organisations, of business units and functions within an organisation, of other elements within functions and of other teams within the elements. In logistics, this could be performance of the various supply chains, the logistics department and the warehouse team. The term used for comparisons is **benchmarking**.

Stephen Hanman, principal of Benchmarking Success, says that benchmarking is more than a comparison tool; it is also an improvement technique that managers can use to assist their performance. Many organisations see benchmarking and KPIs as the same thing; however, KPIs are a performance management tool and can facilitate an improvement process as one part of a benchmarking project.

Successful process-based benchmarking requires KPI comparison and validation. Discussion of the process among members of a benchmarking group, drawn from selected enterprises, ensures that quantitative comparisons are valid. It is dangerous to form conclusions and develop improvement strategies on quantitative comparisons alone; understanding the processes and the definitions behind these performance comparisons is important.

To be effective, the measurements need to compare 'apples with apples'; therefore, ensuring compatible measurement (for example, what are the company's and customers' definition of 'on time') is fundamental to the credibility of the measurement process. The establishment of a benchmarking process is best done by an independent organisation that identifies the measurement criteria and maintains the confidentiality of participants.

Benchmarking reports identify the participant companies by a code. Therefore, when the participants come together (using the independent organisation as facilitator) to discuss the results and how overall performance can be improved among the participants, the identity of the person responsible for a particular performance is not known. The best-practice benchmark is simply the best KPI in the relevant area. This is a moving target because organisational improvement is a dynamic process.

One of the challenges is to ensure that when managers set targets they give members of the team a motivation to perform. If targets are set too low it can be a lost opportunity; however, if they are set too high, the target can become de-motivational. Target setting should be a dynamic process within the organisation, as an understanding of the process evolves. Benchmarking has a significant role to play in establishing achievable targets.

Chapter review

This book has provided a framework for logisticians to build their knowledge base of the factors required to be successful and of the range of inputs required to be a successful manager in supply chains. A person who is able to build a team that understands the objectives of the organisation and how they are to be achieved, and who is sufficiently confident in their role, is able to let the team perform well and take credit for its success.

Chapter questions

Operational

1. Ethics has received much attention in the business media. What do you consider are the ethical priorities of a senior manager and supervisor in a logistics environment?
2. Identify the common perception problems that a manager or supervisor might have. How would you as a manager or supervisor attempt to minimise the perceptions that you may hold?
3. Figure 16.5 identifies the five most important motivators in the work environment. Consider the similarities and differences in these motivators for the following people:

   a. you
   b. a skilled maintenance person working in a distribution centre
   c. a distribution centre manager
   d. the management accountant at the distribution centre.

   Why are they different and how may an organisation address these motivators within one business and management model?
4. Payments to employees can help organisations attract and retain capable people. If incorrectly structured, payment can also cause dissatisfaction. There are three aspects to pay: equity (comparison with others), expectancy (valuing own worth) and reinforcement (employer recognition of value). When recruiting a 'hard to fill' job in logistics, what emphasis would you put on the following and why:

   a. base pay plus overtime
   b. merit pay
   c. annual salary
   d. annual hours salary, with overtime paid in excess of those hours
   e. skills-based pay
   f. gain-sharing plan
   g. lump-sum performance bonus
   h. non-pay performance bonus, e.g. a holiday for two
   i. bonus share issue—no-cost or subsidised shares in the company
   j. flexible benefits—the employee selects from a 'menu' of payments or equivalent up to the annualised value of the position?

Planning

5. Why may organisations sometimes fail in the implementation of major organisational change projects? How may multicultural factors have influenced the outcome in multinational companies?
6. You are the logistics manager of a company in your home country. Your employer has merged with a company of similar size in another country in the Asia–Pacific region (you select that country). You have been asked to provide input to the following questions:

   a. What are the most likely cultural and performance problems the new joint logistics team will encounter?
   b. What actions will be required to help overcome the problems?
   c. What cultural issues may be of particular concern?

7. Select a management role in an area of logistics.

   a. Describe the likely management challenges for this person.

   b. How can these challenges affect the productivity and performance of the team or department for which the manager is responsible?

8. The concept of self-managed teams has been accepted and rejected by different organisations. Research self-managed teams and consider the following in (A) a warehouse and (B) a logistics planning group setting:

   a. In what specific ways is a self-managed team different from a more traditional work team in these settings?

   b. In what circumstances do self-managed teams work and why is this? Can self-managed teams work in the settings identified?

   c. How would you as a manager implement self-managed teams in a logistics setting of your choice?

Management

9. Are management examples from North America, Western Europe and Japan sufficient for logisticians working in the Asia–Pacific region, or should lessons from other countries in the region be provided? Justify your response.

10. Theories of organisation behaviour can be criticised for being based only on study and experience of Western (mainly Anglo-Saxon) cultures. Discuss whether the often-quoted theories (Maslow, McClelland, Hertzberg etc.) are valid to a 'Western' logistics manager working in a business based in Asia.

11. Benchmarking is stated as being an improvement technique. Structure a plan for implementing benchmarking as part of performance improvement with logistics in an enterprise

References and links

Khanna, T. & Palepu, K.G., 'Why Focused Strategies May Be Wrong for Emerging Markets', *HBS Working Paper*, No. 98–100, 1998.

Maslow, A., *Motivation and Personality*, 3rd edn, Harper and Row, New York 1954.

Orton, T., 'Leadership across Cultures in times of Change', *Leadership*, Autumn 2008.

CASE STUDIES

	Chapter	1. East Asia Chemicals (Hong Kong)	2. OES Company (Singapore)	3. Patties Foods (Australia)	4. Ororo Goldmine (Papua New Guinea)
1	The enterprise, its logistics and supply chains	*	*	*	*
2	Business planning, risk and sustainability		*	*	
3	Logistics in practice				
4	Supply chains in the Asia–Pacific region				*
5	The role of logistics service providers in supply networks	*	*	*	*
6	International trade logistics		*		
7	Transport within logistics	*			*
8	Storage and distribution operations			*	
9	Building external relationships	*	*	*	
10	Inventory—balancing demand and supply		*	*	*
11	Planning and scheduling the enterprise	*		*	
12	Procurement	*			*
13	Accounting and logistics		*	*	*
14	Technology and communications as enablers		*	*	
15	Improving logistics	*	*	*	*
16	Managing logistics operations		*	*	*

	5. Hewlett-Packard (Australia)	6. Big China Store (China)	7. Supercheap Auto Group (Australia)	8. Sabah Furniture (Malaysia)	9. Southern Tea Company (India)	10. Fonterra and KiwiRail (New Zealand)
	*	*	*	*	*	*
	*	*	*	*	*	*
				*	*	*
	*	*		*		*
				*	*	*
	*		*	*	*	*
		*	*			
				*	*	
	*	*	*		*	
			*	*	*	
		*		*	*	
	*	*	*	*	*	
		*	*		*	
	*		*	*	*	*
		*			*	

Case study 1

East Asia Chemicals courier services tender
Hong Kong

Developed by Kerry Hammond

East Asia Chemicals (EAC) is a Hong Kong-based company that produces a range of chemical additives for the construction industry. Sales are mainly to the trade and for major projects. EAC purchases the primary ingredients from international sources. These are diluted and reconstituted to form retardants and accelerants. To gain business from major projects, EAC submits responses to government in business tenders.

EAC has six main operating sites, each complete with a manufacturing facility and sales offices, at the following locations:

* Macao
* Manila
* Guangzhou
* Shenzhen
* Hanoi
* Xiamen.

Deliveries to the six regional centres are *time and office location critical* for government tender boxes. The six sites also send documents to the other sites. There are no remote locations to service.

The international satchels go to:

* London
* Frankfurt
* Chicago
* Stockholm
* Milan
* Sydney.

The business sends approximately 250 satchels per week within the region and 50 international satchels per week. Most deliveries weigh between 1 and 10 kg.

Currently, five courier companies are used for regional deliveries and two for international deliveries. Recently EAC has lost some contracts due to the courier service being late in delivering the bids by the required time. As a part of an improvement project, the company is looking for ways to reduce the number of service providers to one for international and one for regional deliveries.

QUESTIONS

Operational

1. Discuss how the network design of EAC can be both a source of competitive advantage and a major operational weakness.
2. Prepare and present a statement of work (SOW) for this courier services tender.
3. From the perspective of a company bidding for this courier services tender, what questions would you ask EAC?

Planning

4. Develop a methodology for tender response evaluation. Which key criteria will you employ to assess the responses by various bidders?
5. From the perspective of a company bidding for this courier services tender, how would you position your tender response? How could you add extra value to this customer if successful in winning the contract?
6. What KPIs should EAC implement with its new courier services provider?

Management

7. Discuss what other solutions are available to EAC to resolve the challenges they are facing. In your answer you should consider solutions based on integration options, technology, network optimisation, and so on.

Case study 2

OES Company moves towards lean supply chains
Singapore

Developed by Derrick and Grace Phua

Optimum Engineering Standard Company Ltd, or OES, is one of the leading oilfield equipment and services providers to oil and gas companies in the world. Through their oil-well site operations and engineering research facilities, OES develops products, services and solutions for customers that optimise performance in a safe and environmentally sound manner.

Reflecting their belief that diversity spurs creativity, collaboration and understanding of customers' needs, OES employs over 70 000 people of more than 100 nationalities in approximately 80 countries. Knowledge communities and special interest groups within the OES organisation enable teamwork and knowledge sharing, unencumbered by geographical boundaries. With over 20 research and engineering facilities worldwide, in 2008, OES invested over $800 million in R&D.

OES offers solutions for applications to optimise the artificial lift and production of oil. These solutions range from onshore applications to complex offshore, deepwater or sub-sea electric submersible pumps (ESP) applications. OES not only supplies ESP components but also provides monitoring systems, surface electrical equipment, engineering services and optimisation services to complement the ESP system. By integrating technology and service, OES can provide a lift system for customers to optimise oil pump and oil well performance while reducing operating costs. Standard ESP components include high-efficiency pumps, high-efficiency ESP motors, modular ESP protectors, ESP cables and multiphase ESP gas handling systems.

Gracia Lambert is a veteran OES employee with 25 years of experience. She is the manager for demand planning and inventory control for five of the OES product centres located in Canada, USA, Ireland, Russia and in Singapore, where she is based. She is currently the focus of attention in a situation attributed to both customer demand and a corporate office directive that is in response to the customer demand.

Gracia reports functionally to the head of operations for all five product centres in terms of inventory-related deliverables. She also has a direct line report to the head of global demand planning, who has recently joined the head of operations to be based in Singapore.

Currently end products are assembled to order, due to the high cost of holding finished products in stock. Sub-assemblies are made to stock through machining processes and some machined sub-assemblies purchased from suppliers. To a small extent, lean manufacturing is practised for both assembling finished product and machining components. Raw materials are purchased from both local and overseas suppliers in each country.

The business system OES uses in Singapore to plan and schedule the manufacturing operations is a 15-year-old legacy system that can handle only single plant/centre operations. It has been used since the days when Singapore was responsible for just its own manufacturing.

The operations group is responsible for the customer service and demand planning function. It requires that the product centres maintain high inventory level, as it has been traditionally believed that high customer service level is synonymous with high inventory levels. However, one of the corporate key performance indicators (KPI) is the amount of inventory against sales.

Beyond the boundaries of OES's internal operations is its dependence on material suppliers. The current lead time for delivery of component materials ranges from two weeks to one year.

In response to customers' changing demands, OES corporate now wants four-week delivery ex-works to support business and customer requirements and at the same time to achieve the industry standard inventory turn of four; that is, every three months. To meet this objective, corporate wants the Singapore manufacturing facility to 'go lean', followed by the other overseas product centres.

QUESTIONS

Operational

1. What are the key challenges facing OES?
2. What logistical trade-offs do you see evidence of in this case?
3. Discuss the human aspects of the challenges facing OES and what solutions are available.

Planning
4. How is OES positioning itself for the future?
5. What is the OES competitive advantage?
6. What role does technology play in enabling OES to meet its customers' requirements?
7. What industry-specific peculiarities does this business have to contend with?

Management
8. Discuss how well the lean approach translates from manufacturing to a broader supply chains environment. What are some of the complexities associated with such transitioning?
9. You have been hired by corporate OES as a business consultant to advise Gracia concerning her new role of managing the planning not only for the Singapore product centre but also the four international centres. You are mindful of the changing industry demand and customers' expectations. Consideration must be given to the OES corporate directives for implementing 'lean' manufacturing operations and new objectives (KPI) in inventory planning. Where will you begin? How will you address the challenges? Who will you talk to? What approach and methodology will you use?

Case study 3

Patties Foods distribution network project
Australia

Developed by Mark Kluver

Patties Foods (Patties) is a publicly-listed company on the Australian stock exchange that has its roots in a family business, developed with a passion for quality and customer satisfaction.

Patties is the largest manufacturer of pastry pies in Australia and is based in Bairnsdale, a town in regional Victoria approximately four hours' drive from Melbourne. Its brand portfolio includes Four 'N Twenty, Herbert Adams, Nanna's, Patties, Wedgewood and Snowy River. The company has expanded the business to include frozen fruits in the Creative Gourmet and the Chef Pride ranges. Patties products are available through retail, private label and food services distribution channels.

The factory operates seven days a week, producing approximately 400 pallets of product a day. The factory has a small staging warehouse that holds 500 pallets. From here the product is distributed to three separate 'picking warehouses', located in metropolitan Melbourne; these are operated by three storage and distribution service companies. Each picking warehouse provides a national service for either the retail, private label or food service channels.

Off-peak production volume is approximately 1700 pallets a week; however, in peak seasons this can increase by almost 50 per cent, leading to the need for overflow external warehousing near the factory in Bairnsdale.

A new group manager logistics (GML) has joined Patties with an initial task to develop a solution for this problem. The GML has assessed the situation and validates senior management's belief that Patties need to redesign its distribution network. To facilitate this, a plan has been developed to reduce the number of LSP-managed warehouses in Melbourne from three to one and build a 10 000 pallet freezer warehouse on the Bairnsdale manufacturing site.

The design of the new freezer has a 5700 square metre area (including staging and docks) and seven levels of racking. The building is north-facing, with stock entering the site from the factory via the south-western corner of the building. It is to be planned and operated using a 'commercial off-the-shelf' (COTS) warehouse management system (WMS), which replenishes the new 'picking warehouse' in Melbourne, coordinated by the newly created role of inventory controller.

For operational purposes it has been agreed that 85 per cent utilisation should be considered a 'full' warehouse. It is also part of the planning criteria that vehicles need to be loaded or unloaded within 60-minute 'windows' in order to accommodate the safe operating procedures for freezer warehouses.

The total upgrade to the business over the course of three years is expected to require an investment of $22m by the company. This will increase the production capability, with additional pie manufacturing lines and the development of a gluten-free manufacturing area, in addition to the new onsite freezer warehouse and distribution network.

QUESTIONS

Operational

1. Identify the current logistical challenges faced by Patties Foods.
2. Map the company's original and newly developed distribution network.
3. What are the key issues faced by the Patties team in transitioning from the original arrangement to the new solution?
4. What are the areas of focus for the inventory controller as new procedures are established?

Planning

5. Discuss the target level of utilisation in the new warehouse. What should that level be in your view? Explain the rationale behind your decision.
6. What techniques and tools could Patties use to maximise the vehicle turn-around at the site?
7. Given that the operation has seven-high racking within a freezer environment, what technological solutions might Patties consider to aid facility management?
8. Develop a warehouse layout document detailing the number and type of docks, racking requirement and layout and any other key elements of the new warehouse. Include in your design a future expansion plan to double the size of the warehouse you are currently designing. Explain the rationale for the choices you have made.
9. Explain the cost savings you anticipate with your design to double the size of the warehouse. In what areas do you expect a cost increase?
10. Consider the consolidation of the three picking warehouses in Melbourne into a single facility. Discuss the basis of the inventory policy you would institute in this single facility. What information would you need to make a decision about the amount of space needed in this new facility?

Management

11. Assume you are a logistics consultant engaged to assist the group manager logistics in development of the business case for the new warehouse. Compile a list of questions for the GML that will assist in your task. (Tip: consider issues such as land size, cost and access.)
12. Construct a high-level business case and operational plan for the proposed solution. You may make any assumptions that are necessary. Document the assumptions made.
13. Evaluate the viability of the proposed solution. Develop a financial model that could be used to underpin the business case.
14. Develop alternative solutions to the challenges you identified in Question 1.
15. Patties Foods has been working with an S&OP process over the past 12 months. Discuss the role of forecast accuracy in the validity of the S&OP output. Refer to the key factors that contribute to inventory accuracy or inaccuracy from the perspective of Patties' sales team, manufacturing, logistics, retailers and consumers.

Case study 4

Ororo Goldmine
Papua New Guinea

Developed by Laurie Le Fevre

Every day a convoy of six or more semitrailers carries bulk diesel fuel by road to the Ororo Goldmine mine site in Papua New Guinea (PNG), 100 km inland from the port of entry. The company uses diesel fuel exclusively for fuelling the electricity generation at the mine and its extensive vehicle fleet. The fuel is a high strategic and high-risk item of supply; therefore, a high level of vehicle maintenance is required to ensure integrity of the vehicle convoys.

A consequence of the convoys is that more than 100 tyres come into contact with gravel roads. Although a relatively low-value contract in dollar terms, tyre repairs must be undertaken en route to maintain a high level of convoy service. The tyre puncture repair contractor accompanies every convoy and makes repairs on the road as required. The contract for tyre repairs was put in place following a competitive tender process.

The mine management has become aware of the progressively diminishing reliability of the tyre repairs service in convoy. The initial contract was awarded on price. The low profit margin in the contract has made skilled repair mechanics difficult to recruit, as the payments offered by the contractor to potential contract tyre repair staff are not competitive. The contractor is talking about walking away from its contractual responsibilities.

Ororo Goldmine management is divided on how to return to the former high level of service confidence. One manager takes a hard line, proposing that the external contractor must ensure that contract KPIs are met. Another manager, perhaps with a more pragmatic view, is proposing that Ororo Goldmine fund the repair contractor for new generation repair tools, plus a proposed service enhancement in that a larger support vehicle carrying an additional 20 complete wheel/tyre assemblies will be provided.

The new procurement manager has undertaken a company-wide review, using internal resources, of the company's buying, the objective being to better understand the relationship with the supply markets, the expenditure on services in the total procurement spend and the allocation of its procurement staff resources. He was surprised to discover that the majority of the spend was largely an exercise in price taking; procurement was largely a reactive process. Furthermore, the company had neither the team structure nor the processes for early or strategic involvement in the supply market. It is hardly surprising that when surveyed, other teams in the organisation had the common view that procurement is a reactive process and that it provides a sub-optimal service.

QUESTIONS

Operational
1. Identify the key stakeholders in this scenario.
2. How might the stakeholders be engaged in developing a solution?
3. Conduct a high level risk assessment. Identify the risks, evaluate their likelihood and severity and propose some mitigation strategies, recognising the inherent challenges of operating in PNG.
4. What can the procurement team do to change its position of being seen in the company as a reactive team?
5. How could the procurement team increase the service level provided to the organisation?
6. What are the merits of having contractual relationships with suppliers? Are there any drawbacks?

Planning
7. What procurement tools would you use to address the general and specific buying challenges at Ororo Goldmine?
8. Would the greater good be served if a new contract were negotiated? If you were to re-tender the tyre repair contract, how would you evaluate the tender responses?
9. Develop the documents to support the procurement model: *Identification of Need, Statement of Work, Specification, Negotiation of Contract*, and *Management of Contract*.
10. Is there a zone of potential agreement in the management of Ororo Goldmine concerning how the tyre repair contract problem may be resolved?
11. How can the level of service provided by the procurement team be evaluated and managed?
12. Discuss the implications of not having contracts for both the customer and the supplier.

Management
13. Discuss the change management aspects of this case.
14. Is the PNG location a factor in how the situation is resolved? Consider a similar situation developing in other countries in the region. How would this affect the situation?
15. What strategies should now be put in place to better manage the corporate spend as a total? What tools might be used?

Case study 5

Hewlett Packard: reducing emissions and saving costs
Australia

Developed by Tony Clarke

The Imaging & Printing Group (IPG) is a division of Hewlett-Packard Australia (HPA) and an integral part of Hewlett Packard's (HP) global business. The Australian business commenced in 1967 when HP purchased its local agency business, with offices in Melbourne and Sydney. The company then grew until there were sales offices in the capital city of each State.

Throughout its existence, HPA has primarily been a sales and distribution organisation, importing products for resale from HP divisions located throughout the world. Due to the distances involved, a major challenge has always been managing the cost of final distribution to customers.

In earlier days when computers were expensive, it was viable to import using airfreight, resulting in a lower cost of holding expensive inventory while in transit and in local warehouses. As the price of electronic products reduced, transport by ship became the preferred method for the majority of products in the consumer market. This meant that the cost of transport decreased as inventory increased—in transit and in Australia.

There are five main points of entry into Australia for seaborne cargo: Fremantle, Adelaide, Melbourne, Sydney and Brisbane. Fremantle is the port closest to Singapore, but the central distribution office (CDO) is in Sydney—a distance of nearly 4000km from Fremantle.

Before 2008, all IPG hardware was being delivered nationally from the CDO, with 40 per cent of supplies landing in Fremantle and then being delivered via rail to customers nationally. A significant 40 per cent of hardware from the CDO was delivered to Melbourne by truck. The deliveries from the CDO were not optimised and did not use larger trucks. As a result, in 2008 HPA was emitting CO_2 at the rate of 6400 tonnes per annum.

The continual reduction in the price of computer peripherals required a full review of transport arrangements. In 2008, HPA worked regionally across the HP organisation and with DHL and Star Track Express, the domestic logistics service providers (LSP), to develop a new model for moving freight from the factories in the Asia–Pacific Japan (APJ) region to end customers in Australia.

Elements of the review were that HPA buys product from the global divisions on a letter of credit (LC) arrangement, so the imported products are a part of HPA inventory when they leave the production facility. Also, freight rates are structured by the conference lines of shipping companies to be similar for all the main Australian ports. It was therefore preferable to have inventory in low-cost ships rather than travelling in more expensive trains and trucks.

The outcome of this cost-based review was that HPA changed its main ports of entry from Fremantle to Melbourne and Sydney; this increased the distance travelled by sea and decreased rail and truck movements to deliver goods into the major retail markets. It also decreased the material handling and storage required at the CDO.

Concurrently, HPA implemented a project to optimise the land freight delivery into outlying markets, by using trucks with higher storage capacity and therefore minimising the total number of trucks required.

Further analysis by IPG identified that in addition to direct cost savings, there was a reduction in CO_2 emissions from product deliveries via all modes of transport including sea, rail and truck. By the close of FY 2009, the division's annual CO_2 emissions from freight delivery were reduced from 6400 to 3776 tonnes. The saving of more than 2600 tonnes is equal to 8.74 hectares of forest preserved from deforestation or 66 666 trees grown from seedlings for 10 years.

This was the largest CO_2 saving project in the HP Asia–Pacific Japan (APJ) region for 2009 and illustrates that reducing CO_2 emissions in supply chains can also save money for the business. This example also shows that for continued effectiveness, supply chains must be reviewed on a regular basis, or when major changes occur in global business and the mix of material movements.

As an example of a regular review of the supply chains of a business, the next project has been to reduce the transport requirements for the reverse logistics of products returned by consumers to retailers. In the past, HPA collected the products on demand from individual retailers and sent them to the CDO in Sydney for disposal and writing off of the value of the assets.

The new process is that a LSP which specialises in reverse logistics collects the products on a 'milk-round' route from retailers in each major population area and arranges to locally recycle the products. When notified of the disposal, the CDO electronically writes off the asset. This saves the transport costs of multiple part-loaded truck movements and the long delivery distance to Sydney, plus the double handling of products for pick-up and at the CDO.

This project also provides savings in CO_2 emissions, which contributes to the HPA IPG goal of reducing distribution CO_2 emissions by a further 20 per cent by 2013.

QUESTIONS

Operational

1. Complete a network diagram of the initial and the improved distribution pattern. Identify whether the distribution can be further improved and how.
2. What are the areas of IPG operations that present most opportunity for better ways of working and distribution directed at improving sustainability? Explain your answers.
3. Select a city and assume there are 10 retail outlets that sell an electronic product. The retail outlets are located at roughly equal distances around the perimeter of the city. Identify the travel and time savings when changing from a pick-up on demand of returned products to a 'milk-run' collection.

Planning

4. If the conference lines serving Australia decided that freight rates would reflect the actual cost of serving each port, meaning that deliveries from Asia to Fremantle and Brisbane would be cheaper than to Sydney and Melbourne, how might the current IPG distribution policy change? What factors would need to be considered to ensure that CO_2 emissions did not increase?
5. Some retailers in developed countries are implementing a store-ready merchandise policy, whereby items are delivered from an international or domestic distribution centre as ticketed and priced products, ready to be displayed in the retail shop. IPG sells many consumable items (ink cartridges, paper, etc.); should these be planned as a separate supply chain from the electronic products such as printers and scanners? Explain your decision. Is your solution expected to provide additional savings in CO_2 emissions?

Management

6. What types of additional projects can be considered by HPA IPG to meet its 2013 target to reduce distribution CO_2 emissions by a further 20 per cent?
7. Select either the logistics department of a product company or a distribution services company. Construct a plan of action to:
   a. identify areas of savings in CO_2 emissions that may also reduce operational costs
   b. implement the proposals.
8. Companies may be able to establish a good perception in the eyes of customers and consumers by their actions to reduce pollution. Use the plan of action you created in the previous question to construct a press release that explains the value to the community of the plan.

Case study 6

Big China Store: retail DC start-up
China

Developed by George Zhou

Modern retailing entered China in the mid-1990s through international retailers such as Wal-Mart and Carrefour. Big China Store group (BCS) operates in the competitive retailing market of greater Beijing, the capital city of China. The retailer has 70 convenience stores and 710 suppliers providing approximately 8000 major SKUs from an authorised product selection list of 32 000 SKUs. Currently, most suppliers make direct deliveries (using their own vehicles or a transport service provider) to the stores, which independently order their own resupply.

Table 1 opposite summarises the current seasonality of sales for BCS.

Table 2 below identifies the major SKU profile (20 per cent of SKUs that contribute 80 per cent of sales).

BCS is planning further expansion to double the number of stores. To ensure success and enable control of this expansion has meant that BCS will centralise the business. Buying of retail products will be conducted from head office and storage and distribution will be contracted to a specialist distribution services provider (3PL).

The initial challenge for BCS is to select a suitable 3PL, because there is little expertise in the company concerning the establishment and operation of a retail distribution centre (DC). The project will be a turn-key project which includes:

- initial requirements design and planning
- site selection
- DC layout
- DC equipment purchasing
- WMS IT application requirements and selection
- project planning and execution
- go-live and immediate post-live management of the DC. This requires both engaging local transport companies and working within local industry practice and 'bad' habits.

Lott Global (Lott), a major international logistics service provider (LSP), has been selected as the organisation to establish the new distribution centre and provide the resupply of BCS shops for an initial period of one year. The contract is based on an 'open book' agreement, with BCS responsible for all capital costs.

Given the move from distributed to central ordering, only about 50 per cent of SKUs will initially go through the DC. Operationally, the DC will provide a cross-dock facility, with the warehousing capability expanded as more SKU are centrally purchased.

The set-up and implementation schedule is tight and will provide many challenges. The most immediate are:

- the scale of change management required in BCS to transition from store ordering to central ordering
- the staged implementation of the WMS IT application that must be capable of supporting the revised retail process, while being Chinese-localised
- the limited site options, as most facilities are traditional flat warehouses built for non-system aided operations.
- the longer time it will take to build a new DC rather than acquiring an existing building
- BCS is very price conscious and wishes to buy on price rather than any other criteria.

Lott needs to act fast and develop creative solutions to overcome these pressures.

After an extensive search, few suitable warehouses are found and the cost is not acceptable for either the existing racked DC or a new facility. The final selection is therefore a warehouse that has been used to store bagged grain. The facility consists of a row of 5 x 2000m² buildings, each divided into two halves by a firewall, creating 10 spaces of 1000m² each. The clear height is 5 metres. It has been decided to take only three warehouses for the first stage, which total 6000m². The remaining two warehouses can be rented at a later stage.

The design is for the central building to be used for receiving, marshalling of delivery orders and cross-docking activities and the two outside buildings to be racked for storage and picking. The location of stock will be adjusted in accordance with seasonal changes, promotion and other merchandising requirements. Even to meet the initial requirement of about 50 per cent of SKUs going through the DC, will require many suppliers to deliver on a daily

Month	Sales % by month
Jan	12.3
Feb	13.3
Mar	5.9
Apr	7.0
May	8.0
Jun	5.9
Jul	5.9
Aug	5.9
Sep	10.0
Oct	8.9
Nov	6.9
Dec	10.0
	100.0

Category, SKU number and sales		
Category	SKU	Sales %
Fresh	N/A	6
Frozen/daily	650	14
Food	1700	19
Candy/liquor/drinks	1350	20
HBA	1500	22
Houseware	800	5
Major/electrical	600	9
Office supply	400	
Apparel/domestic	1000	5
Total	8000	100

basis. This demand requires the goods receiving area to be upgraded; also, the local authority requires lobbying to repair the entry road.

Due to the height restriction of the site, there are only four tiers of racking; the bottom level is a picking location, with storage on the other tiers. The final number of slot locations is close to 6000. The order profile shows 80 per cent single pick and the remainder case picked, so there will not be enough slots to accommodate all the SKUs. This requires a reconfiguration of the racking to lower the bottom racks in order to accommodate more SKU. Some bin locations are divided into four, six and eight for slower-moving items.

As a part of the competitive rental agreement, Lott has to recruit at least 70 per cent of the people from the warehouse owner. The additional task will therefore be retraining the operatives (who are State-recruited employees), from handlers of bulky and bagged products into operatives of a high turnover DC. Some will need to be trained in using the WMS and all will be performance measured through the 20 KPIs set by BCS and Lott.

The selection of a suitable WMS application has also become a challenge. Although a European WMS was initially proposed by Lott, its inflexibility for customisation deemed it not suitable. As other WMS did not meet the requirements, it was decided to develop in-house a basic retail-focused WMS application. This will require the employment or contracting of an IT team working to a tight timeline.

The decision relating to the choice of warehouse equipment has caused a lot of tension between the two organisations. Ultimately, BCS decides in favour of the cheaper option (Brand B). As an example of the challenges this decision presents, the difference between the final two brands of forklift truck are as follows.

Functions	Brand A (more expensive)	Brand B
Turning radius	1540mm	1750mm
In-China market	Well established	Just entered
After-sales service network	Extensive	Just commenced

This decision means that aisle widths must be wider, reducing the number of racking slots available. Lott will still have to meet its KPI while dealing with a supplier that is new to the market and with an untested after-sales service capability.

This is the first time a major Chinese retailer has outsourced its DC operations to a 3PL and the first 'open book' contract logistics operation in China. There is an ongoing balancing act between the retailer pursuing the lowest cost solution and the 3PL seeking efficiency, value for money and the responsibility of meeting the KPI measures. The gap in values, perceptions and process can sometimes strain the relationship.

The situation is now as follows.

- The selection of hardware for the DC has been completed, but the equipment has yet to be delivered and installed.
- The 'bare bones' WMS application is being tested, but has not been implemented.
- The training plan for the staff has been completed but training has not commenced.

Despite the challenges of getting the DC into an operational state and successfully managing the operations, the parties have entered discussions concerning the extension of the current contract into a seven-year agreement. BCS is anxious for this to happen so that its executive team can achieve their business objective to grow the retail business and list the company on the stock exchange. Lott Global executives would like to be a part of a growing and successful relationship, as it would assist in gaining further business opportunities with other Chinese companies; however, the challenges already faced show that the relationship may be difficult and not necessarily profitable.

QUESTIONS

Operational

1. What are the key challenges facing the retailer? Provide alternatives for overcoming these challenges.
2. From the perspective of Lott Global, what are their key success factors for this project?
3. Discuss the implications of the seasonality and SKU profile information on the decisions being made in the DC design and later in operating the DC.
4. What are the key considerations in making layout decisions for this DC? Develop an outline drawing of the DC layout.

5. What decisions are required concerning the space and operational practice of the cross-dock part of the DC?
6. Discuss the trade-off situation arising from the decision concerning the width of the aisles necessary to accommodate the forklift turning circle.

Planning

7. Develop a high-level project plan for the tasks that need to be completed by Lott Global to deliver this project on time and on budget.
8. What functionality should be available within the in-house developed WMS?
9. Even working on a 24/7 basis, can Lott Global successfully meet the challenge of supplying the increasing number of retail outlets?

Management

10. As a Lott Global executive, what risks would need to be evaluated prior to deciding whether to accept the proposed seven-year contract?
11. Should an LSP accept new business that may not be profitable, but which enhances its reputation in the market? If so, will it put contracts with other clients at risk if the new business fails?
12. Discuss the cultural challenges that may arise as the project is implemented and how they might affect the logistical performance of the project.
13. Discuss the impact of the decision by BCS to select a less-than-optimum distribution facility and buy equipment on the basis of lowest price. From the perspective of Lott Global, how would you seek to influence BCS to make future buying decisions based on other criteria?
14. What metrics would you use to measure success of the training program for staff at the distribution facility?
15. Develop the change management approach for transitioning the DC staff to think and behave as operational staff of a growing and successful commercial enterprise.

Case study 7

Supercheap Auto Group Limited
Australia

Developed by Carter McNabb, Partner, GRA Pty Ltd at www.gra.net.au

Supercheap Auto Group Limited (www.supercheapautogroup.com.au) has grown at a compound annual growth rate of over 25 per cent to become one of Australia and New Zealand's largest retailers with more than 300 stores, 5000 staff and annualised sales in excess of $800m.

The group comprises three businesses and sells known brands and house brands (that is, own label products) through:

* Supercheap Auto retail stores
* leisure retailing through BCF (boating, camping and fishing) retail stores and the recently acquired Ray's Outdoors retail stores
* bicycle retailing through Goldcross Cycles.

The company's business plan that was unveiled in 2006 provides direction for the group and includes the improvement of procurement and supply chain capabilities. This is based on the premise that the difference between good and high-performance retailers is providing products and solutions that consumers want in a timely manner—it is about speed and excellence of execution.

Products for resale are purchased domestically and through the China-based overseas sourcing office (OSO). China-sourced products are handled by LSPs through to the group's network of five distribution centres that were established in 2007/08 to support the planned growth and deliver cost efficiencies. The warehouse management system (WMS) was upgraded to support the growth objectives of the individual businesses.

An initial project within the business plan was to reduce the working capital requirements of the group, through the use of both strategic and operational/tactical inventory optimisation techniques. The results were:

* $100m invested in opening new stores over three years with only $40m increase in net debt
* in FY06, the group added 30 new stores or $60 million in revenue without any additional investment in inventory

- inventories reduced by 17 per cent (that is, operating cash flow improved by $23 million), while increasing service levels via advanced demand management and inventory optimisation techniques
- the need for an additional distribution centre (that is, a fixed asset investment) avoided due to inventory and operating efficiency improvements.

Based on the success of the inventory optimisation project, the 'store friendly' (that is, store-ready merchandise) project has now commenced. The DCs will be focused on reducing the workload of stores while reducing out-of-stocks and improving service; this is targeted to increase service levels from DC to stores from the low 80 per cent to the high 90 per cent.

QUESTIONS

Operational

1. Is the implementation of an ERP system a prerequisite for an inventory optimisation project? Explain your reasoning.
2. Is a fully functioning WMS a prerequisite for an inventory optimisation project? Explain your reasoning.
3. Would the 'store-friendly' project have the opportunity for success without having undertaken the inventory optimisation project? Explain your reasoning.

Planning

4. Identify the strategic and operational/transaction optimisation techniques the company would have used and why.
5. Would similar benefits accrue to any retailer using the same techniques? If so, why?

Management

6. Based on the information provided in the case, is inventory optimisation a source of competitive advantage or a cost-reduction technique? Explain your reasoning.
7. As the logistics manager at a similar-sized retail chain, how would you communicate the importance of improving supply chains to the senior management, who may have the perception that supply chains are just trucks and warehouses?

Case study 8

Sabah Furniture exporting challenges
Malaysia

Developed by Ranjeet Singh, Director TransEco Pty. Ltd at www.transecopl.com

Sabah Furniture (SF) is a large and long-established furniture manufacturer based in Sabah, East Malaysia. SF produces high-quality outdoor furniture sourced from plantation wood for export. The challenges that face SF are similar to those encountered by other island and remote communities in the Asia–Pacific region when developing sustainable industries.

The company exports to the UK, Japan, Germany and Sweden, but sales have declined by more than 9 per cent in the period 2004 to 2008, while the exports of furniture in the same period from competitor countries, such as Vietnam, have increased. SF has been approached by a major international retailer to substantially increase sales through producing a private-label range for the retailer. To help fund the expansion required in SF, the retailer will pay for each order in full against shipment documents. However, to be assured of continuing and uninterrupted supply, the retailer requires a guarantee of delivery in full, on time and without errors in documentation; SF will be charged substantial penalties for non-compliance.

Before accepting this offer, the family shareholders and management of Sabah Furniture have engaged you as the consultant to identify the supply chain challenges the company will face in meeting the retailer's requirements and to recommend action that will reduce the risks. The CEO expects that your report will be the basis for a submission to the government of Sabah concerning action to be taken that will assist with improvements to all supply chains in the State.

You have identified the following situation.

The export process

The process to satisfy the customer's order is based on a pull system commencing at the start of manufacturing. Timber for production is taken from SF's inventory of seasoned wood. Other materials required for the manufacturing process are sourced from three suppliers in West Malaysia and these are shipped on a CIF basis. The manufacturing process is then completed and the finished goods despatched for export on an FOB basis via Port Klang or Port of Tanjong Pelepas (PTP), both in West Malaysia.

Sabah Furniture is entirely dependent on the shipping agent to arrange despatch. The shipping agent provides a shipping schedule and the required 40-foot (FEU) containers are ordered; there is usually a delay of two to three days in receiving the containers as there is no pooling of containers between shipping lines. The containers are stuffed and sealed before hauling to nearby Sapangar Bay for shipment to Kota Kinabalu (KK).

The shipping feeder service from KK in Sabah to West Malaysia is reliant on Malaysian-registered ships, due to the Malaysian government's cabotage policy between Malaysian ports. Direct export is not currently available, as 'mother vessels' destined for Europe and major ports in Asia are yet to visit the ports of Sabah, citing a lack of volume.

For Europe and Scandinavia, the company has a choice of Johan Shipping, which takes two months to reach Europe from West Malaysia, and Maersk Line, which takes one month. A delay in shipment time contributes to higher inventory holding costs. Estimated value of goods in a (FEU) container is RM70 000.

The earlier part of the timber supply chain is buying future timber supplies against forecasts of orders for furniture. Due to the potential for scarcity in the supply of timber, SF maintains a higher than normal raw material inventory, compared with competitors in West Malaysia that use the more readily available rubber tree wood.

The company purchases timber from a single saw miller on an FOB basis and to secure its raw material supply, maintains a deposit of RM50 000 in favour of the sawmiller. Inbound transport averages about RM100 per tonne to the furniture factory. The wood is then treated and seasoned, a process which takes two months. The company operates its own kiln drying facilities that are flexible in use and enable high-quality standards to be maintained.

Constraints in the process

INCOME

* Standard export payment terms from a customer are 30 per cent on verification of shipment of goods followed by the balance (70 per cent) paid on receipt of goods through a letter of credit (LC). Longer delivery increases the accounts receivables outstanding.
* Exporters are unable to explore new markets due to the lack of shipping connections to Thailand, Indonesia, the Philippines and northern Australia.
* While there is a double tax deduction on ocean freight charges (only applicable when making profits), the specific freight charges are difficult to identify because total charges are quoted on a door-to-door basis.

STATE COST PENALTIES

* Prices for many goods imported from West Malaysia are 20 to 30 per cent higher in East Malaysia (Sabah and Sarawak) than in West Malaysia.
* Cabotage rules affect the export industries of furniture, palm oil and seafood that use the natural resources of Sabah.
* Sabah is a poor state with low tax revenue. Therefore, there is:
    o insufficient investment in skills training
    o insufficient trained local labour
    o a reliance on foreign contract labour.
* Companies in Sabah can only source foreign labour from Indonesia and the Philippines. However:
    o West Malaysians require a work permit to work in East Malaysia
    o in West Malaysia, labour can be sourced from anywhere.

ROAD TRANSPORT COST PENALTIES

* Road freight rates are based on distance, not time.
* Road transport incurs added costs in Sabah:
    o Only a low vehicle mass is allowed, due to poor roads and bridges—34 tonnes allowed versus 38 to 44 tonnes in West Malaysia. As a result transport companies incur more trips and higher costs.

o More powerful vehicles are required to handle the hilly terrain of Sabah. In Sabah fuel consumption is higher at 0.9 to 1.0km per litre, as opposed to in West Malaysia where it is 1.8 to 2.0km per litre.

o The average road speed in Sabah is 60 km/h, whereas it is 80 km/h in West Malaysia.

o Cost inputs, such as tyres and batteries, are 15 to 20 per cent cheaper in West Malaysia.

o For journeys between Sabah and Sarawak, permits and taxes are required to cross Brunei.

o There is an excessive regulatory compliance cost in Sabah to obtain a 'removal pass' for every movement of timber related products in the State.

o There is a shortage of skilled truck drivers in Sabah and therefore a higher cost to retain trained drivers.

WAREHOUSING COST PENALTIES

- Terminals and warehouses are labour intensive.
- The added value of the sector fell by 16 per cent between 2002 and 2006.

CARGO HANDLING AND STEVEDORING COST PENALTIES

- Port services have been 'privatised' to a government-linked company (GLC) called Sabah Ports Sdn Bhd (SPSB). Licensed port service providers, such as bunkering and port equipment maintenance are carried out by 'sister' companies of SPSB. Regulations require that these companies be owned by Malays (the Bumiputra policy). These companies contract out to labour hire companies who use foreign labour and therefore have a less motivated workforce and a low container handling rate, at 14 to 16 containers per hour. In West Malaysia materials handling equipment supply companies can handle up to 30 containers per hour.

- There is a traditional accounting approach to pricing, with establishment costs recovered by low volumes; therefore, unit charges are high.

LOGISTICS SERVICE PROVIDER COST PENALTIES

- The international net margin for LSP companies is about 6 to 8 per cent. (Note that TOLL, the largest LSP in Australia, has a net margin of 6 per cent). However, in:

o West Malaysia the after-tax profits on sales for freight forwarders is 3 to 8 per cent

o Sabah the after-tax profits of freight forwarders to 2006 was more than 20 per cent and after 2006 reduced to less than 15 per cent

- Delays of around 10 days in Sabah and West Malaysia, owing to inefficient transport and logistics services processes, translate to an inventory holding cost of RM94 per container shipped (based on 7 per cent per year interest rate).

SHIPPING COST PENALTIES

- Sabah to Port Klang sailing time is seven days. The factors that can affect this time are:

o Ship delays can be one to three days plus cancellations.

o Current ships are operating at full capacity, therefore suitable and timely shipping capacity for exports and imports can be difficult to secure.

o There is a lack of available FEU containers and a container interchange facility between shipping lines.

o The connection in West Malaysian ports are unreliable, therefore 'mother ships' at West Malaysian ports do not accept bookings from Sabah until the transhipment vessel reaches the West Malaysian port. Additional documentation, storage and port charges are incurred.

- The dominant flow of containers is from West Malaysia to East Malaysia. Approximately 75 per cent of the containers used for imports from West Malaysia return empty due to insufficient export volumes and are returned on an ad hoc basis, without reference to the forward demand for containers.

- International transhipment cargoes represent approximately 5 per cent of the containers handled. Therefore, specified containers are not always available when required.

- Export containers from East Malaysia are backhauled by the Malaysian shipping lines and so there is an erroneous expectation of lower shipping rates.

- Total ocean freight charges for export cargoes are higher due to the need to tranship at West Malaysian ports. This cost penalty is estimated to be USD400 per FEU container.

- Two shipping companies control 60 to 70 per cent of the East to West Malaysia service, although nine companies ply the route.

- o The average age of ships used between East and West Malaysia is more than 25 years. The level of technology is low and costs are high, but low volumes on the route do not justify investment in new ships.
- o Bunker costs in East Malaysia are high, at 40 per cent of ship operating costs.
- Intra-Malaysia shipping lines added value fell 9 per cent between 2002 and 2006.

Shipping freight charges

The quotation from shipping agents for ocean freight charges is on a lump-sum basis, without a breakdown of the two separate legs.

Sample of shipping charges February 2009
Origin: Sabah (Kota Kinabalu)
Destination: United Kingdom (Southampton)

Description	Container type	Amount in Malaysian currency (RM)
Ocean freight charges	40 foot high cube	2547.30
Bunker adjustment factor	40 foot high cube	2183.40
Crane hire charge (KK)	40 foot high cube	100.00
Terminal handling charge at port of loading	40 foot high cube	440.00
Document fee export	40 foot high cube	80.00
Total		**5350.70**

Comparison of shipping rates

Sabah (East Malaysia) to:	RM	Port Klang (West Malaysia) to:	RM
Tokyo	3,610	Tokyo	2,770
Rotterdam	10,260	Rotterdam	7,220
Southampton (UK)	5,350	Southampton (UK)	2,775
USA West coast	23,000	USA West coast	12,540
Hong Kong	equal charge	Sabah	equal charge

Source: TransEco Pty. Ltd, www.transecopl.com.

QUESTIONS

Operational
1. Develop a process map for Sabah Furniture exports.
2. Discuss the essence of push and pull manufacturing processes.
3. Is Sabah Furniture employing a true pull process?
4. How could the process be amended to deliver more value to Sabah Furniture?
5. Consider the current Incoterms arrangements (CIF, FOB). Is this the optimal arrangement for Sabah Furniture?

Planning
6. Refer to the process map developed in Question 1 above. Discuss strategies for reducing SF's lead time to customers.
7. Discuss the specifics of the Sabah location and its inherent challenges to providing customer service for export clients.

Management
8. Discuss the impact of each group of constraints noted in the case on Sabah Furniture's competitiveness.
9. How may Sabah Furniture leverage their role as a key exporter with the State government?
10. The decision to manufacture private-label products can be a complex strategic decision. Discuss whether taking on a private-label contract is a viable option for Sabah Furniture.
11. Based on the information in this case, what are the inherent logistics challenges for businesses established in island and remote areas of the region? What actions would you propose to reduce these disincentives?

Case study 9

Southern Tea Company: a different approach to export
India

Southern Tea Company is a long-established business based in southern India. It began growing tea bushes in plantations and selling the green tea leaves to a factory for processing. These were then packed in bulk plywood cases for onselling to tea exporters. As Southern expanded its business, it built a tea factory on the largest estate (which also processed the green leaf from its small estates) and then sold the processed tea directly to exporters. The next stage of development was to export the processed tea in bulk directly to tea marketing companies in Europe, which then packed the tea under their own or retailer's brand names. This is illustrated in Figure 1.

Figure 1

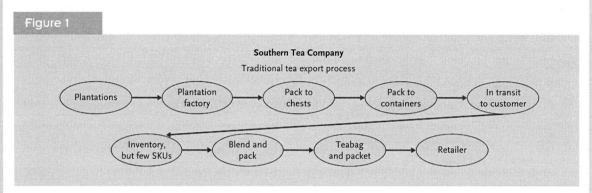

The standard process is as follows: companies in Europe order three months in advance of their requirements, allowing for a shipping time of 17 to 23 days, plus the time from the plantation factory to the export port. Inventory cost and risk lies with the importers as they buy against an LC.

It is now time for the fourth stage of development for Southern Tea Company. The company is proposing to change its business model and become a packaged tea business. The raw tea will be purchased and processed by the company and packaged under contract for marketing companies and retailers in Europe.

The company will sell its plantations and the capital raised will be used to develop a major tea packing operation, located to suit the growing areas from where raw tea leaves will be purchased and the export ports and airports. The proposed new export process is illustrated in Figure 2.

Figure 2

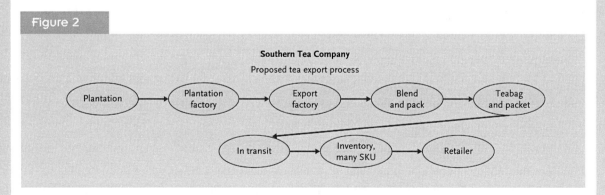

The new business model is designed not just to benefit from lower labour costs in India (the usual reason quoted for production in a developing country), but as a change in the risk profile for Southern and its customers in Europe. The business plan is designed to allow customers in Europe to increase their return on assets (ROA) and reduce inventory risk. The proposed benefits are as follows.

1. Increased ROA for importers

In India to achieve this:

* tea is to be supplied exclusively to one European importer. This reduces the risk of customers dealing with many plantation-based suppliers of tea
* tea is to be blended and packed at the export factory to customer's specification—the factory assumes the final quality risk
* contract tea tasters are based in the growing regions. The tea tasters certify quality; therefore the quality risk is assumed at the plantations.

In Europe to achieve this:

* importers are to close their packing operation to save on re-equipment costs and to reduce staff costs
* the packing factories are to be sold; these are located in redevelopment areas of cities and so ensure a capital return to the owners
* retailers will hold their buying price because:
  o the importer takes a smaller margin but receives a higher ROA because they are without packing facility assets
  o the export factory takes a higher margin to cover the risk and investment in the export factory.

2. Reduced European importers' inventory risk

In India to achieve this:

* the current three-month order cycle time is to be maintained
* lower-value tea is to be processed and packed to stock
* higher-value tea is to be processed and packed to order
* forecast accuracy is to be improved by using inventory optimisation application software
* the export factory will incur the cost and risk of imported packing material. There are:
  o minimum order quantities for low-volume products
  o multiple SKUs—additional packing material is held in inventory at the factory.

In Europe to achieve this:

* higher-value tea is to be imported by air
* there is to be no inventory of high value tea held by European importers
* for lower-value tea:
  o the base forecast is sent by sea
  o when actual sales are above the forecast, the additional quantity is to be sent by air
* the value of inventory is to be only slightly increased over traditional methods.

The main business cost considerations are as follows.

1. While total labour costs in the factory will initially be 22 per cent lower in India than in Europe, total labour costs are increasing in India, especially for educated and trained staff.
2. It is estimated that it will cost Rs 25crore ($10m) to build and equip the factory. As a result, there is a need to attract a real estate investor to share the cost.
3. New tea bag and box-packing machines from Italy cost approximately Rs 1.32crore (AUD$515 000) each, including import duty of 54 per cent. The central government should be lobbied to reduce the duty on packing machines from 54 per cent to 5 per cent.
4. The objective for both factory and export shipment is for continuous use (24/7). This high-volume business will require a steady flow of orders from customers and good relations with the supplier plantations.
5. All packing materials will be imported to ensure product quality (expected reject rate 0.1 per cent) and lower machine downtime.
6. Automated packing machines require few staff to operate. However, the workforce must be:
   o educated and well trained; therefore the challenge will be to attract and keep these staff members
   o prepared to work either rotating eight-hour shifts or four 12-hour shifts and three 12-hour shifts over two weeks.

QUESTIONS

Operational

1. Compare and contrast the value chain of the original and the proposed tea export processes.
2. What are the implications of the proposed change to the tea export process for the logistics structure of Southern?
3. Consider the geography and logistics infrastructure of southern India. Discuss what opportunities and challenges it offers to Southern.
4. The factory and export shipment operations are expected to be 24 hours per day, seven days per week. What shift structure would you propose and why?

Planning

5. Structure an inventory policy to support the new approach. Discuss your approach and the reasons for your selection.
6. What attributes should the planning and scheduling application contain to cope with the proposed business plan?
7. What steps would you propose to improve the accuracy of sales forecasting at Southern?
8. How would you use the inventory optimisation application to minimise the investment in inventory at Southern?
9. What steps would you propose to retain trained operators at Southern?

Management

10. You are the supply chain director for Southern and have been asked by the CEO to review the proposal.
    a. Is the proposed business model reasonable and viable, given that the 'textbook' approach is that consumer products should be packed close to the customer?
    b. Are the gains for all parties realisable?
    c. What are the risks associated with this change? How could these risks be mitigated?
11. The positive impact on the European importers is outlined in the case. Discuss the implications of the proposal on the ROA and risk profile of Southern. How may Southern compensate itself for these effects?
12. You have been asked by the CEO to be part of the team that will sell the proposal to customers in Europe. How will you sell the final proposal to the interested parties from a supply chains and logistics viewpoint?
13. Explain how the proposal will be implemented.
14. You are a consultant engaged by the supply chain director of Southern. You have been asked to develop an alternative supply plan for the next stage of company development, considering the supply chains and logistics effects. Justify your proposal.

Case study 10

Fonterra and KiwiRail: exporting dairy products
New Zealand

New Zealand's dairy exports began in 1846. The result of refrigerated shipping, the country's temperate climate and an efficient industry based on farmer-owned cooperative dairy companies has enabled dairying to grow into New Zealand's most important industry, at about 20 per cent of total export goods. Over the years and in response to competitive forces, consolidation of the farmer cooperatives occurred, which ultimately led to the creation in 2001 of Fonterra, the largest business in the industry. Fonterra now handles 90 per cent of New Zealand's milk production.

Dairy exports are valued at $11b, with 95 per cent of all dairy production exported and equal to about 35 per cent of the global trade in dairy products. The United States is New Zealand's most important dairy market. In addition to China, there are a further seven countries in Asia that are among New Zealand's top 15 dairy exporting countries.

The North Island has about 80 per cent of dairy farms, with more than 30 per cent located in the Waikato/South Auckland region. The South Island provides 20 per cent of dairy farms.

Fonterra

The Fonterra Dairy Co-operative Group has a group turnover of NZ$16b and is the world's leading exporter of dairy products and responsible for more than a third of the international dairy trade.

At the peak of the milk season, the company collects 3000 tanker loads of milk a day and delivers them to 26 manufacturing sites, which produce 2.2m tonnes of product annually (about 85 000 TEU), destined for 140 global markets and distributed through 80 current warehouses that are being progressively reduced to about 45 hub warehouses. It is the largest general user of rail freight in NZ and has selected Auckland, Tauranga, Napier and Lyttelton as its main export ports.

KiwiRail

The rail turnaround plan for KiwiRail puts the focus on the main Auckland–Christchurch route, with one of the objectives being to reduce the average time that a train takes between Auckland and Wellington in the North Island from 13.5 hours to no more than 11 hours (a truck takes about nine hours). The plan also identifies an upgrade to the ferries which carry the railway rolling stock across the Straits between the North and South Islands of New Zealand.

This approach can be challenged concerning the provision of best value. There is an argument as to whether KiwiRail should focus its operations on internal passenger and goods movement or whether it should be an integral part of the goods exporting effort. The point can be made that export freight movement is not time sensitive, so does not need to have the speed of road transport—but it does need to be consistent. Also, the inter-island ferries will require replacement in approximately 10 years and new ferry designs do not allow for the railway rolling stock to be carried. Therefore, focusing on the Auckland–Christchurch route is a short-term view that will have to be revisited.

One option is that KiwiRail could operate as a service within each island, feeding the respective hub ports. In the North Island these are identified as the ports of Auckland and Tauranga and in the South Island the ports of Otago (Dunedin) and Lyttelton (Christchurch) which will combine to operate as one entity. KiwiRail could also enter into an alliance with a coastal shipping company to offer a service that links Otago/Lyttelton in the South Island with the North Island ports of Tauranga and Auckland. This approach could provide intermodal efficiency, linking rail and ports to meet shippers' varying demands.

There is a potential difference between the objectives of the rail service and those of its largest customer. This illustrates that logistics service providers and any one customer may not always agree on objectives, because each is responsible to its own shareholders.

QUESTIONS

Operational

1. Develop a network map of Kiwi Rail as it services Fonterra.
2. Discuss the nature of the export dairy product range and how it affects the overall logistics solution.
3. Discuss the suitability of an intermodal solution for this particular product.

Planning

4. Consider the New Zealand rail network from an export freight viewpoint. What routing and structure would you consider to be necessary?
5. How is the economy of scale approach traditionally associated with railways compatible or incompatible with Fonterra's needs?

Management

Answer the following questions from the perspective of Fonterra's supply chain manager.

6. What alternatives are available for moving Fonterra's export shipments to the ports?
7. How would you negotiate to achieve the most flexible outcome for Fonterra? Specifically, discuss which areas could be negotiated and which are non-negotiable.
8. As the largest customer of KiwiRail, what position would you take in working with the company, and why?
9. In the event that you are unable to reach an agreement, what is your alternative solution for the distribution of your company's product?

INDEX